Greenhill
Books

The Guns that Won the West

The Guns that Won the West
Firearms on the American Frontier, 1848–1898

John Walter

Greenhill Books, London
MBI Publishing, St Paul

The Guns that Won the West
Firearms on the American Frontier, 1848–1898

This edition published in 2006 by Greenhill Books/Lionel Leventhal Ltd
Park House, 1 Russell Gardens, London NW11 9NN
and
MBI Publishing Co.
Galtier Plaza, Suite 200, 380 Jackson Street, St Paul, MN 55101-3885, USA

British Library Cataloguing-in Publication Data available
Walter, John, 1951–
The guns that won the West: firearms on the American
frontier, 1848–1898
1. Firearms – West (U.S.) – History – 19th century 2. West
(U.S.) – History, Military
I. Title
623.4'4'0978'09034

ISBN-10 1-85367-692-6
ISBN-13 978-1-85367-692-5

Library of Congress Cataloging-in Publication Data available

For more information on our books, please visit www.greenhillbooks.com, email sales@greenhillbooks.com, or telephone us within the UK on 020 8458 6314. You can also write to us at the above London address.

Printed and bound in Great Britain by
Creative Print and Design (Wales), Ebbw Vale

CONTENTS

LIST OF ILLUSTRATIONS

Line Illustrations

Plates (between pages 128 and 129)

The author and publisher wish to thank Butterfield & Butterfield, Fine Art Auctioneers and Appraisers, for permission to use plates 1–15, and Joseph Rosa for plate 16.

INTRODUCTION

'He was supposed to be about eighteen, but looked older when you saw him closely. He was sunburned and not much to look at . . . Everything he had on would not have sold for five dollars – an old black slouch hat; worn-out pants and boots, spurs, shirt, and vest; a black cotton handkerchief tied round his neck, the ever-ready Colt double-action .41 pistol around him and in easy reach; an old style .44 rim-fire brass-jawed Winchester . . .'
Frank Collinson describing an encounter with Billy the Kid in 1878.

Law in the wilder parts of the West bore little resemblance to the choreographed jurisprudence known to Easterners. All too often, it was dispensed at gunpoint or on the end of a lynch mob's noose. It was so much easier to accept the testimony of the victors and simply bury the losers on Boot Hill. If the cause had been just, recriminations would be short lived; had it been unjust, the wrong would soon be avenged by the victims' friends . . . and peace would be restored. This had an odd kind of symmetry and reduced the violence to what most Westerners – if no one else – could accept. If the levels ever rose too far, Federal marshals and even the US Army could be called to restore sanity.

However, the 'Wild' West remained a magnet for adventurers, the unscrupulous, outcasts and the lawless – particularly in the years immediately after the Civil War, when the bitterness among victorious Northerners and vanquished Southerners was at its height. The murderous exploits of guerrilla bands in 1863–5 (Quantrill's attack on Lawrence, for example) and the effects of continual small-but-bloody skirmishes with Indians had made death cheap currency. Certainly, quarter was rarely sought and equally scarcely given.

The age of the gunfighter lasted little more than a quarter-century. And even though a few men, such as Butch Cassidy and the Sundance Kid, plied their trade for a few more years, most of the best-known badmen had met violent deaths or hung up their guns by 1900.

Yet the threads of truth and legend are still often difficult to unravel. Stories customarily grow in the telling, and most cultures have mythical heroes whose exploits once had a basis in reality. The Wild West was no different. Remote and mysterious, even romantic in the minds of many Easterners, the stories were adapted, exaggerated and often bowdlerised by the dime novelists. Some Western fiction is now often regarded among landmarks of early 20th-century American literature – e.g. Owen Wister's *The Virginian*, published in 1902, or Zane Grey's *Riders of the Purple Sage* (1912) – but most were destined for uncritical popular consumption, and errors of fact counted for little.

Consequently, some truly bad men were cast in the light of society's victims; some not-so-bad men were painted much more blackly than they deserved; and comparatively good men were unfairly sketched as villains. The concepts of 'outlaw as hero' and 'lawman as villain' were by no means uncommon. Perhaps outlaws were simply so much more interesting!

Some of the outlaws did nurse grievances which were often shared in their home states. This was particularly true of those who had been raised in territories with Confederate sympathies, such as the James Brothers, and others whose family life had been destroyed by death or disaffection. William 'Billy the Kid' Bonney, now seen as a psychopathic killer, is still often viewed as a victim; and his eventual nemesis, Sheriff Pat Garrett, lionised at the time by those who saw The Kid as a threat, sometimes stands accused of killing Bonney 'without giving him a chance'. Garrett, in his turn, was shot down in 1908 in what was accepted as self defence – but, as the only witness was a confederate of the assailant, was more probably just another cold-blooded righting of a perceived wrong. Just or unjust, fair or foul: no one knows to this day.

Jesse James, the Younger Gang, Butch Cassidy and the Sundance Kid have all been fictionalised as victims of a society which had failed them, though degrees of innocence vary; Wild Bill Hickok and Buffalo Bill Cody owed their fame less to reality and more to the dime novel or the Wild West Show. Wyatt Earp owed his renown partly to the writer Ned Buntline (a pseudonym of Edward Judson), and also to a biography by Stuart Lake, published after Earp's death, which took excessive liberties with the truth. Simply by outliving contemporaries who may have taken the real story of the OK Corral to their graves, Earp was able to ensure that his own colourful depiction of events gained common currency.

And the real Martha Jane Cannary – 'Calamity Jane', nothing like the glamorous character played by Doris Day on the cinema screen – was fated to die young, in drunken obscurity, in Deadwood in 1903.

The Guns of the West

Even if the advent of railroads removed a major inhibition to the distribution of fireams in the West, major problems remained. As late as 1898, many places were still hundreds of miles from the nearest railroad station; ammunition, the vital component in the use of repeating firearms such as the Winchester lever-action rifle and the Colt revolver, was often in such short supply that it had to be carefully husbanded.

These factors alone restricted the distribution of guns which required unusual or proprietary cartridges, and killed many promising projects; secondly, they allowed the cap-lock muzzle loader (especially shotguns and small-calibre 'squirrel rifles') to survive in the remotest areas well into the twentieth century.

The concentration of the firearms industry in the industrialised north-eastern states was also a great handicap. Although the spiritual home of gunmaking was to be found in Pennsylvania, where the emigrant German gunsmiths had settled before the War of Independence, mechanisation had taken its greatest hold in New England.

Samuel Colt is customarily given the credit for perfecting the mass production of firearms, though, in the USA at least, the honour is really due to Eli Whitney. By developing unsuccessful French efforts to produce standardised military weapons in large numbers, Whitney and his son, Eli II, laid the basis for the machine-made gun – i.e. with parts which would interchange from gun to gun with minimal (preferably no) handwork.

Whitney struggled greatly with the first musket order he obtained from the US Government in 1798, taking seven years to complete work instead of the allotted two, but had neither experience to guide him nor the benefit of efficient machine-tools. The Whitneys were forced to design virtually all of their tools from scratch.

It was the younger Whitney who threw Colt a lifeline after the failure of the latter's Paterson venture, making the Walker and early Dragoon Colts in the Whitneyville Armory in 1847–8. The subsequent success of Colt's own factory in Hartford, Connecticut, has tended to obscure the early co-operation between Colt and Whitney and painted the two men as deadly rivals.

The major gunmaking businesses concentrated in the north-eastern corner of the USA. In addition to Colt, in Hartford, Whitney worked in Whitneyville and then New Haven, Connecticut; the Sharps Rifle Company worked in Hartford and subsequently Bridgeport, Connecticut; Remington worked in Ilion in New York State; Winchester and Marlin settled in New Haven, Connecticut; Peabody traded in Providence, Rhode Island; Spencer in Boston, Massachusetts; Sharps & Hankins in Philadelphia; and Starr in Yonkers, New York. And the principal government armoury had been built in the small Massachusetts town of Springfield.

Virtually all the major participants, therefore, were based in New England. The story was much the same with ammunition, with E. I. Du Pont de Nemours, the major propellant maker, trading nearby in Wilmington in Delaware. Most of the first cartridge-loaders worked in the same districts. Crittenden & Tibbals worked in South Coventry, Connecticut; Fitch & Van Vechten and Jacob Goldmark traded from New York City; C. D. Leet operated in Springfield, Massachusetts; and the Sage Ammunition Works was sited in Middletown, Connecticut.

No 'mass producers' of firearms or ammunition ever operated in the Wild West. Although sporting guns were made in New Orleans and cap-lock Hawken 'Plains Rifles' were made in St Louis in some numbers, they were largely hand-made by traditional gunsmithing methods. Frank Freund made a few Sharps-type breechloaders in Denver, but there was no real manufacturing base west of the Mississippi or south of the Mason-Dixon Line.

Some Westerners relied on distributors such as Benjamin Kittredge of Cincinnati or John P. Lower's 'Sportsman's Store' in Denver for their guns and ammunition. Others relied on mail order, delivered originally by the overland stagecoach services and latterly by the railroads.

Shortages of guns were reflected in the mining industries west of the Mississippi, where even the most productive districts imported most of their tools. The needs of the farmer were also satisfied from the East. The problems testified to the meagre population west of the Hundredth Meridian (which added to the difficulties of distributing goods in sufficient numbers to be profitable), and to the violent and unsettled nature of the territories.

Although most Western towns had their gunsmiths, few were capable of anything other than basic repairs. Their supplies came from the East, or from the larger regional distributors. However, because the distributors and travelling salesmen were given the best discount rates by the true mass-market gunmakers, only the wares of a handful of major companies were commonly seen once the glut of old Civil War guns – a spectacular variety not always matched by utility – had finally worn off.

A deep-seated belief that the Westerners were armed exclusively with Sharps buffalo rifles, Winchester repeaters and Colt revolvers is misleading, although the grip Sharps, Winchester and Colt had on the distribution network ensures a basic truth. Other manufacturers did attempt to sell their goods into the Western markets, achieving localised and often temporary success, but they were greatly in the minority.

Consequently, a broad range of firearm can be legitimately associated with the Wild West, ranging from the tiniest single-shot self-defence pistol or 'derringer' up to target rifles showing considerable sophistication.

A guide to the efficiency of individual types of gun is given by the weapons of the gunmen. Realising that their lives depended not just on speed of fire but also its certainty, gunslingers were discerning. Whereas many Westerners were content to leave firearms in drawers or hanging on walls once the worst of the Indian wars was over, shooting only 'for the pot', the gunmen realised that their lives depended on their weapons. The simpler the gun, the easier it was to repair. Colt revolvers were favoured, partly because they were readily available and partly because they fired ammunition which was easy to acquire. Though the cap-and-ball Colts were weak in the frame, and though the original Peacemaker could not be carried safely with the hammer down on a loaded chamber, very little went wrong with a Colt. When it did, the local gunsmith could usually replace a broken spring, hammer or trigger pawl. Solid-frame Remingtons were sturdier than open-frame Colts, but prone to jamming.

When the first double-action and self-ejecting guns appeared, they were eagerly sought. The Smith & Wessons and the Forehand & Wadsworth patterns were more complicated than the single-action Peacemaker, gradually losing favour with the professionals, but the double-action .38 and .41 Colts introduced in 1878 sold in surprisingly large numbers for designs which are now popularly regarded as failures. Billy the Kid was one devotee of the double-action Colt, but there is little doubt that the fragility of the lock work was accompanied by breakages; consequently, the 'Lightning' and the 'Thunderer' – names bestowed by Kittredge – disappointed men used to the sturdy single-action Peacemaker.

The strictures applied to handguns hold true for the rifles. The most popular of the single-shot designs were the dropping-block Sharps and rolling-block Remington, both of which proved to be durable and dependable. Their greatest advantage was the ease with which they could chamber powerful long-case cartridges, offering sufficient hitting power to knock down a buffalo at long range.

The supremacy of these guns was challenged from time to time by designs such as the Ballard and the Whitney Phoenix, but few of their rivals were made in large enough numbers to mount serious competition. The Browning-designed single-shot Winchester, which is often seen as a rival, was not introduced commercially until 1885 and did not reach the West until buffalo-hunting had ceased.

Winchesters reigned supreme among the earliest magazine rifles, partly because they were made in large numbers but also because they were comparatively simple and trouble-free. The only major problem prior to 1876 lay in the use of nothing but low-power pistol-type cartridges, owing to a lack of strength in the locking mechanism. The advent of the 1876-type gun, based on a patent granted to Luke Wheelock in 1871, allowed Winchesters to handle ammunition which rivalled the cartridges of the single-shot guns. However, not until the first Browning-designed guns appeared in 1886 were the inherent shortcomings finally overcome.

The success of the 1866- and 1873-pattern Winchesters encouraged the introduction of many rival designs. Although many of these were interesting – the best of them were often superior technically – the Winchester Repeating Arms Company had such a stranglehold on distribution that few lever-action guns prospered prior to 1900 other than the sturdy and efficient Marlins. Winchester had cleverly strengthened its position by acquiring the business of Fogerty, Adirondack (Robinson) and others in the 1870s, and, as Fogerty had already incorporated the remnants of the Spencer Repeating Arms Company, few rivals remained in 1870 to challenge Winchester's supremacy.

Colt attempted to introduce a lever-action rifle designed by Andrew Burgess, but Winchester let it be known that if Colt persisted, revolvers would soon emanate from New Haven to challenge the Peacemaker. Wise counsel prevailed, and the Colt-Burgess disappeared after less than 10,000 rifles and carbines had been made. A slide-action Colt appeared in 1885, known as the 'Lightning', but the action proved to be too weak to survive the arduous usage common in the West and production ceased in the early 1900s.

Guns such as the lever-action Bullard were promoted on the basis of specific advantages – some could be loaded from the top or the bottom, or would operate upside-down – but the backers could rarely compete with Winchester and were usually forced into liquidation.

Substantial quantities of 'Trapdoor Springfield' rifles were sold by the US Army, first when the .50-calibre guns were superseded in the 1870s and then when the .30-calibre Krag-Jørgensen magazine rifles were introduced in the 1890s, though the old 'Trapdoors' were never distributed in sufficient numbers in the West to supersede the Sharps and the Remington. However, many Westerners were content to use military-pattern rifles remodelled in half-stock 'sporter' style; even Buffalo Bill Cody and George Armstrong Custer used .50-70 rifles of this general type.

Bolt-action rifles appeared in small numbers from the 1880s onwards, inspired by government trials with Remington-Lee, Chaffee-Reece and Winchester-Hotchkiss designs, but official hostility and their basic unfamiliarity restricted popularity prior to 1917; even repeating shotguns had attained far greater acceptance prior to 1900.

Acknowledgements

I am pleased to acknowledge assistance given by Joseph Rosa, author of *The Gunfighter: Man or Myth?* and the standard biography of Wild Bill Hickok, and rightly regarded as the finest of all 'Old World' Western historians. I am also grateful for the help of Ian Hogg, and to Tom Griffin, of the Lyman Products Corporation of Middletown, Connecticut, for supplying details of the performance of key nineteenth-century cartridges. Dr John P. Langellier provided helpful hints concerning the good and bad men of the West, and I hope that I have not misrepresented the authors of the books listed in the bibliography, whose tireless research has allowed a few corners to be cut.

By far the majority of the illustrations appear by courtesy of the Patent Offices in Britain and the USA, and from the wonderful sales catalogues published by San Francisco auctioneers Butterfield & Butterfield: not just fascinating reference tools, but also works of art in their own right. I am particularly grateful to Greg Martin, Specialist in Charge of the Arms & Armor Department, and to Ms Katja Kaiser, Departmental Manager, for their assistance with the processing of the photographs.

That *The Guns that Won the West* has appeared at all is due largely to the indulgence of my publisher, Lionel Leventhal of Greenhill Books, who has supported the project through an assortment of trials and tribulations which could form a book in themselves. And, of course, I would not have made progress without the love of Alison and Adam. I promise to remove everything from the dining-room table . . . until the next edition!

John Walter, Hove, 1999

CHRONOLOGY OF THE WEST

1801. Census assesses population of USA as 5.3 million. Thomas Jefferson becomes third President of the USA (4 March).

1803. The Louisiana Purchase (from France) doubles the size of the USA. The land was sold to fund Napoleon's military campaigns, but New York and Massachusetts threatened to withdraw from the Union as the purchase had not been ratified by the Senate.

1811. New Orleans slave riot put down, with more than sixty Black dead (10 January). Battle of Tippecanoe; Shawnee Indian army destroyed by US troops led by General Harrison (7 November).

1812. The USS *Constitution* destroys the British frigate HMS *Guerrière* (19 August). John H. Hall patents his breechloading rifle. The 'War of 1812' begins.

1813. Battle of the Thames (Ontario, Canada); US General Harrison defeats British and Indian forces under General Proctor (5 October). Tecumseh is killed in the fighting.

1814. Most of the Library of Congress in Washington DC burned down, allegedly with British assistance. A US force defeats a British naval squadron in the 'Battle of Plattsburgh' on Lake Champlain (11 September). End of the War of 1812.

1815. British forces are destroyed with the loss of 700 men at Battle of New Orleans (8 January), after the peace treaty has been signed.

1817. Mississippi becomes the twentieth State of the Union. The Ohio Indians cede four million acres of land to the US Government. The sternwheeler steamship *Washington* makes the first voyage from Louisville, Kentucky, to New Orleans and back (3 March). The border between the USA and Canada is established as the 49th Parallel from Lake of the Woods to the Rockies (20 October).

1818. Artemus Wheeler and Elisha Collier patent a mechanically revolved flintlock revolver in England.

1819. Spain cedes Florida and all possessions east of the Mississippi to the USA. Alabama becomes the 21st State of the Union.

1822. Joshua Shaw patents a percussion cap in the USA.

1823. President Monroe declares the 'Monroe Doctrine': 'The American continents are not to be considered as subjects for future colonisation by any European Power . . .'

1825. Opening of the Erie Canal (26 October), connecting the Great Lakes with the Hudson River and thus the Atlantic.

1830. The first section of the Baltimore & Ohio Rail Road is opened (24 May).

1833. Captain Benjamin de Bournville begins a three-year expedition to explore and chart the Rocky Mountains.

1835. Samuel Colt patents a mechanically operated revolver in England.

1836. The Colt revolver is patented in the USA (February). Missionary Marcus Whitman leads wife Narcissa Whitman and Eliza Spalding to the Pacific Ocean, the first white women to cross America. The Battle of the Alamo (6 March). The Battle of San Jacinto (21 April) results in the capture of Mexican President Antonio de Santa Anna and ends the Texas–Mexican War, allowing Texas to declare independence. The first railway in Canada links Laprairie with St John's (2 July).

1841. The first emigrant wagon-train arrives in Oregon Country after a trek of 2000 miles, often across hostile Indian territory.

1844. Fifteen Texas Rangers armed with Paterson Colt revolvers, commanded by Colonel Hays, attack 300 Comanches. About 125 warriors are killed.

1845. Texas is annexed by the USA.

1846. President James Polk declares war on Mexico (13 January) after negotiations to purchase New Mexico have broken down. US forces commanded by General Zachary Taylor defeat the Mexicans at Palo Alto (8 May) and Reseca (9 May), forcing the Mexicans to retreat across the Rio Grande. The Black Bear Rebellion begins on 14 June in the Sacramento Valley, as settlers declare the Republic of California independent of Mexico. The Oregon Treaty (15 June) agrees to continue the 49th Parallel separating British and US territories westward of the Rockies.

1847. More than 200,000 people flee the famines in Ireland, mainly bound for North America. This has an important effect on Western settlement. Colt supplies a thousand .44-calibre 'Walker Colt' revolvers to the US Dragoons, with the help of the Whitney factory. US forces led by General Zachary Taylor crush Santa Anna at the Battles of Buena Vista (23 February) and Cerro Gordo (18 April).

1848. Colt founds a factory of his own in Hartford, Connecticut, where the first Colt Dragoon and pocket-size revolvers are made. Christian Sharps patents his breechloading rifle. The treaty of Guadalupe Hidalgo (2 February) ends war with Mexico. Mexico sells the USA all the land north of the Rio Grande, including California, for $15 million.

1849. Gold is discovered by James Marshall near Sutter's Mill, California (24

January), the prelude to a 'Gold Rush' involving more than 6000 prospectors.

1850. Senator Henry Clay introduces a 'Compromise Bill' (29 January) to reduce tension between northern and southern states over slavery. California is admitted as the 31st State of the Union (9 September).

1851. Colt exhibits his revolvers at the Great Exhibition in London (opened 1 May), though his contributions are largely overlooked in favour of the guns displayed by his English rival, Robert Adams.

1853. Introduction of the perfected Sharps 'Slant Breech' rifles and carbines.

1854. Passing of the Kansas–Nebraska Act, and the beginning of border warfare in Kansas.

1855. Introduction of the first .58-calibre 'Springfield' rifle-musket and the Springfield carbine-pistol. The first two regiments of US Cavalry are raised in this period. Grant of a patent to Rollin White, protecting a revolver with bored-through chambers in its cylinder. Smith & Wesson formed. The Volcanic Arms Company, predecessor of Winchester, is formed in New Haven, Connecticut.

1856. Colt closes his unsuccessful London factory, which had been opened only four years earlier.

1857. The New Haven Arms Company, successor to Volcanic, is formed. The Mountain Meadows Massacre (11 September) occurs when more than 300 Ute Indians, led by Mormons, kill almost all of the 135 emigrants accompanying the Fancher wagon-train.

1858. The US Cavalry test the Merrill, Latrobe & Thomas carbine without success. E. Remington & Sons introduce a revolver designed by Fordyce Beals.

1859. Colt's Patent Fire Arms Mfg Co. introduce a shoulder stock for revolvers. John Brown raids Harper's Ferry Armory (16 October). Federal troops under Colonel Robert E. Lee overpower and capture Brown (18 December). Brown is hanged for treason in Charleston (2 December).

1860. The .44-calibre Colt New Model Army Revolver (or 'M1860') appears. Fort Defiance, New Mexico, is attacked by a thousand Navajo Indians after the soldiers have slaughtered the Indians' sheep and goats for food (30 April–3 May). The attacks are repulsed, but only at great cost. Abraham Lincoln is elected President of the USA (November), but discontent with the Union is increasingly heard.

1861. The American Civil War begins with the bombardment of Fort Sumter (12 April). The Battle of Ball's Bluff, on the Potomac river, gives the Confederate army its first important victory (2 October). On 1 November Lincoln entrusts General George McClellan with overall command of the Federal army. McClellan immediately begins training 200,000 men. Kansas becomes the 16th State of the Union. Colt introduces the .36-calibre New Model Navy Revolver. Remington introduces the New Army and New Navy revolvers. Springfield Armory begin to make a new-model rifle-musket. Richard Gatling is granted a US Patent protecting his mechanically operated machine-gun.

1862. Production of Henry's improved rimfire cartridge begins. Confederate forces under General Henry Sibley seize Santa Fé (4 March). The first naval battle of the war allows the Confederate iron-clad *Merrimack* to destroy the Federal frigate *Cumberland* and damage *Congress* (8 March); a day later, CSS *Merrimack* and USS *Monitor* pound each other in a stand-off from which both emerge relatively unscathed. The Battle of Shiloh (6–7 April) is inconclusive, with horrendous casualties on both sides. A Sioux uprising in Minnesota under Little Crow (beginning on 17 August) is suppressed; nearly forty warriors are hanged on 26 December. Confederate troops commanded by Generals Jackson and Longstreet defeat Union forces commanded by Pope at the Second Battle of Bull Run or 'Manassas' (30 August); the Battle of Antietam (17 September) is inconclusive; but Confederate General Robert E. Lee routs Union forces led by General Ambrose Burnside at the Battle of Fredericksburg (13 December). Samuel Colt dies at the age of only forty-eight. Passage of the Homestead Act.

1863. On 25 January, Lincoln replaces Burnside with General Joseph 'Fightin' Joe' Hooker. Confederate forces commanded by Lee defeat Union forces (1–4 May), but Stonewall Jackson dies of his wounds on 10 May. General George Meade replaces General Hooker as commander of the Army of the Potomac (28 June). The turning-point of the war comes at the Battle of Gettysburg (1–3 July), when Lee's Confederate forces are defeated. The fall of Vicksburg to General Grant (4 July) gives control of the Mississippi to the Union. Draft Riots affect the northern cities, especially New York, from 11 July; the costs include about 1200 dead. Confederate forces commanded by Braxton Bragg defeat Union forces at the Battle of Chickamauga, but only at a terrible cost. On 19 November, President Abraham Lincoln dedicates the national cemetery at Gettysburg with the famous 'Gettysburg Address', which effectively frees all slaves. At the Battle of Chattanooga (23–25 November), Bragg and his Confederate troops are routed. Remington improves the New Army and New Navy revolvers.

1864. General Ulysses Grant is made Commander-in-Chief of the Union armies (10 March). Lee defeats Grant at the Battle of Cold Harbor (1–3 June). Confederate forces beat General Sherman at the Battle of Kenesaw Mountain (27 July). Sinking of the Confederate commerce raider *Alabama* by USS *Kearsarge*, off Cherbourg. Fire destroys most of the revolver-making facilities in the Colt factory in Hartford, allowing other companies to make unlicensed copies and Remington to supply tens of thousands of revolvers to the Federal armed forces. At the Battle of Franklin (30 November), Union forces backed with Gatling Guns defeat Confederate units led by General Hood.

1865. Charleston, South Carolina, surrenders to Union navy (18 February). General Ulysses Grant takes Richmond, Virginia (3 April). Lee's surrender at Appomattox Court House effectively ends the Civil War (9 April). President Abraham Lincoln is assassinated by John Wilkes Booth in Ford's Theatre, Washington (14 April); Booth is hunted down and killed on 26 April. The infamous guerrilla leader William Clarke Quantrill is shot by Union troops in May. The first Allin 'Trapdoor Springfield' conversion is approved.

1866. Nelson King receives a US Patent protecting improvements to the Henry rifle, resulting in the first lever-action Winchester rifle.

1867. Abilene, Kansas, becomes the major junction on the cattle trail running northward from Texas. The Dominion of Canada is formed (29 March), and the USA buys Alaska from Russia for $7 million (30 March).

1869. A metallic-cartridge conversion for Colt revolvers is patented by Alexander Thuer. Expiry of the Rollin White patent. First .44-calibre Smith & Wesson revolver patented in England. The Union Pacific and Central Pacific Rail Roads meet at Promontory Summit, Utah (10 March), completing the first transcontinental railway.

1870. Smith & Wesson revolver accepted for service with the US Army.

1871. Metallic-cartridge conversion for Colt revolvers patented by Charles Richards. First 'Russian' and 'Schofield' Smith & Wessons.

1872. Colt makes a few thousand open-frame revolvers chambered for metallic cartridges, and begins development of an improved solid-frame design.

1873. The Colt Single Action Army Revolver (alias 'Model P' or 'Peacemaker') is introduced. The improved M1873 lever-action Winchester appears in .44-40. The perfected .45-calibre 'Trapdoor Springfield' rifle is approved after a year of tests. Barbed wire, invented by Henry Rose, is exhibited at the Illinois State Fair. Subsequently made in large quantities by Glidden & Haish, it allows crops and livestock to be enclosed, and becomes an important catalyst in the taming of the West.

1874. Gold is discovered in the Black Hills. Lieutenant-Colonel George A. Custer leads an expedition to the Black Hills.

1875. Remington introduce a New Model Army revolver chambered for metallic-case ammunition. Alexander Graham Bell invents the telephone.

1876. The Centennial Exposition opens in Philadelphia. Custer and 263 officers and men of the 7th Cavalry are slaughtered at the Battle of the Little Big Horn (25 June). Wild Bill Hickok is murdered in Deadwood,

Dakota Territory, by gambler John McCall (2 August). US Army trials with Colt, Remington and Smith & Wesson 'Schofield' revolvers.

1877. The first double-action Colt revolver appears.

1878. US Army tests Colt and Merwin & Hulbert revolvers. Introduction of the Smith & Wesson New Model No. 3 revolver.

1881. The Gunfight at the OK Corral. President James Garfield is shot by Charles Guiteau (2 July). Billy the Kid killed by Pat Garrett (15 July). Death of President Garfield from gunshot wounds (19 September).

1882. Suicide of Colonel Schofield. Murder of Jesse James by Robert Ford.

1883. William F. Cody founds 'Buffalo Bill's Wild West' show. Invention of the recoil-operated 'Maxim Gun' by Hiram S. Maxim (1840–1916).

1886. The 'Haymarket Massacre' occurs in Chicago (4 May), during a protest by the Knights of Labor against working conditions; more than thirty people are killed.

1887. The Canadian Pacific Railway reaches Vancouver.

1889. Colt introduces a .38-calibre double-action revolver with a swing-out cylinder, which is adopted by the US Navy.

1890. The Remington Arms Company introduces an improved solid-frame army revolver. The arrest of Sitting Bull leads to his murder (15 December) by an Indian policeman, Red Tomahawk, after a skirmish with reservation police. The Battle of Wounded Knee (29 December) leads to the deaths of about 250 Indian men, women and children at the hands of US cavalrymen. The Superintendent of Census declares that the Western Frontier no longer exists.

1892. Winchester introduces the M1892 lever-action rifle. The US Army adopts the .30-calibre Krag-Jørgensen magazine rifle.

1894. Winchester introduces the M1894 lever-action rifle.

1895. Winchester introduces the M1895 lever-action rifle. John Wesley Hardin is killed in El Paso by John Selman (19 August).

1897. John Browning patents his first semi-automatic pistols. The USA annexes the Hawaiian Islands (16 June), a decision ratified by the Hawaiian Senate on 9 September.

1898. The destruction of USS *Maine* in Havana Harbour (15 February), with a loss of 260 men. A US Navy Court of Enquiry concludes that the explosion has been caused externally. Publication of the report (28 March) blames Spain, war commences on 22 April. US Navy victories at Manila Bay (1 May) and Santiago Bay (3 June) destroy the Spanish battlefleet, and the land Battle of San Juan Hill (1–2 July) also ends in defeat for the Spanish.

1900. The population of North America is estimated at 81 million people.

CHAPTER 1

FIELDS OF GOLD

Opening the Frontier, 1848–61

'I have no hesitation now in saying that there is more gold in the country drained by the Sacramento and San Joaquin rivers than will pay the cost of the war with Mexico a hundred times over.'

Colonel R. B. Mason, US Army, military governor of California, after touring the goldfields in 1849.

Definitions of the 'Wild West' can be legitimately varied with the passage of time. This was largely due to the California Gold Rush, which fixed the image of the little-known Spanish settlements on the Pacific coast firmly in the minds of the Easterners, and to the march of settlement westward across the central USA.

Much of the confusion can be resolved by studying a map of the United States of America, paying particular attention to geology. The Appalachian mountain system in the east separates a narrow coastal plain bordering the Atlantic – broadening as it runs south-westward to the Gulf of Mexico – from a vast triangular-shaped area of plains and lowland. This tapers downward from the border with Canada to western Texas, and is blocked to the west by the vast natural barrier of the Rocky Mountains.

A plateau region of hostile sun-baked desert must then be traversed before reaching the western mountains (the Cascades and the Sierra Nevada) that separate the desert plateau from the narrow Pacific coastal margins.

A major handicap to exploration was provided by the major rivers. Most of those that rise in the mountain ranges customarily flow seaward, back the way most settlers had come, and the systems of the Great Plains often flowed southward. The Mississippi and Missouri, boon though they were to north/south trade, represented a huge barrier to east/west movement.

Although there was a long-established Spanish presence in California, few settlers ventured west of the Appalachians before the War of Independence. By 1820, however, the Mississippi had been crossed, and, by 1840, the western frontier was generally regarded as the Hundredth Meridian. Yet the 'Wild West' of legend was short lived in its pristine form; by 1890, the year of the

Wounded Knee massacre, the Superintendent of Census was reporting that no single frontier line was discernible anywhere on the map.

The progress of settlement is evident in the dates of incorporation of the individual states. Those that lay between the Mississippi and the Hundredth Meridian were all granted statehood prior to the Civil War – Louisiana in 1818, Missouri in 1822, Arkansas in 1836, Texas in 1846, Iowa in 1847 and Minnesota in 1858. Excepting California and Oregon (incorporated in the Union in 1851 and 1859 respectively) the status of territory westward of the Hundredth Meridian, however, took years to resolve. Nevada was incorporated in 1865, largely owing to the discovery of great mineral riches, and Nebraska followed in 1867. Then came Colorado (1877); Dakota, Idaho, Montana and Washington (1890); Wyoming (1891); Utah (1896); and finally Arizona and New Mexico, where grants of statehood were delayed until 1912.

Any attempts to cross the mid-nineteenth century USA faced terrible hardships. Explorers such as Lewis and Clark tried hard at the beginning of the nineteenth century to find safe routes, followed by Fremont and others in the 1840s, but were often defeated by the towering faces of the Rockies and the arid desertland which backed them to westward. Gradually, however, the USA grew.

The Louisiana Purchase of 1803, from France, was followed by the annexation of Florida (1812) and Texas (1845); by the acquisition of Oregon Country (1845–6); and by the cession of the south-western part of the USA by Mexico in the Treaty of Guadalupe Hidalgo (1848).

The discovery of gold on 24 January 1848 near Sutter's Mill, a little known township in California, was a major catalyst in the growth of the Wild West. News of the lucky strike travelled slowly at first, but eventually reached the eastern USA. Chaos ensued as thousands of men and their families set out on the dangerous journey across the uncharted Great Plains towards the foothills of the Rocky Mountains.

The Gold Rush persuaded the brave – and the foolhardy – that the risks were worth taking, creating a rapid population boom which established California as an important and fast-growing, if isolated, State of the Union. The first overland routes from east to west were the Settler Trails. Gradually, however, the need to communicate rapidly with California and the otherwise isolated far-west states created alternative routes.

Many men began their journeys from towns such as Cincinnati or St Louis, striking westward along the Oregon Trail and the Platte river until they reached Fort Laramie. The route led westward through Wyoming to Forkham, where the California Trail began at the head of the Snake river. Prospectors who had survived to Forkham turned south-westward for Sacramento, San Francisco and the Pacific Ocean, and the staging posts along the route grew into important townships.

Other routes included the Upper Emigrant Trail, the Bozeman Trail, the Taos Trail, the Atlantic–Pacific Trail, the Fort Smith–Santa Fé trail, and, eventually, the routes taken by the stagecoach and mail routes. The Central Express ran from Missouri to San Francisco by way of Ogden, Reno and Sacramento; the Butterfield Overland Express connected St Louis with Los Angeles and San Francisco by way of New Mexico; and the San Antonio Express, as its name suggested, ran from the Texan town of San Antonio to San Francisco. The Pony Express and the Overland Stage also contested these routes for a few years.

The east/west emigrant trails were eventually cut in many places by the Beef or Drove Trails, which were used to herd cattle from the fertile plains of western Texas northward to the burgeoning markets provided by first the 'Railway Towns', then the stockyards of the north-east, which led to the growing population of the industrial districts surrounding the Great Lakes, which, in concert with the growing railway network, allowed many a fortune to be made in Canada and the New England states. The Beef Trails all struck out from the Texas town of San Antonio. The Shawnee Trail ran to Fort Worth, then forked west to Junction City or east to Kansas City. The Chisholm or 'Chizzum' Trail ran by way of Wichita and Newton to Abilene. And the Western Trail reached the quaintly named Beans Store before running on to Ogallala.

However, the trek westward to California was quite as dangerous as it was arduous. Men, women and children died of thirst on the plains and deserts, or froze to death seeking elusive paths through the mountains. Others were killed by marauding Indians, who felt threatened by the settlers' incursions. Some simply disappeared without trace, until the creation of the transcontinental railways finally eased the hardships of westward migration.

Not everyone, of course, dared risk the direct overland route. Yet the alternatives were no less unpleasant; the protracted sea-haul south to Cape Horn and then north to California was fraught with danger, and the pestilential Isthmus of Panama killed many of those who dared to cross from the Atlantic to the Pacific.

By 1850, what had once been small Spanish colonial towns had often become hotbeds of saloons, brothels and tricksters. The population of California tripled in a year, and had reached more than ten times its 1848 levels by 1851. Fortunes were won and lost at gaming tables, where life was cheapened to the point where the *Illustrated London News* could report in the summer of 1851 that:

> The crime of homicide continues to prevail all over the country to an extent which [elsewhere] would be taken as proof that civil society was completely disorganised. Our 'Homicide Calendar' for June, lately published in the *San Francisco Chronicle*, the 'total of Killed' for the first six months of the present year

> is set down at 219 persons; and in the same period, 'Hung by the sheriff, 2; hung by the mob, 24'. But whether the two judicial and twenty-four lynch executions are included, I am not able to determine. The number of 'killed' in the month of June was twenty – a fact which it is sincerely to be hoped may be taken as evidence that the homicidal epidemic is abating.

An insatiable appetite for guns brought into the Californian market Colt revolvers, Deringer pistols, Hawken rifles and many other products of the industrialised eastern states, helping to lay the foundations of an arms industry which would eventually fuel a bloody Civil War.

Longarms

Single-Shot Muzzleloaders

The cap lock retained its popularity far longer in the West than in military service, lasting almost into the twentieth century in remote parts of the USA. This was due largely to the scarcity of metal-case ammunition in some Frontier districts, and persuaded men whose livelihood depended on firearms to be wary of innovation.

The single-shot rifle had a long pedigree, descending through the flintlock Trade Guns supplied to settlers and Indians alike during the eighteenth century, to the indigenous Long Rifles. By the 1840s, however, the markets had changed. Cap locks were finding increasing favour not only among gunmakers, but also with hunters who ventured out across the Great Plains in pursuit of buffalo.

Development of what is now known generically as the '**Plains Rifle**' – but was originally known as the 'Mountain Rifle' or 'Hawkins [sic] Rifle' – is usually credited to the brothers Jacob and Samuel Hawken of St Louis, Missouri, though many other gunmakers in the Mid-West made them.

The prototypes were probably the Long Rifles, originating in Pennsylvania, that had shown their deadly efficiency on eastern game. However, the quarry east of the Appalachians were small, and customarily pursued on foot. Consequently, as they had to be carried for considerable distances, the guns were usually light, slender and small-calibre.

The needs of plainsmen were very different; the small-calibre Long Rifles had little effect on buffalo or bear, and much of the travelling was done on horseback. Long-barrelled prototypes, therefore, were adapted to become shorter and heavier guns firing large bullets with exceptionally large powder charges. The Mountain Rifles lost much of the elegance of their predecessors in this transition – in some ways reverting to the hefty construction of the eighteenth-century Jaeger Rifles from which Long Rifles descended – but the general lines could still be detected. Sturdy stocks with strong wrists were essential to protect the guns if they fell from the saddle or had to double as a climbing stick.

Mountain Rifles typically had barrels of 28–32in, bored to 0.50–0.55, and could weigh 12lb or more. This was necessary to ensure that the recoil of guns firing heavyweight bullets with propellant charges which could exceed 200 grains was kept within bounds.

The guns had half- or full stocks with comparatively little ornamentation, as the pierced brass strapwork and silver escutcheons of the Long Rifles had given way to simpler iron furniture. This was probably due to a desire to reduce cost, but probably also owed something to local scarcity of brass and silver and an appreciation that bright metal reflected light too readily on the vast plains.

Barrels, often octagonal, were held in the stock by transverse keys set in oval washers screwed or pinned to the fore-end sides; a patch box (oval or rectangular) was set in the right side of the butt, often accompanied by a decorative patch-box plate; and the trigger guard often had a rearward scroll or spur. Wiping rods were carried in pipes beneath the barrel.

The first Mountain Rifles were flintlocks, but the majority have side-action cap locks. Set triggers are commonly encountered and open 'Buckhorn' sights were standard. Manufacturers included the Hawken brothers, Diettrich, John Gemmer and Horace Dimick of St Louis; Edward Tryon of Philadelphia; Henry Leman of Pittsburgh; Carlos Gove, John Lower and Morgan Rood of Denver; and Jasper Maltby of Galena, Illinois.

The 'Golden Age' of the Mountain Rifle stretched from the early 1820s to the end of the Civil War in 1865, when its supremacy was erased by competition provided first by the Sharps and subsequently the Remington breechloaders.

Jacob Hawken had died in May 1849, at a time when his products were already being challenged by similar guns made elsewhere in St Louis, and Samuel Hawken sold the business to John Gemmer in 1862. Gemmer continued to make cap-lock rifles for some years, but then became better known as a distributor of breechloading cartridge firearms. The last true Hawken Rifle was made by Samuel shortly before he died in 1884.

The steady progression in the design of **military firearms** in the middle of the nineteenth century was accompanied by a regular disposal of obsolescent guns, which were sold at auction or occasionally to soldiers who had completed their terms of service. This meant that a steady flow of old muskets and carbines reached the West prior to the Civil War, to be followed after 1865 by a much greater variety of muskets, rifle-muskets and breechloaders.

The history of the firearms of the US Army prior to the Civil War was essentially similar to that of most European states. Beginning with a gradual diminution of calibre and the rifling of many otherwise obsolescent large-calibre weapons, it had led in the 1850s to the universal adoption of rifle-muskets firing self-expanding Minié projectiles.

The first regulation cap lock, a cadet musket authorised in 1841, was followed by better known weapons such as the .54 Model 1841 rifle, the .69 Model 1842 musket, and a .54-calibre Model 1842 pistol made by Henry Aston of Middletown, Connecticut.

The M1841 rifle was about 48.8in long and weighed 9lb 12oz. It had a conventional cap lock, a walnut stock with a brass patch box, and two brightly polished brass bands. The trigger guard was also brass. The 33-inch barrel, rifled with seven grooves, had a standing back sight for fifty yards. Known as the Mississippi or Yaeger Rifle, it was made at Harper's Ferry (25,296 in 1846–55). Other contractors included E. Remington & Sons of Ilion, New York, who took over an abortive contract granted to John Griffiths of Cincinnati; Robbins, Kendall & Lawrence and their successors, Robbins & Lawrence of Windsor, Vermont; Edward Tryon & Company of Philadelphia; and Eli Whitney of Whitneyville, Connecticut.

The .69-calibre M1842 musket was essentially similar to the last of the regulation flintlocks, but had a cap lock and a bolster on the right side of the breech to accommodate the nipple. It was 57.7in long, had a 42-inch smoothbore barrel and weighed 9lb 3oz. Furniture was iron. Though originally smooth-bored, most survivors had been rifled after the introduction of the M1855 rifle-musket; 14,292 were adapted in 1856–9, though not all were given new Minié-ball sights. The revised back sight had a single leaf with a slider, graduated to 900 yards.

Surviving M1841 rifles were altered at the same time, their bores being reamed-out to .58 and re-rifled to handle conical bullets. They were also given new long-range sights. The original 1855 rifle-musket pattern had a single leaf with a slider and a stepped base, but was replaced in 1858 by a simpler pattern with two small folding leaves. Some guns were subsequently fitted with a screw-adjustable back sight of superior performance.

A new sabre bayonet was attached either by a conventional spring, groove and stud, or by a cumbersome system of rings. Some bayonets relied on split rings while others had a pommel ring sliding over the front sight until the guard-ring could be locked on the muzzle by a thumb-screw. Guns converted after 1859 usually accepted socket bayonets.

The Musketoon Model 1847 was adopted for cavalry, artillery and sappers on 12 March 1847, production continuing until 1856. The original guns had standing-block back sights and swivel rammers; post-1851 examples had chain rammers and an improved sight with holes for 300 and 500 yards in the leaf, plus a 700-yard notch on the leaf edge. A sling bar and ring ran from the second barrel band to the breech.

After the M1855 rifle-carbine had been approved for the cavalry, 1847-pattern musketoons were made exclusively for artillerymen and sappers. Guns for the artillery were issued with socket bayonets; sapper examples took distinctive sabre bayonets, and had swivels under the butt and band.

Many old flintlock muskets were modernised at Springfield Armory in the 1850s, 30,431 Model 1822 and 26,841 Model 1840 guns being fitted with cap locks in 1851 alone. Some of the best survivors were rifled and resighted for expanding-ball ammunition in the late 1850s.

Remington converted 5000 Model 1816 muskets by exchanging the old flintlocks for cap locks with Maynard Tape Primers, and many flintlocks that survived into the early days of the Civil War were converted in 1861–2. These simply had the old breech cut away and a plug carrying the nipple-bolster screwed into the barrel.

The advent of the Minié expanding ball brought new small-calibre weapons. Approved on 5 July 1855, the series comprised a rifle-musket, a rifle, a rarely encountered rifle-carbine (only 1020 were made in 1855–6) and a pistol-carbine. The .58-calibre rifle-musket was typical of its genre, firing a self-expanding Minié ball from a 40-inch barrel in which three grooves made a turn in 72in. It was 56in long, weighed 9lb 2oz and had iron furniture.

The enthusiasm of Jefferson Davis, the Secretary of War, ensured that the Maynard Tape Primer was adopted for all the 1855-type guns excepting the rifled cavalry carbine. The Ordnance Department was less certain, but the Maynard system had performed well enough on trial to allay the worst fears.

The official endorsement in July 1855 also accepted .58-calibre for all small arms. It also noted that the 'present rifle, modified by the adoption of the new calibre and primer lock, will be ... issued to the sappers instead of the sappers' musketoon, the manufacture of which will be discontinued'. The single-shot pistol carbine was to be used 'as a carbine by light artillery and mounted troops'. It was universally disliked, as it was far inferior to the Colt Dragoon revolvers.

Changes made to the basic M1855 musket included the adoption of a simple two-leaf back sight in 1858, together with substitution of an iron fore-end tip for the older brass pattern and the appearance of a butt-side patch box in 1859.

About 2500 M1858 cadet rifles were made at Springfield Armory in 1858–60, similar to the M1855 rifle-musket but with a 38-inch barrel and a short-bladed bayonet. The Model 1855 rifle was a two-band variant of the musket, its 33-inch barrel accepting a sabre bayonet. Measuring 49.4in overall and weighing about 10lb without its bayonet, it had iron furniture. It was originally equipped with a detachable cross-hair front sight, held against the existing sight block by a binding screw to facilitate accurate shooting. The delicacy of the sight meant that it was normally carried in the patch box on the butt-side.

Single-Shot Breechloaders

One of the most interesting of the military rifles produced in the USA prior to the 1850s was the work of John Harris **Hall**, born into a prosperous mercantile family in Portland, Maine, in 1778. After unsuccessfully experimenting with shipbuilding, Hall began work on a breechloading rifle. This was patented on 21 May 1811 in collusion with William Thornton, a Washington architect.

Confident of its merits, John Hall immediately offered the gun to the US government. The first exhibition aroused great interest in the army, and Hall supplied substantial quantities of prototype and semi-experimental weapons, most of which were made in his workshops on Richardson's Wharf, Portsmouth, New Hampshire.

The US Army formally adopted the Hall rifle as the 'Model of 1819', spending more than $150,000 on perfecting it. Hall superintended efforts to make the guns on an assembly-line basis, designing many of the machine-tools personally. Indeed, it has been claimed that the Hall rifle was the first to offer complete interchangeability of parts and by so doing finished the work begun by Eli Whitney and Simeon North. It appears that some handwork was still needed before the guns could be passed by government inspectors as fit for service, but it seems churlish to deny Hall the credit he deserves; unlike most earlier breechloading rifles, which had remained as prototypes, curiosities or small-scale trials issue, the Hall rifle was distributed in surprisingly large quantities.

Prior to his death in the Missouri town of Moberly in February 1841, Hall had received nearly $40,000 – a staggeringly huge sum for the day – in royalty and patent-licensing fees. Production of Hall-system guns was surprisingly large by the standards of the day, even though manufacture taxed facilities to the utmost. By 1842, when production ceased, about 23,500 rifles had been made by the government armoury at Harper's Ferry and gunmakers such as Henry Deringer, R. & J. D. Johnson, Reuben Ellis and Simeon North; production of carbines had amounted to 13,684 by 1842, though orders were still being fulfilled and the final total is difficult to determine.

The essence of the Hall system was a removable chamber embodying the lock. Although this permitted a tighter-fitting bullet and undoubtedly enhanced accuracy, gas leaked from the interface between the chamber and the bore and reduced the value of what was otherwise a creditable design. No attempts seem to have been made to improve the seal (cf. the Sharps rifles), other than to reduce manufacturing tolerances and improve the metal-to-metal fit. Changes made in the basic action by North & Savage, principally concerned with the locking mechanism, were too few to allow the Hall to compete satisfactorily with even the first rifle-muskets.

Tests undertaken in 1826 showed that the Hall could be fired much more rapidly than muzzleloading rivals: a hundred shots were fired during the time in which the standard flintlock service rifle managed forty-three and the musket could muster merely thirty-seven. Unfortunately, even though muzzle velocities were lower, the Hall powder charge was much heavier than the muzzleloading equivalents to compensate for the loss of gas at the breech.

Experiments at West Point in 1837 revealed that penetration in oak at 100 yards was one inch for the muzzle-loading musket, .93 for the muzzleloading rifle and only .34 for the cap-lock Hall. The trials also showed that the muzzle velocity of the Hall-North carbine was merely 1240 ft/sec compared with 1687 ft/sec for the Jenks carbine, which fired the same seventy-grain charge and had a barrel of comparable length.

The original or 1819-type Hall rifle had a .52-calibre 32.7in barrel, measured 52.5in overall, and weighed about 10.25lb without its socket bayonet. The barrel was rifled with sixteen-groove right-hand or 'clockwise' twist making a turn in 96in. Reaming-out 1.5in of the muzzle gave the appearance of a smooth bore. A hundred-grain powder charge fired a .525-diameter ball weighing about 220 grains (0.5oz). Priming was ten grains of fine powder.

A contract sealed on 19 March 1819 permitted the US Government to make 1000 Hall-system rifles in Harper's Ferry armoury. However, even though John Hall was employed to oversee the contract, continual problems delayed completion of the first order until 1824. Construction of another 1000 began immediately, and a third 6000-gun contract followed on 22 April 1828.

Although the comparatively meagre facilities in Harper's Ferry were enough to satisfy the needs of the US Army, they could not handle orders placed on behalf of the militia forces of individual states. In accordance with the Militia Act of 1808, therefore, the government ordered additional Hall rifles from Simeon North. The last of North's 5000 guns was delivered by 1836.

A Hall-system carbine appeared in 1833, with a 23-inch smooth-bored barrel. The first cap-lock firearm accepted for service in the US Army, it was 43in overall and weighed 8lb 3oz. The carbine also introduced a rod bayonet, which slid in the fore-end beneath the barrel. There were two barrel bands, and a large sling ring lay beneath the under-edge of the butt in the extremity of the trigger-guard. Some carbines had a patch box let into the butt, but this feature does not seem to have been universal.

A series of .69-calibre smooth-bore carbines, made for the Regiment of Dragoons in 1834 and the Second Dragoons in 1836–7, often incorporated old stocks and other components which had been held in store. They were similar to their predecessors, retaining the rod bayonet, but had shorter barrels, an eye bolt through the stock-wrist to retain a sling, and a hole bored through the hammer.

On 3 March 1840, the Secretary of War approved a 21-inch carbine barrel and the substitution of a ramrod for the fragile rod bayonet. Five hundred Model 1840 carbines had been delivered by 2 May, fitted with a folding elbow- or 'L'-shape breech lever designed by government arms inspector Nahum Patch, but the operating lever was unpopular; from August 1840 until June 1843, therefore, 6000 were made with a 'fishtail' pattern credited to Captain James Huger of the US Army. The .52-calibre M1842 carbine was the last of the regulation-pattern Halls, 1000 being made in 1842–3. These had Huger-pattern breech levers; in addition, the design of the trigger-guard bow and the brass furniture differed from earlier guns.

A few improved or 1841-pattern cap-lock rifles were made at Harper's Ferry after Hall's death. Their receivers lacked a flash guard; the catch plate was integral with the trigger guard; a Huger-type breech lever was used; and the barrel was rifled with seven grooves extending to the muzzle. Production apparently exceeded 2500 in 1841–3, though documentation is lacking.

The Hall-North carbines, often listed officially as the 'Improved Model of 1840' (or M1843), had a side-mounted breech lever protected by US Patent 3686 granted to Henry North & Edward Savage in July 1844. About 11,000 carbines were made in 1842–50. Lacking rod bayonets, they had 21-inch .52-calibre smooth bore barrels and measured 40in overall. A sling bar and ring ran from the second barrel band back along the left side of the receiver.

Simeon North was asked to deliver 1000 carbines of the original model in 1843 (with the Huger fishtail lever), together with 500 guns with the North & Savage lever. Subsequent deliveries of the improved guns, at the rate of 500 every six months, were to be made until 3000 had been delivered into government stores by 1 July 1846.

Some Hall and Hall-North guns, long since declared obsolete, remained serviceable until the Civil War; others, displaced from military service by better weapons, were still serving settlers out on the Frontier. Federal ordnance records reveal that 1575 Hall rifles and 3520 Hall carbines were bought back into store from state reserves, and it is assumed that these saw service during the war alongside comparable guns remaining in the hands of militia and volunteers. Others served the Confederacy.

The 1843-pattern Hall carbine featured in one of the more intriguing scandals of the war. New York Arsenal sold 5000 Hall 1843-model carbines in 1861, for $3.50 apiece, to Arthur Eastman of Manchester, New Hampshire. Eastman then re-sold the Halls to Simon Stevens of New York, who rifled and rechambered them. The carbines were offered to Major-General Fremont, commanding the Army Department of the West, who so desperately needed firearms that he paid $22.00 for each gun. Rumours surrounding the deal soon reached the US Treasury, and, outraged, Congress authorised an immediate investigation. No collusion between Eastman, Stevens and Fremont was proven, but it was discovered that Eastman's offer to rifle and refurbish the guns for a dollar apiece had been rebuffed by the government!

The breechloading carbine patented in May 1838 by William Jenks of Columbia, South Carolina (US no. 747) may have been the best design of its day. The first musket-length gun – a flintlock – was tried in 1838, followed by a hundred .64-calibre smoothbore carbines. Concurrently, the US Navy bought a few 'Model 1839' .54 cap-lock muskets, with 36-inch barrels and an overall

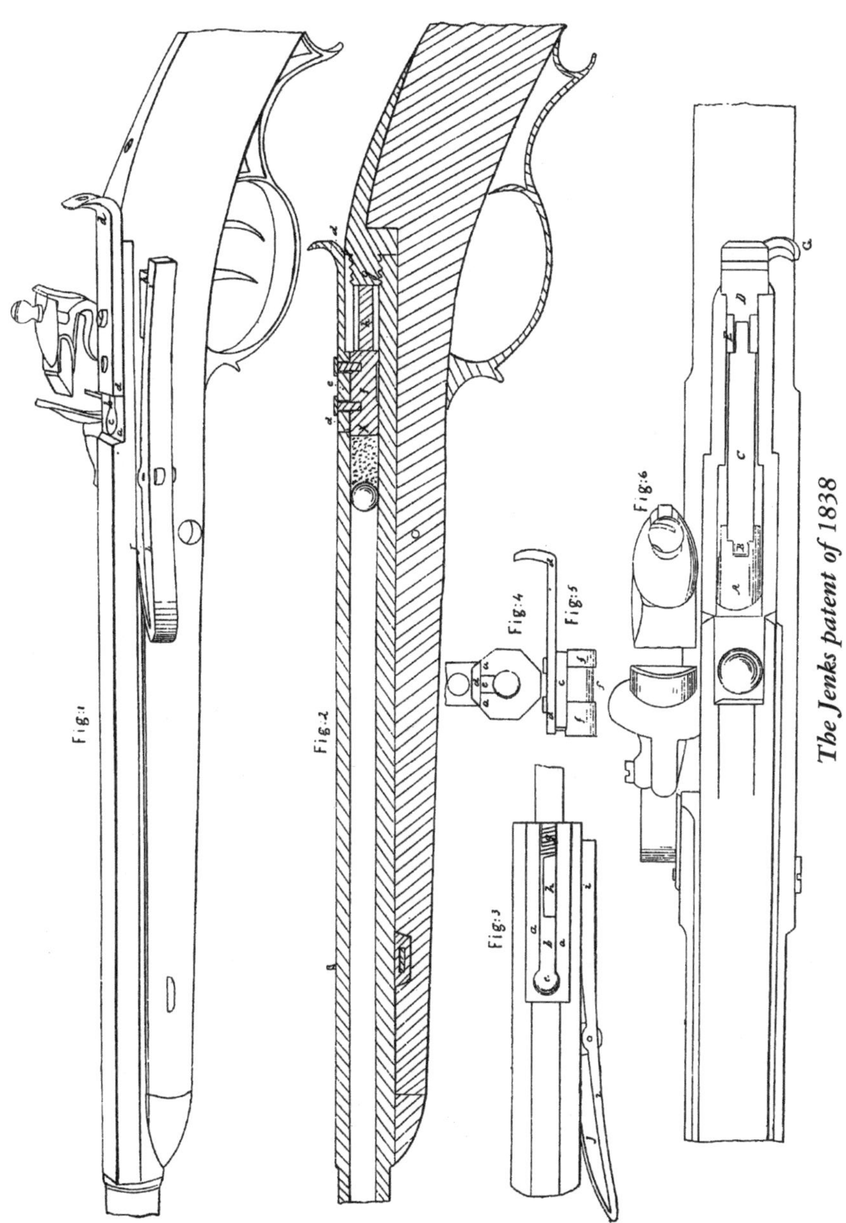

The Jenks patent of 1838

length of 52.5in. Weighing only about 7.6lb, these guns were very lightly built, featuring three brass barrel bands and brass furniture.

The army's flintlock Jenks carbines were soon supplemented by forty cap-locks, twenty based on the guns supplied to the navy and twenty specially rifled for trials with the dragoons. Trials undertaken in 1841 soon confirmed the potential that lay in the design, and a protracted endurance test at Fort Adam ended only when the nipple split after 14,813 shots had been fired. It seems very unlikely that any rival breechloading system available in 1840 could have withstood this treatment without failing.

The perfected cap-lock Jenks had a very distinctive side hammer, earning it the sobriquet 'Mule Ear'. Its toggle-type breech was opened by an elongated breech cover pivoted at the back of the action. Raising the lever broke the lock and withdrew the breech-block or 'piston' from the chamber to permit reloading. The mechanism sealed surprisingly well, and the breech lever deflected escaping gas down and away from the firer's face.

A Board of Officers representing the army and the navy, convened in Washington Arsenal in 1845, recommended immediate adoption of the Jenks carbine. However, troop trials proved catastrophic. Attempts had been made to load the Hall carbine cartridge – which was much too large – into the small Jenks chamber, or to fire standard musket cartridges instead of loose powder and ball. The failure of these trials, which was due as much to bad practice as anything, brought the career of the Jenks carbine in the US Army to an abrupt halt.

Yet although the army rejected the Jenks after the disastrous field trials, the navy remained convinced of its potential. A thousand rifles and 4200 carbines with Jenks breeches were ordered in 1841–5 from Nathan Ames, and 1000 carbines from E. Remington & Son. The Remington-made guns were the first martial arms to incorporate the Maynard Tape Primer and a cast-steel barrel. They also had double-ear actuating levers and straight-shank hammers.

By 1860, surviving guns had all been withdrawn to store. Although a few unaltered carbines did see limited service during the Civil War, most of the survivors had been transformed by James Merrill (q.v.) into conventional side-hammer cap locks.

The unlucky failure of the Jenks Carbine in army service, which also prevented its commercial exploitation, proved a boon to Christian **Sharps**. Born in Washington, New Jersey, in 1811, Sharps was apprenticed to a local gun-making business before finding employment in the Harper's Ferry Armory in 1830. There he worked under the tutelage of John Hall and came into direct contact with the first truly successful breechloading rifle.

When work on the Hall ceased in Harper's Ferry in 1844 and the production line was closed, Sharps moved northward to Cincinnati, Ohio, where he worked on an improved sliding-block breech mechanism patented on 12 September

1848 (US 5763). Sharps's breech relied on a massive block which slid downward in a substantial receiver when the operating lever was depressed, the combustible paper (later linen) cartridge being ignited by an externally mounted side-hammer striking a cap.

Tested by the US Army as early as 1850, the earliest examples had a distinctive breech lever outside the conventional trigger guard, but this was soon replaced by a sturdier operating lever doubling as a trigger guard. An improved design appeared in 1851, with a breech-block which moved obliquely (the so-called 'Slant Breech Sharps'), a combined operating lever and trigger guard, a tape primer ahead of the hammer, and a hammer carried inside the back-action lock plate. The contours of the receiver were distinctly rounded, compared with the angularity of later guns.

A typical 1853-type sporting rifle had a 25-inch .38-calibre octagonal barrel and a conventional external hammer. Sporting guns usually chambered .36, .44 or .52 linen-case combustible ball cartridges, though .52 shot loads were made in small quantities and .56-calibre carbines were made for trials in Britain. The Model 1853 provided the basis for carbines submitted to the US Army prior to the Civil War, and then for the many weapons used during the conflict.

Among the most famous Sharps carbines were the 200 purchased in 1857 by the Massachusetts–Kansas Aid Committee. Destined for Abolitionists – the anti-slavery faction – in Kansas, the carbines were shipped in the summer of 1857, but were impounded in Tabor, Iowa. They were subsequently retrieved by John Brown, who had obtained authority to sell a hundred to the Kansas Abolitionists and retain the remainder to arm anti-slavery forces raised in his own state.

After Brown's unsuccessful attack on Harper's Ferry Armory in 1859, 104 carbines and 160 boxes of Sharps Patent Pellet Primers were retrieved. Stored in Harper's Ferry, unclaimed by the Massachusetts Aid Committee, they were subsequently seized by the Confederacy, refurbished in Richmond and issued to rebel cavalry.

As a Sharps Carbine was carried by John Brown, so the genre acquired the nickname 'John Brown Sharps' or, alternatively, 'Beecher's Bibles' after the fiery Brooklyn preacher Henry Ward Beecher.

A few Model 1853, Old Model or 'Slant Breech' Sharps carbines saw action during the Civil War. Generally made in .52-calibre, 37.8in overall with a 21.6in barrel and brass furniture, the guns had Sharps's patented pellet magazine in the lock plate. This relied on a slender brass tube of waterproofed priming discs, fed automatically each time the hammer was thumbed back to full cock.

The Model 1853 was supplemented by the Model 1855, 400 being ordered by the US Army in April 1855 and 200 rifles by the navy in March–September 1856. The .52-calibre half-stocked rifles were 44.3in long, had 28.3-inch barrels and weighed 9lb without their sabre bayonets. The back sights were graduated to 800yd. Furniture and the single barrel bands were brass.

The carbines were essentially similar to the 1853 pattern, with the distinctive slant breech, but Maynard Tape Primers replaced Sharps's own pellet feeder. Though Sharps's Rifle Manufacturing Company marks appeared on the carbine barrels, with 'EDWARD MAYNARD/PATENTEE 1855' on the tape-primer gate, the guns were made by Robbins & Lawrence in Hartford, Connecticut. Governmental property marks and inspector's initials (e.g. 'U.S.' over 'J.H.-P.') will sometimes be found on the rear of the barrel.

Trials of an 1853-model Sharps Carbine, undertaken in 1854, showed that accuracy was poor. However, penetration of more than seven inches of pine at thirty yards showed the Sharps to be appreciably more powerful than Hall or Jenks patterns.

The 1853-pattern Sharps action, sturdy and durable though it was, leaked a considerable amount of gas. Most of the breechloading designs of the mid-nineteenth century were prone to leaking, owing to the use of combustible ammunition. However, the sharpened upper edge of the Sharps breech-block was designed to shear the base off the chambered cartridge as the action was closed, inevitably scattering a few grains of powder on the upper surface of the breech. When the gun was fired, flash from the cap (or sometimes emerging through the breech-block/barrel face joint) customarily ignited the loose powder grains and could make even a slightly worn gun unpleasant to use.

The problem was recognised very early in the career of the Sharps, and many attempts were made to develop a suitable gas-check system. An expanding collar patented on 1 April 1856 by Hezekiah Conant of Hartford, Connecticut (US Patent no. 14,554) was the first successful design – so successful, indeed, that the Sharps Rifle Company is said to have paid Conant $80,000 for rights to his invention. Yet although the Conant seal was unquestionably an improvement on earlier attempts to seal the Sharps breech, it did not work as well as had been predicted.

The next step was taken by Richard Smith Lawrence, a partner in Robbins & Lawrence and part-owner of the Sharps Rifle Company. Lawrence was a talented but opinionated engineer, with such a strong self-promotional streak that it is now difficult to determine how much credit is rightfully due for inventions and improvements he claimed as his own.

Born in 1817 in Chester, Vermont, Lawrence was raised in New York State and served the US Army – briefly – during the Canadian Rebellion of 1837. He left the army to join the metalworking business of Nicanor Kendall, who was making guns in what had once been Windsor prison. Lawrence's untutored skills were honed so quickly that he had been made factory foreman within six months, and by 1843 was trading in partnership with Kendall. Kendall & Lawrence obtained a government order for 10,000 1841-type cap-lock rifles in

1844 and, with the aid of a local businessman, formed Robbins, Kendall & Lawrence. Robbins and Lawrence bought the ageing Kendall's share of the business in 1847 and the reputation of 'Robbins & Lawrence', as it had become, grew rapidly. A contract to equip the British Royal Small Arms Factory with machine tools was accepted in 1851, followed by orders for British rifle-muskets and short rifles.

A new factory opened in Hartford, Connecticut, when Robbins & Lawrence successfully tendered to make Sharps firearms in 1852. No sooner had work begun, however, than an attempt to manufacture railroad freight cars ended in disaster. Robbins & Lawrence failed in 1854, but the Hartford factory was acquired by the Sharps Rifle Company; Lawrence, who seems to have held shares in the new business, was retained as the factory superintendent until retiring in 1872 to serve the civil authorities in Hartford until his death in 1892. In addition to work with firearms, Richard Lawrence is remembered as a skilled designer of barrel-making machinery and machine tools.

The Lawrence gas-seal was patented in the USA on 20 December 1859 (no. 26,501). By 1860, the Marine Corps was optimistically reporting that 'all the earlier troubles encountered with Sharps Carbine' had been corrected. However, the problem was eliminated only by converting cap locks to fire metal-case cartridges after the Civil War had ended.

Although only 5540 Sharps breechloaders had been acquired prior to 1861, no fewer than 89,653 were officially purchased by the Federal government during the Civil War.

Breechloading trials guns included carbines designed by Lieutenant Colonel James Durrell **Greene** of the US Army, best known for an underhammer cap-lock rifle-musket with Lancaster's oval-bore rifling, and 200 guns with a rotating breech-block made in accordance with a patent granted to John Symmes of Watertown Arsenal, Massachusetts, in November 1858.

One of the most forward-looking steps was taken by Samuel **Morse**, who presented a breechloading carbine to the US Army in 1857. Morse's cartridge was not especially powerful, but it had an internal primer and was genuinely self contained. The conversion of 2000 muskets was authorised in September 1858, but progress was so slow that only sixty had been completed by the end of 1859; very little had been done when Confederate forces seized Harper's Ferry Armory in April 1861. Ten thousand Morse conversions of .69 Model 1842 muskets were ordered in 1860 from the Muzzy Rifle & Gun Manufacturing Company of Worcester, Massachusetts, but it is believed that only a handful were ever completed.

Among the most successful of the pre-1860 designs, excepting the Sharps, was the **Burnside** carbine. Ambrose Everett Burnside, born in Liberty, Indiana, in 1824, graduated from the US Military Academy in West Point in 1847. After tinkering with breechloading rifle designs, he resigned his commission in

1853 and, after protracted experiments, founded the Bristol Fire Arms Company in Bristol, Rhode Island, in 1855. A patent was granted to Burnside in March 1856 to protect a breech block which was dropped by an operating lever curling around the base of the side-hammer mounted on the right side of the frame. The distinctive copper cartridge case, which was conical, was inserted backward into the block through the top of the frame. As the action closed, the protruding bullet seated in the chamber-mouth. Ignition was provided by the flash of a conventional cap passing through a hole in the centre of the cartridge-case base. A seal of thin waterproofed paper protected the powder charge from moisture.

The first Burnside carbines were originally made by the Bristol Firearms Company of Bristol, Rhode Island. Distinguished by the separate breech-lock lever beneath the hammer, they also lacked a fore-end. The US Army purchased 200 of these guns in April 1856, followed by 709 in September 1858.

The earliest Burnside was acceptably reliable, but its accuracy was poor. One gun tested at Washington Navy Yard in 1859 fired 500 shots without malfunctioning, though thirty of 470 aimed shots missed the eight-feet square target at 500 yards. This was probably due to the quality of the ammunition. Penetration at thirty yards proved to be 6.15 inches of pine.

However, though grudgingly agreed to be the 'best of the imperfect systems' submitted to army trials in 1857–8, no large-scale orders were placed and the Bristol Fire Arms Company was liquidated.

Ironically, the new controllers of the patents, reorganised as the 'Burnside Rifle Company', made many carbines for the Federal Government during the Civil War. The breech-locking lever on the later guns was incorporated in the trigger guard, a fore-end was added, and substantial changes were made to the action of the breech mechanism to improve efficiency.

Designed by the inventor of the popular tape-priming system, the carbine developed by Edward **Maynard** was also successful. Maynard – born in Madison, New York, in 1813 – was a very interesting man. Resigning his place in the US Military Academy after his first year, owing to poor health, Maynard turned instead to dentistry and practised in Washington DC from 1836 virtually until his death in 1891. Renowned for the many advances he made in dental science, Maynard held several professorships, received honorary degrees, and was feted not just in the USA but also in Europe.

Yet Maynard remains best known for his firearms. Patented in 1856–9, the Maynard Carbine was an unconventional dropping-barrel gun locked by a trigger-guard lever. Like the earliest Burnside, it lacked a fore-end. Made by the Massachusetts Arms Company, Maynard carbines fired a copper-case pierced-base cartridge, ignited by the flash from a cap struck by a centrally hung hammer.

A test undertaken in 1859 showed the Maynard gun to be more accurate than Burnside's, probably owing to its better bullet-seating system, as all the aimed shots fired at 500 yards hit the regulation target. Even at 1300 yards – a long range for such a short-barrel gun – fourteen shots out of 43 hit a target ten feet high by thirty feet broad, penetrating an inch of pine. No misfires had been registered, and the maximum rate of fire proved to be a praiseworthy twelve rounds per minute.

In 1860, Major Colston reported to the Commissioners of Virginia Armory that the paper-cartridge Smith carbine (described below) loaded easily when clean, but became so foul after sixty shots that it could not be loaded at all; the essentially similar Merrill had proved solid and gas-tight even after a hundred shots; the Burnside shot admirably, with no evidence of fouling; and the Maynard (which Colston regarded as very powerful) shot the best of the special cartridges. Unfortunately, Colston concluded that he could not recommend the Burnside or Maynard carbines owing to use of special ammunition.

Multi-Shot Guns

The revolver-rifle had a lengthy pedigree. Manually operated guns of this type had been tried in Europe in the seventeenth century, but the most important advances had been made early in the nineteenth century by Elisha Collier and Artemus Wheeler. Collier's was the first revolver to incorporate a mechanical linkage to rotate the cylinder; unfortunately, a combination of high price, delicacy, and flintlock ignition conspired to prevent real progress being made. Thus promotion of the Collier failed, even though the later guns reverted to manually indexed cylinders in a bid to reduce cost.

Samuel Colt is now generally given the credit for perfecting the mechanically revolved cylinder, though the loss of many early records when the US Patent Office in Blodgett's Hotel, 'E' Street, Washington DC, was burnt to the ground in December 1836 has allowed other claimants to be forwarded. It is probable that the whole truth will never be known; it cannot be proven if Colt was aware of the existence of the 1819-type Collier revolver, though Colt's claim that his work was inspired by the spokes of a ship's (or, alternatively, Mississippi riverboat) wheel is probably just as much hokum as the cure-alls he sold in his youth.

Samuel Colt was born in Hartford, Connecticut, in 1814. The early death of his mother and the failure of his father's business forced the young Colt into apprenticeship with a bleaching and dyeing company when he was just ten. Expelled from preparatory school a few years later, Colt signed as a seaman on a voyage to India in 1830, where he subsequently claimed to have made his first wooden model. Work continued throughout the early 1830s, a series of handguns and longarms being made in Baltimore by a gunsmith/mechanic named John Pearson. These worked well enough to encourage Colt to apply for patents in Britain, France and the USA. The grants included the master US

Patent of 25 February 1836, and a small factory was opened in Paterson, New Jersey, to make the guns in quantity.

The hammerless 1836-pattern Colt-Paterson rifle had a ring-type cocking lever ahead of the trigger; the improved 'Model 1837' had an external hammer and a small detachable rammer to seat the bullets in their chambers.

The Colt revolver, initially in its rifle form, was immediately brought to the attention of the US Army: backed by a dubious career selling patent medicines, Colt was never one to tread warily. However, the board of officers responsible for trials of Colt, Hall, Cochran and 'Baron Hackett' guns reported on 19 September 1837 that the Colt was complicated, too prone to accidents and totally unsuited to service.

When the Second Seminole War began in Florida in 1838, however, Colt defiantly exhibited his revolver rifles in Charlestown, South Carolina, and let it be known that the army was ignoring a most effectual weapon. On 9 March 1838, a Board of Officers convened at Fort Jupiter in East Florida to re-examine the rifle. A recommendation that guns should be acquired to equip part of a dragoon regiment was immediately countersigned by the commander of the US Army in Florida, Major-General Jessup, and fifty rifles were ordered.

The Colts proved to be delicate, but worked reliably if they were loaded with care. Most of the dragoons regarded them much more highly than regulation flintlock muskets, but more than half of them were lost in a small skirmish at Caloosahatchie and the remainder were recalled to ordnance stores in Baton Rouge, Louisiana, in 1843.

In August 1839, Samuel Colt was granted US Patent no. 1304 to protect a loading lever or 'rammer' mounted permanently on the gun; the 1839-type rifle, therefore, was little more than the 1837 pattern with the new rammer. Yet a US Navy trials board reported in May 1840 that the advantages of the eight-shot cap-lock Colt-Paterson revolver rifles were still not clear enough. The guns were still too complicated and delicate to withstand rigorous service, and tended to chain-fire.

A few rifles were purchased to arm expeditions, but the quantities involved fell far short of Colt's hopes. These were dashed still further when a Board of Officers, convened in the summer of 1840 at the Dragoon School of Practice in Carlisle, Pennsylvania, recommended the purchase of only a few carbines for field trials. About 160 guns had been delivered by July 1841, but experiments showed that they were still too delicate.

The failure of the Paterson venture in 1842 ended production of the mechanically operated Colt revolver rifles, though manually operated rivals continued to be made in small numbers elsewhere. Surviving examples usually prove to have been made in accordance with US Patent no. 203, granted on 11 June 1829 to James **Miller** of Brighton, New York. Miller died in 1843; his business was then split between his brother John and William Billinghurst, who each made guns to the master patent. A few Billinghurst guns even had a smooth-bore barrel doubling as the cylinder axis pin, later to achieve greater notoriety in the Le Mat revolver.

Production was confined largely to the State of New York, where Miller-pattern guns were made by Holmes of Oswego; Perry of Fredonia; Patrick Smith of Buffalo; William Smith of New York; Charles Bunge of Geneva; Calvin Miller of Canadia; and Benjamin Bigelow of Rochester – although Bigelow moved to Marysville, California, with the Gold Rush.

Miller-type guns had sturdy bullet deflectors and manually rotated cylinders indexed by a catch at the cylinder-mouth. Many of the original J. & J. Miller guns were pill-locks, though caps were favoured by the copyists.

Only a few Miller-type revolver rifles reached the West, probably accompanying settlers who had made the long journey from New England. The same was probably true of the rifle credited to **North & Savage** of Middletown, Connecticut, more than 500 being made in accordance with US Patent no. 8982 granted in June 1852 to Henry North and Chauncey Skinner. These guns were operated mechanically by pulling the front of the trigger guard down, removing the supporting wedge and rotating the cylinder, but the hammer was cocked manually. Rifles were also made by the Springfield Arms Company (250?) and James Warner (400?) on the basis of the cap-lock revolvers described below.

Although detachable shoulder stocks were issued with Colt's Dragoon and Army revolvers in the early 1850s, no progress with Colt revolver rifles was made until a patent was granted in 1855 to Elisha King Root, the Master Armorer of the Hartford factory.

Renowned for the side-hammer Colt which is now generally linked with his name, Root deserves to be remembered as one of the best production engineers of his generation. Born into farming stock in 1808 in Ludlow, Massachusetts, Root was apprenticed to a machinist in his teens and became a lathe operator with Collins & Company of Hartford in 1832. Root soon demonstrated his talents, rising rapidly to become factory superintendent and transforming Collins & Company from a workshop to the USA's principal manufacturer of axes and tools.

Aware of the engineer's abilities, Samuel Colt offered Root superintendency of the new Hartford arms factory – then still in the planning stage – in 1849. When the factory opened, much of the credit for its success was due to Root. In addition to machine tools such as barrel riflers, stock turners and cartridge-case makers, Root patented an efficient drop-hammer which became a great commercial success. When Colt died unexpectedly in 1862, Root assumed the presidency of the company and held it until his own death three years later.

The 1855 or Root Model side-hammer revolver rifles shared the action of the essentially similar small-calibre revolvers. They enjoyed considerable commercial success, in rifle and shotgun form, and 4612 were purchased by the Federal government during the Civil War (for $204,487); others were purchased privately to arm militia and volunteer units.

Briefly offered as an alternative to the revolver rifle, the 'Turret Repeater', characterised by a disc-like cylinder with chambers bored radially, enjoyed a brief vogue in the USA. However, only a handful of these strange-looking guns could have reached the West. One or two are known to have gone to California with prospectors heading for the Gold Rush, but few other instances are documented.

The best known of the turret repeaters is the **Monitor**, patented on 28 April 1837 by John Cochran (US no.188) and made by Cyrus Allen of Springfield, Massachusetts. Under-hammer Monitors had a horizontal cylinder, but proved much more popular as a pistol than a .44-calibre seven- or eight-shot rifle. A similar gun, patented in September 1856 by Edward Graham of Hillsborough, New Hampshire, sought safety by placing the ball in a chamber at an angle to the propellant, and the guns made by George Foster of Taunton, Massachusetts, for Patrick 'Parry' **Porter** of Memphis, Tennessee (in accordance with US Patent no. 8210 of 18 July 1851), had vertical disc cylinders. Porter's 'Cap Box Revolving Rifles' were .36 or .50-calibre eight- or nine-shot firearms with special tape-primer locks and offset sights. Later guns of this type, including those made after 1856 by C. D. Schuberth (Foster's successor), were made alongside similar guns using 'Colt's Metal-Lined Cap'.

Numbers on Porter rifles run as high as 427, but the inventor is said to have been fatally wounded by a chain-firing incident during a demonstration to Samuel Colt (or, alternatively, the Board of Ordnance). As some of the radial chambers pointed backward, safety could never be guaranteed with a turret gun.

An alternative approach to repeating-rifle design was made by Walter **Hunt** of New York. Hunt was another of those enterprising men who combined careers as engineers or machinists with an interest in firearms design. Born in the New York township of Martinsburg in 1796, Hunt moved to Brooklyn in 1826 in an unsuccessful bid to exploit his invention of a flax-spinning machine. This was followed by a series of inventions which, in different circumstances, could have made Hunt his fortune. However, he lacked the backing to do much other than sell rights to his designs as they appeared. Among Hunt's ideas were a nail-making machine, a safety pin and a primitive sewing machine – never patented – which presaged the essentially similar, but outstandingly successful Howe pattern.

Walter Hunt was also responsible for one of the first successful self-propelled cartridges, patented in the USA in 1848, which he called the 'Volitional Ball'. It consisted of a hollow lead bullet with a large enough cavity in its base to hold propellant. The cavity was closed at the rear by a thin cork disc, pierced by a central channel, which held a separate primer. Tests showed that the ammunition worked surprisingly well, though lacking in power compared with more conventional loadings. Encouraged, Hunt patented a repeating rifle in August 1849.

Although perhaps only a solitary twelve-shot piston-breech rifle was ever made, with a tube magazine beneath the barrel and a 'straightline' firing pin driven by a coil spring, experiments showed that the basic principles were correct. It is probable that Hunt then sold rights in his guns and ammunition to George Arrowsmith of New York City, who appears to have been a small-scale entrepreneur, and a gunmaker named Lewis **Jennings** was subsequently asked to hone the design of the Hunt Rifle for series production.

On Christmas Day, 1849, Jennings was granted a patent to protect a .54-calibre pill-lock rifle with a 34-inch barrel, a twenty-shot tube magazine, and an overall length of 53in. However, Arrowsmith had soon sold his interest to a syndicate financed by the railroad magnate Courtlandt Palmer. Optimistically, Palmer ordered 5000 Jennings-type rifles from Robbins & Lawrence, but the project failed after no more than a few hundred had been made.

There were two types of pill-lock Jennings rifles, each about 44in overall with 26-inch .54 barrels rifled with seven grooves. The earlier pattern had its ring trigger/operating lever inside a conventional guard and a magazine tube ending level with the muzzle; the later gun dispensed with the guard entirely, and had a magazine which ended behind the muzzle.

Some of the improvements in the Jennings rifle are believed to have been due to Richard Lawrence, junior partner in Robbins & Lawrence, but the self-promotional Lawrence subsequently claimed so great a part in the transition from the Jennings to the Volcanic that his true contribution is impossible to judge. A far greater part may have been played by one of Robbins & Lawrence's machinists, Benjamin Tyler Henry.

Robbins & Lawrence collapsed in 1854, though Palmer may already have cancelled the contract for Jennings rifles; the last few guns are known to have been completed as single-shot muzzleloaders. Rights were subsequently reassigned to a newly formed partnership of **Smith & Wesson.**

Born in Worcester, Massachusetts, in 1825, Daniel Baird Wesson was apprenticed in 1843 to his elder brother Edwin Wesson. When Edwin Wesson died in 1850, still a young man, Daniel inherited rights to his brother's patents and continued to make the Wesson & Leavitt revolver in partnership with a syndicate of heirs and interested parties in the 'Massachusetts Arms Company'. No sooner had trading begun in earnest, however, than Colt sued for patent infringement. After a celebrated verbal duel between Edwin Dickerson and Rufus Choate, two of the most famous attorneys of their day, Colt won punitive damages large enough to force the Massachusetts Arms Company into liquidation in 1853.

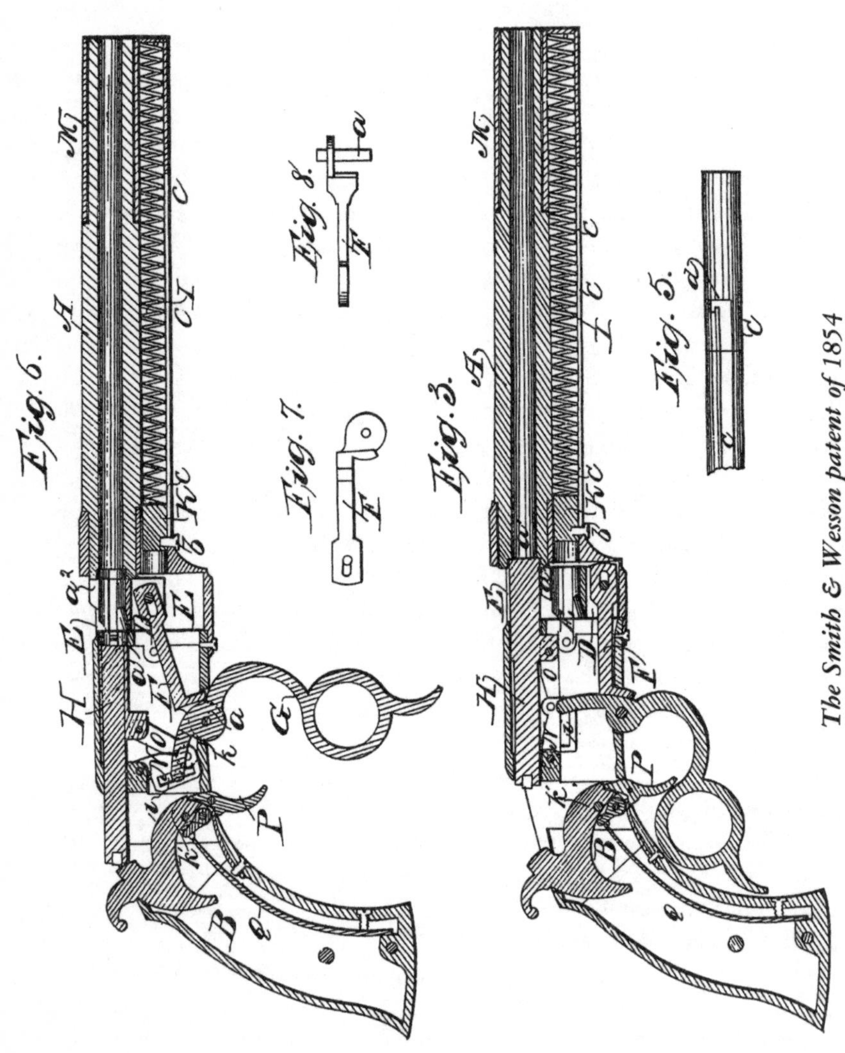

The Smith & Wesson patent of 1854

Daniel Wesson joined the well-known gun-barrel making business of Allen, Brown & Luther, where he met Horace Smith. Finally, in June 1854, Smith & Wesson opened a small workshop in Norwich, Connecticut, to exploit – among others – the Hunt and Jennings patents.

Horace Smith and Edwin Wesson patented an improved magazine pistol in 1854, and series production began immediately; although a few carbines were made, however, handguns predominated. Eventually, Smith & Wesson decided there was far more promise in the Rollin White patent than in the 'Volitional Ball' repeaters and sold interests in the latter to a group of New Haven clockmakers, bakers, grocers, carriage makers and entrepreneurs, who eyed the lucrative arms trade being built up in neighbouring Massachusetts with envy.

Forming themselves into the **Volcanic** Repeating Fire Arms Company, the new proprietors continued work on the Volitional Repeaters. Daniel Wesson was retained as works superintendent until the spring of 1856, but Horace Smith had retired and Benjamin Henry returned to Robbins & Lawrence.

The unexpected death in December 1856 of the president of the Volcanic company, mining entrepreneur Nelson Gaston, gave control to a successful shirt-maker named Oliver Winchester. Gaston and Winchester each held stakeholdings in Volcanic, in addition to advancing large sums of money secured on the Hunt, Jennings and Smith & Wesson patents. Yet Volcanic was trading insolvently by the summer of 1857.

Sales had never been large enough to make a fortune, and the unstable nature of fulminate powder, which sometimes blew the magazine tube off the breech, had proved to be a great handicap. A reversion to the separately primed black-powder propellant of the original Hunt Rocket Ball cured the problems, but only with a marked loss of power. The muzzle velocity of the .36-calibre Volitional Ball ball was only about 500 ft/sec with a fulminate charge, and any reduction in power was clearly unacceptable.

Volcanic firearms made before the sale of the company to Winchester were invariably .40 calibre. They included pistols with ring-tipped operating levers, and a selection of carbines whose appearance presaged the much more successful Henry rifle of 1860. The longarms were made with barrels of 16, 20.5 and 25in, with magazines of 20, 25 and 30 shots respectively.

The formation on 1 May 1857 of the **New Haven** Arms Company, to purchase the Volcanic patents, allowed Oliver Winchester to gain $40,000 for tools and inventory in addition to the patent rights. He immediately persuaded Benjamin Henry to return as works superintendent, reorganised the factory, and continued to make 'Volcanic Repeating Fire Arms'.

An 1859-vintage broadsheet advertised carbines in 'No.2' bore (0.40), with barrels of 16, 20 and 24in; two .40 'Navy' pistols with barrels of 6 or 8 inches; a No.1 (.31) target gun with a 6-inch barrel; and a .31 pocket pistol with a 4-inch barrel. The largest carbine had a thirty-round tube magazine beneath the barrel.

Broadsheets issued by Oliver Winchester contain the most magnificent claims, backed up by 'testimonials' from clipper-ship captains and Winchester's St Louis agent. Self-contained Volcanic ammunition was much more efficient than cap-and-ball rivals, particularly in damp conditions, and claims to have fired 'over 200 shots . . . without even wiping the barrel' and to have had the pistol 'at sea for more than eighteen months, on a voyage around the world, and [to have found]. . . the Balls as good now as when I left New York' may have a ring of truth. Those that relate epic feats of accuracy are much less convincing.

Despite Winchester's best efforts, the New Haven Arms Company failed to prosper. When the Civil War began in the spring of 1861, insolvency loomed. Fortunately for business, however, Benjamin Henry had developed a new lever-action rifle chambering a .44-calibre metal-case cartridge with rimfire ignition and a 216-grain lead bullet. The muzzle velocity of 1150–1200 ft/sec was a vast improvement on the weak Volitional Ball.

Henry's rifle was to be the salvation of the New Haven Arms Company once fighting between North and South began in earnest.

Handguns

Single-Shot Pistols and Derringers

The legions of small-calibre revolvers produced after the introduction of the first pepperboxes and Colts did nothing to reduce the popularity of the easily concealable single-barrel pistol, which continued in vogue into the late nineteenth century.

The best known personal-defence pistol of this type was the cap-lock made in Philadelphia by the gunsmith Henry **Deringer**, who had made substantial quantities of 1817-model flintlock rifles for the US Army in the 1820s. Deringer turned to handguns in the 1830s, making a range of weapons from a large duelling pistol to a tiny gun which could be hidden in the palm of the hand.

The popularisation of 'derringer' as a generic term for an easily concealable pistol is popularly supposed to have arisen from the assassination of Abraham Lincoln by John Wilkes Booth on 14 April 1865; however, attention has also been drawn attention to the killing of General William Richardson by Charles Cora in San Francisco in November 1855. Local newspapers described the murder weapon as a 'derringer'.

William F. 'Buffalo Bill' Cody purchased a pair of genuine Deringers in 1865, while Leon Czolgosc used a double-barrel Remington equivalent to fatally wound US President William McKinley in September 1901.

The classic Deringer amalgamated a back-action cap-lock with a rifled .41-calibre seven-groove barrel within an overall length of just 4½in. Invariably marked 'DERINGER PHILADEL.' on the lock plate, genuine guns had distinctive side plates and pineapple-pattern escutcheons retaining the transverse barrel key. Barrels were finished in a false damascus twist, achieved by streaking; locks were case-hardened; and metalwork was customarily blued, apart from trigger guards and escutcheons which could be plated with silver.

Deringer pistols achieved notoriety during the California Gold Rush, when many gunmakers attempted to exploit their success in the saloons, gaming halls and bordellos of the West Coast. Copyists included Slotter & Company and A. J. Plate of San Francisco. A Philadelphian tailor named Jacob Deringer made a small fortune by licensing the use of his name to gunsmiths seeking to legitimise their wares.

Henry Deringer died in 1867. Although his executors took action against copyists who were content merely to duplicate the distinctive miniature caplock, some gunmakers were more ambitious. Jesse **Butterfield** of Philadelphia produced a .38-calibre near-facsimile of the Deringer with a patented priming tube, mounted vertically ahead of the hammer, to feed a pellet over the nipple each time the hammer was cocked.

Another oddity was the smallest **Lindsay** 'Young America' single-barrel caplock pocket pistol, with two sequential charges fired by separate hammers. In practice, however, unless the charges had been carefully separated by greased wads, the first hammer fired a two-shot volley as flash from the front charge ran back around the second ball.

Pepperboxes and Revolvers

When the Gold Rush began in 1849, very few revolvers were available in quantity. Colt's Paterson venture had failed some years earlier, and the first of the Dragoon Colts were only just reaching the US Army. Though small-calibre pocket revolvers were emanating from the Hartford factory, Colt was unable to supply them in large enough numbers to suit the burgeoning California markets.

Consequently, substantial quantities of 'pepperboxes' – the name did not enter common currency until after the London Great Exhibition of 1851 – found their way westward. Some were made in New England, while others had been imported from Europe. Often in relic condition, guns of this type have been retrieved from many Western sites. Some were buried with their owners along the settler trails; others come from abandoned home- or farmsteads; and a few have even been found in long-abandoned mines. Several from the Pike's Peak district of Colorado, where gold was not discovered until 1859, confirm that pepperboxes were still being used at the time of the Civil War.

Inspired by multi-barrel flintlock antecedents, the pepperbox had owed a great debt to the advent of the percussion cap. Caps allowed each barrel to be primed separately, and ignition was reasonably certain as long as the caps could be held efficiently on the nipples. Most pepperboxes consisted simply of full-length barrel clusters mounted on a axial pin, each barrel, capped separately, being turned successively beneath the hammer. The barrel clusters of the earliest guns were rotated manually, and fired by single-acting trigger systems.

The guns were simple, sturdy, easy to make, and effective enough at close range. However, keeping the size of the barrel cluster within acceptable bounds restricted the diameter of the bore to .28 or .31 and limited the 'hitting power' of the ball. Some large, long-barrel guns were made (such as the .36-calibre Allen & Thurber 'Self-Cocking Dragoon Revolver'), but they were almost always heavy, cumbersome and unpleasant to fire.

Purchasers regarded small calibre as a reasonable price to pay for additional shots, but short-barrel guns were prone to 'chain-fire' – discharging all their barrels simultaneously when either the flash of a cap radiated outward to other flash-holes or flame from the firing chamber ignited its neighbours. Chain-firing tendencies could be reduced by careful loading, sealing each barrel with a properly greased wad, or by erecting fences between the nipples; indeed, short-chamber revolvers suffered the same problems until efficient mechanical rammers were introduced.

Many of the guns used in the USA in the middle of the nineteenth century were imported from Britain and Europe by entrepreneurs such as Lewis & Tomes. A particular favourite was the '**Mariette**', allegedly developed in the 1830s by a French or Belgian gunmaker of the same name, which was customarily distinguished by a double-action ring trigger and fired the lowest barrel of its cluster to minimise disturbance in the hand.

Guns made by Barton & Benjamin **Darling**, initially in Shrewsbury, Massachusetts, are generally regarded as the earliest of all the self-rotating pepperboxes and have even been used in attempts to discredit Colt. However, there seems no real substance to claims that the Darlings were the rightful recipients of the patent granted to Colt in 1836 to protect the Paterson revolver. The first Darling guns had a thumb trigger on top of the butt, but this was rapidly superseded by a much more conventional design. Production was never large and the pepperboxes had no significant effect on firearms history.

Much more successful than the single-action Darling was the double-action or 'self-cocking' pepperbox patented by Ethan **Allen** in November 1837, the patent being reissued twice in 1844. Improved by US Patent no. 3998 of 16 April 1845, the Allen pepperboxes were made by Allen & Thurber in Grafton, Massachusetts (until 1842), Norwich, Connecticut (1842–7), and then in the small Massachusetts town of Worcester. Later guns were made by Allen & Wheellock, successors to Allen & Thurber in 1856. Guns with a patented short barrel-cluster axis pin were made for a few years after 1857, and were still being offered by Tryon of Philadelphia as late as 1864. The longevity was often influenced by price, as a double-action pepperbox cost only about a third as much as a Colt revolver in the 1850s.

The Allens were typically .32 or .36-calibre five- or six-shot smoothbores with bar hammers and double-action triggers. The best of them were made prior to the grant of the April 1845 patent, when ribbed barrel fluting, nipple shields, engraving, silvered escutcheons and similar refinements were gradually abandoned. Six-shot guns gave way to five-shot types, which were smaller and lighter, and a few were even made with ring triggers in an attempt to reduce manufacturing costs.

Among Allen's major rivals were **Blunt & Syms**, established in 1837 in Chatham Street in New York City. This partnership of Orison Blunt and George Syms made a double-action pepperbox with a concealed hammer mechanism protected by US Patent no. 6966, granted on Christmas Day 1849. Undoubtedly inspired by the Mariette, these guns were made in substantial quantities; the US National Census recorded that '2600 guns' (presumably including guns other than pepperboxes) had been made in the year ending 1 June 1850. John Syms, 'late Blunt & Syms', was still selling guns of this type in 1860.

George **Leonard** of Charlestown, Maryland, and Shrewsbury, Massachusetts, designed a distinctive double-action, ring-trigger pepperbox with fixed barrels. Protected by US Patent no. 6723 of 18 September 1849 and improved by no. 7493 of 9 July 1850, this gun was also made by Robbins & Lawrence of Windsor, Vermont, prior to 1853.

Pecare & Smith of New York City, a partnership of Jacob Pecare and Josiah Smith, active in 1849–53, made double-action pepperboxes in accordance with US Patent no. 6925, granted in December 1849 to protect a folding or 'concealed' trigger (though some of the last guns have fixed ring triggers).

Pepperboxes were also made in 1849–52 in Worcester, Massachusetts, by **Stocking** & Company. Distinctive single-action guns with an extended hammer spur and a spurred trigger guard, they were never made in large numbers.

Among the **lesser makers** of pepperboxes were Bacon & Company of Norwich, Connecticut; the Manhattan Fire Arms Company of Newark, New Jersey; William Marston of Newark, New Jersey, and New York City; the Union Arms Company of Hartford, Connecticut; and the Washington Arms Company of Washington, DC. Most of these were double-action guns with bar hammers, though Bacon's followed a single-action underhammer pattern.

However, marks of retailers, sporting-goods promoters and other agencies will often be found on European and American-made pepperboxes. For example, John G. Bolen of New York City sold pepperboxes as 'Life and Property Preservers'. Bolen specialised in cased pairs – two identical guns, or one large and one small – but guns were purchased from differing sources and may not match each other in detail.

The first **Colt** cap-lock rifles, made in Hartford in 1832 and then in Baltimore, were successful enough to encourage applications for what became

English Patent 6909, granted on 22 October 1835, and comparable US no. 136 of 25 January 1836. Each claimed novelty in ease of loading, and in rapidity of fire by connecting the hammer and cylinder-rotating pawl.

In 1835 – confident of success – Colt founded the Patent Arms Manufacturing Company in Paterson, New Jersey, in part of an under-employed silk mill. The earliest revolver-rifles were accompanied by '**Paterson Revolvers**' with triggers which sprang down beneath the frame when the hammer was thumbed back for the first shot.

About 180 'Number 5 Holster Pistols' were acquired by the government of the independent State of Texas in 1839–41 for the navy; withdrawn when the navy was soon disbanded, they passed to the Texas Rangers – but not before an incident between the Texan and Mexican navies on 16 May 1843 (the 'Battle of Campeche') provided the inspiration for the maritime battle-scene rolled into the cylinder peripheries of many Colt revolvers in the 1850s.

Colt's enthusiasm for his own products did not ensure success in a traditionally cautious market, and the Patent Arms Manufacturing Company was forced into liquidation in 1842.

When war with Mexico began in 1846, an army commanded by General Zachary Taylor was sent southward to the border between Mexico and Texas. Taylor's men included Samuel H. Walker, who had become acquainted with Paterson Colts during service with the Texas Rangers.

When the problems in Mexico multiplied, Walker was ordered northward to recruit volunteers and obtain firearms. He immediately sought out Colt, to whom the 1836 US master patent had reverted, and the two men successfully refined the Paterson Colt into a battle-worthy weapon.

A thousand-gun government contract was obtained in January 1847. As Colt no longer had facilities of his own, the revolvers were sub-contracted to the factory of Eli Whitney in Whitneyville, Connecticut. The cumbersome 1847-vintage six-shot **Walker Colts** were more than 15in long and weighed more than 4½lb, but combat showed them to be effective enough to bring another order. The strength of success persuaded Colt to take a further risk, by laying the foundations of a new factory in the small Connecticut town of Hartford in 1848.

The .44 Model 1848 or **Colt Dragoon** revolver – confined to 1848–50 – initially embodied old Whitney-made parts, but improvements were soon made. Guns of this type could be identified by square-back trigger guards and ovoid cylinder-stop slots. The Second Model of 1850–1 had squared cylinder-stop slots, pins between the nipples, a roller on the hammer and a leaf-type main spring; the Third Model, available until 1861, had a round-back trigger guard, an improved back sight and could accept a shoulder stock.

A transitional pattern incorporating Walker-Colt parts was made for the US Army in 1848, to replace defective Walker-type revolvers; 239 of the latter are known to have failed in service, mostly owing to ruptured cylinders.

The Dragoon revolvers brought Colt his first real success; about 20,000 were made in 1849–55, 9380 being purchased by the US Army. Their success inspired the introduction in 1848 of the first .31 five-shot Colt pocket revolver, known colloquially as the '**Baby Dragoon**', which had a distinctive square-back trigger guard and rounded cylinder-stop slots. Excepting the last guns, Baby Dragoons lacked rammers beneath the barrel. They were customarily reloaded simply by substituting cylinders, though the cylinder axis pin was specifically designed to double as a rammer if required. About 15,000 guns were made in 1848–50.

Baby Dragoon barrels measured 3–6in. A motif showing Texas Rangers chasing Indians was rolled into the surface of the cylinders, but was replaced by a stagecoach robbery scene on transitional guns made in 1850. Next came the .31 **Colt Pocket** Revolver, essentially similar to the Baby Dragoon but now misleadingly designated 'Model 1849' by many collectors.

The .31 revolvers were made with cylinders holding five (standard) or six (uncommon) shots. Barrels measured 3–6in; the cylinder-stop slots were squared; and the stagecoach-robbery cylinder scene was customary. Most of the guns were blued, with some colour case-hardening, and the grip straps were often silvered. However, optional extras included engraving, ivory grips and virtually any barrel-length the purchaser suggested.

The most sought versions of the .31 'M1849' Colt revolver include early guns with a small trigger guard; the so-called 'Wells Fargo' pattern, which lacked a rammer; and a special 3-inch barrel gun with a greatly abbreviated rammer.

Helped by an extension of the 1836 master patent to 1857, owing to a successful lack-of-profit claim filed in the US courts, Colt's Pocket Revolver proved to be such a great success that about 314,000 guns were made in Hartford and another 11,000 in London, numbered in their own special number-series. The last 1850-type Pocket Revolver did not leave Colt's warehouses until 1873.

The greatly improved .36 **Navy Colt**, otherwise known as the 'Old Model Belt Pistol' (or Model of 1851), was a contemporary of the .31 Pocket Model. Made in substantial quantities – 215,348 in Hartford (1850–73) and about 40,000 in London – it was 13in overall, had a 7½-inch barrel and weighed 2½lb. Naval connotations arose partly from the small calibre, but also from an engraving commemorating the Texan victory over the Mexican Navy in the Battle of Campeche (16 May 1843). Few guns ever saw the sea, most being used during the land campaigns of the American Civil War or on the plains of the Old West.

Navy revolvers ranged from the plainest military issue – the first thousand-gun consignment was accepted by the US Army in 1855 – to gems of the gunmaker's art. The earliest guns had square-back trigger guards, and a barrel wedge which lay above the retaining screw. Second-pattern guns had the wedge below the screw. The third pattern had a small round-back guard, and the otherwise identical fourth type had a large round-back guard. A few shoulder-stocks were sold with post-1859 Navy Colts, but the low level of sales reflected their great unpopularity.

Many Westerners favoured the Navy Colt for its light weight and excellent balance. Though some of this popularity waned after the harder-hitting .44 Army revolver appeared in 1860, the .36-calibre Navy pattern was still to be seen in large numbers into the 1870s. Among the most famous owners of .36-calibre Colts was James Butler 'Wild Bill' Hickok, who had a pair of guns. Robert Kane witnessed him offering 'to do a little shooting for us . . . outside the city limits . . . His last feat was the most remarkable of all: a quart can was thrown by Mr Hickok himself, which dropped about 10 or 12 yards distant. Quickly whipping out his weapons, he fired alternately with right and left. Advancing a step with each shot, his bullets striking the earth just under the can, he kept it in continuous motion until his pistols were empty.'

Developed by Elisha Root, superintendent of the Hartford factory, the Model 1855 or '**Root Colt**' pocket revolver supplemented the original .31 Pocket Model. The new guns had solid frames and sheath triggers, but the most

WILD BILL HICKOK

Born in May 1837 in Troy Grove, Illinois, James Butler 'Wild Bill' Hickok left home in 1856 to become involved in the Kansas 'Free State' troubles. The killing in 1861 of David McCanles in Rock Creek, Nebraska, gave Hickok a reputation which he skilfully turned to advantage after the Civil War. Appointed sheriff of Hays County and then marshal of the Kansas cow-town of Abilene, Hickok became a legend thanks largely to lurid descriptions of his exploits in the popular press and dime novels.

He toured briefly with Buffalo Bill's Wild West show in the mid-1870s, but drifted to the Black Hills goldfields in search of easy gambling pickings. He was murdered by Jack McCall in the Number Ten Saloon in Deadwood, Dakota Territory, in 1876, playing what thereafter became the 'Dead Man's Hand' – reputedly the aces and eights of spades and clubs, and the jack of diamonds. The murder weapon was an unidentifiable .22 'Suicide Special'.

Although Hickok has been the subject of many thousands of words (Joseph G. Rosa's biography *Wild Bill Hickok: The Man and His Myth* is by far the best), comparatively little is known about Hickok's guns. He undoubtedly made good use of a pair of .36 1851-pattern Colt Navy revolvers with engraved frames and ivory grips, and is also said to have owned a pair of .41-calibre Williamson cartridge derringers.

obvious feature was the 'cranked' side-mounted hammer allowing the axis pin to enter the cylinder through the back of the frame. A 'creeping' rack-and-pinion rammer was used, in Root's words, to combine 'the plunger of a many-chambered rotating-breech pistol ... with a lever with a cogged sector engaging the cogs of a straight rack'.

Although the new Colt revolvers were sturdy and undeniably very well made, the expiry of the original master patent in 1857 exposed them to competition afforded by cheaper and cruder guns. There were two major variations – five-shot .28 and .31 – with barrels of $3\frac{1}{2}$ or $4\frac{1}{2}$in. Barrels were cylindrical, excepting for a few octagonal $3\frac{1}{2}$-inch examples made in the late 1850s. A few guns were made with full-flute cylinders, but most of the side-hammer Colts display either a log cabin and Indian motif or (more rarely) the standard stagecoach-robbery pattern on the cylinder surfaces. Production in 1855–70 amounted only to about 40,000 guns.

The success of the Colt revolvers encouraged many other gunmakers to compete with them. Made by the Massachusetts Arms Company of Chicopee Falls, the Wesson & Leavitt guns relied on a manually rotated cylinder patented on 29 April 1837 by Daniel Leavitt (US no. 182) and a mechanically rotated adaptation designed by Edwin Wesson. Protection for the latter had been granted posthumously in 1850, allowing Wesson's assignees to produce the gun.

The first Wesson & Leavitt revolvers relied on bevel gears to rotate the cylinder. They included a huge .40-calibre six-shot army revolver, weighing 4lb 2oz in its final form, which was nearly 15in long. A 7.1-inch barrel, hinged to the standing breech alongside the side hammer, was held to the sturdy cylinder axis pin by a swivel-latch.

Wesson & Leavitt revolvers could be reloaded simply by pressing the latch, raising the barrel, and pulling the cylinder forward and off the axis pin. About eight hundred .40-calibre guns were made in 1850–51, alongside a thousand .31-calibre six-shot Belt Models with barrels measuring 3–7in.

The advent of the Wesson & Leavitt revolvers did not escape the notice of Samuel Colt, fortified by an extension of his patent until 1857, and a patent-infringement lawsuit ensued. Colt won in court, gaining substantial damages which forced the original Massachusetts Arms Company into liquidation in 1853. About a thousand .31 Belt Model revolvers were made in 1851–7, with manually rotated cylinders locked by a latch in the trigger guard ahead of the trigger. Almost all had Maynard Tape Primers, while a few made after 1853 had a rammer patented by Joshua Stevens. Two hundred were supplied to Abolitionists by the Massachusetts–Kansas Aid Committee in 1856, many eventually reaching John Brown.

The **Massachusetts Arms Company** also made .28-calibre Pocket Model revolvers with $2\frac{1}{2}$in or 3in octagonal barrels, Maynard Tape Primers and a single frame-mounted nipple serving all six chambers. The first thousand guns had manually rotated cylinders, locked by a button inside the trigger guard, but an attempt to circumvent Colt's patents was then made with a mechanism patented in August 1853 by Joshua Stevens (US no. 9929). Thumb-cocking the hammer operated the Maynard priming system, and pressure on the trigger unlocked, rotated and then secured the cylinder, finally tripping the hammer at the end of the stroke. The original Stevens action was rapidly superseded by an improved version patented on 2 January 1855 (US no. 12,189) which allowed the trigger to rotate the cylinder before the hammer was cocked.

Production of Stevens-patent Massachusetts Arms Company revolvers has been estimated at 50 Belt and 300 Pocket Model guns (1853 type), plus about 1500 large-frame .28 or .31 Pocket Models with the later or 1855-type action. These had round or octagonal barrels measuring 3–3½in.

The complexity of the Stevens-patent guns was abandoned when the Massachusetts Arms Company reverted to simple hammer-rotated cylinders in 1857, owing to the expiry of Colt's master patent. About 2000 'hammer-rotation' guns were made, and some 300 unsold 1855-patent Stevens action guns were converted to the simpler mechanism.

Dissatisfied with the inability of its proprietary revolvers to challenge the supremacy of Colt, the Massachusetts Arms Company obtained a licence to make the British **Beaumont-Adams** revolver. However, only about a thousand of the .36-calibre six-shot Navy Model and less than 5000 .31 five-shot Pocket Model guns of Beaumont-Adams pattern had been made when the Civil War began in 1861.

Beaumont-Adams revolvers were protected in the USA by patents granted to Robert Adams on 3 May 1853 (no. 9694), to Frederick Beaumont on 3 June 1856 (no. 15,032) and to James Kerr on 14 April 1857 (no. 17,044) – though the larger revolvers showed the date of the Adams patent as 1858, and the smaller version erroneously dated the patent protecting the Kerr rammer to 7 April.

A few hundred American-made .36 Beaumont-Adams revolvers were purchased by the Federal authorities during the Civil War, survivors often bearing the marks of government inspectors William Thornton ('WAT') or Lucius Allen ('LCA'). Some imported English-made examples saw service with the Confederate forces.

Revolvers made by the Springfield Arms Company resembled Wesson & Leavitt designs externally, but relied on a hammer-rotated cylinder patented by James **Warner** on 15 July 1851 (US no. 8229). The earliest guns were all-metal .40-calibre six-shot 'Dragoon Pistols' with a distinctive nipple shield and a safety gate, but the perfected guns also had pivoting rammers and conventional wooden grips.

Springfield also promoted the 'Jaquith Patent Belt Model', though acknowledgement to an irrelevant patent granted to Elijah Jaquith on 12 July 1838 was little more than a ploy to confuse Colt. The .31-calibre six-shot revolvers, made with round barrels of 4–6in, were superseded by the similar Warner 'Patent Belt Model'. This incorporated a modified Jaquith cylinder-rotating hand, with a separate locking bolt, and (after 1852) a two-trigger mechanism. Retracting the hammer to full cock allowed pressure on the front trigger to index the cylinder; pressing the rear lever then dropped the hammer to fire the gun. Most guns had an early form of Warner's patent rammer.

A few .36-calibre six-shot Warner 'Patent Navy Model' revolvers were made in the mid-1850s, mostly with the twin-trigger mechanism. The principal difference from the .31 belt patterns concerned the rammer, pivoted on the barrel lug instead of the cylinder arbor, which allowed the barrel of the navy guns to be removed without detaching the rammer first.

The cylinder of the .28-calibre six-shot Warner 'Patent Pocket Model' revolver could be rotated by the hammer, a ring trigger or the perfected two-trigger system; some were rifled, others were smooth-bored; and several differing ratchet patterns and cylinder-arbor locks were used – even though total production amounted only to about 1500.

The failure of the Springfield Arms Company in the early 1860s allowed Warner to continue work under his own name. A .28 Warner pocket model was most common. Originally made with a 3-inch octagonal barrel, it was given a round barrel after about a thousand guns had been made. The calibre was then enlarged to .31. Guns of this type, with barrels measuring 2.6–4in, were still being made when Warner died in 1870. Total production is believed to have been 9,250–10,000.

Remington's first cap-lock revolver was a five-shot .31 pocket pattern patented by Fordyce Beals – who had previously designed the 'Walking Beam' revolver for Whitney (q.v.) – on 24 June 1856 and 26 May 1857 (no. 15,167 and no. 17,359 respectively).

Only about 5000 **Remington-Beals** guns were made from 1857 until production ceased in favour of the Rider pattern described below, shortly before the Civil War began. The earliest had an external arm and pawl actuating the cylinder, but the second version of 1858–60 had a disc and pawl, and the otherwise similar third type had a lever rammer protected by US Patent 21,478 granted on 14 September 1858. Third-model Remington-Beals revolvers, which weighed about 14oz, also had barrels of 4in instead of the earlier 3in type.

The perfected .31 Remington pocket revolver was the subject of patents granted to Joseph **Rider** on 17 August 1858 (no. 21,215) and 3 May 1859 (no. 23,861). Weighing about 10oz, the odd little gun had a solid frame and a distinctive 'mushroom' cylinder. The 3-inch barrel carried a small brass-pin front sight, which was used in conjunction with a sighting groove in the frame-top above the cylinder. Offered in blue or nickel-plate finishes, with grips of gutta-percha, ivory or pearl, the Rider revolvers were surprisingly popular: they were still being dispatched from the Remington warehouses in the early 1880s, and total production has been estimated at 85,000–100,000.

The first **Whitney** revolvers were inspired by the success of the Walker-pattern Colt, which had been made in the Whitneyville Armory in 1847. However, the all-enveloping nature of Colt's 1836 patent ensured that Whitney's first attempts were poor. The earliest seems to have been a crude brass-framed gun with a bird's head butt and a manually rotated cylinder with a most distinctive guard. Next came a much more conventional design, with a manually rotated cylinder locked by a trigger-like lever ahead of the square-back trigger guard. Guns will still be found with frames of brass or iron, and straps and trigger guards of iron or brass; however, production is assumed to have been meagre.

On 1 August 1854, Eli Whitney received US Patent no. 11,447 to protect a ring-trigger revolver with a frame forged 'all in one piece, with a top bar, not only to strengthen the frame but also to serve as a foil with a comb of the hammer to strike against to prevent battering the cones [nipples]'. Whitney's failure to claim this frame-style as a novelty cost him dearly, losing a chance to make a fortune in royalties.

Very few 1854-patent guns were made, as work was concentrated on a ring-trigger revolver patented on 26 September 1856 (US no. 11,715) by Fordyce Beals. Known as the '**Walking Beam**', the cylinder of an essentially quirky design was rotated by an oscillating bar. The trigger lever was pushed forward once the hammer had been retracted manually, rotating the cylinder; pulling the trigger lever back again locked the cylinder in place before tripping the hammer.

Solid-frame cap-lock 'Walking Beam' revolvers had ring triggers and an oscillator housing covering the lower part of the cylinder aperture on the left side of the frame. The .28 version is particularly rare, but even the five-shot .31 guns are scarce; production was never large.

About 1000 .22 rimfire six-shot **Remington-Elliott** or 'Zig-Zag' derringers were made shortly before the Civil War began. They were made in accordance with patents granted to William Elliott on 17 August 1858 and 29 May 1860 (no. 21,188 and no. 28,461 respectively).

The revolver patented by Henry North on 17 June 1856 (US no. 15,144) was made by Edward Savage and then **Savage & North** of Middletown, Connecticut, until an improved version was patented jointly on 18 January 1859 and 15 May 1860 (no. 22,566 and no. 28,331 respectively). Both patents were assigned to the Savage Revolving Fire-Arms Company.

The first guns had a distinctive ring-tipped operating lever, which protruded from the frame below the trigger; the addition of a spur-like protector ahead of the operating lever gave the appearance of the number '8'. Pulling back on the operating lever revolved the cylinder and cocked the hammer; releasing the lever allowed a wedge to press the cylinder forward until the chamfered chamber mouth rode over the end of the barrel to give a surprisingly efficient gas seal.

The clumsy .36-calibre six-shot revolvers were 14in long, had 7-inch barrels and weighed 56oz empty. A rammer pivoted beneath the octagonal barrel; a 'spur' or saw-handle grip was fitted; and a long-nose central hammer projected above the frame.

One brass-frame Savage & North gun was tested by the US Army in June 1856, performing well enough to allow a hundred more to be delivered in the late spring of 1857 for field trials. The second pattern had an iron frame and a creeping rammer patented by Henry North in April 1858.

The third variation reverted to a brass frame, although its sides had been flattened and the spur on the back strap was rounded. The US Navy ordered 300 revolvers in July 1858, and a 500-gun army order soon followed. The navy contract was not fulfilled until the end of 1860. A very few fourth-model guns, with a flat iron frame and an improved 1860-patent cylinder adjustor, were made in 1860–1. However, production of all the 'figure 8' Savages probably did not exceed 2000.

Sturdy solid-frame **Allen & Wheelock** revolvers ranged from tiny five-shot .31 and .34-calibre double-action bar-hammer guns to a perfected .44 six-shot 'army' pattern. Protected by patents granted to Ethan Allen on 13 January 1857 (US no. 16,367) and 15 December 1857 (18,836), they indexed their cylinders with uncommon precision. A third patent – US no. 21,400 – added a projection on the cylinder to deflect propellant gases away from the cylinder-axis pin, reducing fouling.

A cranked side hammer was required to clear the axis pin, which entered the cylinder through the rear of the frame similarly to the Root-model Colts. Allen & Wheelock guns also had a unique rammer which formed the major part of the trigger guard, yet could swing forward around a pivot in the lower front of the frame. The unique method of rotating the cylinder relied on a transverse bar in the recoil shield, rotated by the hammer, engaging a groove cut across the rear face of the cylinder.

Frames came in four sizes, and a spring-loaded rammer latch was eventually substituted for an inefficient friction pattern. Side-hammer guns were made in .28, .31, .34 (five shots apiece) and as a six-shot .36; their octagonal barrels measured 2½–8in. Production amounted to perhaps 4000 guns, .31 examples being marginally the most common.

Repeating Pistols

The first **Smith & Wesson** pistols were derived from the original Hunt and Jennings rifles of the late 1840s, chambered for self-contained rocket-ball ammunition. The lever-action repeaters were loaded through a port cut in the underside of the under-barrel magazine tube near the muzzle. Blunt tipped 'Volitional Balls' were supplied in calibres of .31, .36 (often advertised as '.38') and .44.

Pistols were made in several sizes with magazine capacities of eight to ten projectiles. However, despite impressive testimonials, they were comparatively expensive and inaccurate. There was no room in the small projectiles for a large charge of propellant; in addition, mercuric fulminate was exceptionally corrosive. Unless cleaned carefully and regularly, the bores deteriorated rapidly.

Business declined steadily until it had no future, but Smith & Wesson – still apparently financed largely by Courtlandt Palmer – had acquired a patent granted to Rollin White in which the US Patent Office had allowed a claim that novelty lay in a bored-through cylinder loaded from the breech.

Realising the potential that lay in this one small claim, Smith & Wesson sold the rocket-ball patents to a syndicate of New Haven businessmen in the summer of 1855; in August, the tools, fixtures, gauges and existing components were removed to a factory in Orange Street, New Haven, Connecticut. Volcanic-type pistols continued to be made in small numbers, but the promoters then failed again and rights to the original patents found their way to Oliver Winchester.

Winchester did not continue with the Volcanic handguns, but the metamorphosis of the basic action into the Henry and then the Winchester rifles made him a fortune after the Civil War had ended.

CHAPTER 2

TO HELL AND BACK

The Civil War, 1861–65

'Our Regiment with the Henry Rifle stood like Veterans, and never left the Line of Battle until the battle ceased. Our men often said ... that with this rifle and plenty of ammunition they could safely meet four to one men ...'

Major Joel Cloudman of the 1st District of Columbia Cavalry, commenting on the regiment's part in a skirmish near Ream's Station, August 1864.

The drive to open up the West brought clashes between the forces of slavery and Abolitionists opposing them. The problem was highlighted in the ever-growing contrast between the northern states, where industrialisation was at its most vibrant, and the largely agrarian south where tobacco and cotton held sway.

Several states had already declared their rights to repeal federal laws, Virginia doing so as early as 1798, but the periodic compromises rarely lasted; South Carolina had attempted to repeal or 'nullify' a federal law in 1832, provoking a crisis so severe that President Andrew Jackson threatened to send in the Federal army unless the state complied with his wishes.

The so-called Compromise of 1850 arose when California asked to be admitted to the Union. The basis of representation was that each state, regardless of size or population, should elect two men to the Senate. The admission of California, whose constitution expressly prohibited slavery, would have given the Abolitionists a majority. However, as the slavery question had not been resolved in Mexican territories ceded to the USA in 1848 by the Treaty of Guadalupe Hidalgo, Senator Henry Clay proposed that the admission of California as a free state should be counterbalanced by the organisation of New Mexico and Utah with slavery to be resolved by 'Popular Sovereignty'.

Backed strongly enough to be implemented immediately, Clay's well-meaning proposals succeeded only in postponing the slavery question until, in 1854, Kansas Territory demanded a settlement by Popular Sovereignty. This caused the bitterest violence in the years preceding the Civil War. In addition, Clay's harsh Fugitive Slave Law turned many a liberal conscience into a rabid Abolitionist.

Finally, the election of Republican Abraham Lincoln to the presidency in 1860 caused South Carolina to leave the Union. President Lincoln refused to recognise the right of the states to secede, and so, after a tense stand-off, the USA was plunged into the Civil War – the most shattering event in the history of a nation which, when the first shots were fired in anger, had spanned less than eighty years.

The secession of the first rebel state was followed by others, until Virginia, the Carolinas, Tennessee, Arkansas, Texas, Alabama, Georgia, Louisiana, Mississippi and Florida (declaring themselves on 8 February 1861 to be the 'Confederate States of America') ranged together against the remainder. Though now seen largely as a conflict of slavers and Abolitionists, the demarcation was far less clear-cut and often had territorial or political influences. Consequently, the 'Union' or Federal faction included 'slave states' such as Delaware, Kentucky, Maryland, Missouri and West Virginia, and the unincorporated Nebraska, Utah, New Mexico, Washington and Indian Territories.

The protagonists were not evenly matched. In 1861, the population of the states comprising the Union outnumbered the Confederacy by about 2.5 to 1; when the slaves were taken into account, the imbalance in the adult male population (i.e., those who could fight) was more than four Federals to one Confederate.

The North had all the raw materials it needed: nearly forty times as much coal, fifteen times as much iron ore, and a factory output ten times that of the South. Manufacturing industries were concentrated in the north-eastern USA, and the Confederacy had such a poor manufacturing base that virtually everything – including firearms and ammunition – had to be imported through ports which were vulnerable to blockade, especially as the Federal navy outnumbered and outgunned the Confederates more than twentyfold when the war began.

One of the key 1861 statistics concerns the production of firearms, which was more than thirty times greater in the North than the South; indeed, when war began, not one single large gunmaking factory could be found in the southern states, with the exception of the government-owned armoury in Harper's Ferry.

The Union even had greater amounts of farm acreage and livestock, and produced substantially more wheat and corn than the Confederacy. Only in cotton did the South have an advantage – by a huge margin – but the advantages were undermined by the concentration of textile production in the North, forcing the Confederacy to rely during the Civil War on exports. Not only were the shipments vulnerable to interception by the Federal navy, but the dispatch of so much raw material to the mill-towns of Europe soon glutted the market and greatly reduced the value of the crop.

A nation at war

Hostilities commenced on 12 April 1861 with a brief bombardment of Fort Sumter, which surrendered after a token resistance. However, neither side was prepared for war on a grand scale. The raising of huge armies at first created little other than untried mobs, buoyed by scarcely more than popular sentiment, and, for a while, almost no fighting of note took place.

By 21 July, 30,000 troops massing for an attack on the rebel capital – Richmond, Virginia – were halted at the First Battle of Bull Run (also known as 'Manassas') and driven back on Washington by Confederate forces commanded by Generals Jackson and Beauregard.

The unexpected defeat, and the spectacle of their forces fleeing in disorder through the streets of the nation's capital, galvanised the Union into raising the half-million strong Army of the Potomac under the command of General George McClellan.

In 1862, however, hostilities took a deadly turn. The North or 'Union' side attempted to strangle the Confederate South by blockading the southern ports, to seize the principal inland river supply routes, and to neutralise the chain of western forts. The Federal authorities were also keen to invade the South and capture the Confederate capital, Richmond, in the hope that this would destabilise the southern nation.

The Confederate goal was largely to defend the territory of the secessionary states, though the proximity of Washington DC to the border between the protagonists encouraged limited invasions of Union territory. Better generalship soon brought Confederate gains, but the Union authorities soon learned from the mistakes they made in bloody fighting in Virginia and Pennsylvania.

The first major campaigns began in the spring of 1862, when General Ulysses Grant captured Confederate Forts Henry and Donelson in western Tennessee. This was followed by the capture of New Madrid, Missouri, and the bloody but inconclusive Battle of Shiloh (Tennessee) on 6–7 April 1862. By June, the Union forces had occupied Memphis, Tennessee, while Commodore David Farragut and the Union navy had gained control of New Orleans.

McClellan, meanwhile, had landed a 100,000-man force near Fort Monroe, Virginia, in another attempt to take Richmond. Erring too much to caution, McClellan's Army of the Potomac was turned back by Confederate Generals Lee, Jackson and Johnson at the Seven Days Battles contested from 26 June to 2 July 1862.

At the Second Battle of Bull Run (Manassas), 29–30 August 1862, Lee drove a Union army under General John Pope out of Virginia and then invaded Maryland. This seemed to pose a great threat to the border states, especially in those such as Delaware where there were strong pro-slavery feelings. However, fortified by advance knowledge of the Confederate battle plan, McClellan stopped Lee at the Battle of Antietam on 17 September.

The setback proved temporary, as Lee, after regrouping, defeated Union forces under General Ambrose Burnside at the Battle of Fredericksburg (13 December 1862). Whatever his merits as a firearms designer, Burnside proved to be out of his depth as a commander of large-scale forces and was superseded by General Joseph 'Fightin' Joe' Hooker.

Joe Hooker decided on an immediate offensive, but was comprehensively defeated by Lee at Chancellorsville, Virginia, at the beginning of May 1863. Lee then reinvaded the Union, dodging through Maryland and onward into Pennsylvania. However, a series of skirmishes developed into the climactic Battle of Gettysburg (1–3 July 1863). Under a new commander, General George Meade, the Union forces turned a defensive position into one of strength: decisively checked, Lee and his men fell back into Virginia.

Concurrently, Ulysses Grant captured Vicksburg in the West, a notable success which, once the last Confederate outposts on the Mississippi had fallen, brought the Tennessee and Mississippi rivers under Federal control. An important Confederate supply route from the Gulf of Mexico had been cut once and for all. In the east, however, General Rosecrans was defeated by Confederates at Chickamauga, Georgia, and Grant was recalled to replace him.

Taking personal charge of the Army of the Potomac, Ulysses Grant elected to grind the Confederacy down, confident that his superiority in manpower and armaments would be the telling factor, and had soon penned Lee's forces by Petersburg.

Grant and his principal lieutenant, William Sherman, drove the Confederate General Braxton Bragg out of Chattanooga in late November 1863; Sherman took Knoxville, allowing the remaining rebels to be cleared from Tennessee. Grant's success persuaded Lincoln to give him supreme command of the Federal armies in the spring of 1864.

In 1864, with the Federal maritime blockade beginning to bite, Ulysses Grant invaded Virginia and the end of the war became a matter of time. Battles such as the Wilderness and Spotsylvania (May 1864) sapped both sides' resources, but Sherman captured Atlanta and began his famous – or infamous, depending on viewpoint – scorched-earth 'March to the Sea' through Georgia and South Carolina, and effectively cut Confederate territory in two by reaching the Atlantic coast at Savannah on 10 December 1864.

By the spring of 1865, therefore, the Confederate forces were starving, short of ammunition and equipment, and penned in their territory with nothing to do but wait. Grant began his final advance with a minor battle at Five Forks, on 1 April, then took Richmond two days later. On 9 April, General Robert E. Lee surrendered his Confederate army at Appomattox Court House, and the capitulation of General Johnson in North Carolina on 26 April effectively ended the war.

The aftermath of war

When the dust had settled, and reflection had become possible, the cost of the Civil War in human terms was seen to have been awful. Of the 2.2 million men mustered by the Federal armies, 360,000 had been killed or died of wounds and about 275,000 had been injured. The toll of more than 635,000 represented about 29 per cent of those engaged. Comparable figures for the Confederate States were far worse; with a much smaller manpower base, the armies had mustered just 800,000 men. About 258,000 had been killed – more than one in three of those engaged – and another 125,000 had been wounded. Confederate casualties, therefore, reached almost one in every two men and contributed to an overall casualty-count of about one man in three. Not only did the physical effects of the war last for decades, with many amputees testifying to its grim horror, but deep-seated mental scars inhibited the development of the USA for some time. Not until 1877, indeed, were the last Federal troops withdrawn from south of the Mason-Dixon Line.

A triumph of northern industrialisation and free-labour capitalism over the 'plantation autocracy' and slave-labour economy of the south, the Civil War changed the face of America. It fuelled pre-war demands for a railroad link with the western Territories, and, by promising each settler who ventured west of the Mississippi 160 acres of 'government land', the Homestead Act of 1862 had an important effect on westward migration. This in turn promoted more efficient agriculture, increased mechanisation, better irrigation and fertilisation, and the introduction of new strains of cereal crops. But it also brought railroads and the concept of enclosing land, which led directly to the long-lived Range Wars between the farmers and the cattle barons.

Longarms

The Civil War ended the brief heyday of the rifle-musket by testifying to the supremacy of the breechloading rifle and metallic-case cartridge, even if these vital advances were not heeded immediately by the Ordnance Department.

The advantages were partly hidden by the profusion of guns, differing cartridges, suspect ignition and poor-quality propellant. In addition, the earliest metal-case cartridges were heavy enough to worry senior officers concerned with the supply and replenishment of ammunition. A Spencer carbine being loaded with the assistance of a Blakeslee cartridge box could fire twenty aimed shots a minute. When its cartridges had been expended, however, even the Spencer was impotent.

Most of the senior commanders active in the Civil War had seen their active service many years previously, and the notoriously conservative Chief of Ordnance, Brigadier General James Wolfe 'Old Fogey' Ripley, had entered West Point Military Academy during the War of 1812! When the Civil War began, Ripley was sixty-five. He had made significant contributions to the development of US Army small-arms as commandant of Springfield Armory (1841–54), but remained convinced that the only firearm suited to the rank-and-file was a cap-and-ball muzzleloader. His antipathy towards breechloading weapons was so great that he was retired in 1863 on the express order of President Abraham Lincoln. Yet Ripley remained active as Inspector of Armaments until shortly before his death in 1870.

When war ended in 1865 and the progressive part-time commanders had returned to civilian life, therefore, magazine rifles such as the Spencer and the Henry were still regarded scornfully by most of the regular officers. Attitudes had changed far enough to permit the adoption of a breechloading rifle, but the Board of Ordnance and Fortification subsequently chose the slow-firing Springfield-Allin or 'Trapdoor' conversion system for its rifle-muskets in 1866, condemning troops to poor extraction for more than twenty years.

Single-Shot Muzzleloaders

Widespread dissatisfaction with the Maynard Tape Primers of the 1855-pattern **Springfield rifle-muskets**, which had proved to be susceptible to damp, led to the adoption of the Model 1861. This was practically identical to its predecessor, with three sprung bands and iron furniture, but was fitted with a side lock and a nipple for standard percussion caps.

Springfield Armory made 265,129 M1861 rifle-muskets from the beginning of 1861 to the end of 1863, apparently including a few two-band derivatives with 33-inch barrels made for artillerymen. The short-barrel guns often incorporated brass components in their furniture.

Adoption of the new weapon coincided with the start of the Civil War. To accelerate production, the patch box was discarded and contracts were placed with leading gunmaking firms. Colt's Patent Fire Arms Manufacturing Company of Hartford, Connecticut; the Amoskeag Manufacturing Company of Amoskeag, New Hampshire; and Lamson, Goodnow & Yale Company of Windsor, Vermont, all made the so-called 'Special Model 1861'. This had screw-retained bands, lacked the vent screw in the nipple cone, and had a hammer of special shape. None of these parts could be exchanged with those of the standard M1861.

The .58 Rifle-Musket Model 1863, approved on 9 February 1863, was essentially the regulation 1861-pattern gun incorporating many minor changes permitted in the Special Model – including screwed bands and omission of the vent screw. Springfield made 273,265 M1863 guns in 1863–4.

Additional changes were authorised on 17 December 1863, when solid bands reappeared, the back sight was changed, and the ramrod head was slotted. Blueing barrel bands and trigger guards was abandoned to simplify production. By the end of 1865, 255,040 M1863 rifle-muskets had been made in Springfield Armory.

In addition to Colt, Amoskeag, and Lamson, Goodnow & Yale, Special Model 1861 and Model 1863 rifle-muskets were made by Addison Burt of New York; the Eagle Manufacturing Company of Mansfield, Connecticut; C. B. Hoard's Armory of Watertown, New York; J. T. Hodge of New York; Alfred Jenks & Son of Philadelphia and Bridesburg, Pennsylvania; William Mason of Taunton, Massachusetts; James Mowry of Norwich, Connecticut; William Muir of Windsor Locks, Connecticut; James Mulholland of Reading, Pennsylvania; the Norwich Arms Company of Norwich, Connecticut; Parker, Snow & Company of Meriden, Connecticut; the Providence Tool Company of Providence, Rhode Island; E. Remington & Sons of Ilion, New York; Edward Robinson of New York City; Sarson & Roberts of New York City; the Savage Revolving Fire Arms Company of Middletown, Connecticut; Casper Schuberth of Providence, Rhode Island; W. W. Welch Company of Norfolk, Connecticut; and E. Whitney of Whitneyville, Connecticut.

Most of these contractors can be identified by name. However, the lock plates of Burt-made guns simply displayed 'TRENTON'; Jenks used 'BRIDESBURG'; the Norwich Arms Company used 'NORWICH', which may be confused with the place-name (cf. Mowry); and Welch adopted 'NORFOLK'.

A few guns made in New York in 1863 display 'U.A. CO.' for the Union Arms Company, which accepted a 25,000-gun contract in November 1861 but probably delivered less than a thousand.

Colt made 113,980 guns to Federal and state orders, Jenks made 98,000, the Providence Tool Company contributed at least 70,000 and there were 50,000 from Lamson, Goodnow & Yale.

A special derivative of the Model 1863 rifle – with an 1841-pattern barrel and lock, the 1855-pattern stock and 1863-type bands – was made by E. Remington & Sons of Ilion, New York during the Civil War. It had a distinctive brass patch box.

Although many of the rifle-muskets were subsequently converted by the addition of the Allin-pattern breech mechanism, large numbers of unaltered rifle-muskets, sold by the Federal authorities after the end of the Civil War, found their way into the Wild West. Most of them were used without alteration, but some had their barrels shortened and others had the fore-ends shortened to half length. Some were converted to shotguns, by boring out the barrels.

A particularly interesting derivation of the regulation-pattern rifle-musket was the **Lindsay** Double Musket. This was patented in the USA on 17 December 1863 by gunmaker John P. Lindsay, its principal claim to fame being the double-hammer lock fired sequentially by a single trigger. The goal was to fire two shots from a single .58 barrel, which, or so Lindsay believed, would be particularly valuable during Indian attacks. It was well known that the Indians feinted to draw the fire of defenders before pressing home the attack during the reloading phase; an unexpected second shot could be the difference between driving off the attackers and losing a scalp.

Federal authorities ordered 1000 Lindsay rifle-muskets for trials, and the guns proved of value on at least one occasion when Indians unwisely pressed home an attack on the assumption that soldiers had fired their volley. Experience showed that both charges fired simultaneously unless great care was taken during the loading process, and the Lindsay muskets had soon been discarded. They were undoubtedly sturdy enough to withstand firing two shots together, but recoil was fearful and the theoretical advantages of a rapid second shot had been lost. Breechloaders chambered for metal-case ammunition achieved the same goal much more efficiently.

The rapid expansion of the Federal and Confederate armies during the Civil War could not be satisfied by the meagre supplies of weapons in store, nor by the comparatively limited manufacturing facilities at Springfield Armory. Ordnance representatives scoured the warehouses of minor manufacturers, wholesalers and distributors, and emissaries were dispatched to Europe in search of **emergency weapons**.

Federal ordnance papers recorded the purchase of 1,472,614 Springfield rifle-muskets, 428,292 Enfields and 795,544 assorted 'Rifles & Muskets' from 1 January 1861 to 30 June 1866 – together with nearly a half-billion .577 and .58 cartridges, 230 million cartridges for the non-regulation muskets, and 1.2 billion percussion caps.

The acquisitions ranged from 12,471 efficient Spencer rifles to 1673 'Suhl Rifles' – old Prussian Jägerbüchsen – and 5995 'Garibaldi Rifles'. There were also 29,201 'Foreign smooth-bore muskets', a category into which anything that could not be more accurately classified was relegated. The poverty of the acquisitions is evident in the report of the arms inspectors who condemned five-sixths of a consignment of 3000 Austrian muskets as unserviceable.

One member of the 148th Pennsylvania Infantry Regiment complained in the winter of 1862 that the calibre of ancient rifled muskets issued in his unit 'may be reckoned as .69, although the bore is so irregular that, whilst in some instances, .69 caliber ammunition fits the bore tightly, in others it falls from the muzzle to the breach [sic] ... The locks are soft iron and many of them are already unserviceable from wear [and the] rifling adds nothing to the accuracy or effectiveness of the weapons.'

The .577 British P/53 **Enfield** rifle-musket and P/58-type short rifles, used by Confederates and Federals alike, were regarded as the best of the imports. Owing to the ready availability of British ammunition, the P/53 was the preferred alternative to regulation M1855 rifle-muskets – particularly as Springfield rifle-muskets would fire .577 and .58 ammunition interchangeably. As many as half the infantry regiments raised in New York State in 1861–2 were armed with P/53 Enfields.

Not everyone was impressed with the British guns. Writing in 1861, General William Smith suggested that guns 'were [often] exceedingly rough, and tear men's hands to pieces when they are going through the [drill] manual'. In addition, claimed Smith, few parts could be interchanged: 'no bayonet, as a general thing, will go on any rifle, except the one it is intended for. But in the case of the Springfield rifles, any one bayonet will fit them all.'

The Enfields acquired by the Federals were generally bought from the Gun Trade in Birmingham; the stock was often poor sapwood, furniture was often sub-standard, and standards of finish were generally low. For once, the South fared rather better than the North. Confederate purchasing agents acquired most of their Enfields from the London Armoury Company. Though customarily lacking the fine finish of British regulation arms, these particular Enfields were not only superior to the 'Trade Patterns' but were also largely interchangeable.

Single-Shot Breechloaders

The American Civil War was the first conflict in which breechloaders firing metal-case cartridges were used in quantity. Owing to the unmatched entrepreneurial capabilities of the US gunmaking industry, an incredible variety of guns was sold to regular, militia and volunteer units. Not only did the war provide a unique chance to try the merits of so many competing designs under combat conditions, but it also made (and sometimes also lost) many a gunmaker's fortune.

The breechloaders are listed here in order of importance on the basis of Federal purchases. It must be acknowledged that this system is imperfect, as it fails to recognise that vast quantities of guns entered military service with militia and volunteer units which had been supplied from sources other than Federal stores. Many others were sold commercially. The ranking of some guns, therefore, does not necessarily reflect their true value: e.g. the Ballard was very successful after the war had ended, and the Wesson, the least important statistically of the Federal government purchases, sold surprisingly well in several individual states.

It has been argued that some of the Civil War breechloaders never reached the West, particularly those which had been purchased in comparatively small numbers. However, demobilisation was often accompanied by distribution of weapons, and periodic sales of equipment from even the most remote army posts in post-war days contained an interesting variety of guns.

Veterans mustered out of the Federal Army in the summer of 1865 to return to their home states and territories west of the Mississippi river, for example, took with them '. . . a total of 1169 Spencers, 683 Sharps, 193 Maynards, 135 Joslyns, 84 Smiths, 19 Gallagers, and a few Cosmpolitans, Starrs and Merrills'. And an 1867-vintage sale of unwanted firearms at Fort Leavenworth included Burnside, Cosmopolitan, Greene, Hall and Wesson carbines.

War-surplus Sharps have been found with the marks of Wells Fargo, Spencers may bear the marks of Wells Fargo or the Union Pacific Rail Road Company, and a Starr carbine is known to have been used during a stagecoach robbery as late as 1892.

It is difficult to be too specific, therefore, about what may be classified as a 'Wild West Gun' in this particular category, but by far the most important of the single-shot breechloading firearms produced in the USA during the Civil War was the **Sharps**. The improved New Model guns of 1859 and 1863 had vertical breeches instead of the slanted or obliquely moving units of earlier designs. They still fired combustible linen cartridges, with nitrated bases to facilitate ignition, and had conventional external side hammers. Though the breech was prone to gas leaks, which varied from gun to gun according to individual fitting and patterns of wear (and were often very small), Sharps firearms were very popular with soldiers and civilians alike. The guns were strongly made, mechanically simple, and much more reliable than many rival designs.

The first US Navy purchase had been made prior to the Civil War, when 900 .56-calibre 1859-model rifles had been ordered on 9 September 1859. Thirty-inch barrels were held in the full-length stock by two iron bands, and an Ames-made sword bayonet could be attached to a bar-and-tenon on the right side of the muzzle.

A second navy order followed in June 1861, shortly after war had begun, when 1500 .52-calibre rifles were ordered through the intermediacy of John Mitchell of Washington DC. At much the same time, the Federal government requested C. C. Bean of New York to provide a substantial quantity – 10,000, perhaps? – of 'Sharps Long Range Rifles with bayonets'. More than 9000 rifles had been delivered into Federal stores by the summer of 1865.

The Sharps army rifles were similar to the navy pattern. However, except for 600 supplied with 36-inch barrels, they had 33-inch barrels held in the stock by three iron bands. Socket bayonets were standard, though a few rifles had bar-and-tenon fittings on the right side of the muzzle to accept swords or sabres.

Although rifle-length Sharps were purchased in quantity, the cheaper, simpler and handier short-barrelled carbines were preferred. The Model 1859 – 39in overall – had a 22in .52-calibre barrel rifled with six grooves. Sharps's name customarily appeared on the barrel, with an acknowledgement of Lawrence's patent pellet-feeder on the lock plate. A cut-off system allowed standard percussion caps to be used when necessary.

Most of the carbines made prior to 1862 had brass furniture, but this was replaced by iron early in the Civil War. The New Model Carbine of 1863 was practically identical to the 1859 pattern, though it was clearly marked 'MODEL 1863' on the barrel. The patch box was abandoned in the spring of 1864 to simplify production, but few other changes were made.

Federal ordnance records reveal that the government purchased 80,512 carbines and 9141 rifles between 1 January 1861 and 30 June 1866, at a unit cost of $27.49 and $36.17 respectively, but many thousands of guns were purchased by militia units and individual volunteers and it is suspected that total production exceeded 150,000. The government also bought 16.31 million combustible paper or linen cartridges, which cost approximately $2.13 per hundred.

Sharps rifles attained prominence in the hands of the two regiments of United States Sharpshooters, formed under the supervision of Colonel Hiram Berdan in September–October 1861. Although Chief of Ordnance Ripley insisted that the élite units carried regulation rifle-muskets, Berdan argued so strongly in favour of the breechloaders that he eventually got his way. A thousand Sharps were ordered on 27 January 1862, followed by another 1000 on 6 February. Their most distinctive features were double set triggers.

Deliveries to the sharpshooters were completed by the end of May, but many other units used the Sharps during the war – including some mounted infantrymen, who probably viewed the full-length rifle as an encumbrance.

Ranking after the Sharps in popularity came the **Burnside** design. Patented in Britain in November 1855, and then in the USA in 1856, a few guns of this type had been acquired prior to the Civil War for extended trials. They fired a uniquely conical cartridge inserted in the front of the breech-block when the action was open, relying on a small hole bored centrally through the base of the metallic cartridge case to transfer flash from a conventional percussion cap to the powder-charge. Consequently, a standard side-hammer cap lock was used.

The absence of large-scale army orders had coincided with a severe economic depression that hit the New England firearms industry particularly badly in the autumn of 1857. Burnside had sold his patents to his creditors, and the Bristol Fire Arms Company effectively ceased to trade.

However, the new proprietors, headed by Charles Jackson, had enough faith in their gun to form the Burnside Rifle Company in May 1860; Ambrose Burnside still held shares in the business, but ceased to take an active part. Tooling began in a new factory in Providence, Rhode Island, and fresh approaches were made to the army.

When the Civil War began, the Burnside company was well-placed to supply guns. The wait was short. In July 1861, the Chief of Ordnance, General Ripley, passed Jackson a request for 800 Burnside carbines from Governor William Sprague of Rhode Island, who required modern weapons for cavalrymen. The order was accepted with alacrity, delivery being promised for the end of 1861.

Modified, 1860- or second-pattern Burnside carbines (tested by the army as early as February 1860) lacked the Maynard Tape Primer and the side-mounted breech latch of the pre-war guns. They were operated by depressing the combination trigger guard/operating lever patented in April 1860 (US no. 27,874) by George Foster, foreman machinist in the Providence factory. A spring-loaded latch was added inside the front of the trigger-guard bow to keep it closed.

The original wrapped-foil cartridge, which had a straight-taper case, was soon replaced with a 'bell mouth' pattern also contributed by George Foster. The new or Foster-pattern cartridges were made in a single piece, with a circumferential groove inside the case mouth containing sufficient wax not only to lubricate the bullet but also to improve the gas seal.

Second-model Burnside carbines had 21-inch .54-calibre rifled barrels, and measured about 39.5in overall. The third pattern introduced late in 1861 was essentially similar, but had a sturdier hammer and a short wooden fore-end held to the barrel by a single iron band.

The New Model Carbine, also known as the 'Model of 1863' or fourth-pattern Burnside, embodied major changes in the breech system. Although the previous guns had proved to be quite popular, assuming their curious cartridges were available in sufficient quantity, the comparatively small projection of the open breech-block above the frame hindered loading, especially if the firer was on horseback. A pattern arm incorporating a double-pivot breech mechanism designed by Isaac Hartshorn (the Burnside Rifle Company sales agent) was deposited with the authorities as early as May 1862, though the relevant patent, US no. 38,042, was not granted until March 1863.

Adopting a double-pivot breech-block and readily detachable hinge pin allowed the block to rise and then tip backward, facilitating loading. The first bulk deliveries of these guns are said to have been made in October 1862. They were followed by the perfected 'Model of 1864' or fifth-pattern Burnside, patented by George Bacon in July 1863.

A pin on the frame followed a cam-track in the side of the breech-block as the action closed, shutting the breech in a single motion. The block of previous Hartshorn (fourth pattern) carbines had to be tipped shut manually before the operating lever was closed, but the mechanism could be jammed if the actions were performed in the wrong order and too much force was applied to the operating lever. Most Burnside carbines embodied the Bacon improvements, however, and generally display 'BURNSIDE'S PATENT' and 'MODEL OF 1864' on the frame.

The Burnside system remained popular with the Federal authorities until the end of the Civil War, perhaps because it was a cap-lock. Government purchases amounted to 55,567 guns between 1 January 1861 and 30 June 1866, ranking the Burnside carbines third only to the repeating Spencer and single-shot Sharps numerically. Each gun cost the US Treasury $25.42, while 21.82 million copper-case 'cone cartridges' were bought for $2.51 per hundred.

Apart from the Spencer, Sharps and Burnside carbines, only the Smith pattern was acquired in quantities exceeding 30,000 – and then only by a small number. Protected by US Patent 15,496, granted on 5 August 1856 to Gilbert Smith, who described himself as a 'Physician of Buttermilk Falls in New York State', the break-action carbine originally fired cartridges with a gutta-percha case. A sturdy spring-steel bar projecting back from the top of the barrel locked over a stud on the standing breech when the action was closed, requiring pressure on a small locking catch or 'lifter' ahead of the trigger lever to release the bar if the barrel was to be opened for loading.

The Smith carbine was tested at Washington Arsenal in the spring of 1860, being praised for its simplicity and an unusually gas-tight breech. Three hundred guns were acquired shortly before the Civil War began, to facilitate field trials. They were made by Poultney & Trimble of Baltimore, Maryland, assignees of Smith's patents.

When fighting began in earnest, Poultney & Trimble obtained a large order from the Federal government. However, this was much too large for the Baltimore workshop and work was sub-contracted to the Massachusetts Arms Company. Production of Smith carbines proceeded satisfactorily until, in August 1863, the Massachusetts Arms Company passed part of the work to Philos Tyler's American Machine Works to free facilities for the rival Maynard pattern.

Poultney & Trimble understandably suspected that the Smith gun was being given a deliberately low priority, shifting the entire contract to the American Machine Works in September 1863. The American Arms Company was formed in Chicopee Falls to oversee work.

Smith carbines had been designed to fire rubber-case ammunition, but Poultney was assigned a patent granted to Thomas Rodman and Silas Crispin in December 1863 protecting an improved 'wrapped-metal cartridge with a strengthening disc or cup'. 'Poultney's Patent Metallic Cartridge', as the Rodman & Crispin design soon became known, undoubtedly transformed the Smith carbine into a better weapon, though power was limited by the weakness of the breech-lock bar.

The .50-calibre Smith had a conventional side-hammer cap lock and a 21.6in barrel, which gave an overall length of 39.5in. Some guns were made with swivels on the butt and barrel band, but most have a ring-and-bar assembly on the left side of the breech.

Federal purchases between 1 January 1861 and 30 June 1866 amounted to 30,062 carbines at $24.80 apiece, together with 13.86 million assorted rubber- and metal-case cartridges obtained for about $2.72 per hundred.

The single-shot breechloading carbine patented in September 1858 by Ebenezer **Starr** of Yonkers, New York State (US no. 21,523), was tested favourably at Washington Arsenal in January 1858, eliciting the comment that it would make a far better weapon than the competing Sharps carbine if the gas seal could be improved. Accuracy had been impressive, and there had been no misfires.

One advantage the Starr had over the Sharps, though not immediately obvious, was that it did not shear off the base of the combustible cartridge when the breech closed. This is believed to have contributed to the poor shooting sometimes ascribed to the Sharps in the reports of the late 1850s, owing to the loss of small, but variable portions of the propellant charge before each shot. The Starr breech-block also had a deep annular recess that fitted over the barrel as the action closed, which had the effect of deflecting gas leaks away from the firer's face and eyes.

The two-piece radial breech-block was locked by a wedge as the operating lever (which doubled as a trigger guard) was closed. Ignition was provided by a side-hammer cap lock, which worked satisfactorily enough provided the lengthy flash-channel through the nipple was kept clean. The standard .54-calibre Starr carbine had a 21in barrel and was about 37.6in long. The furniture was customarily brass.

The external similarity between the Sharps and the Starr has caused occasional confusion, though the Starr was much more angular and had a longer receiver. The tip of the operating lever rested in a prominent latch-post projecting from the underside of the Starr butt.

The proven efficiency of the cap-lock Starr persuaded the Federal authorities to order 3000 guns chambering the .56-52 Spencer rimfire cartridge on 21 February 1865. A new breech-block was developed, fitted with an ejector, and a modified hammer with a short straight shank replaced the recurved cap-lock design. The guns were so successful that an additional 2000 had been ordered within a month, though practically no metal-cartridge Starrs had been issued when the Civil War ended in April 1865.

Apart from some conversions and the earliest new-production batches, the Starr carbines chambered for rimfire ammunition were mounted in iron instead of brass. Federal purchases amounted to 20,603 cap-locks and 5000 metal-cartridge carbines prior to 30 June 1866, each costing $22.92. Supplies totalling 6.86 million combustible cartridges had been acquired at a rate of $2.05 per hundred.

If the Starr was widely regarded as successful, the same could not be said of the **Gallager** even though the latter was purchased in broadly similar quantities. Patented in July 1860 by Mahlon Gallager of Savannah, Georgia, the guns were made in Philadelphia by Richardson & Overman. The essence of the Gallager action was a barrel which moved forward before tipping to give access to the chamber. Doubtless inspired by the Sharps, the Gallager breech lever doubled as a trigger guard.

There was nothing inherently wrong with the Gallager action, though it was comparatively weak; indeed, many similar designs had been tried successfully in

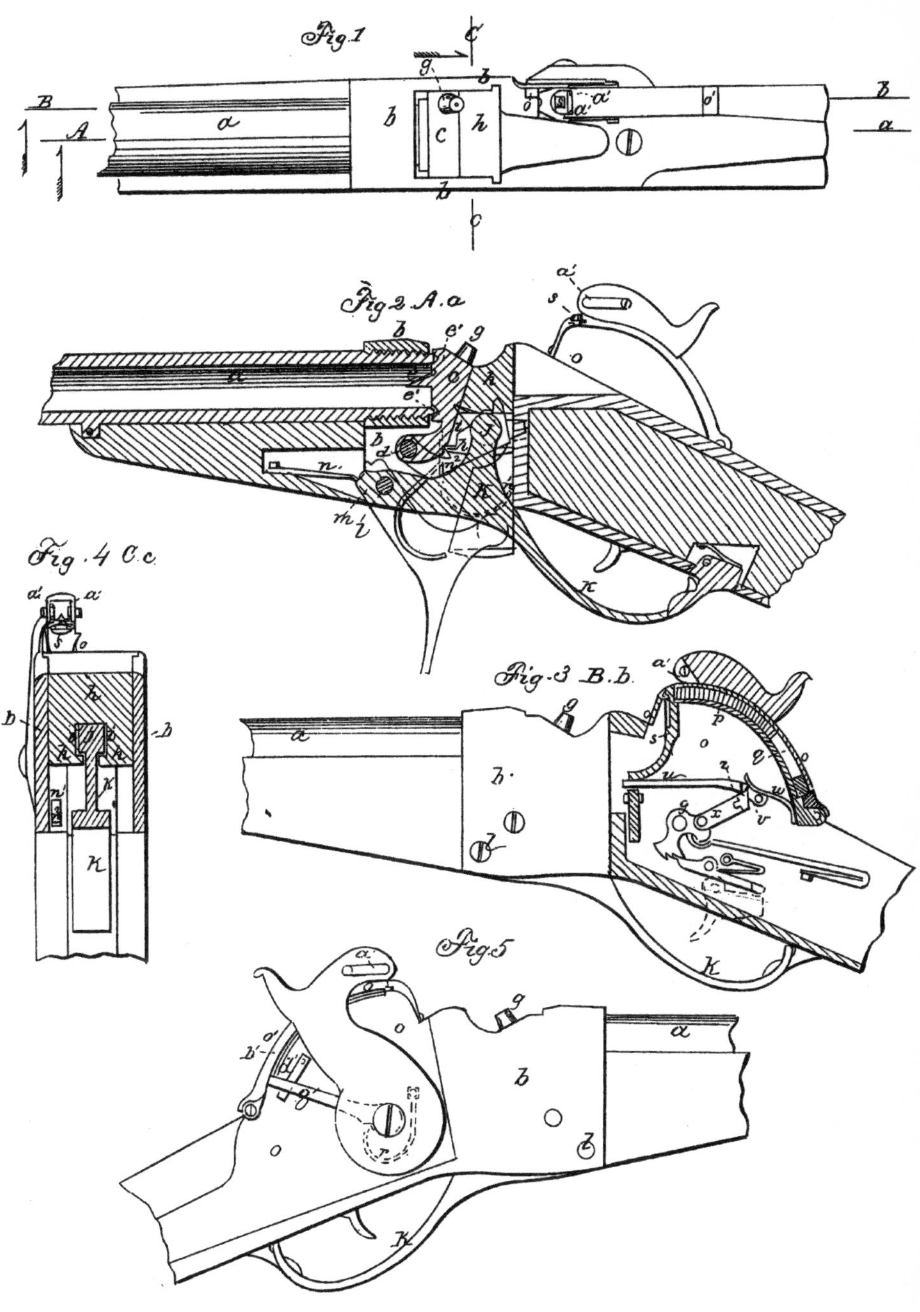

The Starr patent of 1858

Europe. Unfortunately, Gallager elected to place half the chamber in the standing breech and the remainder in the barrel.

The earliest guns fired combustible linen- or paper-case ammunition, but this was replaced during the Civil War by Poultney's or Jackson's patent cartridges – made respectively from brass-and-paper or paper-wrapped iron foil. When the gun fired, the cartridge cases tended to stick inside the chamber walls and sometimes ruptured badly enough along the circumferential joint between the barrel and the standing breech to prevent the mechanism opening efficiently.

It was by no means uncommon for the front portion of the spent case to stick in the chamber while the rear part was torn clear; or, alternatively, for the rear part to stick in the standing breech while the front part was pulled from the chamber. Even though one-piece drawn-brass cases were eventually produced, the extraction of Gallager carbine was notoriously unreliable. A special combination tool was issued with each gun, but it was not strong enough to prise cases free of the breech.

The standard Gallager lacked a fore-end beneath its .50-calibre 22.25-inch barrel, which gave an overall length of about 39.25in. A conventional side-hammer cap lock supplied ignition. Many soldiers hated the Gallager, regarding it as inferior to guns such as the Sharps and Starr. Unfortunately, the Federal government, desperate for serviceable weapons of any type, paid $22.37 for each of 17,738 cap-lock Gallager carbines acquired during the Civil War. About 8.29 million of the special cartridges were bought for $2.55 a hundred.

Five thousand improved guns chambered for the .56–50 Spencer rimfire cartridge were ordered in March 1865, but were delivered into store too late to see service in the Civil War and were subsequently sold at auction. Gallagers found their way West in substantial numbers, often smooth-bored to fire powder-and-shot or powder-and-ball loads.

Although the Gallager breechloading system failed to prosper after the Civil War had ended, the same could not be said of the interesting little **Maynard** carbine.

Edward C. Maynard, a Washington dentist, began experimenting with metal-case cartridges in the mid 1850s. Beginning with a metal tube closed at the base by a waxed paper disc, he eventually developed a closed iron (later brass) tube brazed on to a sturdy perforated base. This combined excellent sealing properties with a rim offering good purchase for an extractor.

The earliest Maynard carbine did not succeed, but its replacement received excellent testimonials. A gun tried in Washington Navy Yard in October 1859 – in the presence of Commander John Dahlgren, Edward Maynard and William McFarland, Maynard's agent – placed all of 237 shots on a target three feet broad by six feet high placed at a distance of 200 yards; at 1300 yards, a significant range for a short-barrelled carbine, it buried a bullet to its length in oak planks. More than 600 shots were fired during the experiments, with scarcely a misfire, while two cartridge cases selected at random each had survived more than a hundred reloads without failing.

Made by the Massachusetts Arms Company of Chicopee Falls, Maynards were light and handy, weighing a mere 6lb; though the ungainly straight-wrist butt suggested otherwise, they handled surprisingly well. The guns were typically 36.5–37in overall and had a 20-inch barrel. The breech was opened by pressing down on a breech lever formed as the trigger guard, tipping the barrel so that a new cartridge could be inserted directly into the chamber. The earliest guns – made in .35 or .50-calibre – had the patented tape primers beneath the hammer, and a folding back sight lay on the tang behind the central hammer. A saddle ring sometimes lay on the lower tang behind the breech lever, but a bar assembly was lacking.

The guns bought by the Federal government during the Civil War, made exclusively in .50 calibre, lacked the tape primer and patch box. They also had a conventional back sight on the barrel above the frame hinge. Between 1 January 1861 and 30 June, 20,002 Maynards were acquired officially, at a cost of $24.47 apiece, and 2.16 million of the distinctive cartridges were acquired for about $3.35 per hundred.

The enviable reputation of the single-shot breechloading **Remingtons** was established by the perfected 'Rolling Block' pattern soon after the Civil War had ended. The carbines used during the war, however, embodied the less effectual 'split breech' action patented by Leonard Geiger and Joseph Rider.

A breech-block containing the hammer moved radially in the high-wall receiver, allowing the nose of the hammer to strike rimfire cartridges through a slot in the top surface of the block. The fall of the hammer locked the breech-block behind the chamber until the hammer was once again thumbed-back manually.

Safe enough with low-pressure loads, the Remington-Geiger action was comparatively weak. Fifteen thousand carbines chambered for the standard .56-50 Spencer rimfire cartridge were ordered on 24 October 1864 for $23 apiece. They were 34.25in long, had 20-inch barrels and weighed about 7lb.

Active service showed that even Spencer ammunition, which was comparatively weak, strained the Remington-Geiger action to its limits. A second order was placed in January 1865 for 5000 smaller guns chambering a weaker .46 rimfire cartridge. Costing the government $17 apiece, few of these had been delivered into store when hostilities ended. They could be identified by the size of their frames, which were notably smaller than .56-50 examples, and by the swivels that often lay under the butt and the barrel band.

Soon after the war had ended, Remington bought back most of the unsuccessful .56-50 carbines for $15 apiece, reselling them to France in 1870 – at a handsome profit – to serve during the war with Prussia.

James **Merrill** of Baltimore was actively promoting carbines designed in partnership with Latrobe & Thomas as early as 1856. These relied on a rotary-tap or 'faucet' breech plug placed laterally behind the chamber, but the gun was too complicated and – like its promoters – had soon failed. However, Merrill persevered with Merrill, Thomas & Company until a satisfactory modification of the Jenks system was made.

The US Navy was the first to test Merrill carbines, though they were little other than Ames-made Jenks adapted to fire combustible paper cartridges. But although the conversions were eventually approved on 26 January 1861, once a side-hammer cap lock had been substituted for the original 'Mule Ear' design, the advent of the Civil War halted progress in the navy.

In June 1861, however, twenty carbines, three rifles, a 'Minnie Musket' and nine converted 1841-pattern Harper's Ferry Rifles were acquired for army trials. These improved Merrills fired regulation combustible paper cartridges or loose powder and ball, ignited by a conventional side-hammer cap lock. Merrill saw this as a great advantage over the Burnside, Maynard and Smith carbines, which all fired special cartridges.

Although clearly derived from the Jenks design, the Merrill action relied on the momentary expansion of an annular copper disc on the piston head to effect a gas seal by expanding outward as the gun fired. A small lug on the actuating lever, which could block the hammer when the breech was open, automatically cleared the spent cap from the nipple while simultaneously ensuring that the gun could not fire until the action was fully closed.

Five thousand carbines were ordered on Christmas Eve 1861, but an additional request for 566 Merrill rifles for the 21st Indiana Volunteer Infantry Regiment (made in March 1862) caused the carbine order to be reduced accordingly.

Merrill rifles proved to be popular – serving with Michigan Volunteer Infantry, Massachusetts Sharpshooters and Kansas Volunteer Cavalry – and attained a reputation for long-range accuracy. Government purchases amounted to only 769 prior to 31 December 1863, but others were doubtless acquired privately.

Typical .54-calibre Merrill rifles were 48.5in long, had 33-inch barrels held in the stock by two brass bands, and weighed a little over 9lb. A bar-and-tenon fitting on the right side of the muzzle accepted a sabre bayonet.

The earliest carbines had 22.25-inch barrels and were about 37.5–38in long. The actuating lever had a flat knurled locking catch, the fore-end was tapered, and the patch box and fittings were brass.

Later guns had a modified locking catch on the breech lever, embodying a sprung plunger; the fore-end tip was crude, and the patch box was eliminated. An eagle and the date of assembly were struck into the lock plates of guns purchased by the Federal authorities, including 14,495 carbines acquired prior to 30 June 1866. Each gun cost the US Treasury $25.86 apiece, with combustible cartridges at $1.92 per hundred.

Testimonials in Merrill broadsheets claimed that carbines equipped a variety of cavalry regiments, but they were not regarded among the best Civil War weapons and did not enjoy the same reputation as Merrill's rifles.

Benjamin Franklin **Joslyn** was one of the more interesting gun-designers of the Civil War, renowned more for constant clashes with sub-contractors and the Federal authorities than the excellence of his wares. Litigation was still being pursued long after the fighting had ceased; ironically, the first breech-loading rifle to be mass-produced in Springfield Armory was a Joslyn conversion of the regulation M1863 rifle musket made in the spring of 1865.

Successful trials of the first Joslyn carbine, known as the Model of 1855, led to the purchase of fifty in November 1857. The breech was opened by a lever running back along the wrist of the stock, which was raised by means of a large finger ring to expose the chamber. The Joslyn accepted a combustible paper cartridge, relying on the momentary expansion of steel rings in the face of the breech to form a gas seal as the gun fired. The .54-calibre carbines had 22.5-inch barrels and measured 38.25in overall.

The army soon lost interest, but the US Navy showed greater faith, ordering 500 .58-calibre Joslyn rifles on 9 September 1858 from an agent, William Freeman of New York. The guns were actually made and marked by Asa Waters & Company in Milbury, Massachusetts, but production problems delayed delivery and only 150–200 rifles were ever delivered in the spring of 1861.

The .58 Joslyn Navy Rifles were 45.8in overall and weighed about 8lb. Rifled with three grooves, the 30-inch barrels were held in the half-stocks by a single band; a bar for a sabre bayonet appeared on the right side of the muzzle. Furniture was brass.

Realising that the combustible-cartridge guns stood little chance of success, Joslyn announced a rimfire design in 1861, series production beginning a year later. The new guns relied on a laterally hinged block or 'cap', which enveloped the standing breech and could be swung open to the left when the locking catch was released. A patent granted in 1862 added cam surfaces to the basic design, improving both cartridge seating and primary extraction.

The Federal authorities purchased 860 Joslyns from Bruff, Bros. & Seaver of New York City between November 1861 and July 1862, all but 200 being sent to units in Ohio.

Joslyn acquired a contract for 20,000 carbines at the end of 1862, beginning the first large-scale deliveries in the summer of 1863, but only about half the guns had been delivered when hostilities ceased.

Made in a factory in Stonington, Connecticut, the 1862-pattern Joslyn carbine chambered .56-52 Spencer rimfire ammunition. It had brass furniture, a

22-inch barrel, and measured nearly 39in overall. The frame had a long upper tang, while the breech cap was hooked and had a single hinge. The extractor plate was retained by screws.

A few transitional guns made in 1864 combined the basic 1862-type action with the improved breech-cap release catch, but were rapidly superseded by the perfected or 1864-model gun. Chambered for .56-56 Spencer or special .54 Joslyn cartridges, this was distinguished by a chequered finger piece let into the underside of the breech hook, to improve the lock; it also had a cylindrical firing-pin shroud, a gas vent on top of the breech cap, and a short upper tang.

Guns numbered above about 11,000 also had improved double-hinge breech caps and iron furniture. They were generally marked 'US' on the right side of the butt, '1864' on the lock plate, and on the back surface of the breech cap instead of the top.

When the Civil War finished, the Federal government promptly cancelled the incomplete contract, claiming that the carbines failed to meet specifications. Government duplicity has sometimes been seen in this, but problems encountered with the Joslyn revolvers – which ordnance inspectors refused to accept as serviceable – suggests that the problems were simply rooted in poor manufacturing standards.

Benjamin Joslyn was still appealing for a review of the situation as late as April 1866, but had been able to sell many of the unacceptable guns commercially. Federal purchases prior to 30 June 1866 totalled 11,261 carbines, each costing the US Treasury $25.09.

Small quantities of the carbine patented in August 1859 (US no. 25,259) by Henry Gross of Tiffin, Ohio, also reached the West after the end of the Civil War. Best known as the '**Cosmopolitan**', after its manufacturer (the Cosmopolitan Arms Company of Hamilton, Ohio), the quirky carbines were also known as 'Gross', 'Gwyn & Campbell' or 'Union' – respectively the inventor, the owners of the manufacturing company, and a mark appearing on some individual guns.

The Cosmopolitan Arms Company was given a contract late in 1861 for 1140 Gross-patent carbines, which were destined for volunteers being mustered in Illinois. The guns were operated by pulling the breech lever downward, exposing the face of the pivoting breech-block. A separate breech cover dropped to allow a combustible cartridge to be pushed into the chamber down an integral loading groove. The Cosmopolitan carbine was fired by a conventional cap-lock with round-shank hammer.

The earliest .52-calibre guns had 19-inch barrels, were about 39in long, and weighed 6.6lb. A serpentine breech lever/trigger guard had a tip which curled to lock into the back of a post beneath the frame. Once the first order had been fulfilled, however, **Gwyn & Campbell** modified the action (US Patent no.

36,709 of 21 October 1862) so that a simple grooved breech-block dropped at the front to expose the chamber.

The Gwyn & Campbell carbine was very similar to its Gross-pattern predecessor externally, but the breech lever locked into the front of the catch-post beneath the butt, and the sides of its hammer were flat. The back sight was also simpler.

The Federal government purchased more than 9000 assorted Gross and Gwyn & Campbell carbines prior to 30 June 1866, the average cost to the treasury being $21.39. About 6.3 million combustible cartridges were acquired at $2.09 per hundred.

The Civil War boosted many gunmaking operations, among them **Sharps & Hankins** of Philadelphia. This partnership owed its origins to the antipathy between Christian Sharps and Richard Lawrence, formerly of Robbins & Lawrence, who had a large stake in the Sharps Rifle Company and was responsible (at least according to his own testimony) for most of the improvements made in the Sharps action in the 1850s.

Sharps eventually relinquished his shares in the Sharps Rifle Company and produced a design for an 'improved' carbine with a barrel which slid forward when the trigger-guard lever was pressed. In 1859, having been granted an appropriate patent, Sharps entered into partnership with a saw-mill owner named William Hankins.

Trials of the new Sharps & Hankins guns were so successful that production began in earnest in 1861. The US Navy ordered 500 .52-calibre rimfire rifles in April–September 1862, chambering the so-called .52-56 Sharps & Hankins cartridge. The guns measured 47.6in overall, had 32.7-inch barrels, and weighed about 8.5lb; the full-length fore-ends were held to the barrel with three iron bands, and the back sight was a Sharps tangent pattern graduated to 800 yards. All but a hundred of them had bar-and-tenon fittings on the right side of the muzzle to accept sword bayonets.

A few Sharps & Hankins carbines armed the 9th and 11th New York Volunteer Cavalry, raised in the summer of 1862, where they performed well enough to attract the attention of the Federal ordnance department. The guns had Sharps tangent back sights, brass butt plates, 23.5in barrels, and measured 38.5in overall. A small slide on the rear of the frame could block the fall of the hammer when appropriate.

Navy issue carbines displayed distinctive inspector's marks (e.g. 'P' over 'H.K.H.'), and had a sturdy leather protector over the barrel to minimise corrosion. The sleeve was held to the muzzle by an iron ring doubling as the front-sight base. The earliest or 'Old Model' guns, made in 1861–2, had the firing pin fixed in the hammer face; post-1863 'New Model' examples relied on a floating pin in the standing breech.

The first Federal government orders were forthcoming in 1863, the army

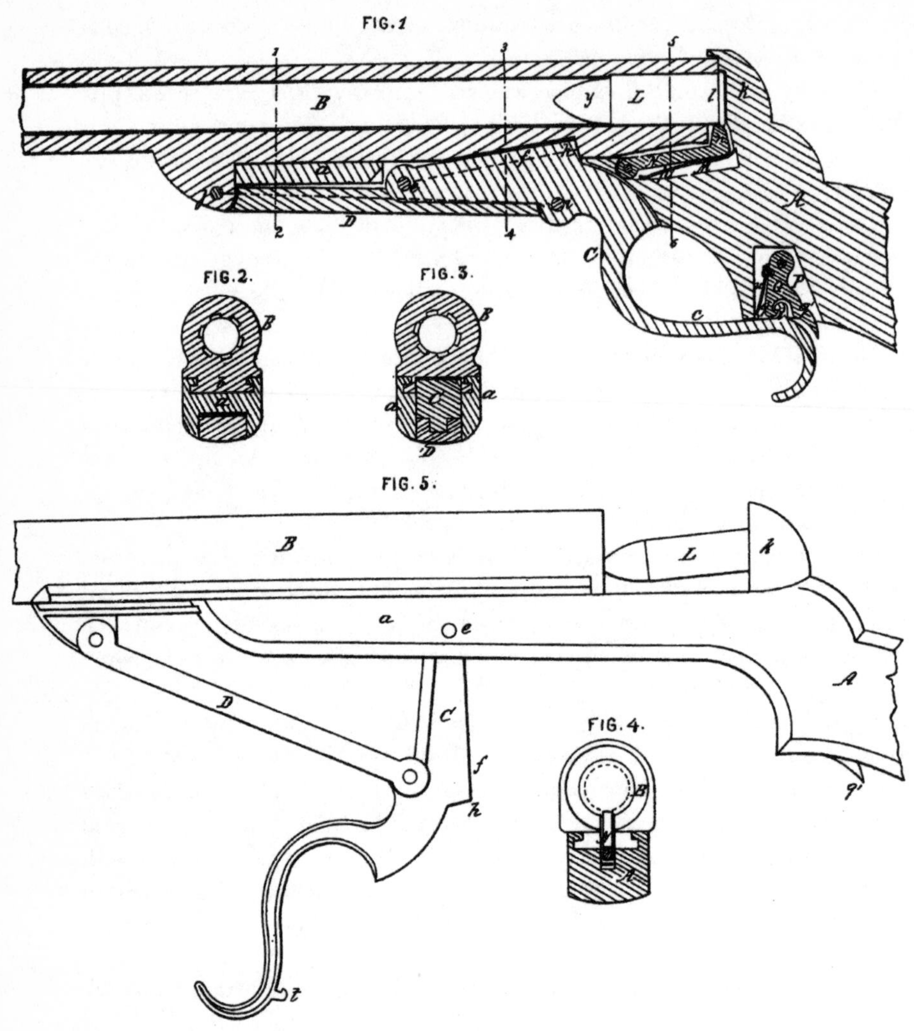

The Sharps & Hankins patent of 1861

eventually receiving 1468 guns and the navy taking 6336. Though some of the prototypes had fired .52-calibre combustible ammunition, service-issue carbines were chambered for .56 Sharps & Hankins rimfire cartridges – 1.01 million being purchased officially in 1863–6 at $2.71 per hundred.

If the Sharps & Hankins carbine had its champions in the Federal ordnance department, the same could not be said of the guns made in accordance with patents granted to James Warner – 41,732 of February 1864 and 45,660 of December 1864. However, the **Warner** carbine enjoyed a greater distribution in the West than some of its better known contemporaries.

It relied on a sturdy cast-brass frame containing a breech-block which could be swung to the right to expose the chamber. Extraction was then accomplished by retracting a lever protruding beneath the fore-end. Unfortunately, the Warner carbine had a very weak butt and was prone to breakages. The proprietary .50-calibre cartridges often jammed so tightly that they could not be dislodged, as the sliding extractor lacked adequate leverage, and spent cases still had to be pulled or shaken from the feed-way.

The original .50-calibre Warner had a 20-inch barrel and was 37.2in long. Pressing the thumb-piece near the hammer allowed the breech-block (which had a lug on the left side) to be swung laterally to the right. The sling ring was customarily held to an eye-bolt running transversely through the frame.

Later guns, chambering .50 Warner or .56-50 Spencer ammunition, were made by the Greene Rifle Works in Worcester, Massachusetts. A sliding breech-block catch – simple and easy to make – lay on the left side of the frame, and a sling bar appeared on the left.

Several small orders totalling 1501 guns, chambering a special .50 cartridge, were placed in January–November 1864; these were followed by a single 2500-gun order, placed on 26 December 1864 for a modified design accepting the .56-50 Spencer rimfire round. The last of the 4001 government guns was delivered into ordnance stores in mid-March 1865; the average cost was subsequently calculated to have been $19.82 apiece.

The distinctive single-shot dropping-block rifles and carbines protected by a patent granted in November 1861 (33,361) to Charles **Ballard** of Worcester, Massachusetts, had very little significance during the Civil War. However, they were destined to be made long after many of their contemporaries had been forgotten.

The earliest Ballards, made by Ball & Williams, were enthusiastically promoted by Merwin & Bray of New York. The breech-block contained the hammer and trigger mechanism, automatically dropping the hammer to half-cock as the action opened. Originally designed to chamber rimfire ammunition, the guns made for the Federal government incorporated a supplementary cap-lock ignition system patented by Joseph Merwin & Edward Bray in January 1864 (US no. 41,166).

Seemingly a backward step, the cap-lock adaptor proved to be useful when metal-case ammunition ran short. Placing a nipple in the block below the hammer nose allowed a percussion cap to be fired as the neck fell. Combustible cartridges or loose powder-and-ball could be used in emergencies, though the breech was far from gas-tight. Alternatively, a hole could be bored in the base of a spent Ballard rimfire cartridge loaded with fresh powder and a new bullet. Firing the gun in this way allowed the brass case to expand to seal the breech.

In view of the sophistication of the design and the enthusiasm shown by recipients, if surviving testimonials are reliable, the meagre Federal government purchases are difficult to understand – merely 35 rifles and 1509 carbines, costing $36.06 and $23.29 apiece. The rifles were apparently purchased in Florida for sharpshooters of the 34th US Colored Infantry Regiment.

A contract had been signed as early in October 1862 to supply 1000 rifles and possibly also 2500 carbines, but the output of Dwight Chapin & Company of Bridgeport, Connecticut, may have been poor enough to force the arms inspectors to reject large numbers of individual guns. Six hundred rifles and a thousand carbines were promptly sold to the State of Kentucky, where the Ballard became popular enough to inspire supplementary orders. An inventory taken in Kentucky in September 1864 revealed 3494 carbines and 4600 rifles. The relative proximity of Kentucky probably explains why original Civil War-type Ballards were surprisingly common west of the Mississippi after 1865.

Perfected Ballard rifles, made by Ball & Williams of Worcester, Massachusetts, in .44, .46 or .56 rimfire, were 45.5in long, had 30-inch barrels and weighed about 8.25lb. Most had three iron barrel bands.

Chambering .44 or .54 cartridges, the carbines had 20-inch barrels and measured 37.25in overall. Wooden fore-ends retained by a single barrel band were standard, often with a swivel under the band; a second swivel lay beneath the butt.

Production of the carbines associated with a patent granted in January 1856 to Lucius **Gibbs**, confined to the Civil War, was eventually curtailed in very unusual circumstances. On 18 December 1861, the Ordnance Department contracted with William Brooks of New York City for 10,000 Gibbs carbines at $28 apiece. An ironfounder specialising in chimney flues, Brookes subcontracted most of the work to the Phoenix Armory on the corner of Second Avenue and 22nd Street. Deliveries commenced in the late spring of 1863.

On 13 June 1863, however, the Phoenix Armory and its contents were destroyed during the New York Draft Riots, and work on the Gibbs carbine stopped after only 1052 had been sent into store at a cost to the government of $26.61 apiece.

The .52-calibre Gibbs operated similarly to the Gallager (q.v.); a lever doubling as the trigger guard tipped the barrel to receive a combustible paper cartridge. A conventional side-hammer cap lock was used to detonate a percussion cap, the flash passing down the nipple channel and out along the axis of a hollow conical spigot which had pierced the cartridge base to facilitate ignition. An annular collar in the breech-face expanded momentarily to act as a gas seal.

A Gibbs carbine typically had a 22-inch barrel, giving an overall length of 39in, and had a conventional wooden fore-end. It could be easily identified by a closed ring on the breech-lever tip.

The carbine patented by William **Palmer** of New York City in December 1863 (US no. 41,017) might have encountered far greater success had it been designed earlier in the war. Made by E. G. Lamson & Company, the first bolt-action pattern chambering metal-case ammunition ever to be adopted by the US armed forces, the Palmer had a collar-type extractor and a spring-loaded ejector. These features alone elevated it far above many other carbines used during the Civil War, even though ignition was still supplied by a conventional external side-hammer.

The first of a thousand guns ordered on 20 June 1864, at $22.90 apiece, was not delivered until the summer of 1865 – too late to see action in the Civil War. Chambered for .56-50 Spencer rimfire ammunition, the gun had a 20-inch barrel and an overall length of about 37.25in.

Another of the quirky Civil War guns was the **Greene** breechloading rifle. A bolt-action carbine patented in 1857 had interested the US Army sufficiently to order a hundred for trials, but James Durrell Greene then patented an improvement (US no. 34,422 of 18 February 1862) on the basis of rifle-musket conversions supplied to Russia.

Greene, Colonel of the 4th Massachusetts Volunteer Militia when the Civil War began, was soon commissioned into the regular army. The sale of a few hundred Greene rifles to the Massachusetts volunteers revived official interest, but tests undertaken in May–June 1862 at Watertown Arsenal were unfavourable. Greene persisted, enlisting high-ranking political assistance, until the purchase of 900 rifles and accessories was approved in January 1863 at a cost of $33,266. That the rifles were delivered on 12 March – an amazingly speedy response by Civil War standards – suggests that they were already in existence, but they were still in store a year later.

The Greene rifles were 52.5in long and weighed about 10lb. Their 36-inch barrels, held in the full-length stock by three iron bands, had British Lancaster-pattern oval bore rifling measuring .530 and .546 on minor and major axes respectively. Another quirk was to be found in the self-contained combustible cartridge, containing a bullet in its base.

The guns were sturdy, but too idiosyncratic to be successful. No one liked the underhammer cap lock, for example, or the way in which the bolt could be retracted only after a release catch had been pressed. The loading cycle was also unique. A single bullet was first seated by pushing the bolt handle forward as far as possible; the bolt was then reopened, a combustible cartridge was dropped into the breech, and the action was closed to its normal (half-forward) position. Rotating the bolt downward then revolved two lugs into seats behind the chamber.

A loaded Greene rifle, therefore, had one bullet ahead of the charge and another acting as a gas-check. Once the gun had been fired, the rear 'gas-check' bullet was pushed forward to allow another cartridge to be inserted. If the chamber became too foul or the special ammunition was unavailable, the rifles could be loaded from the muzzle.

A carbine patented on 29 March 1859 by Edward **Lindner** was also used officially in small numbers, though alterations of guns for militia or volunteers are believed to have been much more common.

The essence of the action was a short grasping handle that rotated the breech sleeve to the left, allowing the cylindrical breech-block to be pivoted upward to receive a combustible cartridge. Ignition was provided by a conventional side-hammer cap lock.

The most basic Lindner was converted from an imported Austrian 'Lorenz' musket, cut down to carbine length. Others were made by the Amoskeag Manufacturing Company of Manchester, New Hampshire, though they rarely bore anything other than an acknowledgement of the 1859 patent on the action.

The Federal ordnance authorities ordered 400 Lindner carbines on 6 November 1861. The guns were to be delivered to Washington Arsenal within eight days, so it is reasonable to conclude that they were supplied from stock. Used by Michigan cavalrymen during the Second Battle of Bull Run (Manassas), the .58-calibre Lindner carbines had a 20-inch barrel and measured about 38.5in overall.

Federal purchases in 1861–5 amounted to merely 892 Lindner carbines, at an average cost of $22.30 apiece, together with special combustible cartridges for $2.26 per hundred.

The scarcest of the Federal Army carbines, to judge from the ordnance returns, was patented by Franklin **Wesson** of Springfield, Massachusetts, in 1859–62. The distinctive frame had two separate apertures, one containing the trigger and the other with a trigger-like latch to release the barrel, which tipped down to expose the chamber. The absence of an extractor meant that stubborn cases often had to be punched out of the chamber with a ramrod.

Measuring 39.5in overall, with a 24-inch barrel, the guns usually bore both Wesson and Kittredge markings on the barrel. Only 151 were purchased officially from Benjamin Kittredge & Company of Cincinnati on 7 July 1863, for $23.12 apiece, and a solitary additional gun came from Schuyler, Hartley & Graham of New York on 1 August. However, Kittredge was an enthusiastic champion of the Wesson system, supplying at least 1366 guns to

Kentucky, 760 to Illinois, and hundreds to individual regiments during the Civil War.

Multi-Shot Rifles

If the Civil War conclusively demonstrated the potential of the single-shot breechloading rifle and the self-contained metal-case cartridge, it also provided a persuasive argument in favour of the repeating rifle – for those who were prepared to listen.

Henry's Patent Repeating Rifle, the forerunner of the Winchester, had the greatest long-term effect. Benjamin Tyler Henry – known as 'Tyler' or simply 'Ty' – was born in Claremont, New Hampshire, in March 1822. Apprenticed at sixteen to a local gunmaking business, Ripley & Co., Henry subsequently went to (among others) Springfield Armory, Kendall & Co. and Robbins, Kendall & Lawrence.

Working for Robbins & Lawrence, as his employer had been renamed following the retirement of Nicanor Kendall, Henry came into contact with the Jennings-patent derivative of the 'Volitional Ball' repeating rifle created by Walter Hunt. He also met Horace Smith and Daniel Wesson; when Robbins & Lawrence collapsed in 1854, Smith and Wesson invited Henry to oversee production for the Volcanic Firearms Company, but Henry was more interested in developing an improved Volcanic chambered for rimfire ammunition and his participation seems to have been limited.

When Volcanic metamorphosed into the New Haven Arms Company, Oliver Winchester invited Henry to become factory superintendent. Henry left Winchester's employ in 1866, possibly after a disagreement over the replacement of the Henry rifle by the 1866-pattern Winchester, but continued to operate an engineering business in New Haven until his death in 1898.

The rifle patented by Benjamin Henry in 1860 (US no. 30,446) was little more than an outgrowth of the lever-action Volcanic. It shared some of the same weaknesses and was by no means easy to load, but had an incomparably better cartridge than the self-contained Volitional Ball. Inspired by the .22 ammunition developed for the minuscule Smith & Wesson No. 1 revolver, the .44 Henry pattern had a short straight-sided case containing about 25 grains of black powder and a 216-grain bullet. Two grams of fulminate spun into the folded-over rim provided the igniter.

Henry rifles had a 24-inch barrel with a bore diameter of .420, rifled with six grooves and a progressive twist which quickened from a turn in sixteen feet at the breech to one in 33in at the muzzle. The frames were initially iron, but later bronze; the straight-wrist butts were hardwood. Overall length was about 42in, and empty weight averaged about 10lb. Among the most distinctive features, which the Henry shared with the Volcanic, were the absence of a fore-end and the comparative fragility of the tube magazines beneath the barrel.

Broadsheets produced by the New Haven Arms Company claimed:

> The prominent feature and great advantage of [the Henry rifle] consists in the great facility and rapidity with which it can be loaded and fired. Any person can, with a few hours' practice, keep up a continuous fire of twenty shots per minute, and an expert from practice can fire it thirty times a minute, which is twice as fast as any other breech-loading gun . . .
>
> In accuracy, power and durability, it is equal to the best Rifles made of corresponding weight and calibre.
>
> The principle of its construction is applicable to Rifles, Muskets and Carbines for army uses, Shot Guns, Target Rifles, Squirrel Rifles, and all other varieties of Sporting or Military small arms.
>
> The main feature is a magazine under the barrel, parallel with the bore of the gun and the same length (which in the size now made hold fifteen metallic cartridges), and a lever under the lock frame, which in two motions (forward and back) cocks the gun, brings from the magazine, and places in the barrel the charge, closes the breech tight, and withdraws and ejects the empty shell; or if the gun misses fire, withdraws the whole charge. When the magazine is filled – which can be done in thirty seconds, or less – and the gun placed to the shoulder, it can be fired fifteen times in ten seconds, without removing it.
>
> . . . [take] the gun in the left hand by the middle of the barrel, and . . . [hold] . . . the lock between the elbow and left side with magazine up. Then with the thumb of the right hand, press the spiral spring in the magazine up to the muzzle tight, so as to release a catch which holds the sleeve from turning; then press to the left with the thumb, the sleeve will turn and open the end of the magazine in which cartridges are then to be dropped until full, with the ball towards the muzzle; when filled the sleeve is turned back.

Series-made Henry Rifles were available from the summer of 1862, enabling many to be sold to state militia and volunteer units. Brigadier General James 'Old Fogey' Ripley, the incumbent Chief of Ordnance, had a particularly harsh view of the new repeater. As early as the autumn of 1861, after reviewing a prototype Henry rifle, Ripley had failed to 'discover any important advantage . . . over several other [single-shot] breech loaders, as the rapidity of fire with these latter is sufficiently good for useful purposes without the objection to increased weight from the charges in the arm itself, while the multiplication of arms and ammunition . . . is decidedly objectionable, and should, in my opinion, be stopped by the refusal to introduce any more.'

After the Spencer rifle had been approved in 1863, however, the attitude of the Federal ordnance department mellowed; 1731 Henry Rifles and the staggering total of 4.5 million .44 rimfire cartridges had been acquired by the end of 1865.

As many as 8000 Henry rifles may have been purchased by state militia and volunteers in addition to the paltry total acquired by the Federal authorities, suggesting that about 10,000 guns saw action during the Civil War. Total production by the end of 1865 is estimated to have amounted to about 11,000.

There is no doubt that the Henry was an efficient weapon, greatly appreciated for its high rate of fire in the days before the 1864-patent Blakeslee Quick Loader elevated the Spencer Rifle to similar heights. Oliver Winchester skilfully capitalised on this praise, particularly if it showed rivals such as Spencer in poor light.

Typical of the 'unsolicited testimonials' was a lengthy letter from Major David Gamble, commanding the 66th Illinois Veteran Infantry Volunteers, written from Washington DC on 1 June 1865. Gamble wrote:

> At no time has the regiment had more than two hundred of these arms in an engagement, yet where other regiments, and even brigades, have given back or failed to press the enemy back, the 66th Illinois, with the assistance of these Rifles, have ever been enabled to hold a position, or take one at pleasure.
>
> On the morning of 9 May, 1864, at Snake Creek Gap, Ga., the 9th Illinois Infantry, armed with the Spencer Rifle, was attacked by Wheeler's brigade of rebel cavalry, and though they fought bravely, and were assisted by the 51st Illinois Infantry, armed with the Springfield rifled musket and bayonet, they were compelled to fall back on the main body of the division and lost a number of ... prisoners to the enemy. The 66th Illinois was ordered forward, and eight companies deployed as skirmishers; and that line of skirmishers alone, without difficulty, checked the enemy's advance, and finally drove him nine miles ... notwithstanding he was reinforced by three regiments of infantry.
>
> The ammunition of the 9th Illinois gave out, a great fault with the Spencer Rifle, it being of the largest calibre – too large for a soldier to carry enough to last through an engagement where repeating firearms are used. Cal. .44 is sufficiently large for every purpose in army use, and enables the men easily to carry a hundred rounds – enough for most battles of the war.
>
> The Henry Rifle is durable – those that we bought of you in 1863 being still serviceable, though some of them has [sic] fired as many as 5000 cartridges. They will continue serviceable longer than the Springfield rifled musket, for the reason that they are the more easily cleaned. Some of the men possessing them traded them for the Spencer Rifle, often getting as much as $30 difference, but in no case where it was done, was the man satisfied. [The Spencer] gets easily out of repair, especially in frosty weather when the catch that draws out the discharged cartridge frequently breaks, which is never the case with the Henry. Your rifle is light, strong, durable, accurate, quick of firing, easily loaded, safe, and not encumbered with a bayonet, and with a cartridge of a better calibre than the Spencer.

It may be hard to argue that the Henry was anything but the best repeating rifle of the Civil War, but it was not without its weaknesses. The fragile magazine tubes were easily deformed, in extreme cases rendering them useless, while the forked firing pin was also prone to fracture. Spencer rifles were sturdier than the Henry and could survive harsher treatment, but suffered from a weak extractor and their rate of fire – even when used in conjunction with the Blakeslee cartridge box – was somewhat less.

The biggest weakness of the Henry, judged as an all-round military weapon, lay in the low power of its rimfire cartridges. It had no peer at short ranges, owing to its rate of fire. Trials undertaken in Switzerland with an 1866-model Winchester indicated that even an untrained rifleman could achieve twenty unaimed shots each minute. When the gun was being fired deliberately, accuracy was such that mean radii of 4in and 24in were returned at distances of 300 and 1200 paces respectively. However, the value of the Henry reduced in direct proportion to increases in range, owing to the steady reduction in striking energy; the Spencer held an advantage in this respect, but both repeaters were greatly inferior to the standard muzzleloading rifle-muskets at ranges greater than about 500 yards.

The Civil War proved as great a godsend to the New Haven Arms Company as it did to many other gunmaking companies, as sale of 10,000 Henry Rifles at $40 apiece finally placed operations on a stable footing. Trade slumped when the war ended, however, owing to the ready availability of war-surplus guns at knock-down prices. Consequently, only about 500 new Henry rifles were sold commercially in 1866.

The major wartime rival of the Henry rifles was the **Spencer**, though a successful transformation into the 1866-pattern Winchester ensured that the Henry had far greater long-term effect on the development of the magazine rifle. The failure of the Spencer to re-establish itself in post-war days allowed Fogerty to buy the Spencer Repeating Rifle Company and then Winchester to buy Fogerty in 1869. Within four years of the end of the Civil War, therefore, a modernised form of the Henry rifle had entirely eclipsed the gun that had been its principal challenger only a few years previously.

ED SCHIEFFELIN

Edward L. 'Ed' Schieffelin is renowned as the discoverer of silver in San Pedro Valley, Arizona Territory, in 1877. The strike was made in Apache land, where Schieffelin was warned that all he would find would be his tombstone. The size of his strike, however, caused 'silver fever' and a boom town soon grew in the most productive district. Schieffelin named the settlement 'Tombstone', with a touch of irony, but sold his claims in 1880 and died prospecting in Alaska in 1897. Among the guns used by Schieffelin were a .44 rimfire Henry repeating rifle (no. 2197), a heavy-barrel M1874 Sharps sporting rifle, and a pair of .44-calibre Smith & Wesson single-action revolvers. The Henry is currently being displayed by the Tombstone Courthouse State Historical Park.

Christopher Miner Spencer was just one of the many talented and versatile engineers to trade in New England. Born in Manchester, Connecticut, in June 1833, Spencer left school early to work in the nearby Cheney Brothers Silk Mills. Broadening his experience by working with a Rochester factory specialising in railroad locomotives (1853–5) and in the Hartford factory operated by Colt (1856–7), Spencer then returned to the Cheney mills. His first patent was granted to protect an automated silk winder, but, even after his interest in firearms waned, Christopher Spencer retained his reputation as an engineer of great skill.

Among his most important designs were a screw-making machine and an automatic turret lathe, both of which were made for many years by Billings & Spencer; he was also responsible for many advances in drop-forging machinery, and continued to work virtually until his death in January 1922.

Spencer's first breechloading firearm was patented (no. 27,393) in the USA on 6 March 1860, and had a profound effect on the progress of the Civil War. The prototypes were apparently made in the Cheney Brothers' workshop, performing efficiently enough to demonstrate their great potential virtually from the beginning of work.

Much has been made of an impromptu trial of a Spencer carbine by Abraham Lincoln in August 1863, implying that the success of the Spencer was entirely due to presidential intervention. The truth is, of course, much more prosaic; the Cheney brothers were friendly with Gideon Welles, Secretary of the Navy, and had simply showed him the prototypes. Welles was sufficiently astute to see that the Spencer had immense potential, passing the information to the commandant of Washington Navy Yard, Captain John Dahlgren. The first trials were undertaken on 8 June 1861, most encouragingly. An inherent weakness was detected in the original extractor, but an improved design, patented in July 1862 (no. 36,062), cured the faults.

On 22 June 1861, therefore, the US Navy ordered 700 .52-calibre Spencer rifles and 70,000 rimfire cartridges to enable large-scale trials to be made. The navy rifles were 47in overall, had 30-inch barrels held in the full-length stocks by three iron bands, and were sighted to 800yd. Empty weight was about 10lb, without the brass-hilted sword bayonet (made by Collins & Company) which could be attached to a bar-and-tenon on the right side of the muzzle. A large delivery of Spencer rifles – totalling 703 – reached the navy ordnance department on 3 February 1863.

Some of the earliest US Navy trials were attended by Captain Alexander Dyer of the US Army. Appointed Chief of Ordnance in later years, Dyer noted the ease with which the Spencer rifle coped with most of the tests, reporting his favourable observations to his superiors. A Board of Officers convened by the commander of the Federal army, Major General George McClellan, successfully tested a Spencer in Washington Arsenal in November 1861, but the Chief of

Ordnance, Brigadier General James 'Old Fogey' Ripley, rejected the recommendation that a substantial quantity of Spencers should be acquired for field trials.

An exasperated Charles Cheney turned once more to Gideon Welles, who convened a meeting between the interested parties and the Speaker of the House of Representatives, James Blaine. Welles then authorised the purchase of 10,000 Spencer rifles for the army, which was an unprecedented step for the Secretary of the Navy to take! The decision was countersigned by Thomas Scott, Assistant Secretary of War, to prevent Chief of Ordnance Ripley from interfering. On 26 December 1861, presented with a fait accompli, James Ripley agreed to accept 10,000 rifles at $40 apiece.

To cope with demand, the Spencer Rifle Manufacturing Company leased half the under-employed Chickering piano factory in Boston, Massachusetts. However, no deliveries had been made by 29 January 1862, when notice was received that the Secretary of War had ordered a review of all existing contracts.

Rumours were even heard that the authorities were going to cancel Spencer orders in favour of rifle-muskets, but the worst that happened was a reduction of the original 10,000-gun order to 7500. A new contract was signed on 19 June 1862, the guns being delivered into store between 31 December 1862 and June 1863.

Progress was still slow, however, when Christopher Spencer met with Abraham Lincoln in August 1863. The president was greatly impressed by the potential of the rapid-firing carbine, listening incredulously as Spencer related (perhaps somewhat misleadingly) tales of high-ranking official indifference to his design. But it was scarcely coincidental that, in no time at all, the progressive George Ramsay had replaced ultra-conservative General Ripley as Chief of Ordnance.

The Spencer was a seven-shot repeater with a radial-block action operated by a lever doubling as the trigger guard. When the breech lever was pulled downward, the upper part of the block dropped into the main portion, allowing the entire breech-block unit to move radially until the extractor pulled the spent case backward out of the chamber and the ejector flicked it out of the gun. As the operating lever was closed, the tip of the breech-block picked up the rim of the first cartridge in the tubular magazine running up through the butt, and fed it into the chamber; at the end of the stroke, with the main portion of the breech-block resting against the breech face, the final upward movement of the operating lever raised the breech-block insert to seal the chamber.

Most Spencers made after 1864 were fitted with a cut-off mechanism patented by Edward Stabler of Sandy Springs, Maryland. Especially popular with high-ranking officers who viewed the fire-rate of the Spencer as a way of exhausting ammunition faster than it could be supplied, the Stabler cut-off

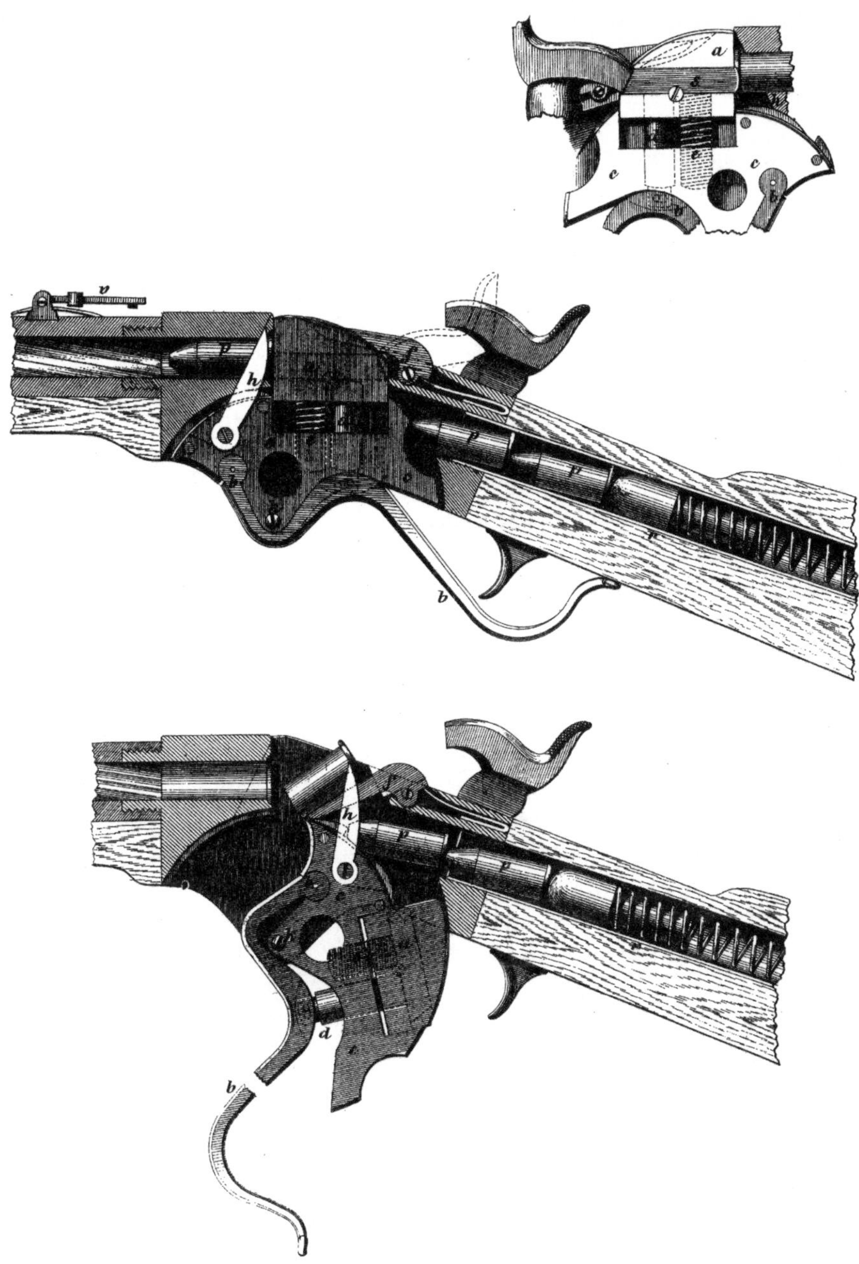

The action of the Spencer carbine

allowed cartridges to be retained in the magazine simply by restricting the backward rotation of the breech-block.

Including the time taken to reload, a Spencer rifle could fire about fourteen rounds per minute. This compared with ten to twelve for the single-shot Sharps Carbine, eight for the Colt Revolver Rifle (which was uniquely time-consuming to load), and only three for a regulation .58 rifle-musket. Loading the Spencer took about fifteen seconds, though this was subsequently reduced to five with the introduction of the Blakeslee loader, with a corresponding increase in fire to twenty-five unaimed rounds per minute. Vigilance was necessary to ensure that the Spencer cartridges were not inserted in the magazine backwards, a potentially dangerous source of premature explosions, but the gun was otherwise very simple to use.

The introduction of a cartridge box patented in November 1864 by Colonel Erastus Blakeslee of the 1st Connecticut Cavalry greatly improved the performance of the Spencer. Made in several sizes, the Blakeslee loader held six to thirteen seven-round tinned sheet-metal loading tubes in a wooden block. The tubes allowed cartridges to be dropped straight into the Spencer butt magazine once the butt-trap had been opened and the magazine spring and cartridge follower had been temporarily removed. Replacing the spring and follower returned the carbine to working order in a matter of seconds.

The Spencer was sturdier than its principal rival, the Henry Rifle, and chambered a much more powerful cartridge. The .56-56 Spencer rounds tested by the US Navy in 1862 contained a 34-grain black powder charge and a .56-diameter bullet weighing 362 grains. Comparable figures for the Henry were a 25-grain charge, a diameter of .44 and a 216-grain bullet.

Adding the muzzle velocities into the equation – estimated at 900 ft/sec for the Spencer and 1125 for the Henry – indicates that the Spencer cartridge had a 40 per cent advantage in muzzle energy. However, if the range exceeded 500 yards, neither of the rimfires was as effective or as accurate as the Minié-type expanding projectiles fired from the regulation .58 rifle-muskets. And, indeed, some commentators suggested that the additional weight of the .56-56 Spencer cartridge compared with the smaller .44 Henry unnecessarily restricted the amount of ammunition which could be carried by individual soldiers.

The first government-order Spencers began to reach the troops early in 1863, though guns had already been sold to state and volunteer units in small numbers; Christopher Spencer, exasperated by official inertia, had been undertaking promotional tours since the summer of 1862. Sergeant Francis Lombard of the 1st Massachusetts Volunteer Cavalry, a personal friend of Spencer, used a hand-made 'pre-production' rifle in a skirmish with Rebel horsemen near Cumberland, Maryland, on 16 October 1862.

Soldiers of Colonel John Wilder's Brigade relied on 1369 Spencers, 323 British Enfields, nine Colt revolver rifles and forty assorted Springfield rifle-muskets to maul a large band of Confederates during the Battle of Hoover's Gap; and the superiority of the Spencer was reinforced at Yellow Tavern, Franklin and Five Forks.

Confederate forces never successfully overcame Spencer-armed Federals, even when the Northern troops were outnumbered ten-to-one. More than 3000 of the first Spencers helped stem the Confederate advance at the first Battle of Gettysburg on 1 July 1863, and the repeaters were soon being demanded in such great numbers that the Boston factory of the Spencer Repeating Arms Company could no longer cope with demand. The problems were solved by sub-contracting 35,000 carbines to the Burnside Rifle Company in June 1864. Burnside delivered 30,496 by the end of 1865.

A typical Spencer-made .56-52 carbine was about 39in long, weighed 8.5lb, had a 22-inch barrel, and was marked 'M-1865' if fitted with a Stabler cut-off. Government inspector's marks customarily appeared in a cartouche on the left side of the butt. Spencers made by Burnside generally had 20-inch barrels chambered for .56-50 rimfire cartridges and were only 37–37.25in long. They were marked 'Spencer Repeating Rifle, Patented March 6, 1860' together with 'Manufd. At Prov. R.I. By Burnside Rifle Co.' on top of the receiver.

Ordnance records published after the end of the Civil War reveal that 12,471 rifles and 94,196 carbines had been delivered into store by 30 June 1866, although only about 50,000 of the carbines had been issued before fighting ceased. Army rifles were identical with the navy pattern, but accepted socket bayonets instead of sabres; each one cost the US Treasury $37.48, compared with $25.41 for a standard carbine.

More than 58 million cartridges had been purchased by 30 June 1866 at a cost of about $2.44 per hundred. The vastness of the total was partly due to a process of standardisation begun at the end of 1863, which ensured that the .56-50 rimfire cartridge was chambered in many other carbines.

The only other magazine firearm to appear in quantity during the Civil War was the work of Albert **Ball**. Born in May 1835 in Boylston, Massachusetts, Ball was apprenticed to a machinist, working for several companies in Worcester before joining Lucius W. Pond shortly before the war began. Though best known as a gunmaker, Pond originally specialised in tools and put Ball to work supervising the manufacturer of planers. There Ball patented his first invention – a machine for polishing flat surfaces – and, inspired by the beginning of the Civil War, followed it with a breechloading rifle.

Pond does not seem to have been interested in the repeating-rifle patent, which was instead bought by E. G. Lamson of Windsor, Vermont. Lamson was making a number of firearms and doubtless saw potential not only in the untried Ball design but also in the single-shot bolt-action Palmer (q.v.). Ball duly became superintendent of Lamson's gun factory, overseeing development of his carbine, but left in 1868 to manufacture a diamond-tipped rock drill.

Prior to his death in 1927, Ball was granted more than 135 patents for drilling equipment, coal-cutters, crushers and pattern-making machinery.

The major novelty in the Ball breech mechanism lay in the design of the cartridge elevator or 'carrier', which took a round from the tube magazine beneath the barrel, transported it to the chamber, then extracted and ejected the spent case as the action opened again. The chamber was formed partly by the rear of the frame and partly by the top surface of the cartridge elevator.

The idiosyncratic method of forming the chamber, though it simplified the movements of the cartridge, ultimately proved to be the Achilles Heel of the design. The carbines seem to have worked well enough when they were new, but chambering became sloppier as the components wore and it is suspected that accuracy may have declined.

Ball originally designed his gun around a special .50-calibre cartridge, but no sooner had work begun than the Federal authorities ordered Lamson to use .56-50 Spencer cartridges to simplify ammunition supply. Perfected Ball carbines would hold nine Spencer or twelve of the shorter .50 'Lamson & Ball' cartridges.

Based on patents granted in 23 June 1863, 16 August 1864 and 6 December 1864 (US nos 38,935, 43,827 and 45,307 respectively), the Ball carbine was most distinctively stocked and had an unusually massive receiver. A tube magazine lay beneath the barrel and a side-hammer was mounted on the right side of the action, relying on a safety interlock to prevent the breech opening unless the hammer was forward.

An extended fore-end was held to the barrel and magazine-tube with two iron bands. The gun was about 37.6in overall and had a 20.8in barrel rifled with five grooves twisting to the right. Empty weight was only 7lb 7oz, which belied its massive-looking construction.

The acknowledgement of a 15 March 1864 patent date on the receiver-side referred to the reissue date of protection originally granted to Ball on 23 June 1863.

Lamson accepted a thousand-gun contract placed by the Federal government on 6 June 1864, at a cost of $25.24 apiece, and a single delivery of 1002 Ball carbines was made on 14 May 1865 – a few weeks after fighting had ceased.

Handguns

Although the reputation of the cap-lock revolver had been established in California in Gold Rush days, the Civil War inspired a search for a weapon which offered a better combination of accuracy, reliability and certainty of ignition. This was eventually found in the rimfire cartridges pioneered by Smith & Wesson, though not before a bewildering variety of infringements and evasions had been touted. Yet although the story of these ammunition developments – and the accompanying firearms – is among the most fascinating in firearms history, only the basic rim- and centre-fire designs stood the test of time.

Major Cap-Lock Revolvers

Samuel **Colt** died unexpectedly in 1862, shortly after the first of the new-type streamlined cap-lock revolvers had been introduced. A culmination of a series of experiments with lightened guns undertaken in the Hartford factory, apparently under the supervision of Elisha Root, the .44-calibre New Model Army Revolver ('Model 1860') replaced the ageing Dragoon Model. The New Model Army was really little more than a .36 1851 Navy pattern with a longer grip, the front half of the cylinder enlarged to take large-calibre projectiles, a change to the frame to accommodate the new cylinder, and an 8-inch barrel with an elegant shroud for the 'creeping' rammer.

Detachable shoulder stocks were introduced shortly after production began, requiring a fourth screw through the frame and additional small (but instantly identifiable) cuts in the lower face of the recoil shields.

Several types of .44 army revolver were made, including one with a 7½in barrel and a fluted cylinder; 55 special guns dating from 1860 had short Navy-style grips, 7½-inch barrels and silvered grip straps, and also lacked the capping recess customarily cut in the recoil shield on the right side of the frame behind the cylinder. Other non-standard guns date from the Civil War, assembled during periodic shortages of standard army-style components. The back straps were iron, though trigger guards were normally brass. Cylinder surfaces bore the same roll-engraved maritime scene as the standard .36-calibre Navy revolvers.

A Board of Officers appointed by the US Army in 1861 to consider the merits of the new revolver was suitably impressed, its president, Acting Inspector-General Joseph Johnston, reporting that 'the decided advantages which Mr Colt has gained for his pistol by the introduction of his recent improvements ... with the 8-inch barrel, will make the most superior Cavalry arm we have ever had...'

The Army Model also provided the basis for some of the most spectacular presentation guns, including matched pairs presented in 1863 by Abraham Lincoln to kings Carl XV of Sweden and Frederik VII of Denmark in an attempt to prevent Scandinavian masts and spars from gracing Confederate blockade runners.

The .36-calibre New Model Navy Colt, now often known as the 'Model of 1861', combined the 7-inch small-bore barrel of the original or 1851-pattern navy revolver with the streamlined barrel shroud and creeping rammer of the .44 army gun. Some 38,843 New Model Navy guns were made in 1861–74, including about a hundred with fluted cylinders and a similar quantity accepting a shoulder stock.

The New Model Police and 'New Model Pocket Pistol of Navy Caliber' both appeared in 1861, though now often known as the Models of 1862. About 47,000 were made in a single number-series, police-type guns being in a small majority. The two five-shot patterns were practically identical, chambering .36-calibre ammunition, but the police variant had a fluted cylinder and a creeping rammer instead of the plain-surface cylinder and hinged rammer of the navy pattern; barrels measured $4\frac{1}{2}$–$6\frac{1}{2}$in. However, fifty police-style revolvers were made in 1862 with $3\frac{1}{2}$-inch rammerless barrels. They were issued with a separate brass rammer, which was simply pushed through the aperture in the barrel shroud when required.

The exigencies of the Civil War meant that few Police or Pocket Navy Model revolvers were extensively decorated, though a few guns were made with the so-called Tiffany Grips prior to 1865 and many more were produced after the fighting had ceased. The grips were white-metal castings, made to the designs of John Ward, and were then often plated in gold or silver. Among the most popular patterns were a Civil War battle scene, the US or Mexican eagles, and an eagle-and-justice motif.

The Federal government purchased more Colts than any other revolver-type during the Civil War, excepting the solid-frame Remingtons. Acquisitions between 1 January 1861 and 30 June 1866 totalled 129,730 examples of the .44-calibre Army Model and 17,010 .36-calibre Navy examples.

The Civil War was initially seen as a short-term affair, and its effect on the gunmakers in the first few months of fighting was comparatively small. When it became obvious that hostilities would not only escalate but continue for some time, many companies began to copy the best-known revolvers. The Colts were particularly vulnerable, as they were not only the market leaders but also relatively easy to make.

Another factor was a terrible fire in February 1864 which had not only destroyed the Hartford 'Old Armory' and administrative block, but also wrecked large quantities of assembled revolvers, machine-tools and the wooden patterns so vital to production. Although Colt's capacity to make rifle-muskets was unimpaired, the fire disrupted revolver production for many months (the buildings were not rebuilt until 1867) and created a gap in the market which less scrupulous manufacturers were keen to exploit. Not surprisingly, therefore, Colt-type guns predominate among the copies.

Among the most notorious of the **Colt copyists** was the Manhattan Firearms Company of Newark, New Jersey, which made .31 pocket and .36 navy-type revolvers acknowledging patent-protection granted to Joesph Gruler and August Rebety on 27 December 1859. This implied that the guns did not infringe Colt's rights, but the Gruler & Rebety patent only protected the inclusion of safety notches on the cylinder (between each pair of cylinder-stop notches) and Colt's attorneys halted production in 1864.

Manhattan had made about 5000 .31 and 80,000 .36 open-frame cap-locks, some with the marks of an entirely spurious 'London Pistol Company'. The small-calibre guns had detachable side plates giving access to the lockwork – unlike the genuine Colts – while all but 10,000 of the .36 examples had five-chamber cylinders instead of six.

Another of the Colt copyists, the Bacon Manufacturing Company of Norwich, Connecticut, also made guns with detachable side plates. This was largely because Thomas Bacon had worked for Manhattan and had simply copied the copy, though the .31 five-shot Bacon revolvers customarily had a ball-type retaining catch on the rammer head instead of the sliding wedge preferred by Manhattan.

Bacon-made Colt copies were often sold through wholesalers, and may be found with markings applied on behalf of Fitch & Waldo; B.J. Hart & Brother; Tomes, Melvain & Company; the Union Arms Company; or the Western Arms Company.

Bacon traded independently until 1867, when his business was purchased by Hopkins & Allen. He had continued to make the side-plate type .31-calibre cap-lock revolvers in post-Civil War days alongside a larger .36 version known as the 'Dictator', most guns displaying a new three-piece rammer unit. Only about 1000 cap-lock Dictators were made, followed by 5000 modified guns chambering .38 rimfire ammunition.

The Colt-type revolvers made by the Nepperhan Fire Arms Company, trading in Yonkers, New York, were essentially similar to the .31-calibre detachable side-plate cap-locks made by Bacon and the Manhattan Firearms Company. However, Nepperhan guns had distinctive brass trigger guards, dovetailed into the frame, instead of the screw-retained wrought iron guards favoured by rival manufacturers.

Colt-type guns were also made in New York City by the Metropolitan Fire Arms Company, deliberately founded in February 1864 to capitalise on the disastrous fire at the Colt factory. Assessment seems to be complicated by the occasional omission of blocks of serial numbers, but it has been estimated that Metropolitan made only about 6000 copies of the six-shot .36 Navy Model and New Model Navy Colt revolvers (the so-called 'M1851' and 'M1861') in addition to a little under 3000 guns based on the five-shot .36 New Model Police ('M1862'). The rammers on the 'New Model' copies were pivoted, instead of the creeping variety associated with the genuine Colts.

Many of the guns made by the Metropolitan Fire Arms Company were unmarked, but others bore the manufacturer's name on top of the barrel; at least one batch was made for H. E. Dimick & Company of St Louis, and was marked appropriately. Many also have a depiction of the Battle of New Orleans (April 1862) rolled into the surface of the cylinder.

The Confederate States of America lacked a firearms industry worthy of the name and was forced to import the majority of the weapons used by the South during the Civil War. However, among the few enterprising gunmaking businesses trading in 1861–5 were those that made **Confederate Colts**.

Among the smallest output – only about 100 guns – was that of the Augusta Machine Works of Augusta, Georgia, which produced copies of the .36 six-shot Navy-model Colt with 7.8in octagonal barrels and six or twelve cylinder-stop notches. Much the same quantity was made by the Columbus Fire Arms Company of Columbus, Georgia, founded by Louis & Elias Haiman in 1862. Dating from 1863, Columbus revolvers were also copied from the .36-calibre Navy-type Colt. Most of them had octagonal barrels, though a few round-barrelled guns were also made. The factory was subsequently sold to the Confederate government and moved to Macon, Georgia, but there is no evidence that revolvers were made after the transfer of ownership.

Modified Dragoon-type Colts were made in .36 and .44 by J. H. Dance & Brothers of Columbia, Texas (also known as 'Dance Bros. & Park'). The first gun was presented to the Confederate authorities on 22 April 1862, but production was comparatively slow. Dance revolvers were readily identified by the absence of recoil shields on the frame behind the cylinder, and by an exploded-cap channel in the breech face. Only about 500 guns were ever made, with the .44-calibre version outnumbering the .36 pattern by about two guns to one.

Tucker, Sherrard & Company of Lancaster, Texas, contracted with the State of Texas in April 1862 to make 3000 Colt-type revolvers. However, no guns had been forthcoming when Labon Tucker withdrew to form Tucker & Son in nearby Weatherford, where he made 100 Navy-pattern Colt copies with round Dragoon-style barrels.

After a hasty reorganisation, Taylor, Sherrard & Company managed to assemble no more than a few sets of parts before collapsing. Clark, Sherrard & Company finally managed to complete about 500 guns, but only after the Civil War had ended.

The failure of these gunmaking businesses typified the parlous nature not only of Confederate ordnance but also of the slow progress of industrialisation south of the Mason-Dixon Line. Excepting the Tredegar Iron Works, the South possessed no large-scale metalworking facilities, and the difficulties facing the gunmakers merely reflected problems faced in other manufacturing industries.

One of the few gunmaking businesses to contribute more than a few hundred handguns to the Confederate cause was Griswold & Gunnison of Griswoldville, Georgia, which made about 3500 .36 six-shot Colt Navy-type revolvers with brass frames and round Dragoon-style barrels from the summer of 1862 until the winter of 1864.

Leech & Rigdon made a few .36 Colt-type revolvers in the Novelty Works in Columbus, Mississippi, before moving to Greensboro (Georgia) in the spring of 1863. The guns had distinctive $7\frac{1}{2}$-inch round barrels. The business was dissolved in January 1864, allowing each partner to continue operations alone. About 1500 revolvers had been made with Leech & Rigdon marks, even though the last batches had been completed by Rigdon & Ansley in Augusta, Georgia. Thomas Leech contributed an additional 100 Greensboro-made revolvers.

Procurement figures published after the end of the Civil War revealed that the Federal government had acquired more Colt revolvers than any other type, but also that **Remingtons** had similarly been acquired in large numbers. Colts accounted for 39 per cent of the official handgun purchases, whereas the Remingtons contributed 35 per cent.

The Colt was generally considered to be superior; though it lacked the sturdy solid-top frame of the Remington, the Colt was better made, easier to maintain, and less prone to jamming. It is assumed that the great fire of February 1864, which effectively destroyed the revolver-making facilities in the Hartford factory, prevented the acquisition of Colt revolvers in 1864–5 and forced the Federal authorities to turn instead to Remington.

The original .44-calibre six-shot Remington Beals Army Revolver was made by E. Remington & Sons of Ilion, New York, in accordance with a patent granted in September 1858 to Fordyce Beals (US no. 21,478). It was a sturdy single-action gun with a solid frame, Beals' Patent Rammer, a brass trigger guard, an octagonal barrel and a characteristic web beneath the rammer shaft. Remington Beals revolvers were about 13.8 inches overall, had an 8-inch barrel with five-groove rifling, and had an empty weight of about 46oz. Finish was customarily blue, with a colour case-hardened hammer.

Federal records show that only 2814 .44-calibre Beals army revolvers were acquired for service before being superseded by the improved 1861 pattern, though it is suspected that at least a similar quantity was sold commercially. There were also about 15,000 of a smaller Beals .36-calibre 'navy' pattern.

The most obvious external change was the substitution of the inefficient Beal rammer by a sturdier pattern patented in December 1861 by William Elliott (US no. 33,932), which allowed the axis pin of the cylinder to be withdrawn without releasing the rammer catch – though the separate cylinder latch could slide forward to jam the action as the gun was being fired.

The 1861-model revolver was otherwise difficult to distinguish from the earlier Remington Beals type. About 19,000 .44 M1861 revolvers were made, all but a handful being purchased by the Federal government. A cartouche containing inspector's initials will be found on the left grip of army-issue guns.

About 7500 .36-calibre M1861 'navy' Remingtons were made in the same serial-number sequence as the .44 army pattern, but the Elliott rammer – which had also proved to be inefficient – was rapidly replaced by an improved design attributed to Samuel Remington. This was patented in the USA in March 1863.

The resulting 'M1863' or New Model Army Revolvers had safety notches between the nipples, and attachment threads were visible where the barrel abutted the cylinder face. They were about 13.8in overall, had 8-inch barrels rifled with five grooves, and weighed 45–46oz. Trigger guards were made of brass. A distinctive 'NEW MODEL' mark appeared on the octagonal barrel, with inspector's initials in a cartouche on the walnut grips – e.g. 'OWA' applied by O. W. Ainsworth.

Federal records show that 125,314 .44-calibre army and about 23,000 smaller .36-calibre 'navy' guns were acquired from 1863 until 30 June 1866, representing virtually the entire production run. One advantage the Remingtons held over the Colts was price: a .44 New Model Army Remington of 1863 cost $13.02 compared with $17.70 for the rival 1860-type Colt.

The huge numbers of Remington revolvers acquired by the Federal army during the Civil War ensured that they survived in quantity in the West. Some of them, still in their original cap-lock guise, were still serving their owners when Remington's business collapsed in 1886 – indeed, some of the small-calibre cap-locks were still in store in Ilion, although production had ceased many years earlier.

The smaller Remingtons included about 8000 .36 six-shot New Model Belt Revolvers, with $6\frac{1}{2}$-inch octagonal barrels. Some guns were made to special order with fully fluted cylinders, but were comparatively uncommon. New Model Belt Revolvers could be supplied in two basic patterns, production amounting to about 3000–3500 single-action guns and 4500–5000 of the double-action equivalent. Purchasers could choose blue or nickel finishes, or, alternatively, combine a nickel-plated frame with a blued barrel. Highly decorated guns were made to order, with scroll engraving and grips of ivory or pearl.

The .36 five-shot Remington New Model Police Revolver was similar to the earlier large-calibre Belt patterns, but had a $3\frac{1}{2}$–$6\frac{1}{2}$in barrel and weighed 21–24oz instead of 36oz. Some 18,000 were made in 1863–70, the last new guns being sold in the 1880s. About 27,500 .31 five-shot New Model Pocket Revolvers made in the same period were distinguished by sheath triggers, though otherwise typical of Remington construction and offered in a variety of finishes. Their octagon barrels usually measured $3\frac{1}{2}$ or $4\frac{1}{2}$in, giving empty weights of 14–16oz.

Starr revolvers were the third most popular among the Federal purchases, totalling about 13 per cent of the handguns acquired between 1 January 1861 and 30 June 1866. They were based on a patent granted on 15 January 1856 (US no. 14,118) to Ebenezer Townsend 'Eben' Starr, a forty-year-old businessman whose family was well known in Yonkers, New York.

A .36-calibre revolver underwent an impressive government trial as early as 1857. The Starr Arms Company of Binghamton, New York, subsequently made good use of testimonials provided by Lieutenant Colonel Alexander of the

Cavalry Bureau, who regarded the double-action .44 revolver as 'the best for Army use', and from Brigadier General Davies, who noted his opinion that the 'mechanical combination of parts in the [Starr] is superior ... to any revolver made'.

Starr described his revolver as 'self-cocking', relying on a 'cocking lever' (which resembled a standard trigger) to rotate and index the cylinder and cock the hammer. If the sliding stop on the back of the cocking lever was upward, the gun would fire as soon as the cocking lever struck the sear-release set into the rear of the trigger guard and tripped the hammer. With the cocking-lever stop downward, however, the hammer remained cocked until the firer released the cocking lever and consciously pressed the sear release.

Although needlessly complicated, this 'hesitation cocking' action allowed the hammer to be released with much less effort than simply pulling through on the cocking lever, improving accuracy if the firer had sufficient time to take a fine aim.

A thousand 6-inch barrelled .36-calibre guns were purchased for the US Navy in 1858, followed by about 1250 for the army when the Civil War began – the first authenticated army issue was made in April 1861 to the 7th New York Regiment of National Guard. The .36 or 'navy caliber' revolver was followed by an enlarged .44-calibre version at the end of 1861. The army revolver had a 6-inch barrel and weighed about 51oz empty; the Federal authorities bought more than 23,000 of them in 1862–3.

Self-cocking Starrs were widely liked, as many people regarded them as superior to the Colts. The standards of manufacture fell below those customarily expected of the products of the Colt factory in Hartford, but were certainly on a par with the Remington. One of the best features of the Starr was the forging of the cylinders and cylinder-axis pins in a single piece, which reduced the number of jams attributable to cap fragments or propellant fouling jamming the cylinder. Sufficient clearance was provided to fit the caps over the nipples.

Starr revolvers could be reloaded merely by releasing the large transverse bolt in the top rear of the frame, which allowed the barrel to move forward to release the cylinder.

The last Starr revolver to be made in quantity was a simplified single-action pattern with an 8-inch barrel and an empty weight of about 47oz. The action was protected by additional patents granted to Ebenezer Starr in December 1860 (US no. 30,843) and to Thomas Gibson in April 1864 (no. 42,435). A bar-type safety patented by Starr on 20 December 1864 – no. 45,532 – may be found alongside the hammers of a few guns made towards the end of the Civil War.

The single-action Starr may have been introduced to capitalise on the loss of Colt's revolver-making facilities in the disastrous Hartford fire of February

1864, when it is suspected that the Federal authorities were forced to look elsewhere for supplies of effectual 'army caliber' (.44) handguns. A little over 20,000 of the 25,000 single-action Starr revolvers ordered in 1864 had been made by the end of the Civil War, though many were delivered only after fighting had stopped. Much of the work is believed to have been undertaken by the Savage Revolving Fire-Arms Company.

Federal government purchases amounted to 47,952 Starr revolvers in the period between New Year's Day 1861 and 30 June 1866. The total included about 1250 .36 revolvers at $20 apiece, 23,250 .44 double-action guns at $25, and more than 20,000 .44 single-action guns at $12 apiece. Thousands more had been sold commercially.

The most numerous of the imported revolvers were French-made **Lefaucheux** designs, Federal purchases totalling 12,374 prior to 30 June 1866 although many more were undoubtedly sold commercially on both sides of the Mason-Dixon Line. However, very little is known about the Federal acquisitions of 1861–2, except that they cost about $13.54 apiece. Nearly 850,000 cartridges were acquired in the same period, at an average of only 49 cents per hundred.

It is suspected that the purchases consisted of a single order for 10,000, negotiated with Schuyler, Hartley & Graham, and that the remaining guns were acquired from dealers such as Hermann Boker of New York City.

Most of the guns fired the regulation French government 12mm cartridge, often identified as '.44' in the USA, though 7mm and 9mm patterns were also acquired in small numbers. It is sometimes suggested that the 10,000-gun order was fulfilled with surplus French navy revolvers, but most survivors prove to be commercial equivalents with spurred trigger guards.

The 1858-model Lefaucheux was a six-shot open frame design with robust single-action lockwork, a 6.2-inch round barrel rifled with four grooves, and a brass trigger guard with a notable spur. Overall length was 11.6in, empty weight being 37.5–38.8oz. The guns were loaded through a hinged gate on the right side of the frame behind the cylinder and had a sliding ejector rod on the side of the barrel.

The essence of the Lefaucheux revolver, however, lay not in the design of the gun – a comparatively flimsy open-frame type with a poor cylinder-locking system – but in the self-contained metal-case pinfire cartridges, which were ignited by striking a small projecting pin downward into a cup-like primer. The ammunition was much more popular in Europe than America, as it was delicate, comparatively weak, and prone to ignite prematurely if the pin was struck accidentally. The 12mm military cartridge contained 9.7 grains of black powder and fired a bullet weighing 208 grains at a muzzle velocity of about 540 ft/sec.

Lefaucheux revolvers seem to have been issued for cavalry service from 1862 onward, initially often without pinfire ammunition! However, they were withdrawn as soon as cap-lock Colts and Remingtons became available in large numbers – though some pinfires remained in service in the West for some time. An inventory taken in the spring of 1864 revealed that 125 were serving in Dakota, Colorado, Kansas and New Mexico, and others came westward with migrants after the Civil War had ended.

A few idiosyncratic North & Savage revolvers (described in the preceding chapter) had been acquired in 1857–60, principally by the US Navy. An improved Savage design, made in accordance with a patent granted in 1859, shared the general lines of its North & Savage predecessor, though the butt spur was cut back and the massive trigger guard ran back to the base of the butt.

Six-shot .36 Savage 'Heart Guard' revolvers were just as clumsy as their antecedents. The cylinder was still rotated independently (by pulling the operating lever) before the trigger could be pressed to release the hammer, but the proven gas-seal system was retained and cylinder indexing was much more accurate than rival designs. A simplified pivoting rammer replaced the original creeping pattern. Some guns were adapted to receive shoulder stocks patented in May 1860 by Charles Alsop (US no. 28,433) or by Edward Savage in April 1861 (no. 32,003).

The Savage revolvers were sturdy and durable, though inexperienced firers sometimes damaged the firing mechanism by mistakenly pulling the ring-lever and the trigger together.

The Savage Revolving Fire-Arms Company sold the first of the .36 or 'navy calibre' guns to the Federal government in August 1861, 700 going to the navy and 200 to the army. The earliest guns were sold through intermediaries, however, and Savage drew little direct comfort from negotiations with the Ordnance Department.

An order for 5000 guns, signed on 10 September 1861, had soon been cancelled; this was due to wrangling over payments supposedly due to Thomas Dyer, an entrepreneur hired by Savage to promote the revolver. Fortunately for the Savage Revolving Fire-Arms Company, a substitute order was negotiated in mid-October and the last of the guns was delivered into store in March 1862.

Although Savage was keen to supply revolvers in far larger quantities, the first approaches were rebuffed by Chief of Ordnance Ripley, who regarded the design as 'not . . . a desirable arm for the service, and not such a one as I would supply, unless in case of emergency'. Yet commonsense prevailed in view of the universal shortages of serviceable firearms experienced in the first few months of the Civil War, and another 5000-gun order was placed in November 1861.

Figures published after the war had ended revealed that the Federal authorities had acquired 11,284 Savage Navy Revolvers from 1 January 1861 until 30 June 1866. Judging by marks on surviving examples, most of these may have finally passed to the Federal navy. Few deliveries were made after the end of 1863, as Savage then agreed to make .44 revolvers under contract to the Starr Arms Company.

Federal purchases of Savage revolvers were only slightly greater than the acquisitions of the much more conventional **Whitney** pattern. The perfected single-action .36 Belt (or Navy) Revolver, introduced after substantial quantities of Colt Navy copies had been made in the old Whitneyville factory, was among the more popular Civil War revolvers. Safety notches were added between each pair of nipples shortly after production began, and alterations were made to the maritime scene rolled into the cylinder surface. A wedge was substituted for the original sprung rammer-locking ball approximately halfway through the production run, five-groove rifling was substituted for a seven-groove type, and the trigger guard was noticeably enlarged to admit a gloved finger.

Made in a new factory in New Haven, Connecticut, the six-shot .36 Whitney Belt Revolvers were about 13.1in long, had 7.6-inch octagonal barrels, and weighed about 41oz. Deliveries amounting to 11,214 guns were made to the Federal army between 1 January 1861 and 30 June 1866. However, 5726 additional guns were procured for the navy and 792 were delivered to the New Jersey State Militia; many others were sold commercially, as production totalled about 33,000. Ordnance records reveal that the army guns cost the Federal treasury $136,690.39 – only $12.19 apiece, which made the Whitneys cheaper even than the Remingtons.

Cataloguing Whitneyesque designs presents a major problem, owing to the existence of Whitney-like guns marked by W. W. Marston (the Phoenix Armory), the Union Arms Company or the Western Arms Company. It is suspected that Whitney supplied ready-engraved cylinders and other parts for completion by these agencies; the nipple recesses on revolvers bearing Union and Western marks are squared rather than rounded, suggesting the supply of unfinished components.

About 800 brass-frame .36-calibre '**Confederate Whitneys**', based on the Whitney navy revolver, were made by Spiller & Burr in 1863. The Confederate government purchased the assets of the partnership in January 1864, moving the plant from Atlanta to Macon, Georgia, where another 750 guns were made until the advance of the Federal army stopped work in November 1864.

A modified Whitney-based revolver was made by Thomas Cofer of Portsmouth, Virginia. Based on the .36 Whitney navy revolver, but displaying a brass frame and a distinctively spurred trigger guard, Cofer revolvers were originally designed to accept a special percussion cartridge patented by Cofer on 12 August 1861. The 'production' version – only about 100 were made – chambered conventional ammunition.

The failure of the Pettengill revolver, described below, left **Rogers & Spencer** with thousands of unwanted components. The problems were eased by the acquisition of the 5000-revolver contract that had once been given to backers of the Freeman pattern.

Designed to use as many Pettengill parts as possible, the single-action Rogers & Spencer revolver was a six-shot .36-calibre cap-lock measuring about 13½in overall and weighing 47oz empty. A distinctive shoulderless black walnut butt gave it a cramped or 'hunched' appearance.

Production problems delayed the first deliveries until January 1865; the last guns were not forthcoming until September, long after fighting had ceased. Although Rogers & Spencer revolvers only cost the Federal treasury $12 apiece, they were never issued for service. Virtually the entire inventory, still in original packing, was sold to Francis Bannerman & Sons for just 25 cents each.

Charles S. **Pettengill** of New Haven, Connecticut, was granted protection for a revolver design in July 1856. The main spring and combination lever were patented by Thomas Austin in October 1858 (US no. 21,730), and improved by protection granted to Edward Raymond and Charles Robitaille in July 1858.

A top-mounted cam revolved the cylinder when the trigger was pulled, placing the main spring under tension with the assistance of a 'combination lever'. The trigger-cam disengaged the sear when the cylinder had been indexed, allowing the hammer to strike the cap and to fire the gun.

The Pettengill had an archaic appearance, as its cylinder, an axial extension of the grip/frame unit, was reminiscent of many of the earliest transitional designs linking pepperboxes with true revolvers. The quirky double-action trigger – especially in its first form – had a particularly unpleasant pull, which discouraged accurate shooting. The guns were typically about 14in long, had a 7½-inch six-groove barrel, and weighed 46–48oz empty.

Rogers & Spencer of Willowvale, New York State, obtained a Federal contract for 5000 'army caliber' (.44) Pettengills on 6 December 1861. These guns were simply enlargements of the pre-war .34-calibre 'navy' model, but army inspectors refused to accept any guns from the first batch on the grounds that they failed to conform with the specifications laid down in the contract.

Modifications were made to prevent fouling jamming the cylinder axis pin, and a trigger patented by Henry Rogers in November 1862 replaced the inefficient cam type. The Ordnance Department finally accepted some of the altered guns, 2001 being delivered between 20 October 1862 and 17 January 1863 at an excessive cost of $20.13 apiece.

The revolvers made by Benjamin **Joslyn** presented the Federal authorities with major problems, something which was also reflected in the story of the Joslyn carbines.

Made in accordance with a patent granted in May 1858, the .44-calibre Joslyn was a five-shot single action design, with a solid frame and the hammer mounted externally on the right side of the frame. Like the Root-pattern Colts, which clearly provided Joslyn's inspiration, the hammer was cranked to allow the cylinder-axis pin to enter from the rear of the frame. The major internal novelty was the incorporation of a 'spring clutch' and a ratchet-type cylinder-rotating mechanism. A three-piece pivoting rammer was used. Guns typically measured 14.4in overall, had 8-inch octagonal barrels rifled with five grooves, and weighed about 48–50oz empty.

Joslyn, who lacked suitable manufacturing facilities, passed the first Federal government order to W. C. Freeman of Worcester, Massachusetts, who agreed on 28 August 1861 to provide 500 revolvers at an extortionate $25 apiece – more than 40 per cent greater than the $17.70 paid for each .44 New Model Army Colt. The first Freeman-made Joslyns had sheet-metal butt caps retained by two screws.

Although Freeman subsequently tried to defend himself on the grounds that he had refused to deliver an 'unserviceable design' to the US Army, the termination of the Federal contract was due to non-delivery. The government authorities subsequently declined an offer of Freeman-made revolvers, partly owing to high price but largely because 225 Joslyns had been purchased in the winter of 1861 from Bruff, Brothers & Seaver of New York. These were guns from the original contract, completed after the order had been withdrawn and sold on the commercial market.

Service soon showed that Joslyn revolvers had serious faults, and the unwanted survivors were passed to Ohio state militiamen at the end of 1861. However, by no means discouraged, Benjamin Joslyn made 2500 additional guns in Stonington, Connecticut. The first examples had wrought-iron trigger guards and lacked butt caps, though the Freeman-type sheet-metal cap reappeared after about 1400 had been made.

The Federal authorities purchased about 875 Stonington Joslyns for the army (1861–2), and 500 were purchased for the navy in 1862. Navy-issue guns are distinguished by an anchor mark on the butt strap or under the barrel.

About 1100 Joslyn revolvers (225 Freeman-made guns and the remainder of the Stonington sub-variety) were accepted by the Federal ordnance authorities prior to 30 June 1866, at a cost of about $22.54 apiece. An attempt had been made to sell 675 additional guns to the 5th Ohio Military Cavalry in 1862 but, remembering problems with a previous consignment, the local commanders speedily declined the offer.

The Rafael or **Raphael** revolver was another of the guns with French origins. Though Federal ordnance records give little detail, it is known that 978 guns of this type were obtained during the Civil War at a cost of $16.55 each. The ammunition was a special centrefire pattern with a straight .53in copper case, lacking a rim, and was fired by an internal primer. The bullet weighed about 170 grains.

The revolvers made by **Allen & Wheelock** had pre-war origins, and are described in the previous chapter. When the Civil War began in 1861, the manufacturer attempted to interest the Federal authorities in modified centre-hammer guns with conventional cylinder-axis pins. Response was minimal, though 536 six-shot .44 or 'army caliber' guns with 7½-inch barrels were purchased for the army in 1861–2. A smaller .36-calibre 'navy' pattern, with round barrels of 4–7½in, was sold commercially – no government purchases are known – and a .36 single-action gun with a sheath trigger was allegedly made for the police department of Providence, Rhode Island, prior to 1865.

Federal ordnance records reveal the purchase of 415 '**Adams**' revolvers during the Civil War. It is assumed that these were Beaumont-Adams guns purchased either from the Massachusetts Arms Company – the US licensees – or from a wholesaler such as Schuyler, Hartley & Graham. Details of the guns will be found in the previous chapter.

Acquisitions of French **Perrin** revolvers were restricted to a single batch of 200 guns, purchased in 1862 at a cost of $4000. Based on patents granted to Perrin & Delmas from 1859 onward, the revolvers (clearly influenced by the British Adams of 1851) had double-action locks and lacked hammer spurs.

The original guns were open-frame patterns with decoratively curved trigger guards and small sprung rammers mounted on a collar around the barrel, which could be pulled out of a locking hole drilled into the frame and turned laterally to the right to align with a chamber and the loading gate. They were chambered for a unique 11mm 'thick rim' cartridge, a primitive centrefire design with an internal primer, but were not particularly successful. A typical cartridge was loaded with a 200-grain bullet and a six-grain charge of black powder; the loaded round was .98in long, the case contributing about .6in.

Lesser Cap-Lock Revolvers

Revolvers purchased by the Federal ordnance authorities were not the only designs to be touted during the Civil War, as many others were bought by individual soldiers for self-protection, or by wives and sweethearts as good-luck gifts.

Alsop revolvers resembled the perfected Savage & North pattern, but were much smaller, had sheath triggers, and were made in 1862–3 in a separate factory in Middletown, Connecticut – even though Alsop family members had stakeholdings in the Savage Revolving Fire-Arms Company.

Protected by US patents granted to Charles R. Alsop between 17 July 1860 (no. 29,213) and 21 January 1862 (no. 34,226), the mechanism embodied a rotary cam which pressed the entire cylinder forward as the hammer spur was thumbed back to provide an efficient gas-seal. Protection was granted in November 1861 to an improved movable-chamber system designed by Charles H. Alsop (US Patent no. 33,770).

Only about 500 .36-calibre six-shot Alsop revolvers were made – with round or fluted cylinders and barrels measuring 3½–6½in – before work was concentrated on a six-shot .31 version with a 4-inch barrel and a plain cylinder. However, only 275–300 small-calibre guns were made before work ceased entirely in 1863. Alsop revolvers were too expensive to compete satisfactorily with rival cap-locks and the first Smith & Wessons.

Army-pattern .44-calibre revolvers were made by C. B. Hoard's Armory of Watertown, New York, in accordance with a patent granted in December 1862 (no. 37,091) to Austin **Freeman** of Binghamton. This protected a unique cylinder-axis pin/locking-catch assembly, which could be pulled forward to disengage the frame and allow the entire cylinder to be taken out of the left side of the gun. The earliest Freemans had a removable side plate on the left side of the frame, but later examples had solid frames with fixed pivot-screws for the hammer and trigger.

The single-action Freeman revolvers had a distinctive angular frame and a 'hump back' wooden grip. They were $12\frac{1}{2}$in overall, weighed about 45oz empty, and had $7\frac{1}{2}$-inch barrels rifled with six grooves. Cylinders were six-chambered.

Hoard received a Federal government contract for 5000 of these guns on 8 May 1864, but delays in production ensured that none was ever accepted. The contract was passed to Rogers & Spencer (q.v.), though about 2500 Freeman revolvers were sold commercially in 1864–5.

The **Butterfield** revolver was another whose archaic appearance belied wartime production. A detachable tube of disc primers ahead of the trigger guard, patented in 1855 by Jesse Butterfield (US no. 12,124), placed an individual primer above the nipple each time the external hammer was cocked.

Butterfield claimed to have accepted a contract for 2280 .41-calibre 'Army Model' revolvers, placed on behalf of the Ira Harris Guard of the 5th New York Cavalry in 1861, but the Ordnance authorities revoked the order on 24 June 1862 after only about 700 guns had been completed by Krider & Company of Philadelphia.

Many Butterfield revolvers eventually appeared in Confederate hands; just how this happened remains unexplained, though a substantial amount of undetected 'cross border' trade was followed during the Civil War.

The five-shot single action Butterfield Army Model Revolver was about 13.8in long, had a 7.1-inch barrel rifled with seven grooves, and weighed about 41oz empty.

Cooper revolvers were difficult to distinguish externally from the .36-calibre Colt pocket models; internally, however, they had a sophisticated double-action lock patented by James Cooper of Pittsburgh on 4 September 1860 and 22 September 1863 (US no. 29,684 and no. 40,021 respectively). A curved trigger lever set well forward in the guard customarily identifies a Cooper gun.

After some 100 revolvers had been made in Pittsburgh, incorporating a safety-notch system infringing the Gruler & Reberty patent exploited by the Manhattan Fire Arms Company, Cooper moved to Philadelphia. Work on five-shot .31 pocket and six-shot .36 navy revolvers began immediately. Most of the guns had 4–6in barrels and iron guards and straps, though brass was soon substituted.

Some of the first navy-calibre (.36) guns had short smooth-surface cylinders, but these were subsequently replaced by a characteristic double-diameter pattern to prevent the cylinder walls rupturing. The frame was cut away to accommodate the new cylinder, and the shape of the barrel lug was altered to allow conical-ball ammunition to be used. The .31 pocket-revolver frame was eventually revised to accept a large-diameter cylinder with a sixth chamber, but only after 10,000 guns had been made. Production had totalled about 15,000 when the Civil War ended, but only a few more were made before Cooper's gunmaking business failed in the depressed post-war days.

In addition to Cooper's own patents of September 1860 and September 1863, marks found on the perfected revolvers acknowledged patents granted to Stanhope Marston on 7 January 1851 (no. 7887) for the lock of a double-action pepperbox; to Josiah Ells on 25 April 1854 (10,812), protecting the extension around the cylinder-axis pin; and to Charles Harris on 1 September 1863 (39,771) to protect a modified cylinder-locking bolt.

Founded in 1864 by Thomas **Bacon** in Norwich, Connecticut, the Bacon Arms Company made about 2000 solid-frame .31 cap-lock revolvers during the Civil War. Distinguished by sheath triggers, but sometimes disguised by a 'Union Arms Co.' mark, these five-shot guns had a 4-inch round barrel with a pivoting rammer. The original Freeman-type cylinder latch was soon replaced by a simple pin retained by a cross-screw.

Although not the most numerous of the cap-lock revolvers used by the Confederate forces, the **Le Mat** was undoubtedly the most interesting. Protected by a patent granted in the USA on 21 October 1856 to François-Alexandre Le Mat of New Orleans (no. 15,925), the major claim to novelty lay in the substitution of an extra barrel for the cylinder-axis pin and the addition of a 'gun-cock with double hammer' to select the type of fire. The principle was by no means new, as guns with superimposed barrels had been made for centuries and cap-lock Miller revolver rifles had been made in the late 1830s to much the same design as the Le Mat.

French-born Le Mat emigrated to the USA in 1843, establishing himself in New Orleans in the mid-1850s as a doctor of medicine. He married a cousin of Pierre-Gustave Beauregard – subsequently one of the Confederate army's best-known cavalry generals – and embarked on an inventing career which encompassed medicine, navigation and firearms design. François-Alexandre Le Mat was made a colonel in the Louisiana militia in April 1859, but returned to Europe during the Civil War to organise production of his revolvers.

Most of the Le Mat guns used during the Civil War had single smooth-bore .67-calibre shot barrel doubling as the axis pin for a cylinder containing nine

.40-calibre chambers. However, the revolvers are believed to have been made in small numbers in the USA, Britain, France and Belgium, and can vary greatly in detail. They share single-action lockwork and an open-top frame, but some barrels are octagonal and others are half-octagon. Lanyard rings customarily appear on the butt, while the hammer has an elongated spur and a barrel selector on its nose. The pivoted rammers vary, as some lie on the right side of the barrel and others appear on the left. Trigger guards may be oval or spurred.

The prototype Le Mat revolvers were apparently the work of Krider of Philadelphia, though one of the better known New Orleans gunmakers has been offered as an alternative source. When the Civil War began, Le Mat and his backers investigated alternative sources of supply. A few guns may have been made in Britain by the Birmingham Small Arms Co. Ltd, but most were apparently the work of A. Francotte of Liége.

Popular with leading Confederate cavalry officers, Le Mat revolvers were cumbersome and badly balanced. Although the rammer and the fire-selector on the hammer nose proved to be comparatively weak, however, the guns gave much better service than most other handguns pressed into service with the Confederate forces.

Le Mat subsequently patented a metallic-cartridge version of his basic design on 14 December 1869 (US no. 97,780), and pin- or centrefire guns were still being made in Europe in the early 1870s.

METALLIC-CARTRIDGE REVOLVERS

When Horace Smith and Daniel Wesson relinquished their interests in what became the Volcanic (q.v.) they did so willingly, realising that the seeds of greatness lay in the rights they had acquired to a revolver designed by Rollin White. The White revolver was too complicated to be worth exploiting, but the patent had allowed a claim to novelty in chambers which were bored entirely through the cylinder. Cap-lock revolvers had 'blind' chambers, closed at the rear to allow flash-channels to be bored into them.

Still irritated by the damage inflicted by Colt on the Massachusetts Arms Company earlier in the 1850s, Daniel Wesson chafed at the bit until Colt's master patent expired in 1857 and **Smith & Wesson** could announce their seven-shot 'Model No. 1' .22 rimfire revolver.

Introduced in January 1858, this tiny, almost toylike weapon proved to be a landmark in firearms history.

However, although Smith & Wesson could see great potential in the design, public opinion was more sceptical and demand proved to be much smaller than anticipated. Only a little over 11,000 guns had been made prior to the introduction of an improved 'second pattern' No. 1 revolver in May 1860, but the Civil War made Smith & Wesson's fortune; by April 1869, when the licensing agreement concluded with Rollin White ended on the expiry of his patent, 271,639 revolvers had been made.

A nice irony was that White had received royalty payments approaching $68,000 on a very poor design, retiring to perfect a steam car.

The Smith & Wesson revolvers, despite their minuscule calibre, proved to be extremely popular with officers (who were not officially issued with handguns) and rank-and-file. Many men carried a Smith & Wesson in a pocket, pouch or haversack as a 'back-up' for the standard large-calibre weapons.

By the time the No. 1 revolvers appeared on the market in the early part of 1858, the expiry of the master patent should have allowed Smith & Wesson to adopt some of the best features of the Colt. Smith & Wesson's method of rotating and indexing the cylinder, for example, was much more complicated and appreciably less efficient than the Colt type. And the omission of a safety or half-cock notch on the hammer of the Smith & Wesson No. 1 promoted accidents with loaded guns.

The ineffectiveness of the short .22 rimfire cartridge was due to an initial inability of Smith & Wesson to make copper cartridge cases strong enough to withstand the pressure of more than about three grains of black powder. As the bullet weighed only 29–30 grains, the tiny Smith & Wesson cartridge compared poorly with .36 and .44 cap-locks.

The worst of the manufacturing problems had been overcome by 1861, allowing a .32 rimfire cartridge to be introduced. A charge of thirteen grains of powder behind a 90-grain bullet, though prone to excessive fouling, represented a significant increase in power compared with the .22 No. 1 round.

The six-shot .32 Model No. 2 revolvers, made with barrels of 4–6in, were joined by the Model No. 1½ in 1864. The No. 1½ – a light five-shot .32-calibre gun with a barrel of 3½in (original) or 4in (later examples) – filled a gap between the puny No. 1 and the sizeable No. 2.

Smith & Wesson refined the No. 1 and No. 1½ after the Civil War ended, fluting the cylinder, fitting round instead of octagon barrels, and replacing the flared grips with rounded or 'bird's head' patterns. A gradual transition from the old patterns to the new designs ensured that an assortment of transitional weapons will still be encountered.

The success of the rimfire revolvers ensured that Smith & Wesson, like Colt before them, were soon being faced with infringements of their licence with Rollin White. However, as a keystone of the licensing agreement, White had agreed to take action against such infringers; though Smith & Wesson paid part of the costs of the most important lawsuits, White's share ate into his royalties.

Realising from the results of the first lawsuits that co-operation would be better than confrontation, E. **Remington** & Sons approached Smith & Wesson for permission to convert cap-lock revolvers. About 4600–4750 .44-calibre Remington army revolvers were altered to fire .46 rimfire cartridges simply by substituting a new five-cartridge cylinder for the original six-shot cap-and-nipple type. A one-dollar royalty was paid to Smith & Wesson on each gun, 25 cents being passed to Rollin White, and the cylinders were marked appropriately. More details will be found in the next chapter.

The **Rollin White** Arms Company also made Smith & Wesson-type revolvers, originally as a legitimate part of the licensing agreement which allowed White to make guns under his own patent. Smith & Wesson even acquired 1000 White-made guns to alleviate a temporary production bottleneck. When the Rollin White company was liquidated, however, its assets were acquired by the Lowell Arms Company. Action was immediately threatened in the courts, as White had no financial interest in the Lowell business and 1853 revolvers 'in course of production' were surrendered.

Guns that transgressed the Rollin White patent were made in a wonderful selection of shapes and sizes. Virtually all the manufacturers operated in the States of Connecticut and Massachusetts, the cradle of the North American gunmaking industry, and it seems strange that they thought they could transgress the Rollin White patent unnoticed.

Lawsuits brought against **Smith & Wesson copyists** began with an action against Herman Boker of New York (a well-known distributor) for selling revolvers made by the Manhattan Fire Arms Company with bored-through cylinders. The case was settled in favour of Smith & Wesson and Rollin White in 1862. Then came suits against Bacon, Moore, Pond and Warner, all of which predictably resolved in Smith & Wesson's favour. However, the defendants were allowed to complete guns 'in the course of manufacture' provided royalties were paid to the owners of the Rollin White patent. Guns of this type were marked 'APRIL 3, 1855' in acknowledgement.

Ironically, Smith & Wesson sometimes bought infringing guns for resale – including 3299 assorted Moore-made revolvers, 1437 .30 rimfire Warners, 4880 .32 rimfire Ponds and 1124 assorted Bacons in .22, .32 and .38 rimfire.

Lucius **Pond** of Worcester, Massachusetts, made guns in accordance with a patent granted on 10 July 1860 to Abram Gibson (US no. 29,126) and partly assigned to Joseph Hale. The guns had a Smith & Wesson-style barrel/cylinder assembly hinged at the top rear of the frame and locked shut with a lever on the lower left side of the bottom strap. Sheath-trigger Pond revolvers had cylinder-stop slots nearer the front of the cylinder surface than the rear, and the cylinder face was recessed in a recoil shield when the action was closed. Six-shot guns were made in .32 and .44 rimfire. The .32-calibre guns usually had 4-inch barrels and were about 8½in long; the larger or 'army' pattern had a 7½-inch barrel.

E. A. **Prescott** of Worcester, Massachusetts, was another of the copyists, making a Smith & Wesson facsimile in .32 rimfire with an iron frame and a sheath trigger. Prescott also made revolvers incorporating a cylinder latch protected by his US Patent no. 30,245 of 2 October 1860. Introduced early in 1862, these included a .38 six-shot rimfire 'navy' gun with an 8-inch barrel, a spurred trigger guard and a saw-handle grip. Seven-shot .22 and six-shot .32 rimfire sheath-trigger pocket revolvers were customarily fitted with 4-inch barrels.

Revolvers made by **Allen & Wheelock** (prior to 1863) and Allen & Company (from 1863) were much more distinctive. Based on the Allen & Wheelock cap-locks, they had central hammers and cylinder-axis pins which entered the frame from the front. They included .32 and .44 lip-fire 'evasions', which, though quite unlike the Smith & Wesson revolvers, still had bored-through cylinders. However, Allen also made small-calibre side-hammer guns in .22 and .32 rimfire.

William **Irving** of New York introduced distinctive .22 and .32 rimfire revolvers in the summer of 1862, with fixed barrels and a button in the tang. Pressing the button released the recoil shield on the right side of the frame to swing up and back to permit loading, relying on a separate rod to facilitate ejection. The rarity of Irving revolvers suggests that production may have ceased after the New York Draft Riots of 1863.

Irving also made convertible solid-frame sheath trigger revolvers chambering either .30 rimfire cartridges or .31 cap-and-ball ammunition. These were protected by US Patent no. 38,336, secured on 28 September 1863 by James Reid of Catskill in upstate New York.

The 'infringement revolver' made by Samuel **Cone** of West Chesterfield, Massachusetts, was a six-shot .32 rimfire solid-frame design with a hinged loading gate on the right side of the frame behind the cylinder. James **Warner** of Springfield, Massachusetts, had been among the sub-contractors employed by Smith & Wesson during the production of the Model No. 1. Warner subsequently made a .30 rimfire derivative of his five-shot cap-lock pocket revolver, with a solid frame, a loading gate on the side of the frame behind the cylinder, and a conventional trigger guard. However, its bored-through chambers infringed the Rollin White patent.

The **Manhattan** Fire Arms Company of Newark, New Jersey, a copyist which had once been the bane of Colt, made close copies of the Smith & Wesson Model No. 1 in .22 (seven-shot) and .32 rimfire (six-shot). The octagonal barrels pivoted upward around the top rear of the frame and were latched in much the same way as the Model No. 1. Smith & Wesson successfully sued Manhattan – one of the most unscrupulous US gunmaking businesses – and the guns disappeared from the market-place.

The **Bacon** Arms & Manufacturing Company of Norwich, Connecticut, made .22 and .32 rimfire infringements. These were often unmarked, perhaps deliberately, to conceal their origins. However, Bacon also made large numbers of six-shot .32 and .38 'navy' rimfire revolvers embodying a swinging cylinder protected by US Patent 35,419 granted on 27 May 1862 to Charles Hopkins and part-assigned to financier Henry Edgerton.

Daniel **Moore** & Company of Brooklyn, New York, made .32, .38 and .44 rimfire revolvers in accordance with a US patent granted on 18 September 1860 (no. 30,079). The Moore 'Seven-Shooter' was an open-frame gun with a barrel/cylinder group that could be rotated laterally to the right, making reloading particularly easy. It had a conventional trigger guard and a spring-loaded ejecting rod under the barrel.

Although most of Smith & Wesson's ire was directed at revolver-like infringements, pepperboxes with bored-through cylinders were made by Elliott, Rupertus and Sharps.

Despite Smith & Wesson's successful lawsuits against many of the infringers of the White patent, they could take very little action against the many attempts to evade the patent by fitting cylinders with chambers which were not bored entirely through.

One of the most successful 'evasion revolvers' was made by **Plant**'s Manufacturing Company of Southington (1860–1), New Haven (1861–6), and then Plantsville and Southington, Connecticut (1866–8). Protected by US Patents no. 24,726 and no. 39,318, granted on 12 July 1859 and 25 August 1863 respectively to Willard Ellis and John White, the Plant revolver fired a self-contained metal case 'cup primer' cartridge loaded from the front of the cylinder. Fulminate priming lay in a rearward extension of the cartridge case instead of within a projecting rim, allowing the nose of the hammer to ignite the priming through a small hole bored in the rear of the chamber.

It was scarcely coincidental that the six-shot .42 rimfire Plant revolvers were modelled on the Smith & Wesson No. 1. Offering plated bronze frames and blued octagonal barrels, they proved to be quite successful. By 1863, however, the tipping-frame design had been replaced by sturdier .28, .30 or .42 solid-frame guns, which were made until 1867. Most of the post-1864 examples featured an improved ejector protected by patents granted to Henry Reynolds of Springfield, Massachusetts, on 10 May 1864 (US no. 42,688) and 22 November 1864 (US no. 45,176).

Markings on the improved guns included those of the Eagle Arms Company of New York; J. M. Marlin & Company of Rock Falls, New York; the Merwin & Bray Fire Arms Company of New York; and Reynolds, Plant & Hotchkiss of New Haven, Connecticut.

Merwin & Bray were distributors, while the Eagle Arms Company, incorporated in November 1865, seems to have been formed simply to sell Plant revolvers. Fire destroyed Ebenezer Plant's factory in 1866; later guns were made by Marlin.

Like James Reid, Plant also offered a range of convertible cap-lock/rimfire cartridge revolvers; Plant's guns featured exchangeable cylinders, whereas the

Reid patterns had detachable screw-in nipples. Plant cup-primer cartridges were also chambered in revolvers made by the **Connecticut Arms Company** of Norfolk, Connecticut, shortly after the end of the Civil War. These single-action .28-calibre guns, with sheath triggers and brass frames, were made in accordance with US Patents granted on 1 March 1864 and 16 January 1866 to Stephen Wood; break-open patterns resembling the original Smith & Wessons, they had a spur-type extractor in the bottom strap.

Daniel **Moore** made the seven-shot rimfire revolvers that achieved temporary popularity thanks to *The Twin Six Shooters* by Major G. W. Manderson, but their bored-through cylinders attracted the attention of Smith & Wesson. After losing the ensuing lawsuit, Moore turned to a teat-fire revolver chambering a cartridge patented on 5 January 1864 by David Williamson. The Moore revolver will also be found marked 'National' or 'National Arms Company', signifying a change of brandname in the mid-1860s.

Ironically, Moore had been granted protection in 1863 for a .32 teat-fire cartridge revolver with a hinged loading gate ahead of the cylinder, but had neglected to claim specific novelty either in the teat-fire system or the insertion of a cartridge from the chamber-mouth. Not only did he have to pay Williamson royalties on ammunition he could have protected a year earlier, but he may also have lost the chance to take punitive action against the promoters of the many other 'evasion revolvers' which loaded from the front of the cylinder.

The Moore .32 teat-fire revolvers had a six-round cylinder, an open-top frame with a sheath trigger, and a bird's head butt. Most of them will bear an acknowledgement of Williamson's patents of 17 May 1864 and 5 June 1864, protecting the combination extractor/cartridge retainer on the right side of the frame beneath the cylinder. A handful of large .45-calibre guns, with a conventional trigger guard, appeared shortly before the Civil War ended.

Another successful evasion of the Rollin White patent was the single-action five-shot .32 rimfire revolver patented by Frank **Slocum** on 27 January (US no. 37,551) and 14 April 1863 (no. 38,204), rights being assigned to the Brooklyn Firearms Company. The principal novelty in Slocum's design was the detachable sliding sleeve or tube in each chamber of the cylinder. This could be pushed forward to allow a conventional rimfire cartridge to be inserted, then returned to its original position to provide support during firing. Apart from a slot for the hammer nose, the chambers were not bored entirely through the cylinder, and thus evaded the Rollin White patent.

The revolver patented in the USA on 3 October 1865 by Silas **Crispin**, and made by the Smith Arms Company of New York, was another hinged-frame design. The major components of the special two-part cylinder could revolve independently, until locked in place by a special .32 cartridge with an annular priming band around the case. The idiosyncratic ammunition was loaded backward through the front section of the cylinder, then fired by a striker between the two halves of the cylinder unit.

The scarcity of special cartridges doomed the Crispin revolver to failure. This was at least partly due to accidents; placing sensitive mercuric fulminate around the periphery of the case made the ammunition vulnerable to ignition by blows.

One of the gunmakers who had transgressed White's patent, Lucius **Pond**, also made an 'evasion revolver' incorporating features from US Patent no. 35,667, granted to John Vickers on 17 June 1862. Separate chambers, lining tubes or 'thimbles', containing conventional .22 and .32 rimfire cartridges, were simply inserted from the front of the cylinder. Offered in seven-shot .22 or six-shot .32 versions, the guns normally had brass frames, sheath triggers and blued steel barrels.

Improvements to the Pond revolver were patented on 8 November 1864 by Freeman Hood of Worcester, Massachusetts (no. 44,953). Guns made in accordance with this patent had a pivoting ejector or 'discharger', attached to the cylinder-axis pin, which was intended to extract spent rimfire cases when the thimbles were withdrawn.

CHAPTER 3

INTO THE UNKNOWN

From Civil War to Centennial Exposition, 1865–76

'Watch-fires gleam over the sea-like expanse of ground outside the city, while inside soliders, herdsmen, teamsters, women, railroad men, are dancing, singing or gambling. I verily believe that there are men here who would murder a fellow-creature for five dollars . . . Not a day passes but a dead body is found somewhere in the vicinity . . .'
Henry Morton Stanley describing the Hell-on-Wheels town of Julesburg, August 1867.

A major factor in the growth of the West was the discovery of mineral resources on a vast scale. One of the best-known sites was the Comstock Lode, discovered in the foothills of Mount Davidson in Nevada and named after Henry Comstock, part-owner of the land in which silver was found in June 1859. Like many comparable seams, the Comstock Lode acted as a magnet; prospectors, entrepreneurs, saloon-keepers, madames, gamblers and a legion of tradesmen made their way westward, eager either to mine the Lode or – alternatively – fleece the miners of their pickings. Some men found their fortune in rich seams which paid out for years; some found seams which played out rapidly; many found nothing at all. Life was cheap not only in the claustrophobic silver-mines, but also in the hurly-burly of a boom town where 'law' was all too often dispensed at the point of a gun or knife.

The importance of the Comstock Lode in attracting settlers was recognised by the admission of Nevada as the eighteenth State of the Union in 1864, and by the opening of a Federal Branch Mint in Carson City a year later. Annual silver extractions peaked at about $35 million in the mid-1870s, but the production declined from 1880 and the rich lower levels of the Lode flooded in 1882. Most of the boom towns disappeared, and the US Mint closed in 1893.

Typical of the largest settlements was Virginia City, Nevada, not to be confused with a similarly named city incorporated in Montana after a gold strike in 1863. Settled in 1859 and named after a prominent prospector, 'Old Virginia' Fennimore, Virginia City was made the seat of Storey County when

Nevada Territory was created in 1861; about four in five of the entire population of the territory were then concentrated in the vicinity. By the 1870s, helped by the formation of the Virginia & Truckee Railroad to connect with the transcontinental system, the population of nearly 30,000 was served by more than a hundred saloons, uncounted brothels and six churches. However, Virginia City was devastated by fire in 1875. Begun in the Bucket of Blood saloon, the conflagration raged unchecked for hours – destroying much of the business district – while rival groups of firefighters are said to have fought a gun battle for supremacy!

Millions of dollars were made by the 'Bonanza Barons' such as George Hearst and John MacKay, and fabulous mansions built in scrubland competed for attention with elaborately decorated public buildings. Yet the importance of Virginia City declined as the mines played out and the lower and most profitable seams flooded. Disincorporated in 1881, becoming virtually a ghost town, Virginia City is now a National Historic District.

The iron riband

When the Civil War began in 1861, the USA was still really little more than two countries separated by vast hostile tracts. In 1849, when the Gold Rush started, the beginnings of an efficient railway network could have been seen on the eastern seaboard, particularly up around the northern New England States and east of the Appalachians. However, only a couple of short lines had been built westward of the Mississippi, and no railroad existed west or north of the Great Lakes except for a couple in Illinois. Though there had been less than thirty track-miles in 1830, the figure had reached 9000 within twenty years; in 1861, it stood at about 31,000 miles.

The construction of a transcontinental route from east to west had been mooted prior to the California Gold Rush; indeed, plans had been under way as early as 1832 and the Whitney Bill, several years in development, had been defeated in 1848. However, the organisation of Oregon Territory (1848) and the incorporation of California (1851), backed by public opinion, persuaded Congress to authorise surveys in 1853. The work had been entrusted to the US Army, but wrangling over routes and details was still raging in 1860 among rival syndicates keen to take the lion's share of government funding.

Yet optimism still prevailed. This was especially true in California, where the output of great mineral strikes such as the Comstock Lode was being moved by stagecoaches and ponderous haulage teams. Although the operators of these businesses opposed the railroads that would destroy their living, contemptuously dismissing their opponents' plans as the 'Dutch Flat Swindle' – Dutch Flat being proposed as the initial westward terminus – public sentiment was greatly in favour of the train.

On 28 June 1861, in the premises of Huntington, Hopkins & Company of

Sacramento – purveyors of 'Nails, Shovels, Picks, Handles, Wheel Barrows, Gas Pipe & Fittings, Rubber Hose, Belting, Powder, Fuse, Rope, Blocks, Pitch & Tar' – the Central Pacific Rail Road of California was duly incorporated. The prime movers were Leland Stanford, soon to be governor of California; Collis P. Huntington and Mark Hopkins, partners in Huntington, Hopkins & Co.; and Charles Crocker, Sacramento's leading dry-goods merchant. The engineer was Theodore Judah, who had been such an impassioned champion of railways in the 1850s that he had gained the sobriquet 'Mad Ted' or 'Railroad Ted'. Judah died in 1863 before much of the work could be started, struck down by disease in the Isthmus of Panama, but the cause he started had gained unstoppable momentum when the Civil War began.

Problems of communicating with the western states and territories convinced the Federal government that urgent action was needed. On 1 July 1862, therefore, while war raged around him, President Lincoln signed an Act permitting a railroad and telegraph line to be built from the Missouri River to the Pacific Ocean. The work was to be the responsibility of the Central Pacific Rail Road of California and the newly formed Union Pacific Rail Road, building eastward from Sacramento and westward from Omaha respectively.

The Union Pacific was the brainchild of Thomas Durant and Sidney Dillon, with the help of the well-known makers of agricultural equipment, Oakes and Oliver Ames. Initial problems were overcome by replacing the first chief engineer, who objected to some of the more unsavoury practices of the railway management, with a professional soldier – General Grenville Dodge – and by placing the labour teams under the control of the brothers John S. 'Jack' and Daniel T. Casement. Another military man, Colonel Silas Seymour, was made consulting engineer and work began in earnest in the autumn of 1863.

Building the transcontinental railroad was a great triumph of fortitude over hardship; not only was work started at the height of the Civil War, when raw materials were in short supply, but virtually everything had to be brought in from the east and shipped across the Mississippi by barges. The loads included a large stationary steam engine, weighing seventy tons, to power the workshops erected by the Union Pacific in Omaha. Constant skirmishes with hostile Indians, which killed two district superintendents among many railroad workers, provided another danger.

Although the first transcontinental railroads eventually brought the 'Wild West' to a close, they also did much to create it in the decade following the end of the Civil War in 1865. Whereas the Beef Trails spawned towns such as Abilene, and the exploitation of mineral riches created San Francisco or Kansas City, the railroads provided the 'Hell-on-Wheels' towns.

The name, coined by Sam Bowles, editor of the Springfield (Illinois) *Republican*, was due partly to an absence of the rule of law, but also to the prefabricated nature of the settlements. Among the first was North Platte, a small town with a population of less than 500, which was transformed within a few weeks in the autumn of 1866 by a mob of 5000 Irish navvies and their camp followers. Construction of a locomotive roundhouse was accompanied by the erection – in a single day – of the 'Railroad House Hotel', which arrived in kit form. Bordellos were imported from Chicago, ready-stocked with their madames and *nymphes du pavé*; and Mississippi gamblers, attracted by the prospects of rich pickings, sailed in from Natchez or New Orleans. The journalist Henry M. Stanley observed in 1867 that in North Platte – 'Paris of Nebraska' as it styled itself:

> Every house is a saloon, and every saloon is a gambling den. Beardless youths imitate to the life the peculiar swagger of the devil-may-care bullwhacker and blackleg; and here, for the first time, they try their hands at Mexican monte, high-low-jack, strap, rouge-et-noire, three card monte, and that Satanic game, chuck-a-luck...

Lucius Beebe added in *High Iron* (1938):

> The roaring towns [a name which vied with 'Hell-on-Wheels'] seethed with settlers and gold seekers, professional gamblers in pearl gray top-hats with Remington derringers in their lace cuffs, cattle drovers with bull whips, engineers and construction workers in jack-boots, tradesmen, newspaper reporters, Mormons, publicans, eastern financiers, strumpets, jobbers, soldiers, rufflers and shady political colonels. Englishmen in deer-stalker caps and Inverness cloaks of outrageous pattern came to see ... and returned to tell their countrymen that Americans were forever shooting each other at table and that every one in the States drank a quart of whisky before breakfast...
>
> Snake-oil vendors shouted their sovereign cures from wagon tails at every corner. Firearms dealers disposed of Colt's Frontier Model .45's and Starr's Navy Revolvers of wall-piece dimensions by the carload lot...

Although Beebe is wrong about the 'Colt Frontier .45's' – they would have been .44 cap-locks in the late 1860s – he does capture the essence of towns populated, in a succinct and memorable phrase, by 'touts, tarts and teamsters'.

By May 1867, the roisterers of North Platte moved on to Julesburg, 477 miles from the starting-point in Council Bluffs. Named after a French trapper who had murdered his wife, Julesburg grew from a population of forty men and one woman in April 1867 to more than 4000 by the end of July. However, the lures of the 'Wickedest City on America' soon began to reduce the efficiency of the railroad gangs, and Jack Casement took decisive action. Arming his ex-soldiers with Trapdoor Springfield breechloading rifles, Casement gave the unwanted gamblers and girls a one-day ultimatum to get out of town. Those who doubted his word – said to have been more than forty – were strung from the town lamp posts and, when space ran short, from the poles of the Overland Telegraph before taking their final journey to Boot Hill.

The facility with which entire 'towns' could be dismantled, loaded on to flat-cars and pack mules, and simply re-erected as the railheads moved became legendary. When the first trainload of knocked-down saloons and brothels rolled into Cheyenne (which was already a small town of note), a brakeman is said to have shouted down to his friends, 'Gentlemen, here's Julesburg . . . !'

The workforce of the Central Pacific, building eastward from California, was largely Chinese. Consequently, the railhead settlements were comparatively trouble free, the unsavoury reputation of towns such as Truckee, Reno, Winnemucca, Carlin and Elko being largely due to miners and their followers. The Union Pacific, forging westward from Omaha, relied largely on Irish labourers and disaffected Civil War soldiers, often Confederate. These men worked and played hard, and the Hell on Wheels townships reflected their drinking, gambling and whoring lifestyle. Towns such as Laramie, Benton, Rawlins, Desert, Bitter Creek, Salt Wells, Bear River City, Wasatch, Corinne and ultimately Promontory all owed their existence to the progress of the Union Pacific track-laying crews in 1867–9.

Photographs taken by the celebrated A. J. Russell and his assistants reveal the true nature of Hell-on-Wheels towns, showing nothing but crudely built log and clapboard shacks, often little more than a frontage to canvas stretched over wooden frames, with streets consisting of trodden earth. Sanitation was non-existent; but signboards – often the most professional and most permanent part of the whole town – advertised the presence of the saloons, lodgings, brothels and sutlers.

The most easterly towns grew rapidly – Cheyenne rose from practically nothing to 4000 people in the winter of 1867 – and, because of the need to form supply bases, had been properly incorporated by the early 1870s. Many of the others, however, had soon packed and gone. Among the most interesting was Tobar, which owed its name to an impressive sign 'To Bar' at its boundary.

The reputation of the transcontinental railroad, so high in 1869, took a dreadful knock in 1873 when the Credit Mobilier scandal implicated in financial chicanery not only Durant and the Ames brothers, but also some well-placed Congressmen. The Union Pacific and, to a lesser degree, the Central Pacific had made vast sums of money out of the railroad; in the UPRR case, this had amounted to more than 24 million acres of land and $27 million dollars of government funding.

Helped by compliant surveyors and engineers, the major participants had each formed companies to build the track, then channelled huge profits from the exorbitant 'construction costs' back into their own coffers. The Union Pacific track was particularly poorly laid, and the Central Pacific had persuaded federal representatives to reclassify the gentle foothills of the Sierra Nevada east of Sacramento as 'mountain territory' to claim bonuses amounting to many thousands of dollars per mile.

The first transcontinental link had wrought an irreparable wrong by bisecting the lands of the Plains Indians, and the tremendous demand for meat to feed thousands of labourers soon put the buffalo herds into irreversible decline.

However, once the scandals abated and some sense of reason had been brought to railroad construction, rival developments began. Where the Central Pacific and Union Pacific led, others followed; by 1872, track mileage had increased to about 67,000. The Southern Pacific Railroad, intending to connect San Francisco with New Orleans, met the Texas & Pacific in El Paso in 1882. The Atchison, Topeka & Santa Fé, having acquired the charter of the defunct Atlantic & Pacific Railroad, then joined the Southern Pacific to complete the route from Kansas City to Los Angeles. The completion in September 1883 of the Northern Pacific – joining St Paul, Missouri, with Portland, Oregon – added yet another east/west riband of steel.

The railroads, though they provided banditry with a new source of revenue – train-robbing became a minor industry – were also one of the greatest catalysts of Western pacification. Gradually, the spread of rails gridlocked much of the American Plains, especially in the southern counties, and, by quickening the movement of goods, fuelled not only the exploitation of the mineral riches of the West but also brought in with ever-increasing efficiency the men who would undertake the hazardous task of extracting them.

The railroad also facilitated the movement of livestock from the fertile Plains and the Texas beef-raising districts to consumers in the eastern margins of the USA. The giant Union Stock Yard in Chicago, for example, received 688,000 hogs, 180,000 sheep and 330,000 head of cattle in 1867; in 1873, after the transcontinental railroad had been completed, the figures had risen respectively to 4,338,000, 292,000 and 761,000.

Cowboys and Indians

By the end of the Civil War, very few of the Indian tribes of the Great Plains had been subdued. Only the Navajo had been largely pacified, as the successes achieved by the US Army at the expense of the Lakota (Sioux) and the Comanche were generally short-lived or confined to the vicinity of the major forts. The country was simply too big and the military establishment was far too small to establish control west of the Hundredth Meridian.

The Indians were surprisingly resilient and, spurred on by their fear and hatred of the 'White Man', soon regrouped for new campaigns. However, most of the fighting between the opposing factions was hit-and-run: a burned farm here, a destroyed Indian village there. Even the most famous battle, Custer's defeat at the Little Big Horn, engaged only a few thousand men – small fare compared with the tens of thousands present at Gettysburg or Shiloh during the Civil War.

The hatred the Indians reserved for the White Men was matched only by the loathing White Men had for their adversaries. Neither side made much attempt to understand the other's beliefs, and the violence associated not only with the raids on settlers but also with reprisals by the US Army succeeded in increasing tension.

Many persuasive attempts have been made to paint the Indian nations as the primary victims of the westward expansion of the United States; and one of the less savoury aspects of post-war expansionism was the gradual disenfranchisement of these native Americans, who were herded into poor-quality reservations from tribal lands which were often rich in minerals or blocking the progress of a railroad. Thousands died during enforced transfers in bleak winters, denied access to traditional hunting grounds where the buffalo were being slaughtered to extinction to feed railroad gangs or Easterners obsessed with 'Things Western'. It is not so hard to see the unfairness in such treatment.

However, this view of unjustified oppression does not always take into account the dread with which settlers feared scalping and burying alive in some godforsaken desert.

Settlers with long memories recalled the killing of missionaries Marcus and Narcissa Whitman and twelve others (1847); the Mountain Meadow Massacre of 1857, when Mormon-led Paiutes had slaughtered all but the eighteen youngest children of a wagon train bound from Arkansas to California; or the destruction by Shoshones of the Ward and Otter wagon trains on the Idaho Trail prior to the Civil War.

Even as late as 1885, a renegade Apache band killed more than forty people in New Mexico and Arizona. Yet the slaughter of Indians by the US Army could be just as bad. Incidents at Bear River (1863) and Sand Creek (1864) cost the lives of scores of women and children, as did the Battle of the Washita (1868) and the Marais River Massacre in Montana in 1870.

Organised military campaigns against the Indians had been waged throughout the Civil War, far to the west of the main battle-zone, and skirmishes continued after the war had been concluded. The notorious Fetterman Massacre of 1866 arose when a Sioux war party ambushed a force of cavalrymen, eighty-one strong, sent out from Fort Phil Kearny under the command of Captain William Fetterman to protect a wood-train. Armed largely with Springfield rifle-muskets, and a few Spencer carbines retrieved from the regimental band, the soldiers were annihilated – though two civilians from the Quartermaster's Department, carrying Henry repeaters, sold their lives particularly dearly.

Colonel Henry Carrington, commanding Fort Phil Kearny, immediately wired his superiors requesting nothing but Spencer repeaters for his men. The army responded by sending single-shot M1866 .50-70 'Trapdoor Springfield' breechloaders, which, though contributing to early successes such as the Hayfield and Wagon-Box fights, could not provide sufficient fire-density to discourage the largest Indian bands.

The so-called Battle of the Washita of 1868 owes its inflated reputation largely to the participation of Custer and the Seventh Cavalry, who, with the regimental band playing 'Garryowen', charged into a Cheyenne encampment under covering fire from Spencer-armed sharpshooters. After initial success, Custer realised that the Indians were being reinforced from neighbouring camps and prudently withdrew.

His official report (claiming to have killed a hundred Indians and a staggeringly large number of ponies) may have been exaggeration, but the public caught Custer's mood and demanded ever-harsher reprisals. Many later commentators believed that the flamboyant cavalryman sealed his own fate by ignoring the treaty – signed only a few months previously – that forbade entry to the Black Hills for all but the Indians.

Settlers and prospectors backed by the US Army were soon making such steady inroads into the area that cattle were grazing and gold was being panned in the southern margins of the Black Hills. A series of skirmishes then led to the vital Sioux Campaign of 1876–7, which gave the Indians their most celebrated victory.

In December 1875, the Indian Agent at Standing Rock received instructions ordering Sitting Bull and the Lakota (Sioux) to move inside the borders of the minuscule reservation prepared for them. The deadline for compliance was set as 31 January 1876. However, the tribe was camped for the winter on the Powder River, more than 200 miles away from Standing Rock across plains which were deepening in snow. A reply that the tribe could not move across Dakota until the summer of 1876 was ignored, and the US Army was ordered into punitive action.

When the smoke had cleared over the Little Big Horn in the afternoon of 25 June 1876, Companies C, E, F, I and L of the 7th Cavalry had died to a man. The only survivor was a single badly wounded horse, inappropriately named 'Comanche', which had been the mount of Captain Miles Keogh. The Springfield single-shot carbines and Colt Single Action Army revolvers of a few hundred men had been no match for the ferocity of 3000 Indians.

Although fighting continued on a small scale, army units commanded by General Nelson Miles and Colonel Ranald Mackenzie eventually convinced the Indians that intransigence was no longer worthwhile. Trouble occasionally flared throughout the 1880s, but only at Wounded Knee (1890), scarcely dignified by the title 'battle', was any real Indian resistance evident.

The Indians had fought long and hard for their rights, but it was not unknown for Indians of one tribe to slaughter Indians of another, and this inter-tribe rivalry often prevented them fielding cohesive forces against the US Army. In addition, though the Indians had evolved an efficient technique for attacking small groups of pioneers, it was based on the premise that the defenders were armed with muzzleloaders. The Indians would simply send out a small raiding party as bait, presenting the intended victims with a choice; withhold fire and risk death at the hands of the raiding party, or fire and be caught by the main Indian force while reloading.

The advent of repeaters such as the Henry and the Spencer changed the situation, however, and many a charge was cut down before gaining its objective. From reports of each incident, Winchester and his salesmen made capital; stories that were already exaggerated needed little attention, others could always be inflated to press the claims.

Yet the problems were not confined entirely to rivalry between Indians and White Men in the West, even though the popular view suggests otherwise. Continual difficulties arose between Hispanos and white Americans, particularly in Texas, and hatred of the Chinese, imported in large numbers to work on the Central Pacific Rail Road and in the mining districts of California and Nevada, ended in a slaughter of more than fifty men in Rock Springs, Wyoming, in 1885.

Longarms

Many pre-1865 guns survived in the aftermath of the Civil War to give good service for many years, though many of their promoters failed almost as soon as hostilities had ceased. Even some of the largest manufacturers were saddled with irredeemable debts, often attracted while fulfilling the enormous or open-ended contracts that were peremptorily cancelled at the end of the Civil War. Among the major casualties of the war was the Spencer Repeating Rifle Company of Boston, which was unable to survive the decline which hit the gunmaking industry – bolstered by four years of war – when peace returned. Spencer traded desultorily for a few years, turning the production line to sporting rifles, but could not re-create markets satisfactorily and was sold to Valentine Fogerty in 1868.

Although the Sharps and Remington dominated the single-shot rifles used for long-range hunting of buffalo and other large game, the advantages of the lever-action repeater were of paramount importance in the West, where most men happily accepted large-capacity tube magazines in preference to the detachable box even though long-range striking power was lost. The straight throw of the classical finger-lever was much more popular than the complicated motion of a bolt, which coloured the thinking not only of civilians but also the US military authorities until the early 1890s.

A few Winchester-made Hotchkiss bolt-action sporters and a few Remington-Keene and Remington-Lee rifles were seen in the West from the

1880s onward. However, their numbers were paltry compared with the many thousands of Winchester and Marlin lever-action repeaters.

Bolt-action rifle with box magazines could be reloaded to suit changing circumstances, fire ballistically superior pointed or streamlined bullets in perfect safety, and withstand far higher chamber pressures than most lever-action patterns. Yet not until the First World War had ended did the bolt action gain widespread favour in North America.

Single-Shot Muzzleloaders

Although the Civil War signalled the end of the muzzle-loading era by demonstrating the advantages of breechloading so conclusively, .58 Springfield and .577 Enfield rifle-muskets remained in regular service for some time. Many of the US Army detachments west of the Mississippi were still carrying them as late as 1867, and guns had been supplied in quantity to the militia raised in Kansas and Colorado Territory; these were marked 'Property Of The State Of Kansas' on the barrels, or 'U.S.' above 'Col. Ter.' on the butt-side.

Inventories taken of wagon-train equipment in the immediate post-war period also often show rifle-muskets as the principal longarms. However, campaigns against the Indians soon showed the folly of opposing large-scale attacks with muzzleloaders, the massacre of Captain William Fetterman and the eighty men under his command (1866) being just one chapter in a sorry story.

Single-Shot Breechloaders

The regulation 'Springfield' rifle-musket was still the single most important military weapon when the Civil War ended, providing the basis for many of the earliest metallic-cartridge conversions tested by the military authorities in 1865–73. Very few of these encountered commercial success, though there were notable exceptions. The Miller transformation, patented in May 1865, cost the Federal treasury $18,000 to prevent a royalty infringement suit; and the Needham or 'Bridesburg' rifle (named after the manufacturer, Alfred Jenks & Company of Bridesburg, Pennsylvania), with a side-hinged breech-block, enjoyed a brief moment of glory in 1867 in the hands of the Fenian invaders of Canada.

The attitude of the Federal Ordnance Department towards the breech-loading rifle had softened after the enforced retirement in 1863 of the Chief of Ordnance, James 'Old Fogey' Ripley. His successor, Brigadier General Alexander Dyer, a much more progressive thinker, noted as early as 1864:

> Use of breechloading arms in Federal service has, with few exceptions, been confined to mounted troops. So far as our limited experience goes, it indicates the advisability of extending this armament to our infantry also ... It is therefore

> intended to make this change of manufacture at our national armories as soon as the best model for a breech-loader can be established ... The alteration of our present model of muzzle-loading arms is also a very desirable measure, both on account of economy and improvement ...

Information had even been sent to interested parties at the end of 1864, seeking suitable conversions of the regulation .58-calibre 1863-type muzzle-loading Springfield. Concurrently, General Dyer asked Erskine Allin, Master Armorer at Springfield, to develop a 'Government Gun' without regard to possible patent infringements. This was intended to accelerate progress at a vital time – the Civil War still raged – but Dyer's instructions were soon to prove costly.

Shortly before the war ended, tests had been undertaken with a selection of single-shot rifles. The trials board recommended standardising the Spencer repeater and the single-shot Peabody in April 1865, but the Ordnance Department, realising that fighting was near an end and that the urgent need of a new gun was receding, merely noted the conclusions. Perhaps the Chief of Ordnance realised that the Allin prototype would not be available for some time, and simply wished to buy time.

The first **Allin** rifle was readied for testing in the late summer of 1865, showing enough promise for a batch to be acquired for field trials. The Rifle Musket Model 1865 – never more than semi-experimental – was a simple adaptation of the .58-calibre 1863-pattern cap-lock, with a new block inserted in a cut-away breech. The block had a transverse hinge at the front of the action, allowing it to swing upward at the rear to expose the chamber. The movement of the block also operated the ratchet-pattern extractor, which lay beneath the chamber. A copper-case .58 rimfire cartridge was developed, to save rebarrelling, while doubts about the ideal calibre were resolved by experiment.

The 1865-type Allin transformation was too complicated to succeed and only about 5000 guns were made. The performance of the extractor and the ballistics of the heavy cartridge were particularly poor. Almost as the first guns were being issued for trials with 12th Infantry, a new Board of Officers convened in Washington DC. Tests with more than forty different guns continued until June 1866.

The M1865 Springfield-Allin, the initial government entrant in the trials, had soon been substituted by an improved gun with a stronger and simpler extractor. In addition, the barrel had been bored-out and then 'lined' or 'sleeved' to reduce the calibre from .58 to .50. The new gun was a considerable improvement on its predecessor; though still prone to extraction failures, these owed more to the use of copper in the cartridge cases than any inherent defects in the Allin breech mechanism.

When the first series of trials had been completed, only a handful of guns remained. The government-backed Allin was challenged only by Berdan, Remington, Roberts and Yates rifle-musket conversions, plus the purpose-built Laidley, Peabody, Remington and Sharps breechloaders.

The Berdan was judged to be the best conversion, the Peabody had proved to be the best new rifle, and (reluctantly, owing to extraction problems) the Spencer repeating carbine was recommended for cavalrymen. The Board also remarked that .45-calibre ammunition was potentially better than the experimental .50 patterns. Backed by both Chief of Ordnance Dyer and army commander Ulysses Grant, the .50 Allin was adopted ahead of the Berdan conversion.

There was undoubtedly some personal antipathy involved – General Dyer and Colonel Stephen Benét of Frankford Arsenal both regarded Hiram Berdan as an untrustworthy opportunist – but there was an understandable preference for a 'Government Gun' to avoid paying licensing fees or royalties unnecessarily. And the enormous quantities of convertible cap-locks told against the robust and efficient Peabody action, which, in its perfected underlever form, could not be used to convert rifle-muskets.

The **Model 1866** rifle was a simplified version of the 1865 pattern, chambering a new inside-primed .50-70 centrefire cartridge. A 'U'-spring extractor had replaced the flimsy ratchet mechanism of the original gun, and the original .58-calibre barrels had been reamed-out to .64 to take a .50-calibre lining tube. This method, suggested by Brevet-Colonel Theodore Laidley, was rapidly perfected in the Springfield factory and an order was given on 26 July 1866 to convert 25,000 rifle-muskets, half of them with varnished stocks and the remainder left plain.

The 1866-pattern Allin conversions, despite their shortcomings, came as a revelation to men used to nothing but muzzleloaders. Shortly after the Fetterman Massacre of 1866 (see above), men under the command of Colonel Henry Carrington, charged with establishing forts and strongpoints along the Bozeman Trail, were issued with some of the first 'Trapdoor Springfield' rifles to reach the West. On consecutive days at the beginning of August 1867, the new rifles showed their value.

The 'Hayfield Fight' occurred when a large Sioux war-party attacked twenty cavalrymen and six civilians, cutting hay near Fort Smith under the command of Captain Thomas Burrowes. A day-long fight repulsed the Indians, inflicting heavy casualties. Burrowes ascribed this largely to the new breechloaders, though (excepting one man armed with a .577 British Enfield) the civilians had a mixture of Henry and Spencer repeaters.

The .50-70 Springfields had proved their worth when the Indians, believing their decoy party had drawn the fire of the defenders, rushed home an attack in the mistaken belief that reloading was taking place. The speed with which the

THE CUSTERS

George Armstrong Custer was born in New Rumley, Ohio, in December 1839. After an undistinguished graduation from West Point in 1861, he had risen to become a brigadier-general of Michigan volunteer cavalrymen by 1863. Custer remains one of the most controversial figures in Western history: flamboyant, reckless and insubordinate, but undeniably charismatic, he was killed on 'Custer Hill' above the Little Big Horn river in the summer of 1876.

George Custer owned a variety of firearms, though the consensus was that his reputation as a marksman owed more to vainglory than skill. A Spencer sporting rifle was specially ordered from the manufacturer in 1866, and he has also been linked with a .50-calibre Burnside-made Spencer carbine, no. 3658, which was allegedly carried in the 1867 Kansas Indian campaign. This particular gun was marked 'G. Custer/7 CAV/USA' on the butt-side.

Among Custer's other longarms was a .50-70 1866-type Trapdoor Springfield rifle modified c.1872 to sporting appearance by reducing the fore-end to half length, and fitting a double set trigger mechanism within a special trigger guard with a long rearward scroll. He also used at least two Remington Rolling Block sporters, one with a straight-wrist butt and another with a pistol-grip type. Both had octagon barrels, and the gun with the pistol-grip butt also had a folding tang sight.

George Custer's handguns included a cased .44-calibre New Model Army revolver (extensively engraved, with ivory grips and a spare cylinder), presented in 1869 by E. Remington & Sons. He also owned a cased .450 Galand & Sommerville 'self-extracting' revolver, made in Britain, which was presented in September 1869 by Lord Berkeley Paget as a memento of a successful hunting expedition. A cased pair of .32 Smith & Wesson No. 2 revolvers – engraved, silver plated, with grips of mother-of-pearl – was presented by J. B. Sutherland in 1869. However, during the last fateful battle on the Little Big Horn, Custer relied on a pair of Webley Bulldogs.

Thomas Ward Custer (1842–76), George Custer's younger brother, carried a nickel-plated Remington New Model .44-calibre army revolver during the closing stages of the Civil War. This particular gun – no. 7179 – had ivory grips and an 1864-vintage presentation inscription from the Ohio Volunteers on its backstrap. Tom Custer also received a cased Galand & Sommerville from Berkeley Paget.

breechloaders could be fired improved the confidence of the soldiers in their weapons, and this composure in turn improved marksmanship.

The 'Wagon-Box Fight' of 2 August repeated the lessons of the Hayfield. A force of more than 200 warriors led by Red Cloud attacked twenty-six cavalrymen and four civilian woodcutters from Fort Phil Kearny, led by Captain James Powell. Armed with brand-new .50-70 1866-type Springfield breechloaders, Powell's men took cover behind box-bodies removed from the wagons.

The Indians pressed home attack after attack for more than three hours, sustaining heavy casualties in the face of withering defensive fire, before retiring in bemused disarray. Poor shots had reloaded guns for the marksmen, allowing one particularly well-practised civilian to maintain a constant barrage by using eight rifles alternately.

A Board of Officers convened in 1868 to examine rifle requirements reported that a 'careful examination of more than 200 monthly reports of Company commanders shows that it [the Trapdoor Springfield] is considered a very powerful, accurate, and serviceable Infantry arm'. Few serious flaws had been reported in the breech mechanism, and the barrel-lining system had proved to be much more successful than its detractors had predicted.

The worst of the problems related to the original inside-primed cartridges, which jammed too regularly, could not be reloaded, and were prone to rupture owing to the absence of reinforcement in the case-head compared with the walls. The drawbacks of the regulation ammunition were clearly shown in the trials of 1872–3, culminating in the adoption of the .45-70 M1873 rifle, where many rival guns performed much better with commercial drawn-brass ammunition than with army-type copper-case patterns. Copper lacked the ability of brass to expand momentarily to seal the breech, then contract just as quickly to permit extraction.

Changes made in the **Model 1868** rifle included the approval of a new 36-inch barrel, retaining the 1866-type rifling – three .0075 grooves making a clockwise turn in 42in. Two barrel bands were used instead of three, a special long-range back sight was developed, and a new short ramrod was held by a stop in the stock which bore on a shoulder about four inches from the rod-tip. The most obvious change, however, concerned the separate receiver. Two-part construction of this type was much stronger than simply cutting a seat for the breech-block into the original barrel.

The **Model 1870** rifle was identical to its immediate predecessor, except that the receiver was shortened. The breech-block was partially cut away behind the hinge, opening farther to prevent unexpected closure as a cartridge was being inserted. A double shoulder was added on the ramrod, and the sights were refined in detail.

However, aware that experiments were being undertaken with small-calibre cartridges, the Ordnance Department sanctioned production of only a few M1870 rifles. They are now sometimes considered to be experimental, instead of a regulation design. The Model 1870 Carbine was built on the same action as the Model 1870 rifle, but was greatly shortened.

Several reduced-scale **cadet rifles** were also made, beginning with about 320 1866-type .50-calibre guns made in Springfield Armory in 1867. They incorporated more than a dozen new parts which could not be interchanged with M1866 rifle equivalents. Made only in small numbers in several versions, including one with a new flat-face hammer, the .50 Cadet Rifle Model 1869 was a diminutive M1868 rifle with two bands and a 29.5in barrel.

Experiments not only to reduce the calibre of the .50 cartridge but also to find an ideal breechloading rifle continued throughout 1871. But although participants included Remington, Sharps and Ward-Burton rifles, the Springfield-Allin system was still preferred. However, progress with ammunition design soon led to a .45-calibre pattern which offered much better performance than the existing .50 type.

When a Board of Officers convened in the autumn of 1872 under the presidency of General Alfred Terry, work centred around the experimental .45-70 centrefire cartridge. More than a hundred submissions had been whittled down to twenty-one by January 1873. Two of them – the British Martini-Henry and the Austro-Hungarian Werndl – were retained merely as a guide to what had been achieved abroad, leaving Elliott No. 80, Freeman No. 76, Peabody No. 63, Remington No. 86, Springfield No. 69 and Ward-Burton No. 97 to wrestle for the ultimate prize of military adoption.

Entered by E. Remington & Sons, the Remington No. 86 with 'Ryder [sic] Power Extractor' was a minor adaptation of the standard rolling-block US Navy rifle (q.v.). Springfield rifle No. 69 was essentially similar to the standard Allin-type M1870 – entered as 'No.48' – except for a lightened lock plate, a screw instead of the original main-spring bolster, a reshaped hammer, and a simplified weight-saving stock. Gun No. 69 eventually proved inferior to the last-minute .45-calibre Springfield entrant, Gun No. 99.

Indeed, none of the triallists could challenge Gun No. 99, which was adopted in a refined form on 5 May 1873 as the **Model 1873** rifle. It perpetuated the Allin system, partly because none of its rivals showed sufficient superiority but also because legislation approved on 6 June 1872 by 'the Senate and House of Representatives of the United States of America in Congress assembled' had included provisions that were biased in favour of the existing breech system. Retaining the Allin breech, which had been developed by government employees, would involve no costs in addition to about $124,000 which had already been paid by the US Treasury to placate the inventors whose systems it infringed. The breech was familiar throughout the army, while production machinery in Springfield Armory could easily be adapted to make the new .45-calibre guns.

The M1873 was a straightforward adaptation of the .50-calibre M1870. The lock plate had been lightened and its edges were squared instead of bevelled; the barrel was made of steel – previous guns used wrought iron – and had been reduced in diameter befitting the smaller bore. The hammer body and the many screw heads were rounded; a screw replaced the trigger-guard swivel rivet; the ramrod was modified; and the top edges of the stock were rounded from the lock plate forward as far as the lower band.

On 28 May 1873, Brevet-Colonel Stephen Benét, representing the Chief of Ordnance, formally instructed Major James Benton, commanding Springfield Armory, that 'The Board . . . having recommended adoption of the Springfield Breech Loading Gun, caliber .45, which has been approved by the Secretary of War as the arm for military service, you will proceed to the manufacture of muskets and carbines on this system.'

Like all brand-new guns, the M1873 underwent many changes. The quirky Rice-Chillingworth trowel bayonet was soon abandoned, and an additional piling swivel was added in the spring of 1874. A few 1873-pattern rifles were also fitted with Metcalfe's Loader, which consisted of a detachable wooden block on the right side of the stock. This held eight cartridges, head upward, to prevent the firer fumbling in his cartridge pouch before reloading.

The Metcalfe Loader was a qualified success, but was never made in large numbers. Indeed, suggestions have been made that only two 'official prototypes' were made in 1874, and that the 1008 guns allegedly made in Springfield in 1876 were destined for state militiamen instead of the regular army.

Derivatives of the M1873 rifle included the Model 1873 Cadet Rifle, essentially similar to the infantry version but lacking sling swivels; and the Model 1873 Carbine, with a short barrel and a half-stock lacking the butt-trap for the cleaning rods. Cadet rifles also had a special stacking swivel on the upper band, whereas the carbine had a stacking swivel attached to its solitary barrel band.

First issues were made late in 1874, when M1873 rifles were supplied to the premier infantry regiments. Among the last to receive new guns were cavalrymen in Texas and – ironically – in Indian country, where receipt was delayed until 1876. Men of the Seventh Cavalry, commanded by Lieutenant Colonel George A. Custer, rode out to the Battle of the Little Big Horn on 25 June 1876 with brand-new Model 1873 carbines.

The events of that fateful day are still well known; Custer and his men met their deaths amid speculation that their carbines had jammed much too frequently. Rumours abounded that copper cases had fused to chamber walls, allowing the extractor to tear through the case rim, but the influence this may have had on the fighting was impossible to quantify – the Indians took all but a few guns from the battlefield, and none of the cavalrymen survived to relate what really happened during the Last Stand.

However, Major Marcus Reno subsequently told the Chief of Ordnance that six of his M1873 carbines had jammed during the fighting on the bluffs above the Little Big Horn (which he ascribed to the breech not locking properly), and a trooper under Reno's command described how one of his officers had spent

A group of longarms with Indian associations. From top to bottom: 1. Associated with the Battle of the Little Big Horn, this old .69-calibre 1808-type flintlock musket has distinctive tack decoration on the side and under-edge of the butt. 2. The brass-framed 1866-pattern Winchester was greatly favoured by the Indians, owing to its gaudy appearance. This gun has tack decoration and a repair to the butt-side. 3. This cap-lock Plains Rifle by H.E. Leman of Lancaster, Pennsylvania, has a 24$^{1}/_{2}$-inch octagon barrel and extensive tack decoration. A fracture in the fore-end has been repaired with a hide binding, and the toe of the butt has broken away. 4. A .58-calibre cap-lock rifle by Eli Whitney of New Haven, Connecticut, this gun has had its barrel cut to carbine length and tack decoration added by its owner. 5. A brass mounted .54-calibre Plains Rifle with a cap lock by Pennsylvanian metalsmith Joseph Golcher. This gun has a 33$^{1}/_{2}$-inch octagon barrel. A break in the butt-wrist behind the bow of the trigger guard has been repaired with rawhide. 6. An 1873-type 'Trapdoor Springfield' single-shot carbine with a rawhide binder shrunk onto the wrist of the butt to make a repair.

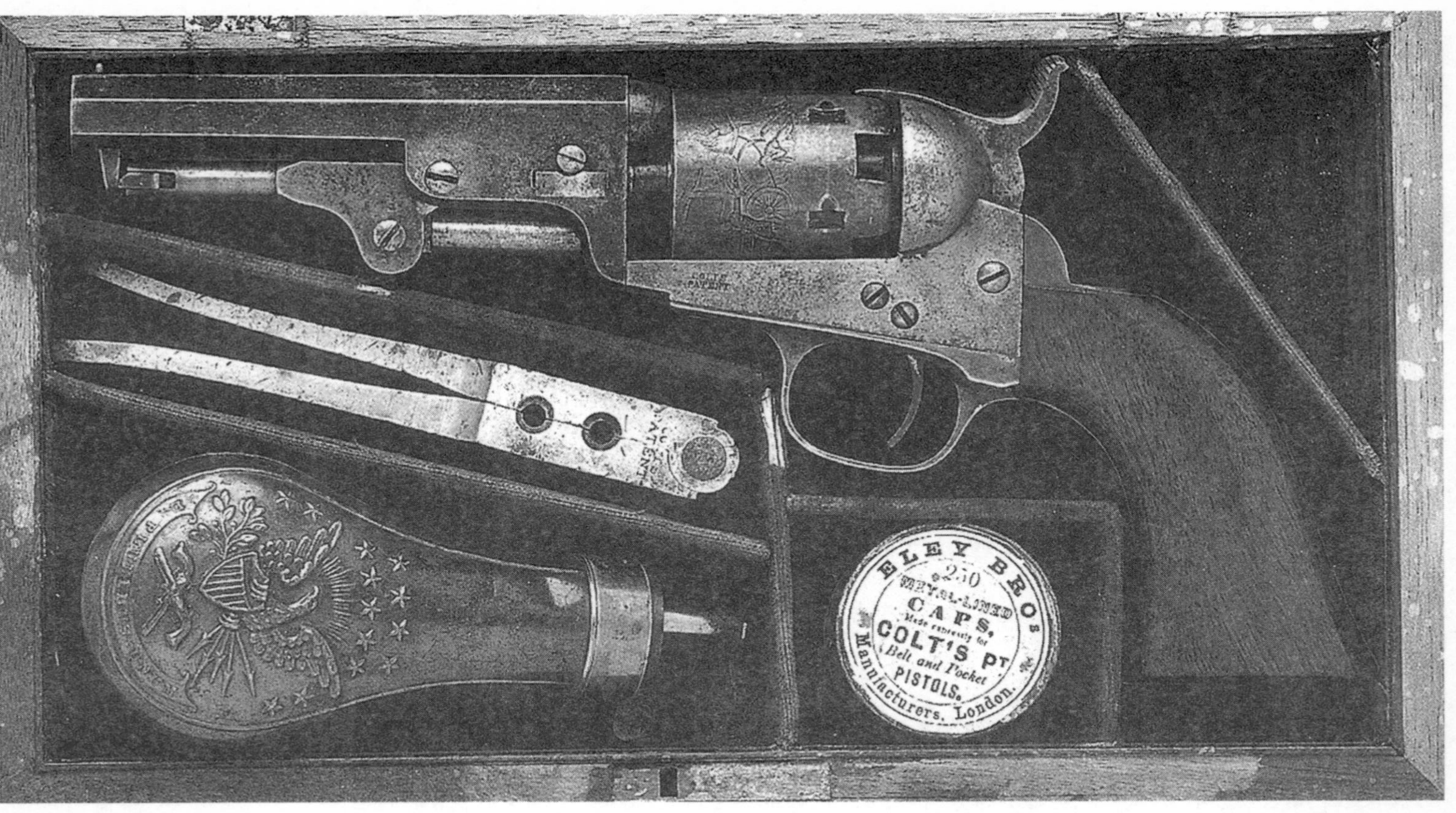

An 1849-model .31 Colt cap-lock pocket revolver, no. 114012, with a one-piece grip and a silvered brass trigger guard/backstrap combination. The octagonal 4-inch barrel bears Colt's New York address and the cylinder surface displays a stagecoach scene. The case contains a two-cavity bullet mould, a powder flask, and a box of Eley caps.

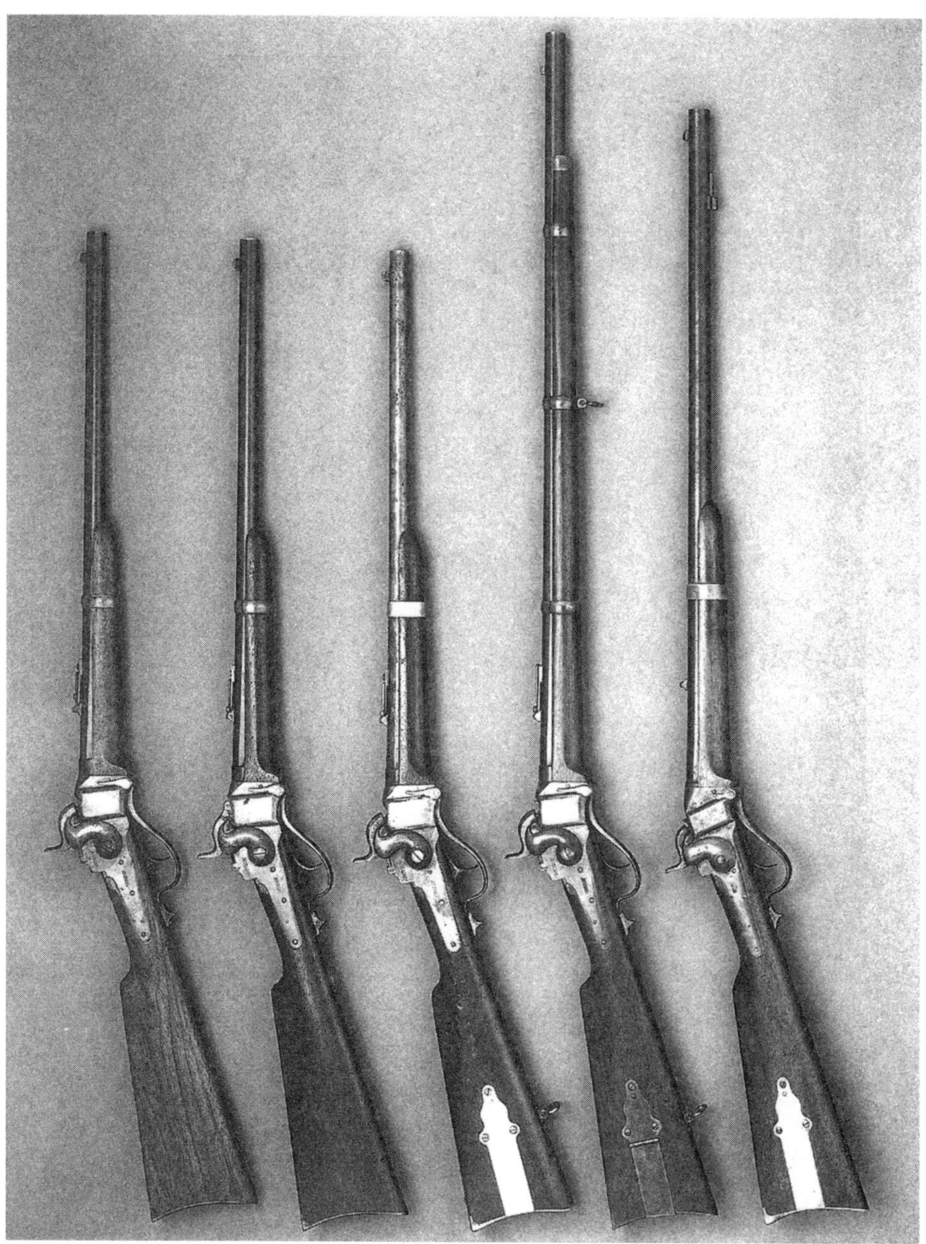

Originally patented in 1848, the Sharps was the best-known single-shot breechloader available in the USA in the mid-nineteenth century. From left to right: 1. A Model 1865 .52-calibre cap-lock carbine, no. C45480, with a 22-inch barrel. 2. A .52-calibre M1865 carbine, no. C44845, converted to fire rimfire ammunition after the end of the Civil War. 3. An 1859-pattern .52 cap-lock carbine, no. 30933. The barrel band, butt plate and hinged-lid patch box are made of brass. 4. A Model 1863 three-band military rifle, no. C39529, with a 30-inch barrel. The patch box, bands and fore-end tip are iron, and a socket bayonet can be locked around the front sight. 5. An 1853-type Sharps cap-lock Navy Rifle, no. 22507, with a half stock and a 27-inch barrel fitted to accept a sabre bayonet. The barrel band, butt plate and patch box are brass. Note the design of the receiver of this 'Slant Breech' rifle, compared with the near-vertical pattern of later guns.

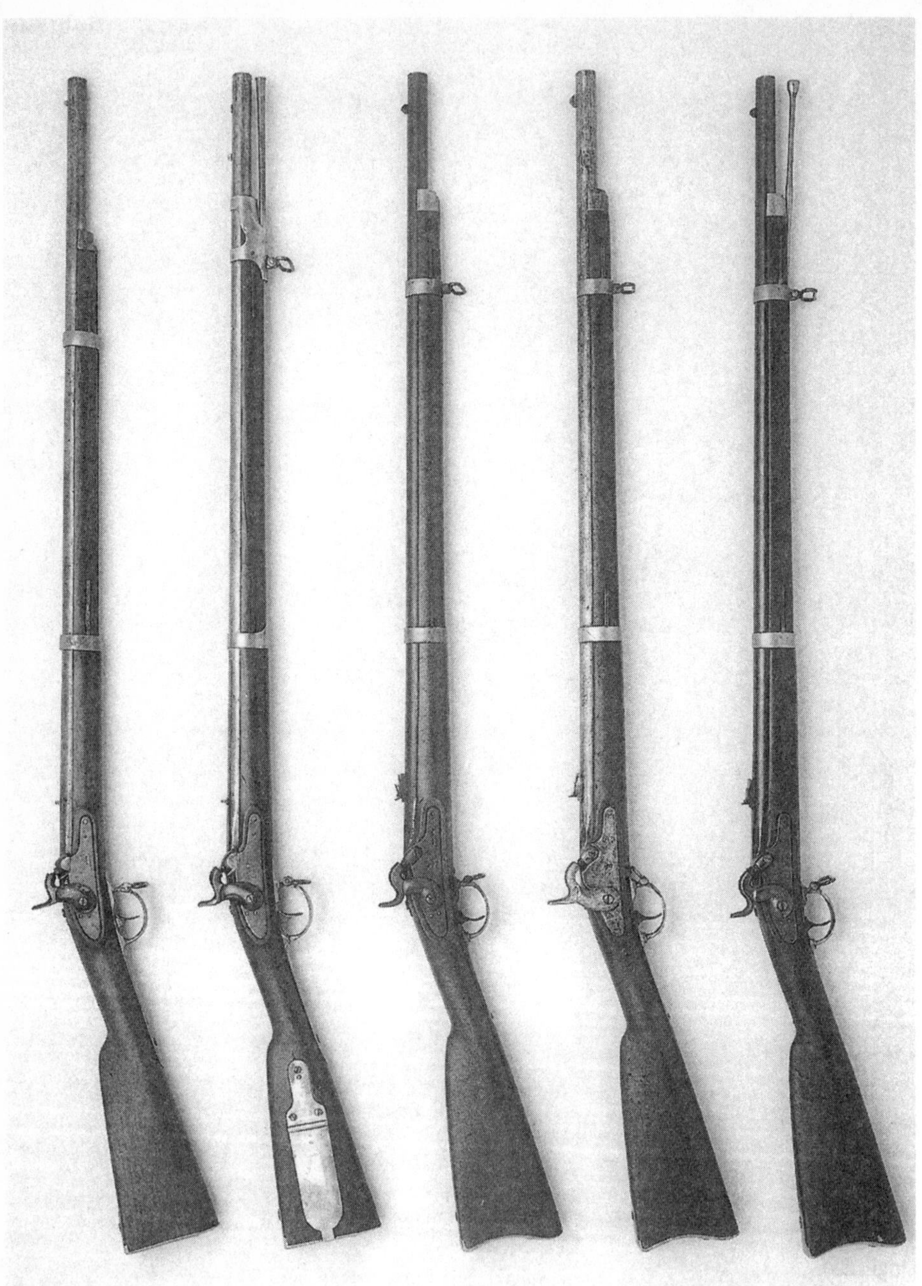

Five cap-lock longarms with Confederate associations. Left to right: 1. A two-band .58 short rifle, without ramrod, made by Greenwood & Gray of Columbus, Georgia, in 1864. The lock bears the mark of J.P. Murray of Columbus. 2. One of about a thousand 1841-pattern cap-lock .54 rifles made for the State of Carolina by the Palmetto Armory. The barrel is marked 'Wm. Glaze & Co.' and dated 1853, whereas the lock is marked 'Palmetto Armory S.C.' with 'Columbia' over 'S C 1852'. Note the bayonet stud on the top surface of the muzzle ahead of the front sight. 3–5. Three .58-calibre cap-lock infantry rifles made by the Fayetteville Armory in 1864, 1862 and 1863 respectively.

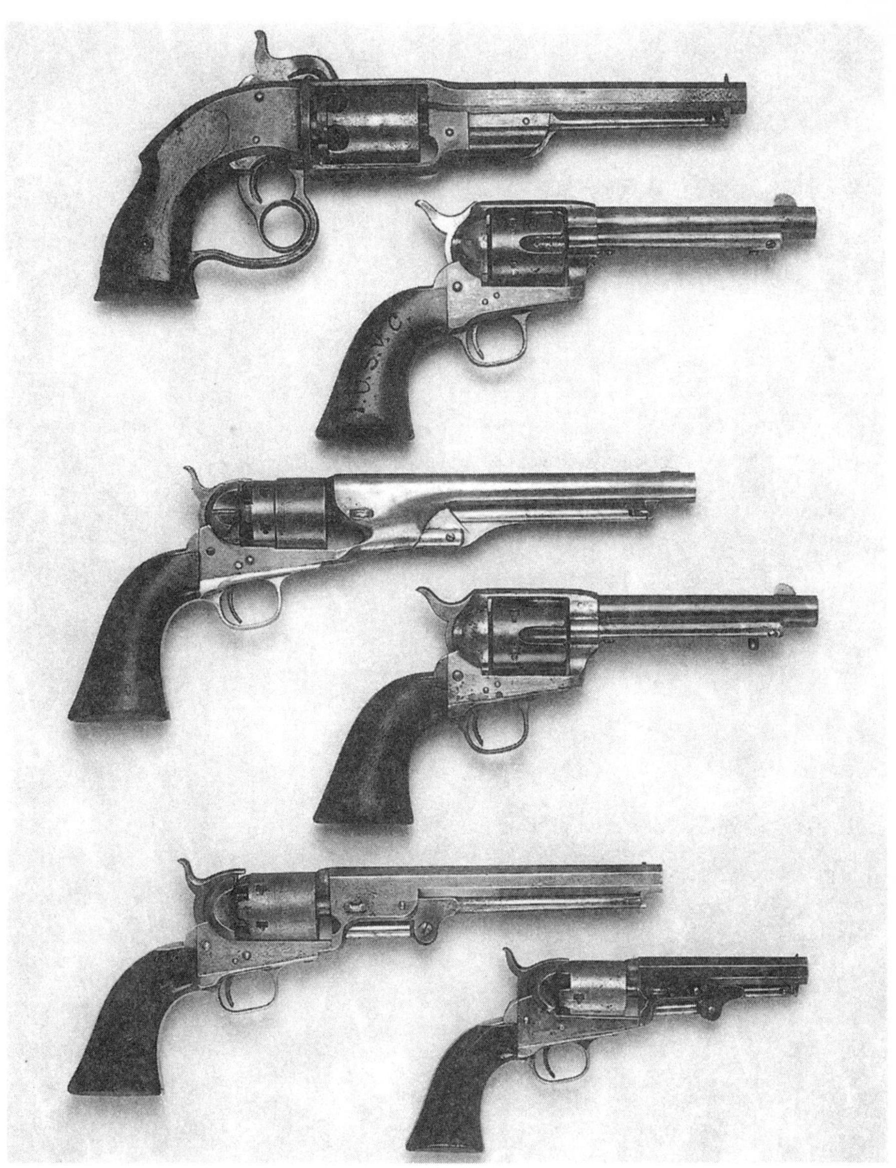

A typical selection of Western revolvers. From top to bottom: 1. A .36-calibre 'heart guard' Savage Navy Revolver, no. 1175. This gun bears an inscription linking it with the 1st Regiment of Connecticut Volunteers, dated 1861. 2. A .45 Colt Single Action Army Revolver, no. 6201, dating from 1874. Marks on the butt of this gun, which has a $5^{1}/2$-inch barrel, suggest use by the 1st US Volunter Cavalry ('Rough Riders') in the Spanish–American War. 3. A .44-calibre Colt Model 1860 Army revolver, no. 45688, with an 8-inch barrel marked with the New York address. It was used in the Civil War by a trooper of the 1st Rhode Island Volunteer Cavalry. 4. Another .45-calibre 'Artillery Pattern' Colt Single Action Army Revolver, no. 115061. This gun was used in the Spanish–American War by a member of Company 'G', 1st US Volunteer Cavalry. 5. A .36-calibre Colt Model 1851 Navy revolver, no. 121. This gun is said to have been exhibited at the Great Exhibition of 1851, and sold when the exhibition closed. It bears the monogram of Major William Scott of the 62nd Regiment of Foot. 6. A five-shot .31-calibre Colt M1849 pocket revolver, no. 87862. Private Horace Souther of the 4th Regiment of Massachusetts Militia Infantry, killed in battle in Virginia in 1861, owned this gun.

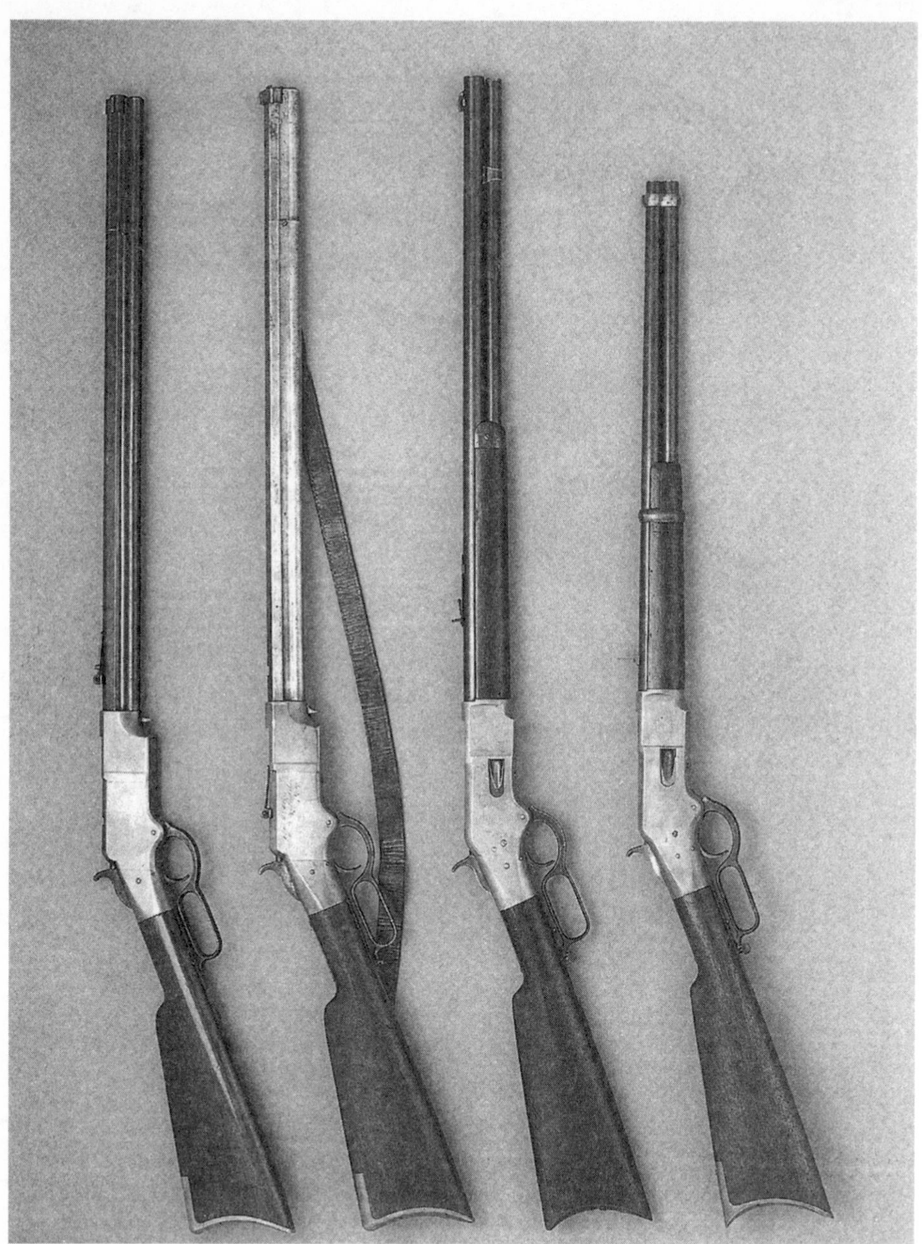

The lever-action Henry rifle and its successor, the Winchester, were very popular in the West. From left to right: 1. A standard .44 Henry M1860 rifle, no. 1616, with a brass frame and the back sight mounted on the barrel. 2. Brass-frame .44 Henry rifle, no. 2909, with the back sight on the frame-top (though the barrel is still cut transversely for the sight base). This gun was owned by J.W. McClure of Company 'D', 57th Regiment of Indiana Volunteers, killed at Kenesaw Mountain in June 1864. 3. The .44-calibre M1866 Winchester rifle could be distinguished from the Henry by the loading gate on the frame-side and the wooden fore-end. This 24-inch barrel gun, no. 152610, dates from near the end of production. 4. A .44-calibre Winchester 'Saddle Ring Carbine', no. 18917. This 20-inch barrel gun has a leaf-type sight hinged to a standing block. Note the band binding the barrel and magazine tube together at the muzzle.

The Winchester rifle underwent continuous improvement, as these five guns testify. Left to right: 1. An 1866-pattern .44 rimfire Winchester saddle-ring carbine, no. 47349, with a 20-inch barrel and folding back sight. These guns had distinctive flat-sided brass frames. 2. An engraved .44-40 Winchester M1873 rifle, with a 24-inch octagon barrel, chequered woodwork and folding back sight. The M1873 had a case-hardened iron frame with a raised panel on the right side. 3. This is an example of the Browning-designed M1886 Winchester rifle, no. 4713, chambered for the .45-90 cartridge. The gun has a 25-inch octagon barrel and a spring-leaf back sight with a sliding elevator. 4. The 1895-pattern Winchester, another Browning design, had a box magazine beneath the frame. This .30-06 saddle-ring carbine, no. 109574, was made shortly before the World War I. It has a 22-inch barrel and a spring-leaf and elevator back sight. 5. The M1894 was an improved form of the M1886; this gun, no. 568639, in .30-30 chambering, has a 20-inch barrel with a King back sight.

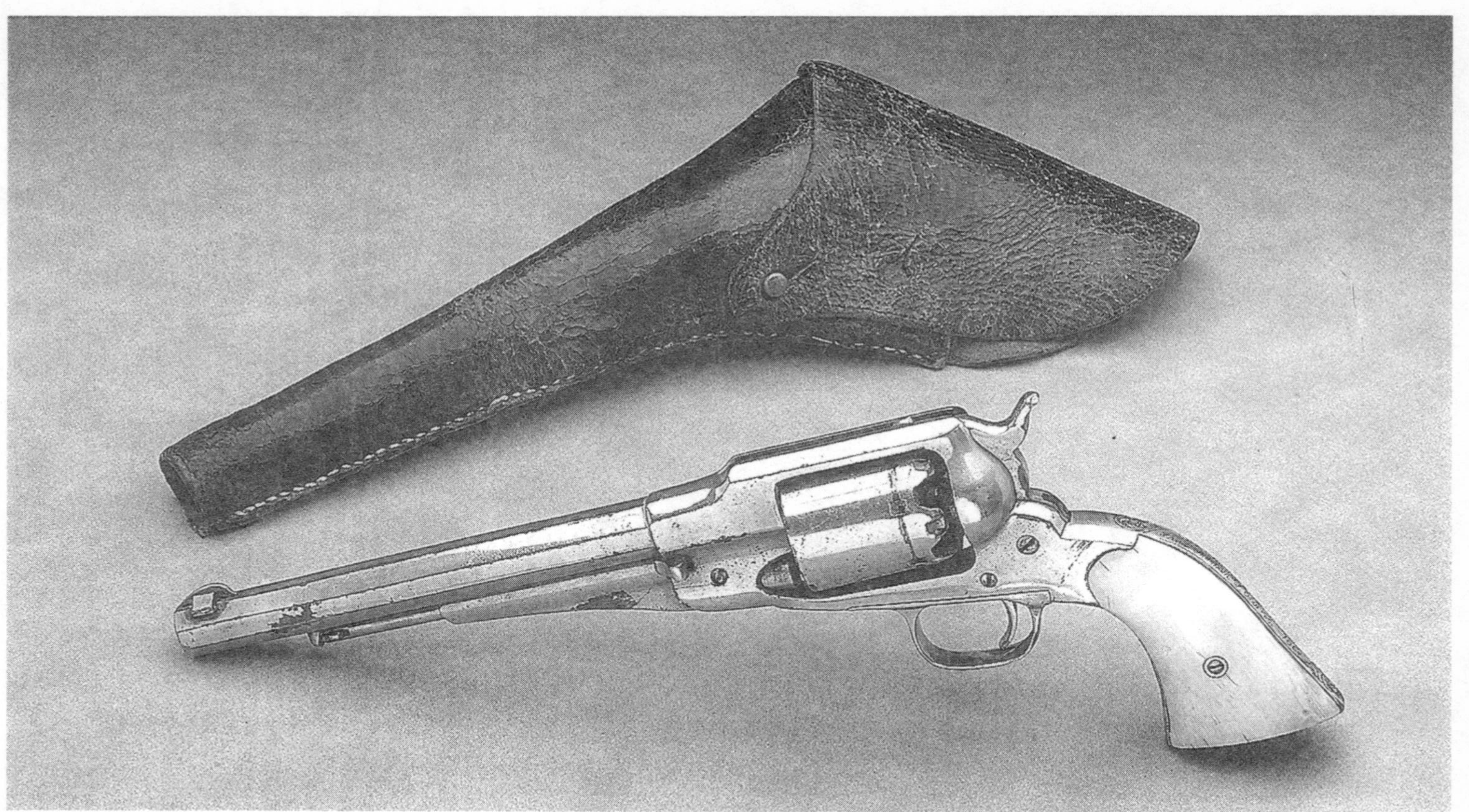

This nickelled ivory-gripped .44 Remington New Model Army Revolver, no. 7179, bears a backstrap inscription (possibly re-worked) suggesting that it had been presented in 1864 to Thomas W. Custer by the men of the Ohio Volunteers. Excepting the gaudy finish, the gun and holster typify the cap-locks of the Civil War era.

This Richards conversion of a .44 Colt M1860 Army revolver, no. 194590, bears inscriptions on the grips which may link it with Robert 'Bob' Ford, cousin and eventual killer of Jesse James. The brown leather holster shows typical military styling.

This round-barrel .38 rimfire conversion of an old Colt cap-lock revolver, no. 2426, is said to have been carried by Jesse James during the catastrophic raid on the First National Bank of Northfield, Minnesota, in 1876. The trigger guard and back strap are brass.

This nickel-plated .44-calibre Smith & Wesson No. 3 'First Model Russian' revolver, no. 28009, with an 8-inch barrel and ivory grips, was surrendered by Cole Younger after the abortive raid mounted by the James–Younger Gang on the First Bank of Northfield, Minnesota, in September 1876.

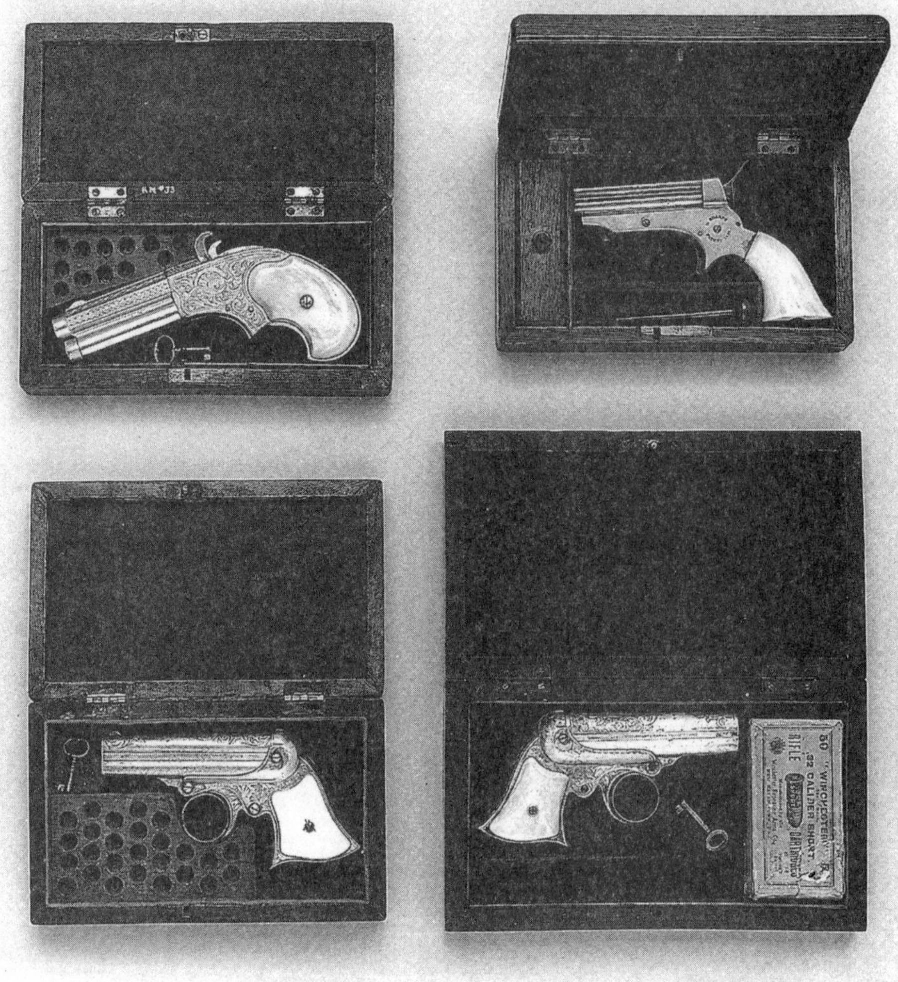

Among the many deringers favoured in the West were a number of multi-shot designs.
Top left: a 32-calibre silver plated Remington-Rider magazine pistol with ivory grips, in its original red-lined walnut case. Bottom left: a .32-calibre Remington-Elliott ring-trigger deringer, no. 20294, with ivory grips and scroll engraving on the frame. This gun was presented in April 1872 to William Dodge by Colonel Squires, Secretary of E. Remington & Sons. Top right: a cased 'factory presentation' four-barrel .22 Sharps deringer, no. 12210, with silver-plated frame and barrel-block. Bottom right: an engraved, silver-plated Remington-Elliott deringer, no. 15598, with ivory grips. The case also contains a box for fifty Winchester-made .32 Short cartridges.

This .41-calibre Colt Thunderer, no. 112719, with nickel plating and ivory grips, was the property of Frank Bailey of Amado, Arizona Territory. Bailey was appointed Marshal of Tucson, Arizona, in 1918.

Once owned by John Ryan, a sergeant in the 7th Cavalry at the time of the Little Big Horn, this Chromolith print of Buffalo Bill and his horse is accompanied by a book – *Thrilling Lives of Buffalo Bill and Pawnee Bill* – and a seven-shot .22 rimfire 'Buffalo Bill'-brand Suicide Special of unknown origin.

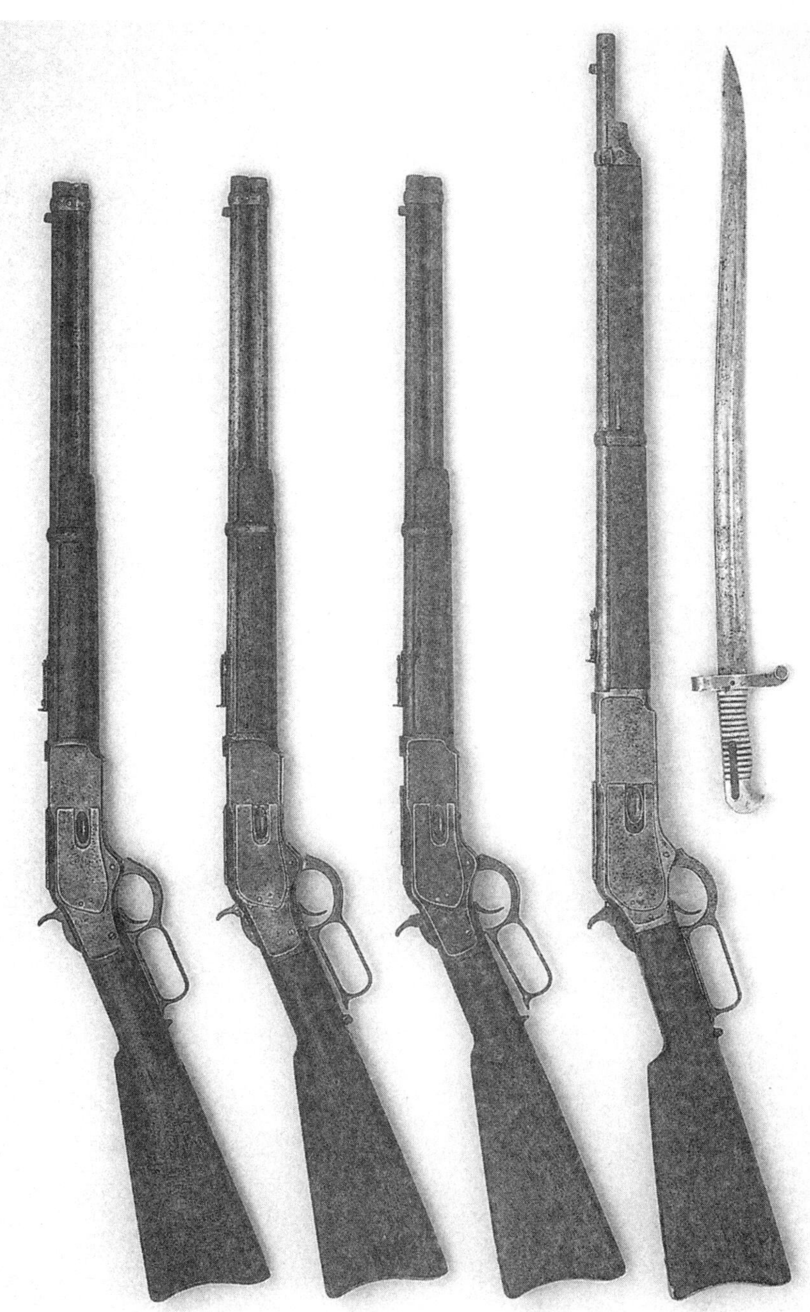

Though lever-action rifles were made by many other companies, often most successfully, the name 'Winchester' soon became synonymous with the West. Left to right: 1–3. Three .44-40 Winchester M1873 Saddle Ring Carbines, no. 397299B, 265143B and 451820B respectively. The guns all have 20-inch barrels and the standard folding back sight. 4. A .45-75 Model 1876 military carbine, no. 62117, with a 22-inch barrel, iron mounts, and a brass hilted sabre bayonet. Note the extra-long receiver, which distinguishes the 1876-pattern Winchester from its short 1873-type predecessor, and the distinctive configuration of the nose cap.

BEADLE'S

Dime New York Library

COPYRIGHTED IN 1881, BY BEADLE & ADAMS.

ENTERED AT THE POST OFFICE AT NEW YORK, N. Y., AT SECOND CLASS MAIL RATES.

Vol. XIII. | Published Every Week. | *Beadle & Adams, Publishers,* 98 WILLIAM STREET, N. Y., January 11, 1882. | Ten Cents a Copy. $5.00 a Year. | No. 168

WILD BILL, THE PISTOL DEAD SHOT; Or, DAGGER DON'S DOUBLE.

BY COLONEL PRENTISS INGRAHAM,

AUTHOR OF "MERLE, THE MUTINEER," "MONTEZUMA, THE MERCILESS," "FREELANCE, THE BUCCANEER," "THE DARE DEVIL," "THE CRETAN ROVER," "THE PIRATE PRINCE," ETC., ETC.

"WALL, PARD STRANGER YER HEV STRUCK IT RICH," CRIED ONE OF THE COWBOYS. "THREE [illegible] THE[illegible] TOES TURNED UP, AN' TWO IN A DURNED UNHEALTHY GRIP," SAID ANOTHER.

The cover of this Dime Novel, dating from 1882, typifies the way in which Western exploits were reported 'Back East'.

time extracting jammed cases, reloading and passing carbines back to the firers. Colonel Ranald Mackenzie subsequently requested Winchester magazine rifles for the Fourth Cavalry, citing the poor fire-rate of the single-shot carbine in support of his argument, but the army authorities were far too satisfied with the Springfield to concur.

One of the most interesting derivatives of the Trapdoor Springfield was the **Officer's Rifle**, or Model of 1875, which was sold to officers who wanted personal weapons of regulation pattern. However, demand was meagre and only about 290 first-pattern rifles were made in 1876–7.

Adapted from the contemporaneous cadet rifle, the **M1875** had a 26-inch barrel and a half stock with chequering on the wrist and the fore-end. The fore-end had a tip of German silver, and foliate scrollwork was engraved on the lock, hammer, receiver, barrel band and butt plate. The wooden ramrod had decorative nickel-plated brass ferrules.

The original Officer's Rifles had a globe-pattern front sight which folded down to allow a pin to serve with the open buck-horn back sight. A Sharps 'peep' or aperture-type back sight, adjustable for drift and elevation, folded down on to the butt-wrist when not required. The special trigger had a normal service-pattern pull, but could be 'set' by pushing it forward.

Although the Trapdoor Springfield satisfied the demands of the US Army, it had no impact commercially until thousands of military-surplus weapons were sold in the 1880s and 1890s. Consequently, several of the best-known Civil War weapons enjoyed a new lease of life in sporting guise.

By far the most common of these was the single-shot **Sharps** breechloading rifle. The Sharps Rifle Manufacturing Company developed the first of its purpose-built cartridge rifles almost as soon as the Civil War had ended; now often known as the 'New Model' or 'Model 1866', they were only made in tiny numbers. The earliest Sharps-pattern guns seen 'Out West' in quantity were conversions of the cap-locks supplied to the Ordnance Department during the Civil War. At least 30,000 of the perfected 1863-type carbines were adapted for the regulation .50-70 centrefire cartridge in 1867–9.

The 'Sharps Improved Breechloading Metallic Cartridge Rifle', often known as the **Model 1869**, was also based on the 1863-type carbine. The first guns, usually offering 26- or 28-inch octagon barrels, were chambered for proprietary .52-70 rim- or centrefire cartridges. Ammunition of this type was also used in many converted cap-lock Sharps rifles and carbines, but proved to be short-lived.

The US Army adopted a .50-70 cartridge to replace the short-lived .58 rimfire, and the Sharps management realised that it was much better to ream-out and then retube old barrels to fire military-pattern ammunition. Sharps sporting rifles altered for the .50-70 round were made in surprisingly large numbers until the US Army changed to .45-70 in 1873.

The 'Improved' Sharps rifles handled a variety of .44 and .45 cartridges, but there were many different loadings and many barrel-length options. Among the earliest Sharps centrefire cartridges were .40 Berdan Short, .44 Berdan Short and .44 Berdan Long, all dating from c. 1870 and subsequently renamed '.40-50 Sharps', '.44-60 Sharps' and '.44-77 Sharps' respectively.

The **Model 1871** rifle, though based on the preceding or 1869 pattern, was strengthened to handle the most powerful sporting cartridges of the day in safety. The guns were made by Sharps Rifle Manufacturing Company of Hartford, Connecticut, until the company failed in 1874. Christian Sharps died in the same year in greatly reduced circumstances, but had long since severed his links with the business.

Sharps rifles had attained such great popularity in the West, particularly for use against large game such as buffalo, that a new promoter – the Sharps Rifle Company – was formed in Hartford in 1874, moving to nearby Bridgeport in 1876. The Sharps Rifle Company was comparatively short-lived, however, lasting just seven years before being forced into liquidation in September 1881.

The **Model 1874** Sharps was practically identical to the preceding 1871 pattern, the change of designation merely reflecting the change in company ownership. Even the earliest catalogues published by the Sharps Rifle Company offered the M1874 with 26–30in octagon, half-octagon or round barrels. An extra-heavy barrel – often as much as 34in long – could raise the gun weight from 8–11lb to as much as 15lb. Characteristic 'Hartford Style' pewter fore-end tips were customary, whilst double set-triggers and a minutely adjustable peep-and-globe sighting system were among the extras.

The 1874-pattern rifles were offered in many chamberings. A catalogue published in 1879 lists options ranging from the straight-case .40-$1\frac{7}{8}$-45 to the awesome .50-$2\frac{1}{2}$-100 round, loaded with a 473-grain paper-patched lead bullet.

BILL TILGHMAN

Renowned as a lawman, Willam H. 'Bill' Tilghman (1854–1924) made his mark in the 1870s as a professional buffalo hunter, reportedly killing more than 7000 – including one shot at a distance 'measured as a mile'. Most of this was accomplished with a .40 1874-type Sharps sporting rifle (no. C53858) with a 32in octagon barrel. Sold by Sharps in June 1874 to gun-dealer F. C. Zimmermann of Dodge City, Kansas, the gun was eventually converted to .50-calibre when its rifling wore out. Tilghman has also been linked with two .45 Colt Single Action Army revolvers, numbered 153926 and 211471. Both had 4.75in barrels with ejector cases, but the former was nickel-plated and the latter, suitably engraved and plated in gold, had steer-head grips of ivory. Tilghman was eventually murdered.

The popularity of the 1874-pattern Sharps rifle inspired the introduction of several derivatives in quick succession. The 'Creedmoor' target rifle appeared in 1874, and then came a plain-stocked 'Hunter's Rifle' in 1875. A 'Mid-Range' target rifle followed in 1876. The announcement of a plain round-barrel 'Business Rifle' in the summer of 1875 inspired Remington to prepare a similar design built on the rolling-block action (q.v.). A few shotguns were also built on Sharps actions in the 1870s, but were never common. Sharps rifles completed in the Bridgeport factory after April 1876 had barrels marked 'OLD RELIABLE.

The **Model 1877** or 'English Model' Sharps was a lighter and more delicate variant of the M1874, said to have been specifically intended for sale in Britain and the Empire where the standard guns were sometimes derided for their clumsy lines. The English Model, therefore, had a slender butt, a minimal fore-end and a special lightweight action. The hammer was also much more delicate than the standard design.

An alternative suggestion that the English Model was originally designed for competitive shooting is worth consideration, the goal being to fit the heaviest barrel practicable within a ten-pound gun-weight limit. Owing to the extent of the revisions, however, this explanation still seems unsatisfactory – even though suitability for competitive shooting may have been a welcome by-product of refinement.

Unfortunately for the Sharps Rifle Company, the English Model was unpopular. It may simply have come too late to compete with British self-cockers such as the Farquharson and the Field – much more advanced technically, though not always as sturdy – and many unwanted 1877-type Sharps actions were shipped to gunsmith John Lower of Denver in 1880.

Although the Sharps Rifle Manufacturing Company was keen to promote the advantages of **Sharps cartridges** loaded with long small-calibre bullets, which offered better ballistics than short large-calibre projectiles of equivalent weight, complaints were soon being received that even the .44-77 round did not always drop a buffalo instantly. This was vitally important, as the single-shot rifle could not always be reloaded quickly enough to facilitate a telling second shot.

The awesome .50-90 'Big Fifty' appeared in the summer of 1872, followed in 1873 by two versions of the .44-90 – one for hunting and the 'Creedmoor' for target-shooting. The range of proprietary cartridges had grown enormously by the time the Sharps Rifle Company failed in 1881, and rifles had also been chambered for Remington and Winchester rounds – the 'Sharps' .44-2$\frac{7}{16}$ was a Remington pattern, for example, and the .50-3$\frac{1}{4}$ 'Big Fifty' was little other than the Winchester .50-140 Express.

The original necked-case .44 cartridges were replaced in the mid-1870s by straight .45 patterns, which were cheaper to make and easier to reload. These were vital considerations in more remote parts of the Great Plains, and explain why oddly loaded cartridges are still occasionally found in collections.

Sharps customarily classified cartridges by case-length, owing to perpetual changes in powder charge and projectile weight. The necked cases included .40-1$\frac{11}{16}$ (.40-50), .40-2$\frac{1}{4}$ (.40-70), .40-2$\frac{5}{8}$ (.40-90), .44-1$\frac{7}{8}$ (.44-60), .44-2$\frac{1}{4}$ (.44-77) and .44-2$\frac{5}{8}$ (.44-90). Among the straight-case designs were .40-2$\frac{1}{2}$ (.40-70), .45-2$\frac{1}{10}$ (.45-75), .45-2$\frac{4}{10}$ (.45-90), .45-2$\frac{6}{10}$ (.45-100), .45-2$\frac{7}{8}$ (.45-120), .50-1$\frac{3}{4}$ (.50-70) and .50-2$\frac{1}{2}$ (.50-90). The .40-2$\frac{1}{2}$ case could contain bullets ranging from 330 to 370 grains, and the .45-2$\frac{6}{10}$ case could be loaded with bullets of 500–550 grains.

The ballistics of the Sharps cartridges make interesting comparisons with contemporaneous Winchester M1873 lever-action repeaters, which were restricted to comparatively weak short-case ammunition. According to handbooks published by the Winchester Repeating Arms Company prior to 1910, the '.40-70 Sharp's Straight' cartridge gave a muzzle velocity of 1220 ft/sec with a 330-grain bullet (1091 ft-lb of muzzle energy), whereas the .40-90 version gave 1357 ft/sec with a 370-grain bullet (1513 ft-lb); penetration of the standard plain-lead projectiles into pine was measured as 11$\frac{1}{2}$in and 16in respectively. Most handloaders were content with muzzle velocities of 1250–1500 ft/sec, though some individuals managed to raise muzzle velocity above 1750 ft/sec by loading lightweight bullets in the .45-2$\frac{6}{10}$ or .45-2$\frac{7}{8}$ cases. Accuracy often declined at these levels, however, as the limits of the efficiency of black-powder propellant and the ability of lead to engrave in the rifling in the barrel-bore were being approached.

By comparison, the .44-40 Winchester round, in the Model 1892 lever-action rifle, fired a 200-grain bullet at 1245 ft/sec (689 ft-lb); penetration into pine was rated at only 9in. Even the Winchester Sharps cartridges – under-loaded by the standards of some other ammunition makers – had a much flatter trajectory than the .44-40 WCF type. The 'mid-range' heights for ranges of 200 and 300 yards were 10.78in and 26.35in for the .40-90 Sharps round, compared with 15.27in and 37.39in for .44-40.

Few changes were ever made to the basic design, though individual gunsmiths were often more enterprising. Frank Freund of Cheyenne obtained US Patent no. 180,567 in August 1876 protecting a modified '**Freund Sharps**' type breech-block which rode in a mortise which allowed a limited backward movement as it dropped (the Sharps breech dropped straight down). When the breech lever was closed, the Freund-patent block moved around its mortise to seat the cartridge-case base by cam action.

Franz Wilhelm 'Frank' Freund had an interesting career. Born in Germany in 1837, he had worked for Remington after emigrating to the USA and served during the Civil War in the Union army. Establishing themselves as gunsmiths in Nebraska City in 1866, Frank and his brother George led a peripatetic life in

Nebraska City, North Platte, Cheyenne, Salt Lake City and Denver. Selling the Blake Street premises in Denver to John P. Lower in 1875, the Freund Brothers subsequently concentrated their efforts in The Wyoming Armory in Eddy Street, Cheyenne.

Frank Freund obtained a range of US Patents in 1874–93, and, together with George, was responsible for the renowned 'More Light' sight patented in June 1880. Although the modification of the Sharps breech was advantageous, Freund Brothers only used it in a handful of 'Wyoming Saddle Guns'.

The **Maynard** rifle, another survivor from pre-Civil War days, had been patented on 6 December 1859 by Edward Maynard. The US Army had purchased 400 tipping-barrel carbines in 1857, and the Federal government had acquired more than 20,000 during the Civil War. Others had been sold commercially.

Among the unique features of the Maynard was its metal-case cartridge, which was ignited by an external side-hammer lock fed with a Maynard tape primer. Made for the inventor by the Massachusetts Arms Company, the guns were operated by depressing a lever which doubled as the trigger guard. Extraction and ejection were accomplished manually.

The original carbines had plain slab-sided butts and lacked fore-ends, but were light, handy and popular. When the Civil War ended, substantial numbers of Maynard carbines and improved **Model 1865** sporting rifles – with new mechanical extractors – found their way westward. External ignition handicapped sales, owing to competition from guns firing self-contained ammunition, but Maynard patented a suitable conversion system on 18 February 1873 (US no. 135,928).

The **Model 1873** Maynard sporter was offered with half-octagon or round barrels ranging from twenty to 32in. Pride of the range was the No. 14 Long Range Creedmoor Rifle, introduced in 1876 to accompany a .44-100-520 cartridge which taxed the Maynard action to its limit, but a variety of hunting rifles was also made. Typical of these was the 'No. 11 Improved Hunter's Rifle', chambered for .44-60 to .55-100 Maynard cartridges. The guns had 26-32in barrels and plain oil-finished walnut butts. An 'Elevating Graduated Peep Sight' was often fitted on the butt-wrist to supplement the open hunting sights.

One of the best features of the Maynard rifle was the ease with which its barrel could be changed, commending it to many Westerners who could substitute a 20- or 28-bore shotgun barrel when necessary.

Though greeted intitially with enthusiasm, the Maynard was ultimately handicapped by its proprietary 'thick rim' cartridges, ranging from .35-30 to .50-100, and sales were far from brisk. While the situation was improved by alterations made after 1882 to chamber more conventional ammunition (including .25-20 Stevens and .45-70 Government), the days of comparatively primitive single-shot rifles such as the Maynard had passed.

Although the **Ballard** rifle had failed to attract much Federal ordnance interest during the Civil War, extensive use by state militiamen in Kentucky had proved it to be much more efficient than many rival single-shot breechloading designs. Originally patented by Charles Ballard in November 1861 (US no. 33,631), the rifle survived long after the war had ended – not only in the hands of Westerners, but also to gain an enviable reputation for accuracy on the target range.

Part of the reason behind the lack of success was a convoluted production history. The earliest Ballards had been made by Ball & Williams of Worcester, Massachusetts, and then, in quick succession, by the Merrimack Arms & Manufacturing Company and the Brown Manufacturing Company of Newburyport, Massachusetts. When a forcible end to Brown's operations was brought by creditors in 1873, rights to the Ballard patent were acquired by Schoverling & Daly of New York.

Finally, in 1875, Schoverling & Daly licensed production of Ballards to John Marlin of New Haven, Connecticut. When the Marlin Fire Arms Company was incorporated in 1881, Charles Daly of Schoverling, Daly & Gales became its first president and production of Ballard rifles continued until 1891 alongside the better known Marlin lever-action repeaters.

The first Marlin-Ballard rifles made from 1876 onward, described in greater detail in the next chapter, embodied 'Marlin's Patent Automatic Extractor and Reversible Firing Pin'. Protected by US Patent no. 159,592 of 9 February 1875, the firing pin could handle rim- and centrefire cartridges interchangeably. Ballards were initially offered in a variety of well-known chamberings, including .45-70 and .50-70, but were then offered in proprietary loadings such as .38-50, .40-63, .40-90, .44-75 and .45-100. The dropping-block action, operated by a lever doubling as the trigger guard, was sturdy enough to handle large powder charges and heavy bullets.

The **Peabody**, among the best of the single-shot breechloading rifles of the Civil War period, struggled to make an impact after the fighting had ceased. Made in accordance with US Patent no. 35,947, granted on 22 July 1862 to Henry O. Peabody of Boston, Massachusetts, the guns were made exclusively by the Providence Tool Company of Providence, Rhode Island.

Peabody had claimed novelty in method of opening the action, which relied on pins on the breech-lever and a slot in the underside of the breech-block. A roller on the breech-lever spring held the breech-block in the loading position.

The patent was reissued in 1866, with a new rider noting that the pin-and-slot depressor featured in the original specification was just one way of operating the breech. Peabody subsequently added a lever-and-slot depressor, and a pivoting extractor struck by the breech-block as it fell. US Patent no. 76,805, granted on 14 April 1868, protected the combination rim- and centrefire striker.

The Providence Tool Company had made 1861-pattern Springfield rifle-muskets during the Civil War, and had experimented with a few Roberts breechloading transformations. However, the Roberts design had not been successful; designs with greater potential were already being sought when Peabody approached the company in search of advice.

Peabody rifles customarily had a most distinctive two-piece stock and an elongated boxlike receiver, and a back-action lock with an external side hammer was let into the right side of the butt behind the receiver. Among their greatest advantages was the dispersion of much of the strain of firing through the rear inner surface of the sturdy receiver, but the position of the breech-block pivot pin also prevented the breech opening prematurely. In addition, the extractor was much more substantial than the earliest Allin-Springfield patterns.

A catalogue published by the Providence Tool Company in 1866, describing some of the many tests undergone by guns submitted to the US Army in 1865, recorded:

> The Board selected four of the eight guns [remaining after the first round] for still further tests, and heavy charges were applied to each. 60 grains of powder and three balls (each of the balls weighing 450 grains) were tried, with no ill effect; the charges were gradually increased to 80 grains and four balls; one of the four guns, however, being blown to pieces by a lighter charge. Two others of the four were thoroughly shattered in the breech by this charge – while the 'Peabody gun' was fired with 80 grains of powder and five balls...
>
> The trial resulted, as was generally anticipated, in a report of the Board of Officers recommending the Peabody gun...

The Peabody was recognised as a better weapon than the Allin-breech Springfield transformation, but could not be created from existing rifle-muskets and was rejected by the Chief of Ordnance in penny-pinching post-war days. Peabody developed a conversion system for rifle muskets, operated by a top lever (US Patent no. 72,706 of 10 December 1867), but this was not as effectual as his underlever design and was abandoned after only a few guns had been made for trials.

Fortunately for Peabody and the Providence Tool Company, enthusiasm for the underlever rifle was far greater abroad than in the USA, and substantial numbers of military-style rifles and carbines were sold to Romania, Spain, Switzerland and Turkey prior to 1874. In a broadsheet submitted to a US Army Board of Officers, convened in St Louis in 1870, Providence claimed to be making a standard 1862-patent .45 side-hammer gun, called the 'Roumanian Model'; a similar .43 'Spanish Model', with a spiral firing-pin retractor spring; and the 1867-patent 'Peabody Self-Cocking Gun', with a top-lever depressor and a coil-pattern firing-pin spring. A self-cocking Peabody-Wessely rifle, chambered for the .42 Russian centrefire cartridge, was also being offered – though probably only ever made in prototype form.

A .50-45-320 Peabody sporting rifle was announced in September 1865, seeking to capitalise on an ability to handle powerful cartridges. The earliest guns apparently had a half-octagon barrel and a side-barred patch box let into the butt. Small metal plates were let into the fore-end, the breech lever/trigger guard had a scrolled rearward extension, and a folding back sight was fitted to the upper tang.

Production of the original sporters was exceptionally small; broadsheets produced in 1866 show a much plainer gun, with a conventional breech lever and an open back sight on the barrel ahead of the receiver. A .45 or .50-calibre military-style rifle with a full stock and a 26in or 28in barrel was offered, accompanied by a carbine with a 20in barrel and a short fore-end. Peabody rifles of this era could be obtained with a 'Sliding Rear Sight' or an 'Elevating Peep Sight' to order.

Rimfire chambering options were restricted to .45-50-330, .45-60-420, .45-70-480 and .50-45-320, but the Peabody had been converted to centrefire by the summer of 1867. A catalogue dating from 1871 indicated that sporting guns were available only in .45, with barrels of 20–28in and the option of sliding or elevating aperture back sights. Military-style muskets, stocked almost to the muzzle, were available in .43, .45 and .50; military carbines were made in .45 and .50 only.

A few deluxe sporting guns were distinguished by superior finish, nickel-plating, German silver escutcheons for the barrel-retaining key, half- or full-octagon barrels, and chequering on the wrist and fore-end. However, the Peabody was expensive – at $40 for even a plain sporter, it cost substantially more than rival Remington and Sharps rifles, which sold for $30–32 apiece.

Remington offered a few sporting guns made in accordance with patents granted to Fordyce Beals. Made only in 1866–8, **Remington-Beals** rifles had a 24-inch half-octagon barrel and weighed 6lb; they were loaded by depressing the operating lever doubling as the trigger guard, sliding the barrel forward and away from the standing breech. This primitive system restricted chambering to .36 and .38 rimfire, and was overtaken by the rolling-block breech system.

The origins of the **Rolling Block** lay in the Civil War, when an early form, known as the 'Split Breech', had been patented by Leonard Geiger. These guns are described in greater detail in the previous chapter.

The perfected Rolling Block, derived from the Geiger split-breech, was largely the work of Joseph Rider. Subject of several patents granted during the late 1860s, it included a sturdy hammer and an interlocking breech-block which moved radially. The action was opened by thumbing back the hammer to full-cock, then pulling the finger spur to rotate the breech-block away from the breech face. Moving the breech-block exposed the chamber, and partly extracted a spent case. The chamber was reloaded, the breech-block was closed and the trigger could then be pulled to drop the hammer. The hammer struck the firing pin and fired the gun.

Careful positioning of the hammer and breech-block pivots gave the Rolling Block its legendary sturdiness, locking the parts as the hammer-shoulder ran forward under the back of the breech-block. Though extraction was often uncertain – the rifles' greatest weakness – Remingtons regularly withstood trials of phenomenal savagery. One .50 gun tested in the Liége proof house withstood 750 grains of black powder behind forty balls. The director, Alphonse Polain, reported that 'nothing extraordinary [had] happened' when the gun was fired.

Remington's sales literature understandably made great play of such durability, camouflaging a weak extractor stroke which depended on the firer flipping the breech-block open as smartly as possible.

The military career of the Remington, which lasted for forty years elsewhere, was brief in the USA. Poor extraction with government-issue copper-case cartridges in the trials of 1872–3 told heavily against it; by the time drawn brass cases had been substituted for copper, the US Army was fully committed to the .45-70 M1873 rifle.

Although the Rolling Block had a short and unspectacular career in the US Army, the navy was more accommodating. Substantial acquisitions of breechloading rifles and metal-case ammunition prior to 1861 showed that the navy ordnance authorities were less conservative than their army counterparts. They were well aware of the difficulties of keeping paper cartridges dry at sea, and that ease of loading was of paramount importance aboard ship.

Issue of Sharps & Hankins and Spencer weapons during the Civil War removed any doubts that remained in the navy about the value of breechloading. Lacking the enormous numbers of muzzleloaders owned by the army, which would otherwise have clouded judgement, the Navy Bureau of Ordnance began trials of its own in March 1869.

Remington Rolling Block carbines had already been purchased in quantity in 1867, and so a preference expressed for the Remington in 1869 was no real surprise. Approval was also given to the regulation army-type .50-calibre Springfield barrel to ensure commonality of ammunition, together with a brass-hilted sabre bayonet and Martin cartridges 'as made by or for the Sharps Rifle Company'.

Although additional trials were undertaken in the autumn of 1869 – with .43 and .50 Remingtons and a prototype bolt-action Ward-Burton – the Bureau of Ordnance decided to retain large-calibre Remingtons until experiments with smaller cartridges being undertaken by the army were finally resolved.

An order for 10,000 **Model 1870 Navy rifles** was placed with Springfield Armory on 3 February 1870, chambered for the regulation .50-70 centrefire cartridge. The 32.6in barrel was to be rifled with three .0075 grooves making a clockwise turn in 42in, and a distinctive brass-hilt sword bayonet with fish-scale decoration and a Bureau of Ordnance escutcheon cast into the grip was supplied by the Ames Sword Company of Chicopee Falls, Massachusetts.

When the guns were completed, navy inspectors realised that the back sights were positioned wrongly and rejected the entire consignment. The discards were subsequently sold to Poultney & Trimble of Baltimore and exported to France during the Franco-Prussian War. So much of the costs of the defective guns were retrieved that Commodore Ludlow Case, the Chief of the Bureau of Navy Ordnance, requested an additional 12,000 rifles on 27 January 1871. These were also made in Springfield.

Inspired by progress with breechloading rifles in the navy, a US Army Board of Officers convened in St Louis in March 1870. After examining a wide range of firearms, only six were accepted for the shooting trials – in order of preference from best to worst, the Remington, the Springfield, the Sharps, the Morgenstern, the Martini-Henry and the Ward-Burton. The final report confided that only the Remington, Sharps and Springfield 'possess such superior excellence as warrants their adoption by the Government for infantry and cavalry without further trial in the hands of troops. Of these . . . , considering all the elements of excellence and cost of manufacture, the board are unanimously . . . of the opinion that the Remington is the best system.'

More than 500 Remington Rolling Block rifles had been made in Springfield Armory in 1868, their characteristics being sufficiently well known for Chief of Ordnance Alexander Dyer to draw attention to inherent defects. His reservations could not prevent field trials: by March 1871, therefore, the National Armory had made 1001 infantry-pattern Remingtons and 1020 Model 1870 Trapdoor Springfields.

These were issued alongside 501 Sharps rifles assembled from Civil War-era actions, 32.5in .50-calibre barrels and 'two-band' Springfield fittings. The remaining Sharps guns had been delivered by midsummer, raising the total to 1001, and 1108 infantry-rifle alterations of Spencer carbines followed in the autumn of 1871. These chambered .56-50 rimfire cartridges instead of the more powerful government .50-70, which was too long to feed through the Spencer action.

Concurrently, the cavalry tried 313 Remington, 308 Sharps and 341 Model 1870 Springfield carbines. The St Louis board had been sceptical about the Remington carbine, recommending that no issues should be made until a half-cock loading feature had been added, but this was not heeded in the rush to complete experiments.

The Spencer was disliked on account of its low power, poor long-range

The action of the Remington Locking Rifle, a rolling-block variant with an auxiliary catch set into the hammer

performance masking its advantages at close quarters. Few of the officers supervising field trials with the experimental rifles had a good word for the Sharps, regarding it as too heavy and inaccurate. The Remington was greeted with greater enthusiasm, though extraction problems had arisen and the mechanism jammed too easily in dusty conditions. And very few respondents liked loading guns at full cock.

The **Model 1871 army rifle** was very similar to M1870 rolling-block rifles made for the navy in Springfield Armory, but included a 'Locking Bolt' in the breech mechanism. The firer thumbed the hammer to full-cock, retracted the breech-block spur to expose the chamber, and inserted a cartridge. When the breech-block was closed, however, the hammer automatically fell to half-cock and the gun could not be fired until returned to full-cock. Army Remingtons had longer barrels than their navy counterparts and accepted socket bayonets.

Remington 'Locking Rifles' were rejected by the Terry Board of 1872–3, though more than 20,000 were issued to the New York state militia. However, although the US Army did not view Remingtons with enthusiasm, foreign governments saw differently. Denmark was an early champion, ordering more than 40,000 rifles and carbines, and the Remington gained a silver medal from the Paris Exposition of 1867.

Sales literature published by Remington in 1873 claimed to have sold 16,500 rifles, carbines and pistols to the US Army, 23,000 to the US Navy, 15,000 Model 1871 Locking Rifles to the State of New York, and 5000 rolling block rifle-musket conversions to South Carolina. Guns had also gone to Spain, for use in Cuba, and to Sweden, Egypt and France. Chile, Cuba, Mexico, Puerto Rico and other New World governments all bought sizeable quantities of Rolling Block rifles in 1875–90, and licences were negotiated to allow production to begin in several European countries.

Remington's 1876 catalogue offered several patterns of military-style rifle – claiming that 'about 1,000,000 arms . . . are now in the hands of troops' – in the hope that they would appeal to impecunious Westerners. They included the .50-calibre US Model 1871; two adapted Springfield .58 rifle-muskets, long and short, which combined the original barrel, stock and furniture with a new Rolling Block action; the .43 or 11mm-calibre Spanish Model, with its socket bayonet; the .43 Civil Guard Model for the 'Spanish or Russian Cartridge', offered with a sabre bayonet; the .43 French Model and sabre bayonet, chambered for the 'Egyptian Cartridge'; and .43 or .50-calibre carbines.

The first commercial Rolling Block was the 1867-vintage **Sporting Rifle No. 1**, offered until 1890 with an octagon barrel of 24–34in and weights, according to an 1876 Remington catalogue, ranging from 8.5 to 15lb. Chamberings in 1876 included .22 Long, .32 Long, .38 Long, .44 Long and .46 Long rimfires, plus .40-50, .44-77, .44 Creedmoor (.44-90), .45-45 and .50-70 centrefire. Optional extras included peep-and-globe sights; set triggers; pistol-grip butts; varnished or oiled and polished stocks.

Patent acknowledgements – which can help to date an individual gun – eventually included 3 May 1864; 7 May, 11 June, 12 November, 24 and 31 December 1872; and 9 September 1873. Guns made before 1886 were marked 'E. REMINGTON & SONS, ILION, N.Y.'; later ones customarily bore 'REMINGTON ARMS CO.'.

From 1867 until about 1892, Remington also advertised the **Shotgun No. 1**, with a plain round barrel chambering 16- or 20-bore cartridges; weight was merely 6.5–7lb, depending on barrel length. The Shotgun No. 2 was simply a smaller or 'juvenile' 30-bore No. 1, built on a smaller action.

Announced in the winter of 1872, the New Model Light Rifle, known initially as the 'Gem' and then as the **Sporting Rifle No. 2**, was chambered for .22, .32, .38 or .44 rimfire ammunition, in addition to the .25-20, .32-20, .38-40 and .44-40 centrefire patterns. Made until c. 1910, the No. 2 had a short octagon barrel, a straight-wrist butt, and a concave butt plate. An open semi-buckhorn back sight was standard, and overall weight, according to a January 1876 catalogue, varied from $5\frac{1}{2}$ to 8lb.

The special **Deer Rifle**, introduced in 1872, was chambered specifically for the .46 Long rimfire cartridge. A 24-inch octagon barrel gave an empty weight of just 6.5lb, though the gun was otherwise similar to the standard No. 1. It was joined in 1874 by the **Buffalo Rifle**, which had a 30-inch octagon or round barrel chambering cartridges ranging from .40-50 Sharps to .44-90-400 and .50-70. Built on the No. 1 action, the plain-finish **Hunter, Business and Black Hills rifles** were all introduced in 1875–6, had 28-inch round barrels, weighed 7.5lb, and were chambered exclusively for the .45-70 government cartridge. Deer and Buffalo rifles lasted until 1890, but the others had been abandoned by 1882.

By the mid-1870s, with the buffalo all but gone, Remington's reputation with the hunting fraternity gradually moved to the target range, where a selection of Short- and Mid-Range guns was offered on the No. 1 Sporting Rifle action. Guns of this type were uncommon in the West until the Western Wars of Incorporation petered out with the beginning of the twentieth century.

The finest of all was the legendary Creedmoor, developed by Lewis Hepburn on the basis of the No. 1 sporting rifle action and named after a rifle range – the first of its type in North America – built in 1873 at Creed's Farm, Long Island, on land that had been acquired by the New York State legislature, the embryo National Rifle Association, and the cities of Brooklyn and New York. Additional details of the rolling-block target rifles will be found in John Walter, *Rifles of the World* (second edition, 1998), and in some of the books listed in the Bibliography.

In tandem with the Sharps, the Remington Rolling Block had swept the buffalo from the Great Plains less than twenty years after the Civil War had ended. One ex-buffalo hunter later ventured his opinion that eight out of every ten buffalo had fallen to guns of these particular makes.

Despite its external similarity to the Remington Rolling Blocks, the **Laidley-Emery rifle** was patented on 15 May 1866 by Theodore Laidley and C. A. Emery (US no. 54,743) – though the barrel markings on later Whitney-made examples misleadingly acknowledged patents dating from 17 October 1865, 26 December 1865 and 16 July 1872. Some of these guns also incorporated improvements protected by US Patents no. 112,997 and 115,997, granted to Eli Whitney in March and June 1871.

The Laidley-Emery system was more acceptable militarily than the Remington, owing to its safety features, but was not as simple. The prototype rifle, which Laidley called 'My Chick', showed sufficient promise to be selected by the Secretary of War to take part in service trials in 1866, alongside the Allin Springfield transformation, the Peabody, the so-called 'Split Breech' Remington and the Sharps. However, only the Peabody survived the rigorous programme of over-load charges, the Laidley being blown apart during the second firing.

The Whitney-made Laidley & Emery rifle contained an auxiliary cam, sharing the hammer-pin, which engaged as soon as the radial breech was closed – even though the breech-block may only have moved a short distance. Unlike the Remingtons, the Whitney rifle loaded at half-cock and its hammer did nothing other than strike the firing pin.

The original guns had a thumb-piece on the right side of the breech-block, whereas the Whitney-made post-1872 production version activated the locking cam when the hammer was drawn back to half-cock. Several changes were subsequently made to improve the action, making it simpler and easier to use. The Whitney-Laidley radial-block guns were offered in military guise, as a carbine or rifle, and as a sporting gun with round, half-octagon or full-octagon barrels of 24–30in. A Creedmoor-type target variant had selected woodwork and vernier peep-and-globe sights.

Dexter Smith, son of Horace Smith of Smith & Wesson, made a radial-block shotgun in 1872–5. Patented by Martin Chamberlain of Springfield, Massachusetts, on 14 February 1871 (US no. 111,814), altered by Smith & Chamberlain in March 1871 (112,505), and then improved by Chamberlain alone in July 1872 (129,393), this 12- or 16-bore gun was externally similar to the Remington Rolling Block. However, the breech-block was locked by the tip of the trigger unit.

Proprietor of F. Wesson Firearms Company of Springfield and then Worcester, Massachusetts, **Franklin 'Frank' Wesson** made distinctive 'two-trigger' carbines during the Civil War. These are described in the preceding chapter.

Wesson continued to offer two-trigger guns in sporting guise after the Civil War had ended, eventually supplementing them with a 'Pocket Rifle' made in accordance with US Patent 103,694, granted on 31 May 1870. He also made 'Wesson Creedmoor' target rifles, apparently patented in conjunction with C. N. Cutter in July 1877 (US no. 193,060). However, business failed a mere two years later and the target rifles are so rare that no surviving example could be traced for examination.

Wesson's Pocket Rifle, offered with a detachable shoulder stock, was little more than a long-barrelled pistol. It was loaded by unlatching and then rotating the barrel to the right around a longitudinal pivot. Adequate enough for a glorified pistol, the breech mechanism was not sturdy enough to suit a heavy-barrel rifle; the Creedmoor rifles, therefore, embodied a dropping-block action with a Sharps-type side hammer. The 'No. 1 Long Range Rifle', and the 'No. 2 Long & Mid Range & Hunting Rifle' had distinctive brass frames.

Guns designed by **Joshua Stevens** became increasingly common in the 1880s. Stevens's first products were tipping-barrel pistols, made to a patent dating from September 1864, and the earliest rifles – enlargements of this basic pattern – made little impact in the West. The first tipping-barrel breechloading rifle appeared in 1871, in .22, .32 or .38 with a 26–30in barrel; and from such an unpromising start, the J. Stevens Arms & Tool Company went on to make a tremendous variety of sporting guns.

Virtually all Stevens tipping-barrel rifles shared the simple transverse barrel-lock system and a sliding extractor powered by a jointed lever attached to a pin in the frame. Company catalogues reveal a bewildering variety, ranging from the No. 1 to the No. 16 Crack Shot, but only the largest guns were powerful enough to make an impact westward of the Hundredth Meridian. They were chambered for cartridges such as .22, .32, .38 and .44 (rim- and centrefire) in addition to proprietary loadings ranging from .32-35 to .44-65. Interchangeable-barrel Stevens rifles often had special quick-detachable extractors, while shotguns built on the same basic action were offered in 10-, 12-, 14-, 16- and 20-bore.

Most tipping-barrel Stevens rifles had been discontinued by 1900, as they were not sturdy enough to withstand high-pressure cartridges. They had been supplemented by the Side-Plate rifle, patented by Joshua Stevens on 8 September 1884 and 11 August 1885.

The action was based on a swinging block. An arm on the breech-block ran forward beneath the breech, where it could pivot loosely on a threaded bolt. The arm was connected with an operating lever, doubling as the trigger guard, by way of an intermediate toggle-link which kept the breech closed when the operating lever was in its upper position. The breech-block activated the rocking blade extractor as it fell.

The rifles made with Side Plate actions, in two differing sizes, were apparently confined to 1885–93. Perhaps only 2000 were ever made. Experience showed that the frame was unnecessarily weakened by the removal of the entire right side to facilitate access to the lockwork.

Changes were made to the frame in the late 1880s, when the small action was adapted to become the 1889-pattern 'Favorite', and again when the larger version metamorphosed into the **Stevens No. 44 'Ideal' rifle**. Introduced commercially in 1893, the inexpensive and exceptionally accurate No. 44 sold in vast numbers; Stevens rifles were customarily renowned for the quality of their barrels, whatever deficiencies may have lain in their actions. The No. 44 was originally chambered for cartridges as powerful as .32-40 and .38-55, but these strained the action too greatly and were rapidly discontinued. After 1897, therefore, the No. 44 accepted nothing more potent than .32-20. This restricted its role almost exclusively to target shooting.

Stevens No. 44 rifles were made in a bewildering variety of styles, the most common displaying a 26-inch half-octagon barrel, a straight-wrist butt and a short wooden fore-end with a schnabel tip. However, guns will be encountered with spur, ring and ball-tip breech levers, pistol-grip butts, hooked Schuetzen-style butt plates, nickel plating, engraving, and specially finished woodwork. The extractor was eventually moved from the left side of the action to a central position, but this did not occur until 1901.

Hopkins & Allen offered a dropping-block shotgun in 12 or 16-bore into the 1880s, built on the company's dropping-block rifle action.

Self-Cocking Single-Shot Designs

The 'first generation' breechloaders, characterised by external hammers which had to be thumb-cocked before each shot, were gradually replaced in the 1870s by self-cocking designs.

Among the first was the **Thunderbolt**, made by the Whitney Arms Company (the Whitneyville Armory), owned by Eli Whitney the Younger. Casting around for an exploitable cartridge rifle at the end of the Civil War, Whitney seized on an underlever rifle protected by US Patent no. 36,779, granted on 28 October 1862 to Sebre Howard of Elyria, Ohio, with improvements made by Charles Howard in September and October 1865 (US Patent nos 50,125 and 50,358). The reciprocating breech-bolt was locked by a toggle system, an internal striker being cocked automatically as the bolt ran back.

Howard rifles had a tubular receiver which was virtually an extension of the barrel. Prototypes made during the Civil War may also have had a sliding tube bayonet, but this had been abandoned before production began.

Made by Whitney for Howard Brothers & Company of New Haven, Connecticut, the Thunderbolt was an unsuccessful entrant not only in the US Army breechloading rifle trials of 1865 but also in those convened by the Adjutant General of the State of New York in April 1867. Neither board liked the absence of an external hammer, and the .46 rimfire New York gun was inaccurate.

The Whitney-Howard sporting rifle could chamber virtually any rimfire cartridge from .44 Short to .44 Extra Long; a 54-bore shotgun version was also made in small numbers. A few of these Thunderbolt rifles found their way west in the late 1860s, but were never popular. Far more successful – particularly in military circles – was the **Peabody-Martini**, which superseded the side-hammer Peabody in 1873.

The essence of the Peabody-Martini was a striker within the breech-block, powered by a coil spring, which cocked automatically as the action was opened. The design was extremely successful not only in its US-made form, but also in the guise of the British Martini-Henry service rifle. Turkey ordered 650,000 rifles in 1873, while others went to Romania and a few equipped US state militiamen. However, only small quantities of sporting rifles were made in .43, .45-70 and '.45 Necked', though a Mid-Range Creedmoor target rifle was offered with a long half-octagon barrel, woodwork of superior quality, and vernier globe-and-peep sights. The Providence Tool Company was never able to establish the Peabody sporting rifles on the market, failing in 1886.

The **Ward-Burton** took a different approach. The experimental .50-calibre 'Model 1871' military rifle had been recommended, admittedly without enthusiasm, by the St Louis trials board. Derived from patents granted to Bethel Burton in December 1859 and August 1868, the Ward-Burton was stocked in the manner of a Trapdoor Springfield but locked by engaging interrupted threads on the rear of the bolt in the walls of the receiver. The extractor and the ejector were both mounted on the detachable bolt head; a bolt-lock catch was let into the right rear side of the receiver. Cartridges were ignited by a spring-loaded firing pin contained in the bolt.

On 31 May 1871, the Chief of Ordnance, General Alexander Dyer, wrote to inform the Secretary of War that 1000 rifles and 300 Ward-Burton carbines had been ordered from Springfield Armory. When the first guns were issued for troop trials in March 1872, official returns showed that 1015 rifles and 317 carbines had been made.

The Ward-Burton deserved a better fate. Among its better features, rare in a bolt-action design of its day, was the retraction of the firing pin into the bolt as the breech opened. However, few of the company commanders supervising its trials reported favourably. A major complaint concerned the absence of an external hammer, which would have allowed the state of cocking to be told at a glance. Some men greeted the Ward-Burton with enthusiasm – when new, it extracted and ejected very well – but their views changed for the worse when parts began to break with exasperating frequency.

Multi-Shot Designs

One of the most basic of all repeating firearms is the two-barrelled shotgun, which was popular west of the Hundredth Meridian even before the Civil War began. Many of the guns were imports, ranging from the cheapest products of Birmingham and Liége to the finest Europe could offer.

Although the development of the self-contained shotgun cartridge owed much to work undertaken in France, many of the greatest advances in shotgun design were British. The top lever was allegedly proposed by Samuel Matthews of Birmingham as early as 1857, though the earliest appropriate patent was granted to Westley Richards on 24 September 1858 (British no. 2149/58). This pre-dated the first grant to Matthews virtually by five years.

Richards is also credited with the design of the 'Doll's Head' bolt, patented in Britain in September 1862, while the classical under-bolt locking mechanism was added by James Purdey in 1863 and the 'Wedge Fast' system was perfected by William Greener in 1873.

Among the earliest of the North American hammer doubles were guns made by **Ethan Allen** in accordance with US Patent no. 49,491 granted on 22 August 1865. A pivoting latch set into the right side of the hinged breech-block locked the block into the frame. The patent also showed a ratchet extractor, operated by a finger-ring, but a conventional trigger guard appeared on guns made in 1868–71.

As far as multi-shot rifled firearms were concerned, the end of the Civil War found the Federal ordnance authorities in disarray. Belated efforts had been made to standardise the .56-50 Spencer rifle cartridge for breechloading weapons acquired after 1864, but had only been partially successful. By 1866, cavalrymen were carrying a variety of carbines. Most of the regulars had Sharps or Spencers, but state units had greater variety: .56-52 Joslyns survived in Nevada and Ohio into 1867. As late as 1869, the Ordnance Department approved the issue of 1000 cap-lock Smith carbines to militia cavalry in the Dakotas.

The Spencer was well proven in battle, but, though temporarily retained for cavalrymen, it lacked sufficient power for infantry use. Although the advantages had been clearly demonstrated by the Civil War, breechloaders were still regarded as too wasteful of ammunition to be trusted to the common soldier.

The .45-70 Springfield rifle was reasonably successful as an infantry weapon, but the cavalry carbine was less popular – particularly with men who had used Spencer repeaters. Groups of men armed with magazine rifles had often repulsed Indian bands many times their size, but the substitution of single-shot Springfields had greatly reduced the margins of superiority.

The Civil War had given the US Army an unrivalled opportunity to test magazine rifles under combat conditions, but the lessons were largely overlooked once fighting had ceased and the military establishment had regained its peacetime status. Union commanders soon forgot how their Spencer-armed men had repulsed Confederates outnumbering them many times over, advocating instead the issue of simple single-shot guns 'the men could understand'.

Yet hopeful inventors still submitted magazine rifles to official trials. Experiments undertaken in 1872–3, leading to the adoption of the .45-70 Trapdoor Springfield, had included repeaters submitted on behalf of Scott, Ward & Burton and Winchester. Even a Swiss Vetterli rifle had been used as a comparison.

The .45-calibre **Ward-Burton** Magazine Musket, no. 97, was the only bolt-action rifle to qualify for the final stages of the 1872–3 trials. Derived from the .50 rifle and carbine models of 1870, which had been issued for field trials, No. 97 combined the bolt mechanism of the single-shot guns with a tube magazine beneath the barrel. A sliding cut-off could hold the contents of the magazine in reserve when appropriate, and the back of the magazine follower was coated with gutta-percha to protect cartridges from recoil. Primers were seated in a deep pocket in the cartridge-case head to prevent premature ignition.

The Board of Officers recommended the purchase of Ward-Burton magazine rifles for trials with the cavalry, but this progressive opinion was rejected by Brigadier General Dyer. Thus the cavalry, which had begun the decade at least partly armed with Spencer magazine carbines, was condemned to the single-shot 'Trapdoor' Springfield for many more years.

Although a few **Spencer** sporting rifles were made in immediate post-war days, the rapid failure of the Spencer Repeating Arms Company – the assets were acquired by Fogerty in 1868 – cleared the field for Oliver Winchester.

The assets and liabilities of the New Haven Arms Company, deep in financial trouble, were purchased by the Winchester Repeating Arms Company in 1865. Oliver Winchester had sold his stake in a shirt-making partnership to become a full-time arms baron, and had gained 1500 $100 shares in the new gunmaking business in return for signing over rights to patents previously controlled by the New Haven firm.

Oliver Winchester had previously obtained a charter from the state of Connecticut permitting him to incorporate the 'Henry Repeating Rifle Company'. Exactly what happened is no longer known, but Benjamin Henry had soon departed, possibly after a disagreement over the transformation of the Henry rifle into the gate-loading Winchester.

The **Winchester Model 1866** was little more than a Henry improved by strengthening the extractor and adding a hinged loading gate designed by Nelson King on the right side of the frame. The gate was a great improvement, as it allowed the firer to reload the magazine virtually without taking his eyes off the target. The loading gate also permitted the magazine tube to be fixed in place, protected by a conventional wooden fore-end.

A minor change was made in the cartridge, where the powder charge was increased from 25 to 28 grains and a reduction in projectile weight (to 200 grains) increased muzzle velocity. Though the new rifle still lacked power, and could still be clogged by mud or dust entering the top of the receiver, it was a far better weapon than the Henry had been.

The Model 1866 was made as a 9–9.5lb rifle, with a 24-inch round or octagon barrel; as an 8.25lb musket, with a 27-inch round barrel; or as a 7.5lb carbine, with a 20-inch round barrel. The rifle and the muskets each held a maximum of seventeen rounds, though a couple of cartridges were customarily omitted to prevent straining the magazine spring; carbines nominally held thirteen rounds.

Comparatively few guns were made in 1866, as the factory moved from New Haven; excepting the first year's production, therefore, all Model 1866 rifles numbered below 125,000 were made in nearby Bridgeport. Guns of this type were still being listed in Winchester catalogues long after the advent of the Model 1873. As late as 1891, 1000 Model 1866 rifles were assembled from old components, chambered for .44 S&W centrefire cartridges and sold to Brazil.

The shotguns made by the **Meriden** Manufacturing Company – and then by Parker Brothers & Company – of West Meriden, Connecticut, were protected by US Patent no. 59,723 granted on 13 November 1866 to William Miller. They were locked by a sprung bar in the top of the breech, which was disengaged by raising a latch vertically ahead of the trigger guard. Meriden guns were sturdy, cheap and efficient enough to find a ready market. Made in 10- and 12-bore, with barrels of 24–32in, they were being marketed commercially by the spring of 1868.

The great success of the 1873- and 1876-pattern Winchester rifles, due as much to good fortune as efficacy, severely damaged the prospects of potential rivals. Among them had been the **Fogerty rifle**, based on patents granted to Valentine Fogerty of Boston, Massachusetts on 23 October 1866 (US no. 59,126) and 6 October 1868 (82,819). The guns were made by the Fogerty Arms Company, which was reorganised as the 'American Repeating Rifle Company' in the autumn of 1867.

Offered in musket, carbine or sporting-rifle guise, the lever-action Fogerty had a tube magazine in the butt. It bore a superficial external resemblance to the Spencer, but the receiver was noticeably more rounded – almost tubular – and the carrier-block fed rimfire cartridges laterally into the breech as the underlever was operated.

The .50-calibre musket was stocked to the muzzle and had three barrel bands; the .45 rimfire carbine had a half-stock and a single band; and the fore-end of the .40 rimfire sporting rifle was held to the barrel by a screw. The sporter also had a pewter or German silver fore-end tip, and could be supplied with a folding vernier back sight on the tang.

Even though the remnants of the moribund Spencer Repeating Rifle Company had been absorbed, production of Fogerty rifles was never large. Fewer than 5000 were made in 1867–9 and, on 6 August 1869, the Winchester Repeating Rifle Company launched a successful bid for the assets and liabilities of the American Repeating Arms Company. The Fogerty rifle disappeared into history, and Winchester resold the production machinery at a profit of $32,000.

On 10 April 1866, **Sylvester Roper** of Roxbury, Massachusetts, was granted US Patent no. 53,881 to protect an idiosyncratic shotgun which amalgamated a reciprocating breech-bolt and a revolving cylinder-type magazine. Retracting the hammer until it was held on the sear not only withdrew the breech-bolt, extracting a spent cartridge from the barrel, but also allowed a spring to revolve the magazine until a new cartridge aligned with the chamber. Pulling the trigger released the bolt to fly forward, chambering and firing in a 'slam bang' motion.

The hammer could be lowered on to the chamber and then pulled back to an intermediate position, from where it could deliver enough of a blow to ignite the cap on the cartridge-base nipple without partially extracting the case.

Made originally in 16- and then also in 12-bore by the Roper Repeating Rifle Company of Amherst, Massachusetts, the slam-fire shotgun was not particularly successful. Most surviving examples incorporate a detachable choke protected by US Patent 79,861, granted to Roper in July 1868, but production was never large.

The Roper Sporting Arms Company was formed in Hartford in March 1869 to exploit the Roper patents, though effectively little more than a partnership between Christopher Spencer and Charles Billings. Small-scale production of .40-calibre rifles and 12-bore shotguns continued into the early 1870s but never made much impact.

Robinson rifles, made by A. S. Babbitt and then by the Adirondack Fire Arms Company of Plattsburg, New York, were another of Winchester's rivals. The earlier rifle was patented on 24 May 1870 by Orvil Robinson of Upper Jay, New York (US no. 103,504). A reciprocating breech-bolt, locked by a pivoting block in its undersurface, was operated by squeezing together two knurled finger-pieces on the rear of the bolt and then pulling them backward: a crude method which lacked the mechanical advantage found in most lever actions.

Robinson may have realised the shortcomings of his first design, patenting an improved 'New Model' on 23 April 1872 (US no. 125,988). The breech was locked by a toggle bar and opened by pulling upward on a retractor protruding from the right side of the gun above the loading gate. Unusually, the New Model Robinson could be loaded from either side of the receiver.

Neither Robinson rifle was made in quantity, as Winchester, taking the threat of rivalry seriously, bought the patent rights in 1874 – Adirondack was then apparently in dire straits financially – and promptly scrapped the rifles. Survivors are invariably .44 rimfire Old Models made to the 1870 patent.

One of the quirkiest of the magazine rifles touted in the USA in the years immediately after the Civil War was the **Evans** Magazine Rifle, protected by patents granted to Warren Evans of Thomaston, Maine, on 8 December 1868 (US no. 84,685) and 18 September 1871 (no. 119,020). Made by the Evans Rifle Manufacturing Company of Mechanic Falls, Maine, and unsuccessfully promoted by Merwin & Hulbert primarily as a military rifle, the Evans was offered as a sporter when the US Army prudently ignored it after a trials gun had comprehensively failed the standard dust test.

The lever action embodied a Spencer-like radial block, but fed from an Archimedean-screw magazine which formed the spine of the butt and could hold up to 34 of the proprietary short-case .44 rimfire cartridges. However, even this perceived advantage could be attained only at the expense of great weight and complexity. The fluted cartridge carrier made a quarter-turn each time the underlever was operated, presenting a new cartridge to the breech.

Evans military rifles were fully stocked, with 30in barrels and socket bayonets; half-stocked carbines had 22in barrels; and the sporters, with 26–30in

BUFFALO BILL CODY

Born in Scott County, Iowa, on 26 February 1846, William Frederick 'Buffalo Bill' Cody began working as a mounted messenger-boy when he was barely eleven; by his teens, he was an accomplished rider and an excellent shot. After serving during the Civil War, he worked for the US Army as a scout and dispatch rider, then became a hunter for the Kansas Pacific Rail Road.

Cody has been credited with downing more than 4000 buffalo in eight months, mostly with the help of a .50-70 1866-pattern single-shot Trapdoor Springfield rifle nicknamed 'Lucretia Borgia'. His wide knowledge of the terrain also enabled him to work as a scout and guide for the 5th Cavalry in 1868–76, taking part in many Indian campaigns.

Cody always had a sense of theatre, starring as early at 1872 in Ned Buntline's play *The Scouts of the Prairie*, and organised his first Wild West exhibition in 1883. Bolstered between seasons by guiding hunting parties of European nobility, Cody was able to project a colourful (if sanitised) image of the Wild West around the world – though never able to keep his own fortune intact. He was still working only a few weeks before his death in Denver, Colorado, on 10 January 1917.

Buffalo Bill Cody was the recipient of many presentation weapons, including a .44 Evans magazine sporting rifle given to him by its promoters in May 1877. Several types of 'Suicide Special' revolver may also be found with 'Buffalo Bill' markings on the cylinders, frames or barrels, but none should be associated personally with the great showman.

octagon barrels, had half-length fore-ends and a selection of sights. A typical sporting rifle weighed about 8lb empty.

The Wesson Fire Arms Company was formed on 27 May 1867 by Daniel Wesson, Franklin Wesson, Horace Smith and J. W. Storrs. The 12-bore drop-barrel **Wesson shotguns** were opened by pushing forward on a thumb-lever above the breech. They incorporated features patented by Daniel Wesson, John Blaze and John Stokes between 17 December 1867 (US no. 72,434) and 24 November 1868 (no. 84,314), but only about 200 guns were made before the assets of the company were sold in 1870 – apparently to Dexter Smith (q.v.).

After toying with a sliding-barrel pinfire shotgun based on the Howard-patent Thunderbolt rifle (q.v.), Eli Whitney the Younger, Charles Gerner and Frank Tiesing received US Patent 93,149 on 27 July 1869. This protected a drop-barrel action locked by a lever ahead of the trigger guard.

The **Whitney shotguns** made in 1869–70 lacked a guard for the barrel-release catch, but an auxiliary bow was subsequently forged in the trigger guard. They were among the cheapest of the double-barrel guns available in the West. One gun was used by part-time dentist and sometime killer John H. 'Doc' Holliday, but sales were not brisk enough to allow work to continue after 1875.

Although the Model 1866 Winchester was very successful, its utility was limited by the weakness of its cartridge. Unlike single-shot Sharps and Remington rifles, Winchesters could not be used successfully for long-range hunting. Attempts to convert the Model 1866 for a more powerful centrefire cartridge, therefore, resulted in the **Winchester Model 1873**.

Offered as a rifle, a carbine, or a military-style musket with a bayonet, it was chambered for .32-30, .38-40 or .44-40 centrefire cartridges, introduced in 1882, 1879 and 1873 respectively. A similar-looking .22 rimfire version, made for twenty years from 1884 onward, was readily identified by the omission of the loading port from the right side of the receiver.

Some guns were made with half-round/half-octagon barrels, while others had half-length magazine tubes, set triggers, rubber shotgun-pattern butt plates or special decoration. The Model 1873 was discontinued in the early 1920s after 720,610 had been made.

The first 'hammer double' **Remington shotgun**, known as the Model 1874, was patented in the USA by Andrew Whitmore on 8 August 1871 (no. 117,843) and 16 April 1872 (no. 122,775). Pushing forward on the thumb-piece of the top-lever withdrew a longitudinally sliding bolt from lugs under the breech. The guns were offered only in 10-, 12- and 16-bore, with barrels of rolled or damascus-twist steel, but action faults hastened their demise in 1878.

The breech of the original **Fox** double-barrelled hammer shotgun, made by the American Arms Company of Boston, Massachusetts, pivoted laterally to the right in accordance with US Patent no. 98,579, granted on 4 January 1870 to

BILLY THE KID

William H. Bonney Jr, was born in New York on 23 November 1859, possibly as William Henry McCarty. He migrated with his parents to Kansas, but his father died and his mother moved first to Colorado – on remarriage – and thence to New Mexico. Beginning his law-breaking exploits in his teens, Bonney, best known by the nickname 'Billy the Kid', roamed the south-western states of the USA. During this period he killed several men and, though the number remains in dispute, had attained considerable notoriety. He was captured near Stinking Springs, New Mexico, in December 1880 by Sheriff Pat Garrett, tried by judge and jury in Mesilla, convicted and sentenced to hang. However, The Kid escaped from Lincoln County Jail in April 1881, killing Deputy Sheriff Bob Ollinger, and remained at large until tracked down by Garrett and his posse. Garrett shot Billy the Kid dead in the evening of 14 June 1881, when the outlaw was hiding on a ranch owned by Peter Marshall.

Billy the Kid is known to have favoured Winchester rifles and Colt revolvers, among them being .44-40 WCF Winchester M1873 carbine no. 20181. Although he carried a new .41 double-action gun in 1878, a .44-40 Single Action Army revolver was surrendered to Garrett's posse in December 1880. He also used Deputy Sheriff Ollinger's own 10-bore Whitney shotgun, no. 903, to shoot the lawman and retained it until killed by Pat Garrett.

George Fox of Boston. The guns did not become available in large numbers until the mid-1870s, and only a few had been made before an improvement was patented by Fox and Henry Wheeler on 6 November 1877 (US no. 196,749). The side-swinging action was simple and strong, but by no means new – many comparable guns had been made in Europe prior to the American Civil War.

On 31 August 1875, William Baker of Lisle, New York, received US Patent 167,293 to protect a gun-lock opened by pressing the front trigger forward. **Baker shotguns** lacked external operating levers or breech latches, and could fool the uninitiated until the secret of the trigger-release was known. Side-lock shotguns and a few European-style combination guns, with two smooth-bore barrels above a single rifle, were made by W. H. Baker & Sons Company of Syracuse, New York, until 1880.

The Model 1873 Winchester rifle was more successful than its 1866-vintage predecessor had been, but still lacked sufficient power to lure buffalo hunters away from their dropping-block Sharps and rolling-block Remingtons merely with a promise of magazine feed.

Buffalo were so numerous on the plains in the early days of the West that it scarcely mattered if a shot was missed. Yet there were outstanding marksmen on the plains, and tales were told of how the best men hardly ever wasted a shot at prodigious ranges.

DOC HOLLIDAY

John Henry 'Doc' Holliday was born in Griffin, Georgia, in March 1852. Graduating from the Pennsylvania College of Dental Surgery in 1872, Holliday briefly practised in Dallas, Texas, before finding his true vocation as a gambler and card-sharp. He may have married Catherine 'Big-Nose Kate' Elder in Dodge City, but had abandoned Elder by 1882. Holliday is best remembered as a lieutenant of Wyatt Earp during the Gunfight at the OK Corral in October 1881, but died from tuberculosis in Glenwood Springs, Colorado, in November 1887. His favourite gun was apparently a Belgian-made 'Meteor' double-barrelled hammer shotgun with the butt cut-down to the pistol grip and barrel merely 12in long. He has been linked with Colt Single Action Army revolver no. 102077, and is also said to have carried small revolvers and cartridge derringers (though none have yet been linked with his name).

The single-shot rifles fired heavy bullets from capacious cartridge cases, to give far higher muzzle energies than .44-40 WCF. Realising that ground was being lost, experiments with more powerful rounds began in New Haven. A .45-70-405 lever-action rifle patented by Luke Wheelock on 31 January 1871 (US no. 111,500), tested unsuccessfully during the US Army repeating rifle trials of 1872–3, was developed into a series of **Winchester Model 1876** prototypes shown publicly at the Philadelphia Centennial Exposition.

Knowledgeable critics acclaimed the rifles, realising that the action was much stronger than preceding Winchesters and could chamber cartridges capable of downing the biggest North American game.

The Model 1876 was eventually adapted to handle .40-60, .45-60, .45-75 and .50-95, gaining favour not so much with the plainsmen – who had already pursued the buffalo to the edge of extinction – but with ranchers and dilettante Easterners who came westward to seek their fortunes or set sail for Africa.

The Winchesters were used by Theodore Roosevelt, who recorded appreciation of his .45-75 rifle in his books. A particularly impressive gun, engraved by John Ulrich, was presented in 1881 to the Civil War hero General Philip H. Sheridan, and full-stock carbines were purchased by the Royal North-West Mounted Police of Canada in the 1880s. When production of 1876-type Winchesters finally ceased, in favour of the Model 1886, 63,871 had been made.

Handguns

Single-Shot Pistols

Designed by Henry Hammond of Naubuc, Connecticut, patented on 23 January 1866 and made until 1868 by the Connecticut Arms Company of Glastonbury, Connecticut, the **Hammond Bulldog** (or 'Bulldozer') was an angular and unattractive derringer chambered for cartridges ranging from .22 Short rimfire to .50. The .32 and .41 rimfire versions were most common. The Hammond barrel was released by a breech-top catch, pivoting to the left to expose the chamber. Long-barrel guns – made only in small numbers – were sold complete with shoulder stocks to convert them into light, but practically useless carbines.

Patented on 2 October 1866, chambering a special teat-fire cartridge patented by David Williamson in 1864, the **Williamson** was a single-shot convertible derringer capable of handling rimfire cartridges or powder-and-ball. The adaptor consisted of an iron tube – resembling an empty cartridge case – with a nipple to accept a conventional percussion cap. Once the hammer had been thumbed back to half-cock and the barrel-locking catch had been pressed, the Williamson barrel could be slid forward to expose the breech. Ignition was supplied by a central hammer, with a blade to fire the cartridges above a small projection to ignite caps.

About 5000 Williamsons were made in 1866–7 by Moore's Patent Fire Arms Company of Brooklyn. They were about 5¼in long, had 2½in barrels and weighed only about 9oz. Frames and trigger guards were brass castings, but were customarily nickel or (rarely) silver plated.

The **Bacon** Arms Company, after falling foul of Smith & Wesson and Rollin White, made single-shot .32 rimfire swinging-barrel derringers instead of small-calibre revolvers.

The **Southerner** derringer was made by the Merrimack Arms & Manufacturing Company of Newburyport, Massachusetts (1867–9), and then by the equally short-lived Brown Manufacturing Company (1869–73). Especially popular below the Mason-Dixon Line, the Southerner originally offered a 2½in barrel which could be swung laterally after a catch set in the frame had been released. Brown produced a handful of long-barrel guns, with square-heel butts instead of the traditional bird's head style, but they were never successful.

The derringer patented on 22 June 1869 by **Charles Ballard**, made by Ballard & Fairbanks in Worcester, Massachusetts, was a single-shot .41 rimfire pistol with a barrel which could be tipped down to expose the chamber once a knurled catch on the barrel-block had been pushed forward to disengage the frame. Most Ballards had a distinctive ejector operated by a toothed rack. They also had frames of brass or iron, often nickel-plated, with a distinctive spur on the backstrap. Grips were rosewood or walnut.

The derringer made by **Forehand & Wadsworth** was another single-barrel .41 rimfire pattern, made in quantity in 1871–3 but available commercially as late as 1889. It resembled the Southerner externally, complete with a bird's head grip, but had a rounded fore-end.

Moore's Patent Fire Arms Company and its successor, the National Arms Company of Brooklyn, made a derringer of their own design alongside the

Williamson (q.v.). Designed by Daniel Moore and protected by US Patent no. 31,473 of 19 February 1861, the .41 rimfire **National** Model No.1 'Knuckle Duster' single-shot pistol – brass framed, often nickel plated – had a sheath trigger and a barrel which pivoted laterally to give access to the breech.

The design was clumsy, but very durable. Guns made before the patent had been granted may display 'PAT. PEND.', whereas later examples have full patent markings, refinements to the hammer, and an improved breech catch. Some guns had blade-pattern extractors, others had none. The Model No. 2 was similar, but the gap between the trigger and the grip was increased to prevent cramping the fingers unnecessarily, and walnut or rosewood grip-plates were fitted.

National was purchased by **Colt** in 1870, though production of the No. 1 and No. 2 derringers continued in the Hartford factory unchanged except for manufacturer's marks. Including a few guns with National markings and others assembled from Brooklyn-made parts before work in Hartford had commenced, Colt is estimated to have made about 7000 No. 1 and 9000 No. 2 derringers; most were sold in matched pairs, decorated with hand-engraved scrollwork.

The .41 rimfire Colt No. 3 derringer or **Colt-Thuer**, designed by F. Alexander Thuer, was another single-shot design. The 2½in barrel pivoted sideways to give access to the breech and had an automatic extractor. No. 3 Colts were made with walnut or rosewood bird's head grips, though ivory and mother-of-pearl could be obtained to order. A few were offered in .41 centrefire, while others differed in barrel length. The earliest guns had a pronounced bolster or reinforcement on the frame beneath the barrel, but straight frames were soon substituted. Changes were made to the radius of the grip, and the height of the hammer spur was raised to facilitate cocking. About 45,000 No. 3 Colts had been made when production finally ceased in 1912.

Easily made, cheap and correspondingly popular, the Colt-Thuer derringer was copied by many enterprising gunmakers. Among the near-replicas were the 'O.K.' and 'Victor' pistols made by John Marlin of New Haven, Connecticut, and the differing 'XL' patterns made by Marlin or Hopkins & Allen. Similar guns could still be obtained from Hopkins & Allen and Forehand & Wadsworth, as late as 1889.

The distinctive **Remington Vest Pocket Pistol** of 1865 had a rolling-block breech and a distinctive saw-handle grip. Offered in .41 and .22 rimfire, in addition to an extremely scarce .32 version, the Vest Pocket Model was quite popular; production prior to 1888 has been estimated at about 50,000 guns.

The .41 version, acknowledging an additional patent date (15 November 1864) was 5½in long, had a 4in barrel and weighed 11–12oz. It was supplied in blue or nickel finish, or with blued barrel and nickelled frame. The standard grips were walnut, lacquered or varnished, but ivory and mother-of-pearl could be supplied to order.

The **Remington-Elliott** 'Deringer Pistol', made in accordance with US Patent 68,292, granted on 27 August 1867 to William Elliott of Plattsburg, New York, was a single-barrel .41 rimfire pattern with a hammer doubling as the breech-block. Although new guns were still available 'from stock' as late as 1888, it seems unlikely that much production had been undertaken after the early 1870s. Remington-Elliott pistols were $4\frac{7}{8}$in overall, had $2\frac{1}{2}$in barrels, and weighed merely 7oz. The standard blued form – with walnut bird's head grips – cost $7 in 1876, compared with $3.75 for the large Vest Pocket Pistol and $8 for the over/under 'Double Repeating Deringer Pistol' (sic).

Among other types of **single-barrel pistol** were those made by Morgan & Clapp: sheath-trigger .32-calibre guns with barrels which could be swung laterally – similar to the Southerner (q.v.), but without the characteristic step in the frame near the hammer. Joshua Stevens and others made some .32 single-shot drop-barrel pistols which could, by stretching the imagination, be regarded as personal-defence weapons.

Revolvers

Many of the cap-lock revolvers used during the Civil War survived into post-war days; indeed, many manufacturing contracts were still being fulfilled long after fighting had ceased. Colt and Remington designs were the most common, though substantial numbers of rimfire Smith & Wessons – generally regarded as toys in the West – were also to be found. Details of the major designs will be found in the previous chapter.

Catalogues published by E. Remington & Sons in 1884 still offered cap-lock revolvers such as the .31 Rider, .31 New Model Pocket or .36 New Model Navy, Belt and Police designs. This confirms that muzzleloaders were still common in the most inaccessible districts of North America long after being displaced in more progressive districts.

Among the most interesting derringers was the '**My Friend**' knuckle-duster revolver, made in accordance with US Patent no. 51,572 granted to James Reid of Catskill, New York, on 26 December 1865. Offered in seven-shot .22, five-shot .32 and five-shot .41 versions, 'My Friends' had flat frames with a prominent finger-hole and an elongated cylinder contained within the solid top. Sliding catches to lock the hammer between the chambers were fitted to some (but by no means all) the .22 and .32 guns, and almost always appeared on the .41 type. About 20,000 guns were made in 1865–80, including only about 500 in .41 rimfire. The barrelless guns were superseded by a short-barrel pattern, but work ceased altogether in 1884.

Realising the value of metallic-case ammunition, and also wary of the litigious reputation gained by Smith & Wesson and Rollin White, **Remington** contracted in February 1868 to convert .44 cap-lock New Model Army revolvers to .46 rimfire. Deliveries totalling 4141 were made to Benjamin Kittredge & Company of Cincinnati between 28 October 1868 and 1 April 1869, plus 400 to J. W. Storrs, 31 to M. W. Robinson & Company, and a single example to Wexell & DeGress.

New five-round cylinders, fitted in Remington's Ilion factory, were clearly marked 'APRIL 3, 1855' in acknowledgement of the Rollin White patent. They were shipped to Smith & Wesson for inspection where, though the first fifty were all initially rejected, 4524 guns successfully passed the tests without problems. Kittredge paid Smith & Wesson \$3.36¼ per gun, a one-dollar royalty being deducted before the monies were passed to Remington. Most of the guns ultimately went westward, making these particular cartridge conversions much more common west of the Mississippi than in eastern districts.

Conversions of the .36 cap-lock New Model Navy Revolver to fire .38 centrefire ammunition were made until the liquidation of E. Remington & Sons, assembly finally ceasing in 1888. However, guns of this type were never made in quantity; the basic design was rooted too firmly in cap-lock traditions to be popular.

The purchase of the Rollin White patent of 1855 by Smith & Wesson, virtually unnoticed, assumed paramount importance for **Colt** after the end of the Civil War. Although the patent supposedly expired in 1869, Smith & Wesson, through a series of appeals, managed to prolong its effect until 1872.

In November 1865, Brigadier General William Franklin, who had assumed the vice-presidency of Colt after the death of Elisha Root, attempted to purchase a licence to the Rollin White patent. Negotiations continued until Smith & Wesson and Rollin White asked for a total of \$1.1 million and the project foundered. Franklin and his advisers calculated that this was too great an investment in a patent that had only three years to run.

The first successful Colt conversion system was patented by F. Alexander Thuer of Hartford, Connecticut, on 15 September 1868 (US no. 82,258). Marketed briefly in 1869–70, Thuer Transformation revolvers were converted from .31 1849 Pocket, .36 1851 Navy, .44 1860 Army, .36 1861 Navy, and .36 1862 Police and Pocket (Navy) cap-locks. Total production was apparently about 5000, though no factory records were kept.

The standard cylinders were shortened or replaced to allow an auxiliary ring to be placed between the cylinder and the recoil shield. The chambers were bored completely through the cylinder, but were loaded from the front with unique tapered copper-case cartridges. The cartridges were fired by the nose of the original hammer striking a rebounding firing pin in the auxiliary ring.

A thumb-piece on top of the unit allowed the Thuer guns to fire normally when turned to the right; rotated to the left, it allowed an ejecting arm in the auxiliary ring to expel either a spent case or a loaded cartridge each time the hammer was cocked and fired.

The ejector arm struck the side of the case-head which – in theory at least – enabled a primed cartridge to be safely expelled. In practice, it carried more than a hint of danger.

Although the Thuer conversion could revert to cap-lock operation, requiring nothing other than a spare cylinder, it was comparatively inefficient. It was tested by the US Army in 1868–9, but was unacceptable militarily; neither could it compete satisfactorily with the contemporary centrefire Smith & Wessons. The Thuer system was abandoned in 1871.

The first large-calibre **Smith & Wesson** revolver was the .41 rimfire Model No. 3, approximately fifty of which were made prior to the Paris exposition of 1867. The gun had a sheath trigger and a four-cartridge cylinder. It weighed only 17oz, but its weak construction attracted so much adverse comment in Europe that the project was abandoned.

The failure of the Model No. 3 left Smith & Wesson without a large-calibre revolver efficient enough to challenge the cap-lock Colts. With the White patent nearing the end of its life, Colt would clearly produce a revolver with a bored-through cylinder as soon as practicable.

The first top-break Smith & Wesson revolver, with the hinge moved to the bottom front of the frame, appeared in 1868. A sturdy latch lay ahead of the hammer, while the new star-plate extractor was attached to a hollow central tube containing a rack mechanism. This extracted spent cartridge cases when the barrel was depressed, enabling them to be shaken free. At the limit of the opening stroke, the extractor snapped back into place to allow the gun to be reloaded.

Mindful of problems that had arisen back in the days of the Massachusetts Arms Company, when a patent-infringement lawsuit brought by Colt had been so costly, Smith & Wesson's attorneys mounted a careful search of existing records. Early in 1869, therefore, the partners acquired rights to a simultaneous extraction system patented by William Dodge of Washington DC on 17 January ('cartridge retractor for many-chambered firearm', no. 45,912) and 24 January 1865 ('revolving firearm', 45,983); a ratchet integral with the extractor for rotating the cylinder, patented by Louis Rodier of Springfield, Massachusetts, on 11 July 1865 (no. 48,775) and assigned to Samuel Norris; and a cylinder and barrel 'swinging away from the recoil shield', which had been patented by Abram Gibson of Worcester, Massachusetts, on 10 July 1860 (29,126) and assigned in part to Joseph Hale.

Acquiring these rights allowed Smith & Wesson to apply for protection in Britain in April 1869, Letters Patent being granted to an agent, Robert Lake, on 17 May 1869. A similar US patent, 94,003, was issued on 24 August 1869 to Charles King, Smith & Wesson's factory superintendent.

The first new Model No. 3 revolver was dispatched in May 1870 to a US Army Board of Officers convened in St Louis. The gun resembled the patent model, though a conventionally guarded trigger had been substituted for the original sheath pattern. Apart from recommending a change from rim- to centrefire ammunition, the Board of Ordnance and Fortification considered the Smith & Wesson 'superior to any other ... submitted'. A centrefire cartridge was produced simply by adapting .44 Henry rimfire to produce .44/100.

The first US Army contract, signed on 28 December 1870, called for 1000 'Model No. 3 Army Revolvers', 800 to be blued and the remainder nickelled. The consignment was delivered in March 1871, the guns displaying a small 'U.S.' on the barrel rib and the mark of government inspector O. W. Ainsworth – a cursive 'OWA' – pressed into the left grip.

Smith & Wesson saw considerable commercial potential in their new guns and shipped samples to their dealers in the summer of 1870; bulk shipments began late in the autumn.

The original Model No. 3, known as the 'First Model No. 3 American' after the introduction of Russian-type guns, underwent many minor variations during the first years of its life. The most obvious change was the deletion of the oil hole in the extractor housing, which disappeared in the region of gun number 1500. The revolvers were blued or nickel plated, and had barrels measuring 6, 7 or 8in.

Production continued after the acceptance of the Russian contract, described below, until the end of 1871. Smith & Wesson then saw the futility of making two separate .44 revolver frames. About 6800 'American' guns were made. Virtually all had chambered .44 centrefire cartridges, though 200 had been assembled by 1870 for .44 Henry rimfire. These had a modified frame and hammer, but otherwise duplicated the centrefire version.

About 9000 **Richards** Transformations or 'Colt's New Breechloading Army Revolvers' were built exclusively on 1860- or Army-pattern frames. Unlike the Thuer system, which was designed as an evasion of the Rollin White patent, Charles Richards used a conventional rimmed cartridge loaded from the rear. The Rollin White patent had expired and Colt could no longer be sued for infringement.

Patented on 25 July 1871 (US no. 117,461), the system relied on a circular disc or 'Conversion Plate' inserted in the breech behind a shortened, but otherwise standard cylinder. Unlike the Thuer disc, which could rotate laterally, the Richards pattern was held in place by the cylinder pin and a projection engaging the hammer channel. It contained a spring-loaded rebounding firing pin.

The original rammer of the cap-lock M1860 was replaced by an ejector case, attached to the right side of the barrel, while a pivoting gate – latched initially by an internal plunger and then by an external leaf spring – was incorporated in the conversion plate.

The conventionally loaded Richards transformation was much more effectual than the Thuer evasion. It attracted sufficient US Army interest for the conversion of 1000 M1860 army revolvers to be approved by the Secretary of War in January 1871. On 21 April 1871, Brigadier General Alexander Dyer, the Chief of Ordnance, informed the officer commanding Springfield Armory that 1153 revolvers had been sent to Colt from differing collection points and that 'with the fifty to which you were directed to apply the Locke Safety Notch [on] January 31 1871, will make 1203'.

Writing in 1873, William Franklin confirmed that 'Twelve hundred of them [M1860 conversions] are now in service with the Cavalry, and we hear excellent reports from them'. Small numbers, apparently totalling 368 guns, were subsequently converted on behalf of the US Navy in 1873–5. These included a variety of 1851- and 1861-pattern .36 navy cap-locks, which were altered to fire .38 centrefire cartridges.

The **Richards-Mason** Transformation was a variant of the Richards pattern, distinguished by a better ejector patented on 2 July 1872 by William Mason of Taunton, Massachusetts (US no. 128,644). The mouth of the ejector case lay nearer to the cylinder than the preceding Richards type. Mason-pattern guns also had an extended hammer nose instead of a rebounding hammer.

The use of newly forged barrels and the quantities involved – the production of Richards-Mason transformations is said to have exceeded 30,000 guns – suggests that this particular conversion was not simply a means of ridding the factory of old parts. The most important numerically was the .38 version of the M1862 Police and Pocket Navy cap-locks, some 24,000 of which were made in a bewildering profusion of styles. In addition, similar conversions were undertaken elsewhere.

The first new Colt cartridge revolver was an open-top .44-23-200 rimfire embodying the classical three-piece construction. Variously known as the New Model Army Revolver, **Colt New Model Holster Revolver**, 'Colt M1872' or 'Open Top Frontier', it had a navy-style grip, a short cylinder with a roll-engraved maritime scene, and a cylindrical barrel with a flat-sided frame lug grooved to receive the Mason ejector case.

Only about 7000 of the open-frame .44 rimfire revolvers were made, variations being restricted to an occasional long or army-type grip, an 8-inch barrel instead of the standard $7\frac{1}{2}$-inch variety, and brass (rather than iron) grip straps.

Most guns were sold in Mexico after the introduction of the perfected Model 1873 (q.v.). They are usually nickel plated and – much more rarely – have ultra-ornate metal or ivory grips of a style popular south of the Rio Grande.

In addition to single-shot derringers (q.v.), **Colt** also marketed .22 'Open-top' and .41 rimfire four-shot Patent House Pistols, the first Colts to be specifically designed for metal-case ammunition. The Patent House Pistol was a curious-looking design. Offered with barrels of $1\frac{1}{2}$ or 3in, it is now known as the 'Cloverleaf' owing to the strange shape of its cylinder.

Among the most interesting features of the Cloverleaf revolver, patented by Charles Richards on 19 September 1871 (US no. 119,048), were the counter-bored chambers. These enveloped the case rims in a way that has since been regularly hailed as an innovation. The ejector rod was contained within the cylinder axis pin, and the cylinder could be turned through 45 degrees to allow the nose of the firing pin to enter a small hole cut between the chambers.

Owing to the narrowness of the frame, the cartridges could fall out of the two side chambers when the gun was being fired. This was prevented by a detachable side plate on the left side of the gun, and by a lug on a collar held in the frame by the cylinder pin.

Frames were bronze, often camouflaged by silver or nickel plating, and the triggers were sheathed. The hammers originally had a high spur, but a lower version was substituted after about 1874. Several non-standard variants were produced, generally with short barrels.

Towards the end of production, a modified pattern with a conventional five-shot cylinder appeared in answer to criticism. The ejector rods were omitted, $2\frac{5}{8}$-inch barrels were standard, and a tiny bead-type front sight appeared immediately above the muzzle.

The **Smith & Wesson** Second Model No. 3 American replaced the First Model in 1871, about 500 hybrid guns being made during the transition. These had 8-inch barrels, were offered in blue or nickel finishes, and numbered either in the Russian series (apparently 3200–3700) or interspersed with the last of the First Model No. 3 Americans.

The Second Model had, among other Russian-inspired revisions, a large-diameter trigger pin, a locking hammer and a revised barrel catch. Numbered from 6800 upward, the perfected guns proved very popular in the West. The basic design was improved in the spring of 1873, in the region of number 18000, when a modified lock was adopted. The new cylinder stop was actuated by the trigger rather than by the hammer as in the previous guns. A shoulder stock was an uncommon optional extra, locking into grooves cut in the base of the butt; only 604 were made, compared with about 20,835 revolvers.

Second Model No. 3 American Smith & Wesson revolvers were offered in blue or nickel finish, though some 'two-tone' guns were made. An 8-inch barrel was regarded as standard, though $5\frac{1}{2}$, 6, $6\frac{1}{4}$, $6\frac{1}{2}$ and 7in options were supplied on request. Some guns featured engraving of the highest order; others were plated with gold or silver. Chamberings were .44/100 or .44 Russian, though 500 .44 Henry rimfire guns were supplied to Mexico in 1872 and an additional 3014 rimfires were made for the commercial market. The earliest of these incorporated the original non-locking hammer. Rimfire .44 revolvers were abandoned in 1874.

THE JAMES BROTHERS

Jesse Woodson James was born on 5 September 1847 near Centerville, Missouri. Raised on a farm by parents with Confederate sympathies, James rode with Quantrill during the Civil War. Beginning with a bank raid in Liberty, Missouri, in February 1866 – part of a gang of ten – Jesse James robbed travellers, stagecoaches, banks and trains from Iowa to Texas, creating a romantic myth comparable in some ways with that of Robin Hood. This owed much to the latent pro-Confederate sympathies of Missourians, who saw in James's exploits blows against the Federal government.

On 7 September 1876, however, the James–Younger Gang mounted a disastrous raid on the First National Bank of Northfield, Minnesota. Met by stiff resistance from armed vigilantes, forewarned of their approach, only the James brothers escaped death or capture (see 'The Youngers').

Jesse James, living under the alias 'Thomas Howard', was killed in St Joseph on 3 March 1882 by his cousin and one-time James-Younger Gang member Robert Ford, the 'Dirty Little Coward' who shot 'Mr Howard' in the back of the head with the help of a .44 Smith & Wesson revolver. Bob Ford also owned a Richards conversion of .44-calibre Colt 1860-type cap-lock army revolver no. 194590; he was eventually killed in Creede, Colorado, by a drunken gambler named Kelly.

A display board of guns owned by Jesse James and 'authenticated by his son' included a M1873 Winchester lever-action rifle, two Colt Single Action Army revolvers, a Schofield Smith & Wesson and a round-butt Merwin & Hulbert. During the raid on Northfield in 1876, however, Jesse James is said to have carried a .38 rimfire conversion of a .36-calibre cap-lock Colt pocket revolver, no. 2426. The gun had a round 3.5in barrel and a brass trigger guard/backstrap combination.

When he was shot by Robert Ford in 1882, Jesse James owned a .45 first pattern Smith & Wesson Schofield revolver, no. 366. Ironically, the murder weapon was a New Model No. 3 Smith & Wesson.

Alexander Franklin 'Frank' James, Jesse's elder brother, was born near Centerville, Missouri, on 10 January 1843. After riding with Bloody Bill Anderson during the Civil War, Frank James joined his brother and the Youngers in a life of banditry. Shortly after the murder of Jesse James, Frank James surrendered to the authorities in June 1882. Subsequently tried for murder and armed robbery in three states, he was found not guilty on all counts – incredibly – and eventually died peacefully on 18 February 1915 in the room in which he had been born.

Frank James carried two .44-40 M1875 Remington revolvers (one being no. 15116). When he surrendered in 1882, Frank James stated that he preferred the Remingtons because they were 'the hardest and surest shooting pistol made', and because they chambered the same cartridges as his Winchester rifle.

The open-top frame of the Colt New Model Army Revolver was weak, even by the standards of the day. The improved Single Action Army Model, '**Colt Peacemaker**', 'Model P' or 'Model 1873' was its successor. Although technically inferior to the contemporary Smith & Wesson Russian Model, the Colt was simpler, stronger and virtually impossible to wreck.

The Peacemaker appears to have been the work of William Mason, who combined traditional Colt features – most importantly, the single-action lock – with a new solid-top frame suited to the increasing power of handgun ammunition.

In 1873, after protracted trials, the US Army adopted the new Colt as the Model of 1873. Captain John Eadie, President of the Board of Officers, reported that he had 'no hesitation in declaring the Colt revolver superior in most respects, and much better adapted to the wants of the Army than the Smith & Wesson'. Subsequently, however, only 37,063 guns were acquired by the army in 1873–91. Fewer still were issued.

Army-issue weapons had $7\frac{1}{2}$-inch barrels marked 'COLT'S PAT. F.A. MFG. CO. HARTFORD CT. U.S.A.', chambered .45 Long Colt cartridges and displayed 'U.S.' on the left side of the frame behind the acknowledgement of US patents issued to Charles Richards on 19 September 1871 (119,048); to William Mason on 2 July 1872 (128,644); and, eventually, another granted to Mason on 19 January 1875 (158,957).

The patent marks took several forms, depending on the age of the gun, and were joined on commercial revolvers by a rampant colt motif. Inspector's marks were to be found on the left grip, often accompanied by the date of inspection (e.g. '1880' above 'DAL' in a cartouche on gun 55407). Among the inspectors were Rinaldo Carr ('RAC'), Daniel Clark ('DFC'), Frank Hosmer ('FH') and David Lyle ('DAL').

Few Colts were as attractive as the eighteen Single Action Army Models made as part of a 300-gun panoply for the Philadelphia Centennial Exposition of 1876. These were engraved with scroll work, featured gold and silver plating, and had plain ivory grips. One of them, no.11088, made in 1874, served as the company exhibition gun until sold in 1894.

Theodore Roosevelt owned two specially decorated .44-40 Single Action Army revolvers. Gun no. 92248 was supplied by Colt to Hartley & Graham in May 1883 and sent to the celebrated engraver L. D. Nimschke. A 'TR' monogram was carved in high relief on the left grip, a bison's head appearing on the right; both grip-plates were made of ivory. The monogram was repeated on the left side of the recoil shield, and the gun was lightly scroll-engraved overall. The other Colt, no. 92267, shipped in June 1883, was completed as a near-duplicate; however, the ivory grips bore only a facsimile of Roosevelt's signature on the right.

Surprisingly few mechanical changes have been made in the M1873 action.

A few rimfire guns were made from 1875, numbered in a separate sequence. With a mere handful of exceptions, they chambered .44 Henry; total production amounted to less than 2000, substantial numbers of which were sold in Mexico.

Shortly after the specimen **Smith & Wesson** had been sent to the US Army, another was presented to General Aleksandr Gorlov. The Russian military attaché was supervising the acceptance of Colt-made Berdan rifles in the nearby

THE EARPS

Wyatt B. S. Earp (1848–1929), James C. 'Jim' Earp (1841–1926), Virgil W. Earp (1843–1906), Morgan Earp (1851–82) and Warren B. Earp (1855–1900) were born in Illinois, then raised in Illinois and Iowa before travelling with their parents to California during the Civil War. Returning to Illinois in 1868, the family moved to Lamar, Missouri in 1870. There Wyatt married, becoming the local constable, but the sudden death of his wife persuaded him to roam the Indian Territory and Kansas. He served as a lawman in Wichita and Dodge City in 1875–7, returning to Dodge City in 1878 as assistant marshal after prospecting for gold in the Black Hills. Travelling through New Mexico and California, Wyatt Earp eventually settled in Tombstone, Arizona Territory, where he acted as a guard in the Oriental Saloon. Virgil Earp, meanwhile, had become town marshal.

A long-running feud between the Earps and the Clantons, which apparently arose over land rights, culminated in the Gunfight at the OK Corral (26 October 1881), where Wyatt, Virgil and Morgan Earp, with 'Doc' Holliday, gunned down three members of the Clanton gang. Virgil Earp was subsequently discharged as marshal – many of the townspeople regarded the gunfight as murder masquerading as rule-of-law – and Morgan Earp was killed by unknown assailants in March 1882. Wyatt and Warren Earp subsequently shot at least two suspects; accused of murder, Wyatt Earp fled to pursue a career of gambling, mining and land-selling before eventually settling in Los Angeles. His reputation was inflated by a biography published in 1931, *Wyatt Earp, Frontier Marshal* by Stuart N. Lake, but this is now regarded more as fiction than fact.

Wyatt Earp is said to have carried an engraved .44 Smith & Wesson Model No. 3 revolver – a gift from the editor of the Tombstone *Epitaph* – during the gunfight at the OK Corral in 1881. Two of the victims, Frank McLowery and Billy Clanton, are known to have carried .44-40 Colt Single Action Army revolvers (no. 46338 and no. 52196 respectively). Virgil Earp owned a nickelled .44 Smith & Wesson New Model No. 3, no. 14289, with a 6.5in barrel and ivory grips.

Wyatt Earp himself acquired a Colt Single Action Army revolver shortly afterwards (no. 69562), eventually shortening the barrel from 7.5in to 5in, and apparently used a borrowed Stevens 10-Bore double-barrel shotgun to kill William 'Curly Bill' Brocius in 1882.

Connecticut town of Hartford. After protracted negotiations, a modified Smith & Wesson 'Russian Model' revolver was accepted for the Russian army and an order for 20,000 was signed on 1 May 1871. Deliveries of the original, first-pattern or 'Old Old Model' No. 3 Russian revolver commenced shortly before Christmas 1871.

The Russian guns chambered a cartridge with a bullet that was appreciably smaller than the case mouth. Consequently, each cartridge chamber had to be 'stepped' rather than merely bored straight through. An unexpected benefit of the change to the .44 Russian cartridge, which contained 23–24 grains of powder and a 244-grain lead bullet, was a substantial increase in muzzle velocity and a marked improvement in accuracy. In addition, the Russians requested a larger trigger pin; a larger cylinder retainer; a limiting tooth in the extractor gear; a hammer that locked the frame shut when down; a firing-pin bush to protect the recoil shield when firing; and a more durable front sight.

Not all these changes were made immediately. The first 3000 revolvers, for example, were accepted with the old-style (small) trigger pin. About 500 revolvers were rejected at inspection, salvaged, given replacement .44/100 cylinders, and sold on the North American commercial market. The Cyrillic barrel-mark was ground away and replaced by the standard company inscription, but the weapons can be identified by the presence of full serial numbers in several places.

About 4655 genuine commercial first-pattern Russian No. 3 revolvers were numbered in the same range as the Second Model No. 3 American. They are identical to the Russian military weapons, but have commercial-style serial numbers and the barrel-rib inscription shows no signs of refinishing. They were originally supplied in blue or nickel finish, had optional lanyard rings and – from March 1873 – could be fitted with a shoulder stock. Barrel lengths varied from 5 to 8 inches.

The grip of the second-pattern No. 3 Russian revolver, subsequently known as the 'Old Model', was modified to prevent recoil shifting the muzzle upward in the hand; a prominent pawl or knuckle appeared on the frame behind the hammer. The hammer thumb-piece was enlarged, and the barrel pivot was modified to eliminate the barrel-pivot locking screw. The cylinder stop was actuated by the trigger, instead of by the hammer, and the barrel length was reduced from 8 to 7 inches. The base of the butt was narrowed and rounded, and a distinctive spurred finger rest was added to the trigger-guard bow.

Though Smith & Wesson heartily disapproved the appearance of the modified revolver, it was adopted by the Russian government in December 1872. A contract dated 15 January 1873 requested 20,000 guns at a cost of $15.33 apiece; on 15 December 1873, after all but the last consignments of the January order had been shipped, the Russians ordered an additional 20,000. Other contracts followed until May 1877, production of second-pattern No. 3

Russian revolvers for the Tsar's forces amounting to about 70,000 in the USA. All displayed the Cyrillic barrel-top legend, amended in later orders to include the gun serial number.

Second-pattern No. 3 Russian-pattern revolvers were particularly popular in Japan and Turkey. The Turks ordered 1000 .44 Henry rimfire guns on 12 August 1874, then took 7000 additional guns in panic during the Russo-Turkish War. About 6200 commercial second or Old Model No. 3 Russian Smith & Wessons were numbered from 32800 upward. These had standard barrel inscriptions, with the additional 'RUSSIAN MODEL'. Large quantities were purchased by Schuyler, Hartley & Graham of New York City and marked with 'SH' in a diamond.

Continued development led to the third pattern or New Model No. 3 Russian revolver, adopted in the autumn of 1874. A contract for 11,138 of these Cavalry Model guns was signed on 27 October 1874, the preceding second-pattern thereafter being designated 'Infantry' in Russian service.

The cavalry revolver was the final variation to be ordered from Smith & Wesson. Its most obvious characteristics were a new spring-loaded extractor catch, which pivoted out of gear to return the extractor to its closed position; a shorter extractor housing; and an improved extractor-gear train. The return spring lay inside the extractor, and the screw retaining the extractor return-spring rod was replaced by a catch. The changes allowed the cylinder to be removed without tools, which was a significant advance.

The subject of a patent granted to Daniel Wesson on 19 January 1875 (US no. 158,874), New Model No. 3 Russian revolvers had 6½-inch barrels carrying integrally forged front sights. Contracts for 10,000 guns apiece were signed in October 1876, January 1877 and May 1877, but these were the last of the lucrative Russian orders. After the last contract had been completed, the Russians ordered 75,000 New Model Russian revolvers from Ludwig Loewe & Company of Berlin, and ultimately started making guns in the Tula arsenal.

Although the Colt Peacemaker had beaten its rivals in the US Army trials of 1872–3, including several guns submitted by Smith & Wesson, the appearance of a gun modified by Major George **Schofield** of the 10th Cavalry presented a serious threat. Patented in the USA on 20 June 1871 (no. 116,225) and 22 April 1873 (138,047), the Schofield Smith & Wesson had a simplified extractor and a latch on the standing frame instead of the barrel extension. The changes were aimed specifically at cavalrymen. There were two models, as alterations were made to the locking latch assembly after production began.

Following a trial in which the Schofield revolver was declared equal or superior to all its rivals, including the Colt, the army ordered 3000 as the Model of 1875. However, respondents who considered the Schofield superior technically were countered by others who saw the Colt as simpler and more durable.

THE YOUNGERS

Thomas Coleman 'Cole' Younger was the eldest, born in 1844 in Lee's Summit, Missouri; his brothers John, James and Robert 'Bob' Younger were born in 1846, 1850 and 1853 respectively. The entire Younger clan had witnessed the Kansas–Missouri border wars at first hand and Cole Younger had ridden with Quantrill during the Civil Wars, befriending Frank James.

When the Civil War ended, Frank James, Jesse James and Cole Younger formed a gang, beginning their bank-robbing career in 1866 in Missouri and the adjoining states. Jim Younger joined the gang in 1868, followed by John in 1869 and Bob in 1872, and the 1873–6 period was characterised by a series of daring train robberies. In March 1874, Pinkerton agents successfully ambushed John and Jim Younger, killing the former, and on 7 September 1876, the James-Younger Gang mounted its disastrous raid on the First National Bank of Northfield.

The outlaws attacked the bank, killing teller Joseph Heywood, but were then confronted by an armed band of vigilantes. Clell Miller and Charlie Pitts were killed in the street, and Bill Chadwell died during the pursuit. The James and Younger brothers escaped, though Jim Younger had been seriously wounded. Jesse and Frank James then struck out on their own, leaving Cole and Bob Younger to protect their injured brother. All three Youngers were captured near Madelia on 21 September.

The Youngers were tried, convicted and sentenced to life imprisonment. Bob died of tuberculosis in jail in 1889, while Cole and Jim were pardoned in 1901. Unable to adjust to life outside the institution, Jim Younger shot himself a year later; Cole Younger, after a few appearances in Wild West shows, died of a heart attack in 1916.

Cole Younger owned a .32 Smith & Wesson Model No. 2, allegedly presented to him by William Quantrill shortly after the sacking of Lawrence, Kansas, in 1863. He also used at least one Colt Single Action Army revolver, and has been linked with a .36-calibre 1851-pattern Colt Navy revolver, no. 109168, which was taken from a drifter (said to have been Younger himself) in July 1876. This particular gun had 'C.Y.' cut into the grips. After the Northfield raid, however, Sheriff James Glispin took a .44 Smith & Wesson 'Old Old Model' Russian revolver, no. 28009, from Cole Younger. The S&W had an 8in barrel, ivory grips and nickel-plated finish.

Charlie Pitts was apparently carrying a .44 third or New Model Smith & Wesson Russian revolver, no. 40369, when he was killed in Northfield.

Supporters of Colt may have gained an upper hand had not Schofield's brother been a major general.

By the end of 1879, purchases amounted to 8285 Schofield Smith & Wessons compared with 20,073 Model 1873 Colts.

Disaster at the Battle of the Little Big Horn led to claims that, as S&W Schofields were easily loaded, the outcome could have been different had cavalrymen been issued with them. One test showed that an experienced cavalryman could reload the Schofield in less than thirty seconds even at a gallop, while the Colt took a minute of undivided concentration.

Unfortunately, the Schofield Model chambered a special short cartridge generating less power than the .45 Long Colt. Colt revolvers would fire both rounds, whereas the S&W could not. Problems arose as soon as Colt cartridges were issued to Schofield-armed units, forcing the army to standardise the Model P. The Schofield was abandoned and by an unfortunate quirk of fate, the inventor took his life with one of his own revolvers in 1882.

The Model 1875 **Remington** revolver, chambered for .44 Remington centrefire, .44-40 or .45 Colt, was another of the many guns developed in the hope of attracting US Army orders. It was offered to the government twice during the mid-1870s, but the authorities retained the Colt as the Remington had little extra to offer.

The M1875 had a 7½-inch round barrel and weighed 44oz. It was blued or nickel plated, except for colour case-hardening on the hammer and loading gate, and had oil-finished walnut grips. Decorative examples with ivory or mother-of-pearl grips were made to order. The revolver, resembling an amalgam of the Remington .44 New Model Army cap-lock and the 1873-pattern Colt, had a prominent web beneath the barrel and a lanyard ring on the butt. About 25,000 were made from 1875 until the demise of E. Remington & Sons in 1886.

The rise of the firearms industry in New England and, particularly, the perfection of small-calibre revolvers by Smith & Wesson and others, encouraged many small manufacturing companies to participate. With the exception of some gunmakers who subsequently rose to prominence, most of the products were '**Suicide Specials**' – a derogatory term, first applied by Duncan McConnell, writing in the *American Rifleman* in 1948, that is now applied to small solid-frame guns made by as many as fifty gunmakers. Often anonymous, their characteristics include detachable cylinders, bird's head butts and sheath triggers. The term 'Suicide Special' is also often applied to a group of cheap break-open auto-ejectors originating in the 1880s, but these are described in the next chapter.

The guns began to appear as soon as the Rollin White patent expired in the spring of 1869, though it was the early 1870s before volume production began. A typical Suicide Special was a seven-shot .22 or five-shot .32, usually chambering rimfire ammunition. The frame was a one-piece forging (some makers seem to have used castings) with a detachable plate on the left side giving access to the simple single-action lockwork. Sheath triggers were customary, butts were square or bird's head types, and the barrels measured 3in or less.

The cylinders were loaded through a hinged gate on the right side of the frame, but could be removed simply by detaching the cylinder axis pin. The guns were blued or nickel plated, and often had poor-quality 'engraving' rolled into the surface of the cylinder. The grips were usually wood or gutta-percha, though mother-of-pearl was sometimes used on the gaudier nickelled guns.

Revolvers of this genre were made in very large numbers, particularly in the 1880s; they were also cheap – Johnson, Bye & Company were wholesaling 'Old Hickory' guns for $35–60 per dozen in 1881, when a Forehand & Wadsworth 'Bulldog' could be purchased from mail-order houses for just $4.75. Production peaked at 600,000 annually by 1885, but then went into a steady decline until virtually none were being made by 1900.

Most of the guns were made in the traditional gunmaking centres in New England. For example, in Massachusetts, known participants included Edward L. Dickinson and Ely & Wray in Springfield; the Forehand & Wadsworth Arms Company, the Harrington & Richardson Arms Company and Wesson & Harrington in Worcester; Johnson, Bye & Company and Iver Johnson of Worcester and subsequently Fitchburg; and the Prescott Pistol Company and Charles S. Shatuck in Hatfield.

Among the companies trading in Connecticut were the Bacon Manufacturing Company, the Crescent Arms Company, the Hood Firearms Company, the Hopkins & Allen Arms Company, the Norwich Arms Company, the Norwich Falls Pistol Company and the Ryan Pistol Company in Norwich; the Marlin Fire Arms Company in New Haven; the Meriden Arms Company in Meriden; Otis Smith in Middlefield and then Rock Fall; and the Whitney Arms Company in New Haven.

Maltby, Curtis & Company and Maltby, Henley & Company traded in New York City, while the Rome Revolver & Novelty Works operated in Rome in upstate New York. Pennsylvania contained the Lee Arms Company of Wilkes-Barre, with the J. Rupertus Patent Pistol Manufacturing Company and William Uhlinger in Philadelphia.

Colt and Remington are also sometimes included among the makers of Suicide Specials, though the quality of their products was incomparably superior to most of the others.

Several hundred brandnames have been associated with Suicide Specials, but identification of individual gunmakers is hindered by the liberal use of wholesalers', distributors' or spurious manufacturers' marks. These include 'Aetna Arms Company' (used by Harrington & Richardson), 'Chicago Arms

Company', 'Enterprise Gun Works', 'Great Western Gun Works' (J. H. Johnson of Pittsburgh), 'Mohawk Mfg. Company' (Otis Smith), 'New York Pistol Company', 'United States Arms Company' and the 'Western Arms Company'.

Wholesalers often commissioned guns from several manufacturers, possibly even concurrently, and so differing guns may bear identical brandnames; it has been alleged that more than thirty differing revolvers were marked 'Defender', made by more than a dozen gunmakers.

Few Suicide Specials have much claim to novelty, though variety may be encountered in barrel-locking systems, ejectors and lock work.

Although best known for its lever-action rifles, the **Marlin** Fire Arms Company also made substantial quantities of small-calibre revolvers. John Marlin's operations had begun in New Haven in 1863, where single-shot rimfire pistols were made. These were modified by the addition of an ejector, patented in April 1870, and then supplemented by a selection of small revolvers. The XXX Standard, sometimes known as the 'Model 1873', was a five-shot tipping barrel gun chambered for .30, .32 and .38 rimfire ammunition.

Another well-known maker of 'Suicide Specials' was Norwegian-born gunsmith **Iver Johnson**, who arrived in Worcester, Massachusetts, during the Civil War and eventually set himself up in a small workshop at 244 Main Street. In 1871, in partnership with Martin Bye, he formed Johnson & Bye to make cheap revolvers.

The earliest identifiable guns were the Favorite and Tycoon, introduced about 1873. These were single-action sheath-trigger revolvers with octagonal barrels, offered in calibres ranging from .22 to .44. They were soon joined by the Encore and Favorite Navy, which had plain cylindrical barrels. The 1875-vintage .22, .32, .38 and .41 rimfire Smoker, similar to its predecessors, had a fluted cylinder and a 'Russian Handle'.

The contemporary sheath trigger .22 rimfire, .32 or .38 Defender had an octagonal barrel, a 'Saw Handle' and a partially fluted cylinder (fully fluted cylinders were optional in .38 only).

Forehand & Wadsworth were formed by Sullivan Forehand and Henry Wadsworth, who joined Allen & Wheelock in the 1850s. Wheelock died in 1863 and the business passed to Ethan Allen – Forehand's and Wadsworth's father-in-law. Ethan Allen & Company made .22 rimfire single-shot 'Allen' target pistols in a factory adjoining South Worcester railway station until production of cheap solid-frame revolvers began. Ethan Allen died in 1871, allowing Forehand & Wadsworth to be incorporated in 1872.

The first products were solid frame five-shot pocket revolvers, chambered for .32 or .38 rim- or centrefire cartridges. Patented on 24 July 1877 (US no. 193,367) to protect the detachable side plate, these guns had round barrels.

Octagonal barrels appeared only in Forehand Arms Company days. Guns made after 1876 are described in Chapter 4.

Gilbert **Harrington** had been employed prior to 1870 by Ballard & Fairbanks, manufacturers of rifles, single-shot pistols and pocket revolvers, but had then joined his uncle Franklin Wesson. William Richardson – another Ballard & Fairbanks man – was enticed to become the factory superintendent, until Harrington bought his uncle's share of the business and formed Harrington & Richardson in 1874. The original Harrington ejector revolver soon found a niche, selling well enough for Harrington & Richardson to begin a steady expansion. It was finally discontinued in 1878. Post-1876 guns are described in the next chapter.

Typical of the better-quality work undertaken in this period was provided by **Hopkins & Allen**. Founded in 1868 by C. W. Hopkins and C. H. Allen, the company started by making vast numbers of inexpensive sheath-trigger guns graced by names ranging from 'Acme' to 'Universal'. Large numbers of revolvers were also made for Merwin, Hulbert & Company (later Hulbert Brothers & Company), sporting goods dealers based in New York City from 1874–5; Hopkins & Allen-made, but Merwin/Hulbert marked revolvers were sold until Hulbert Brothers entered liquidation in 1896.

The Hopkins & Allen XL series, made from 1871, contained a superior brand of sheath-trigger Suicide Special. The XL No. 1 was a seven-shot .22 rimfire; XL No. 2 was a five-shot .32 rimfire; XL No. 2½ was similar, but chambered for .32 Short rimfire; and XL No. 3 handled .32 Long rimfire. By 1875, the series also encompassed the XL No. 4 in .38 Short rimfire; XL no. 5, apparently in .38 Long rimfire; XL No. 6 in .38 centrefire; and XL No. 7 in .41 rimfire.

The **Colt** Open-Top and Cloverleaf revolvers were replaced after 1873 by 'Colt's New Breechloading Revolvers', subsequently advertised as the New Line. There were five major variants, each differing in chambering and frame size. The cylinder-locking bolt and loading gate were the subject of a patent issued to William Mason in September 1874. These features were added progressively to the basic New Line design.

The .22 version was followed, in ascending order of size, by .30, .32, .38 and .41. The three largest calibres were available in rim- or centrefire, the smaller weapons being rimfire only. Excepting the seven-shot .22 pattern, all New Line guns had five-cartridge cylinders. A few weapons also had non-standard loading gates on the right rear of the frame behind the cylinder.

A major change in the mechanism was made in 1876, when the locking slots on the cylinder periphery were moved to the rear face. The New Line guns all had solid frames, sheath triggers and bird's head butts. Except for the smallest gun, which was made of bronze, frames were iron. The barrels, made without ejectors, usually measured 2¼in; however, a few .30-calibre examples had 1¾-inch barrels while .38 and .41 examples could be found with 4-inch barrels. Grips could be walnut, rosewood, gutta-percha, ivory or mother-of-pearl.

The .22 rimfire was sometimes known as the 'Little Colt', the .30 as the 'Pony Colt', the .32 as the 'Lady Colt', the .38 as the 'Pet Colt' and the .41 as the 'Big Colt'. The names were bestowed by Kittredge & Company of Cincinnati, however, and had no official standing.

Like Colt, **Remington** introduced a series of New Line cartridge revolvers in the 1870s. They embodied a lock patented by William Smoot on 21 October 1873 (US no. 143,855); solid frames, sheath triggers and bird's head butts were standard.

The New Line No. 1 of 1873 chambered .30 Short rimfire cartridges and offered a five-round cylinder. The barrel was octagonal, 2.8in long, and had an ejector rod on the right side of the frame web. The rarely encountered New Line No. 2 was identical, except that it chambered .32 Short rimfire.

The 1875-vintage five-shot New Line No. 3 resembled No. 1 and No. 2, but fired .38 Short rimfire cartridges. It had a sizeable $3\frac{1}{4}$-inch octagonal barrel – out of proportion with the comparatively small grip – and weighed about 15oz. Post-1876 guns are discussed in the next chapter.

Repeating Pistols

The break-open **Marston** derringer, patented in 1857, had a monoblock containing three rifled barrels. Chambering .22 and .32 rimfire cartridges, the mechanism embodied a travelling striker that fired the barrels sequentially from the bottom upward.

Christian **Sharps** made thousands of his distinctive four-barrel derringers between 1859 and 1874, when they were licensed to Tipping & Lawden in Britain and North American production ceased. The sheath-trigger Sharps guns were offered in .22, .30 and .32 rimfire, their barrels measuring $2\frac{1}{4}$–$3\frac{1}{2}$in. They were 'cluster derringers', the barrels being arranged as two rows of two in a monoblock. Their barrel-group slid forward to give access to the breech after a catch had been released, while a rotating striker-plate – generally on the hammer, but in the frame of some of those made by Sharps & Hankins – ensured that the chambers were fired correctly. Frames were either blued iron or brass, usually nickel or silver plated; grips were walnut or gutta-percha, though ivory and mother-of-pearl examples will also be encountered from time to time.

The standard **Remington-Elliott** derringer, patented on 29 May 1860 (US no. 28,460) and 1 October 1861 (33,362), had a multi-shot 3-inch barrel cluster that tipped down for loading. It was fired by a revolving striker actuated by a ring trigger. The guns were generally blued, but could be obtained with a nickel-plated frame or full nickel finish. Grips were smooth gutta-percha or, alternatively, mother-of-pearl or ivory. About 50,000 five-shot .22 and four-shot .32 examples were made in 1863–88 with cylindrical and squared barrel clusters respectively.

The cluster derringer group also contained .22 rimfire five-shot sheath-trigger guns produced by the **Continental** Arms Company, which had a rounded barrel block resembling a small pepperbox.

Guns produced contemporaneously by the **Bacon** Arms Company of Norwich, Connecticut, had a frame that extended forward to the front of the elongated cylinder. The cylinder axis pin, which ran through an arbor on the frame-tip, doubled as an ejector rod when the cylinder had been removed.

Wheeler derringers, made by the American Arms Company in 1865–6, featured a two-barrel monoblock that rotated through 90 degrees to give access to the breech. The guns were made in a variety of calibres, including .22, .32, .38 and .45. Some had identically chambered barrels; others had two different ones.

Designed by W. H. Elliott, the **Remington** Double Repeating Deringer (sic), was protected by US Patent 51,440, granted on 12 December 1865 to protect a 'many barrelled firearm'. Introduced commercially in 1866, this gun sold amazingly well; when it was finally discontinued in the mid-1930s, about 150,000 had been made. The essential feature was a pair of superimposed 3-inch .41 rimfire barrels in a monoblock hinged to the frame. The barrel-block swung upward around a pivot at the top rear of the frame when the lever on the right side of the frame was pressed downward, allowing the gun to be reloaded. The firing pin fired the top barrel first, being reset each time the frame was opened. Most of the guns were nickel-plated, although blued examples were produced in small numbers. Their grips may be walnut or rosewood or, alternatively, chequered gutta-percha, mother-of-pearl or even ivory. Double derringers were marked as the products of E. Remington & Sons until 1888, then by 'Remington Arms Company' or 'Remington Arms–UMC Co.'

In the late 1860s, Franklin **Wesson** made a selection of two-shot .32 derringers with a flat barrel block that rotated laterally to the right when the breech catch was released. He also made what he termed a 'Pocket Rifle', which was a .32-calibre single-barrel pistol no more than 6in long. The barrel was released by a latch protruding beneath the frame ahead of the sheath trigger – a poor feature, as the barrel could often open accidentally in the confines of a pocket.

The **Remington**(-Rider) Magazine Repeating Pistol, another product of the fertile imagination of Joseph Rider, was patented on 15 August 1871 (no. 118,152). The pistol had a tube magazine beneath the barrel, holding four .32 Extra Short rimfire cartridges; a fifth could be loaded directly into the chamber. The mechanism embodied a variant of the rolling-block action, relying on an elevator to convey cartridges into the breech. Guns were encountered with 3-inch barrels and weighed 10oz. Some were nickel plated, while others had colour case-hardened frames; grips were varnished walnut, though ivory and mother-of-pearl were also available. About 15,000 of these interesting sheath-trigger guns were made in 1872–88.

CHAPTER 4

BANK, BAWDY HOUSE AND BOOT HILL

From the Centennial Exposition to Wounded Knee, 1876–90

'The life my people want is a life of freedom. I have seen nothing that a white man has – houses or railways or clothing or food – that is as good as the right to move in the open country . . .'
Sitting Bull, 1887.

The Centennial Exposition held in Philadelphia in 1876, marking the centenary of the Declaration of Independence and the beginning of the Revolutionary War, is often held to mark the point at which the United States of America took its first major step from isolation to play a part on the world stage.

Railroads connected the east and west coasts, tremendous mineral wealth was being exploited all the way across the continent, and much of the land had been organised in the States of the Union.

However, though the progress of civilisation seemed to be implicit in the gleaming railroad locomotives and all manner of consumer goods displayed in Philadelphia, the reality of the West was very different. The Centennial Exposition and the Battle of the Little Big Horn, representing triumph and disaster for white Americans, happened almost contemporaneously. Although the Hell-on-Wheels railroad towns had drunk, shot and caroused their way out of existence or into organised cityhood, violence still characterised 'cowtowns' such as Abilene and the booms which accompanied periodic discoveries of gold or mineral resources.

Many of the most notorious figures of the West met their ends in this period – Wild Bill Hickok died, shot in the back of the head in a Deadwood saloon, and a disastrous raid on banks in Northfield had put an end to the James-Younger gang.

Violence still flared regularly as late as 1910, as cattlemen, sheepmen and farmers wrangled over land, but the popular conception that every lawman and

THE DALTONS

Lewis Dalton, an itinerant saloon keeper, abandoned his wife Adeline and fifteen children during the Civil War. Mrs Dalton and her brood moved from Missouri to Kansas and then back to Missouri before settling in Oklahoma Indian Territory in the 1870s. The eldest Dalton boys – cousins of the Youngers – worked as cowboys until 1887, when Frank Dalton, a Federal Deputy Marshal, was killed by whisky runners. Gratton 'Grat' Dalton (1861–92), Robert 'Bob' Dalton (1870–92) and Emmett Dalton (1871–1937) were subsequently sworn-in as lawmen, but found the badges provided excellent cover for horse-rustling and were forcibly discharged in 1890.

This was the prelude to two years of robbing banks, gambling dens and trains in the company of their previously respectable brother William 'Bill' Dalton (1863–94). On 5 October 1892, the Dalton Gang attempted to rob both of the banks in Coffeyville, Kansas. Coming out of the first bank, however, they were faced with a band of armed vigilantes. Grat Dalton, Bob Dalton, Bill Powers, Tim Evans and Dick Broadwell were killed; only Emmett Dalton survived, badly wounded. Tried, convicted and imprisoned in the Kansas State Penitentiary for fourteen years, Emmett Dalton was pardoned in 1907 to live in obscurity for thirty years.

Bill Dalton had returned to Oklahoma by the time of the 'Coffeyville Massacre', joining the Doolin Gang and then forming an outlaw band of his own. On 8 June 1894, however, he was killed by lawmen while playing with his daughter on the porch of his home in Ardmore.

Comparatively little is known about the Daltons' guns, though a .38-calibre Webley Bulldog was taken from the waistcoat pocket of the slain Bob Dalton after the Coffeyville raid. His holster gun was apparently a Colt Single Action Army revolver. An 1886-pattern Winchester rifle was pictured with the corpses, but it is not known whether it was one of the Daltons' own guns.

outlaw carried a Colt Peacemaker and a Winchester rifle – fuelled by western fiction and countless Hollywood films – still dies very hard.

Strenuous efforts have been made in recent years to prove that the Western handguns ranged from tiny derringers and .22-calibre Suicide Specials to the largest revolvers. The most popular handguns prior to the mid-1870s were cap-lock Colts and Remingtons, large quantities of which had either been touted commercially or sold out of military service at the end of the Civil War. James Butler 'Wild Bill' Hickok was presented with a matched pair of scroll-engraved .36 Colt M1851 Navy revolvers in 1869, their carved ivory grips displaying an eagle motif; outlaw Sam Bass was carrying a .44 1860-pattern Colt Army revolver when he was fatally wounded during a bank-raid in Round Rock, Texas, in the summer of 1878.

Lawmakers and lawbreakers alike never agreed on the perfect weapon. Many favoured shotguns, which were particularly deadly at short range and more likely to correct minor deficiencies in aim than a revolver; others used knives or axes in preference to firearms, and a few men even preferred the silence of the bow.

Many of the most notorious Westerners changed weapons when the opportunity arose: balance and handling qualities have always been subjective. Identifying their guns, therefore, may be difficult. The late Hank Wieand Bowman, in *Antique Guns from the Stagecoach Collection*, quoted the collection's founder, Osborne Klavestad, as saying:

> Zerelda Samuels, the crafty old mother of the James bandits, talked my uncle into buying Jesse's 'very own six shooter'. My uncle was greatly elated over his prize until he learned that the female mountebank kept a whole bushel basket of guns on hand to sell to gullible tourists. Legend has it that Borax Smith's Twenty Mule Team would have bent an axle if ... loaded with all the Jesse James guns Zerelda Samuels tearfully parted with.

A display board of guns owned by Jesse James and 'authenticated by his son' included a M1873 Winchester lever-action rifle, two Colt Single Action Army revolvers, a Schofield Smith & Wesson and a round-butt Merwin & Hulbert.

Many lesser guns reached the West. The compact Webley 'British Bulldog' – and a legion of European-made copies – was a popular import, favoured for its large bore, while small-calibre 'Suicide Specials' were preferred for the ease with which they could be concealed. Owing to their ability to fire several shots without reloading, cheap revolvers steadily eclipsed derringers in the last decades of the nineteenth century.

The popular image of the Western duel is wildly inaccurate, as most men tipped the odds in their favour whenever possible. A shot in the back prevented the victim returning fire, and a stealthy attack out of the shadows guaranteed more success than a confrontation in the midday sun. The following extract from Joseph Rosa's fascinating *Guns of the American West* (1985) gives an idea of the performance of the average gunslinger:

> A ... less publicised event took place on 9 March 1877, at Cheyenne, Wyoming, when gamblers Charlie Harrison and James Levy shot it out after a dispute at a gaming table. The pair had been drinking heavily all evening, and the more they consumed the more belligerent they became, until finally Levy pulled a gun on Harrison ... They stepped into the street and Harrison hurried into the Senate Saloon to pick up a revolver. He emerged to find Levy waiting for him outside Frenchy's Saloon. Charlie promptly opened fire, but missed, and Levy shot back. Six shots were exchanged before Harrison fell, struck in the chest. Raising

himself, he fired once more but missed, and then fell back. Levy ran across the street, stood over him, and deliberately fired another bullet into him before ... hurrying away.

The Indians

Ironically, the ultimate subjugation of native Americans arose from a well-meaning attempt to help. In the mid-1880s, Senator Henry Dawes of Massachusetts proposed legislation allowing tribal lands to be granted to individuals on the basis of 160 acres for each householder and 80 acres for each unmarried man. These plots were not particularly generous – the larger was equivalent to a strip a mile long by a quarter-mile wide – and disguised an attempt to 'civilise' the Indians by making them into farmers. They gained US citizenship, of course, but also became subject to Federal Law. The suitability of each grantee was to be decided by the President of the USA, acting through representatives of the Indian Department.

The proposers of the scheme were genuinely concerned with Indian welfare, however misguided their efforts to impose a homesteading lifestyle on nomadic tribal traditions may now seem. But Dawes had too few supporters to ensure the passage of his Act without the belated assistance of speculators who, by insisting on the inclusion of clauses allowing surplus land to be sold publicly, saw a licence to make money.

The Dawes General Allotment (or 'Severalty') Act was ratified by Congress on 8 February 1887, much to the delight of its rag-bag following, but its effects were catastrophic. Few Indians adapted easily to farming life; wanderers no longer had much to seek; tribesmen were easily swindled out of land; and many reservations sunk inexorably into poverty or alcoholism. The effect was to reduce Indian landholding from about 138 million acres (215,600 square miles) in 1887 to less than 60 million acres by 1937. Speculators grew rich on land pickings while the Indians struggled with the enforced changes in their way of life.

In 1889, invoking the Dawes Act, Congress voted to buy out all Indian territorial claims in Oklahoma District. The total amounted to 1.92 million acres, or about 3000 square miles. At noon on 22 April 1889, therefore, the 'Boomers' (as the prospective settlers were called) began their frantic rush by foot, bicycle, ox, horse and railroad train – pre-empted by the 'Sooners', who had illegally grabbed much of the best land the previous night. By nightfall, virtually every exploitable square yard had been claimed and a settlement named Guthrie had grown in hours to a tented city with a population of 15,000.

Within a few months, Guthrie had gained a hotel, three newspapers, several general stores, fifty saloons and uncounted brothels. For a brief period, the 'Hell on Wheels' town returned with the 'Land Grab' seasons. The biggest land rush in Oklahoma occurred in September 1893, when more then six million acres were offered, and statehood was eventually conferred in 1906. Much to the disgust of the inhabitants of Guthrie, who claimed priority, Oklahoma City became the state capital.

The passage of the Dawes Act, which had created Guthrie and sister-towns overnight, added to the Indians' hardships by fragmenting their lands. However, no binding agreement had been reached with the Lakota (Sioux) in the Dakotas by 1890, even though General George Crook and his commissioners had attempted to divide and conquer the nine tribal chiefs by treating with each individually.

The US government demanded that half the Lakota reservation be surrendered, the attitude of the white settlers towards the Indians being pithily expressed by Senator John Logan: 'you have no following, no power, no control, and no right to control. You are on an indian reservation merely at the sufferance of the government.'

The government eventually obtained the consent of the Lakota to cede the land. Yet in spite of reassurances to the contrary, Congress cut appropriations to all Indian reservations in the summer of 1890. The failure of the harvest in an unusually dry growing season sowed the seeds of discontent, while epidemics of European diseases such as measles and diphtheria swept through tribes already weakened by lack of food.

With unutterable hardship came the reappearance of the Ghost Dance, which had originated among the Paiutes in the late 1860s. This promised resurrection of the dead, return of the buffalo – they had long since been exterminated in the Dakotas – and new grass to bury the white men. Indians would be masters of their lands once again.

The Dance was resurrected by a Paiute shaman named Wovoka after a solar eclipse in the spring of 1889. Mingling Christianity with traditional Indian beliefs, foreswearing alcohol and violence, Wovoka promised that the old world known to his ancestors would return and the white men would vanish forever. The attractions of the Ghost Dance were clear to many Indians, though not all who listened voiced their support.

News of the Dance was brought back to Sitting Bull at Standing Rock by Kicking Bear, who had travelled westward – ironically, by railroad – to hear Wovoka. However, somewhere along the line, elements had been added. These included a claim that no bullet could harm any Ghost Dancer who dressed in a white shirt marked with appropriate symbols: a dangerous addition to an otherwise peaceable religion, giving it a new and threatening dimension. Indian Agents reported their concerns to their masters back East. Washington responded by sending General Nelson Miles and 5000 men westward.

Old rivalries died hard, and none was keener to settle an old score than James

McLaughlin, Indian Agent at Standing Rock. McLaughlin seized his chance to brand Sitting Bull as an architect of the Ghost Dance, which the agent saw as a 'pernicious system of religion' and a threat to white supremacy. When the commander of the Indian police in Standing Rock reported that Sitting Bull intended to travel to the Indian stronghold of Pine Ridge to witness the coming of God, McLaughlin made his move.

More than forty Indian policemen were dispatched on 15 December to arrest the old man, followed discreetly by two troops of cavalrymen. But the plan miscarried badly. One of Sitting Bull's followers shot the commander of the police detachment as the escort party emerged; as he fell, Lieutenant Bull Head shot Sitting Bull in the chest with his revolver and, a split-second later, Sergeant Red Tomahawk shot the chief in the back of the head. When the dust of the firefight had settled, Sitting Bull, eight of his followers and four policemen lay dead. Two more policemen were fatally wounded.

The remainder of Sitting Bull's followers, fearful of attack, strove to reach Pine Ridge in the hope that either the problems could be resolved peaceably or they could hide out in the Badlands. But General Miles saw things differently and ordered Colonel John Forsyth and the 7th Cavalry to intercept. By 28 December 1890, the escorted party – perhaps 120 men, 230 women and children – had come to a creek named Wounded Knee.

On the morning of 29 December, Forsyth mustered the Indian men and ordered the surrender of all weapons. Disbelieving denials that guns were to be found, Forsyth ordered the search of all the tents and belongings. Then a shaman appeared, dancing, tossing earth skyward, reminding his audience that they were immune to bullets and that the soldiers would be scattered to the four winds. The mood grew uglier. A rifle was seen beneath a cloak of an Indian whom survivors swore to be deaf to commands to relinquish his gun; a struggle ensued and a single shot was fired – by whom is no longer known.

All hell broke loose as soldiers and Indians shot, knifed, punched and gouged each other at close quarters. When the soldiers finally drew back, their four small Hotchkiss cannon blasted away at the tents containing women and children for what, to the Indians, must have seemed an eternity. The carnage was terrible. Officially, Wounded Knee had cost the Lakota 86 men, 44 women and 16 children; unofficially, the death toll was put at 250 as the Indians had taken some of the dead. US Army casualties amounted to 25 dead and about 30 wounded.

Bitter small-scale fighting raged for a few months before the US Army managed to restore a superficial order, sealed by the final surrender of the Lakota nation on 15 January 1891. By 1900, when the population of the USA had grown to 76 million and more than 21 million people were living west of the Hundredth Meridian, barely 237,000 pure-blood 'Native Americans' remained of those who had fought and died to halt what an 1846 pioneer,

Alfred Robinson, noted was 'The March of Emigration ... to the West, [which] naught will arrest its advance but the Mighty Ocean'.

The Indian nations had made no real contribution towards the history of the firearm in North America. Though many tribes used guns, occasionally to good effect, the weapons were often taken in battle or from settlers; others were obtained through the trading posts, particularly after the passing of the Indian Intercourse Act in 1834.

Flint- and cap-lock trading muskets were popular, often the work of Henry Leman, and the brass-mounted 1866-model Winchester was favoured in later days. These guns can be identified by decorative tacks driven into their woodwork, or by crude wrapped-rawhide repairs to the butt wrists.

Longarms

Single-Shot Rifles

Among the most important changes made to the 1873-type **Springfield** rifle was a new 'Model 1877' back sight in January 1877, with different graduations and an improved sighting notch. The sights were changed again in May 1878, without changing the designation, when a base with curved wing plates replaced the previous stepped design. The height of the arch in the breech-block was reduced from March 1878 to give greater rigidity, creating 'Low Arch' guns; internally, the firing-pin spring and the corresponding shoulder on the firing pin were discarded.

Changes made in October 1878 included an increase in the width of the breech-block and a correspondingly broadened receiver. In addition, the gas escape holes through the receiver sides were deepened and extended rearward.

Only about 135 of the second type of **Springfield Officer's Rifle** were made in 1877–9 and 1885; all rifles made after April 1877 were accompanied by a detachable pistol-grip block. They also had an improved Springfield tang sight, with an attachment block that allowed the leaf to fold closer to the butt wrist. Some of the last guns to be made – perhaps after regular production had finished – had proper pistol-grip stocks with an elongated schnabel tipped fore-end. They often carry improved sights and lack the ramrod, instead carrying the three-piece rod in a carbine-type 'trapped' butt.

Eleven **Springfield Marksman's Rifles** were made in 1881–2, with special adjustable vernier back sights and tunnel-pattern front sights with integral spirit levels. The 26-inch cylindrical six-groove barrel, chambered for .45-80 cartridges, also bore the standard 1879-type buck-horn back sight. The pistol-grip half stock was selected black walnut, distinguished by a German silver nose cap.

The three-piece cleaning rod and the dismantling tool were carried in the butt trap. Engraving and the set-trigger paralleled those of the Officer's Model described above, though the decoration was somewhat more ornate.

A mere 151 **Long-Range Rifles**, destined for competition shooting, were made at Springfield Armory in 1879–80; 24 followed in 1881. Chambered for .45-80 cartridges, they had full-length barrels and two spring-retained barrel bands.

Pattern No.1 had a Hotchkiss-pattern butt plate, a full-length stock, a chequered fore-end and wrist (with a detachable pistol grip), a sophisticated Sharps vernier back sight on the tang above the stock wrist, and a laterally adjustable tunnel-pattern front sight with an integral spirit level.

Pattern No.2, sharing the stock design of its predecessor, had an aperture tang sight designed by Freeman Bull of the National Armory and an adjustable globe-pattern front sight. Pattern No.3 had a Hotchkiss butt plate, a full-length stock, a Bull-pattern back sight on the barrel and a regulation front sight.

Progressive improvements made in the basic M1873 rifle led to the 'M1873 Improved' or 'M1873 with 1879 Improvements'. Dating from January 1879, a standing plate with two projections improved the sight picture. Known as a 'buck-horn', this went through minor adaptations in October 1879, when the drift graduations were placed .04in apart instead of .02in and the buck-horn plate was changed; in November 1879, when the upper surface of the leaf-hinge was flattened; and in July 1880, when the notches in the buck-horn were revised.

A hole was bored up into the ramrod channel from the front end of the guard plate to reduce the accumulation of dirt (April 1879); a lip was added to the face of the hammer in January 1880; a heavier butt plate appeared in August 1881; part of the under-side of the thumb piece was removed to prevent it striking the lock plate (January 1883); a straight trigger was fitted from March 1883; and a detachable front sight protector was introduced in October 1883.

The improved cadet rifle was a minor variant of the rifle, lacking swivels. The revised carbine was also essentially similar to its predecessors; however, from December 1879, a rifle-type lower band replaced the special stacking-swivel band. Unlike the rifle, the carbine had a butt trap for the cleaning rod.

The .45 Rifle Model 1880 was the first to be fitted with a triangular-section rod bayonet, sliding in a channel under the barrel where the ramrod would normally be carried. Though often defended in ordnance correspondence as a means of reducing the soldier's burden – by a whole ten ounces – and saving the US Treasury about 91 cents per man, it was actually a way of avoiding manufacture of socket bayonets. Those in service in 1880 had all been made before 1865.

No socket bayonets had been made in North America for some years, whereas rod bayonets could be created by modifying machinery on which ramrods were made. Colonel James Benton, commanding Springfield Armory, sent a prototype rifle to the Chief of Ordnance, Brigadier Stephen Benét, on 29 May 1880. It elicited sufficient enthusiasm for manufacture of a thousand guns to be approved on 3 June. A total of 1,014 was made in 1881.

Though otherwise essentially similar to the improved Model 1873, 1880-type rifles were easily distinguished by the special nose cap. Their full-length barrels were held by two bands.

The 20-bore Forager shotgun allowed troops stationed on the frontiers to supplement their army rations. Springfield Armory made 250 Foragers by 2 October 1881, the last of 1,376 leaving the factory in 1885. They had a standard 1873-pattern Springfield-Allin lock, dated in cursive script, but lacked rifling. Their plain-tipped tapering fore-end was attached to the barrel by a single screw.

During the 1880s, many obsolete .50-70 Model 1865 and Model 1866 Trapdoor Springfields were converted by replacing the barrel and cutting the fore-end to half its length. These ultra-cheap 12- or 16-bore conversions were supplemented out on the Frontier by 12-bore 'Zulu' guns – ex-French Tabatière breechloaders purchased in Europe after the Franco-Prussian War.

In the late 1870s, the troubled Sharps Rifle Company pinned its hopes on the Model 1878 **Sharps-Borchardt** rifle. Designed by German-born Hugo Borchardt and patented in the USA in December 1876, the dropping-block action was far in advance of its period. Instead of the familiar external hammer, Borchardt introduced a spring-loaded internal striker. As the block dropped, it automatically forced the striker back to full cock and applied the safety mechanism. When the action had been reloaded and closed, the firer could override the safety by pressing a secondary trigger.

Sharps, perhaps optimistically, saw the Borchardt as a military weapon. Sporting guns gradually appeared – including a mid-range target rifle and a Creedmoor pattern. But the unfamiliar appearance of the Sharps-Borchardt inhibited sales in the West; with the failure of the Sharps Rifle Company in 1881, the Borchardt rifle also disappeared.

Although the promoters of the Sharps preferred the advantages of long small-calibre bullets to short fat ones, which were far inferior ballistically, complaints were soon voiced that even the .44-77 round did not always drop buffalo with one shot. This resulted in the introduction of the awesome .50-90 Big Fifty in the summer of 1872, and the virtual end of complaints. Two versions of the .44-90, one for hunting and the 'Creedmoor' for target shooting, were announced in 1873.

Ammunition was loaded by (more probably, for) the Sharps Rifle Company, by the Union Metallic Cartridge Company (UMC), by Winchester, by E. Remington & Sons, and by the US Cartridge Company (USCCo). The products of Sharps and USCCo. are rarely headstamped, though UMC and Winchester both identified cartridges loaded after about 1880. Remington's often bore an embossed headstamp, and are additionally identifiable by their rounded or bevelled-edge case rims.

Cartridges were loaded in Europe by Eley, specifically for Sharps-action rifles sold in Britain by gunmakers such as John Rigby & Company or Daniel Fraser. Some of these were simply American-made guns with British retailers' marks, but others were Sharps actions stocked and barrelled in 'English style'.

The cartridges were loaded with a mixture of plain and paper-patched bullets, the latter being intended to minimise leading in the bore. Light British-style 'Express' bullets were also favoured for some loads, particularly after the Sharps-Borchardt rifle had appeared in 1878.

The range of Sharps cartridges was extensive. In addition, the company chambered rifles for cartridges originally introduced for Remingtons or Winchesters – for example, the 'Sharps' .44-2$\frac{7}{16}$ was a Remington pattern, and the .50-3$\frac{1}{4}$ Big Fifty originated as Winchester's .50-140 Express. The confusion is not helped by mistakes made by the ammunition companies; for example, the 1881 USCCo catalogue listed a '.44-60' straight-case Sharps round, though no such pattern ever existed.

Substantial quantities of Sharps rifles were chambered for the US Government .45-70 and .50-70 rounds prior to 1874. As the years passed, the necked-case .44 cartridges were replaced by straight .45 patterns, which were cheaper to make, easier to reload, and improved extraction.

Sharps also loaded .40-2$\frac{1}{2}$ and .45-2$\frac{1}{10}$ cartridges with greatly reduced powder charges and comparatively light lead balls. These were apparently intended for short-range gallery practice.

A relic of pre-Civil War days, the perfected **Maynard** rifle, announced in 1882, fired conventional centrefire cartridges. However, although they were made of the best materials, the Maynard action was not strong enough to handle smokeless-propellant loadings. Business declined until the assets and liabilities were sold in 1890 to J. Stevens Arms & Tool Company. Edward Maynard, greatly honoured in his lifetime for his services to dentistry in addition to his work with firearms, died a year later.

According to the periodical *Forest and Stream*, Marlin-made **Ballard rifles** were initially offered in nine styles ranging from the standard No. 1, .44 rim- or centrefire with a round 26-30in barrel and a blued frame ($27–29), to the No. 7 'Creedmoor A.1'. The No. 7, sighted to 1200 yards, was offered with .44 cartridges containing up to a hundred grains of powder. It had a 'selected, hand-made pistol grip stock, finest vernier and wind gauge sights, with spirit level' and cost $100.

By 1883, the No. 1 Hunter's Rifle had been dropped to leave the No. 2 as the basic sporting rifle. This had an octagonal barrel, the reversible firing-pin system and an open buck-horn back sight, and could be obtained in .32, .38 and .44 'Colt and Winchester centre fire'. The .32 version was sold with a

28-inch barrel, the others with thirty-inch patterns. Weights varied between 8.25lb and 9lb. Ballards were also offered in the guise of target rifles – No. $4\frac{1}{2}$, 6, 7 and 8 – but these were far more popular in the civilised East than the lawless West. Additional information will be found in the books listed in the Bibliography.

The No.4 Perfection was intended for hunting, being fitted with 'Rocky Mountain sights'. Available only in .38-50 and .40-63, with thirty-inch barrels as standard, it weighed about 10lb. The so-called Everlasting Shells, specifically intended for reloaders, were recommended for this rifle.

Ballard No. 5 Pacific and No. $5\frac{1}{2}$ Montana rifles were essentially similar, introduced in 1876 and c.1879 respectively, each having the heavy barrels favoured out West. They also had cleaning rods beneath the muzzles, unlike the other guns in the series.

The Pacific rifle had a heavy octagonal barrel and double set-triggers, plus Rocky Mountain sights. Chambered for .44-40 and .45-70 cartridges in addition to three Everlasting patterns – .40-63, .40-90 and .45-100 – it had barrels of 30–32in and weighed 10-12lb. The Montana pattern was similar, but even heavier: chambered only for the Sharps .45-$2\frac{7}{8}$ cartridge, it had a 30-inch barrel and weighed 14lb. No. 5 and No. $5\frac{1}{2}$ rifles were generally found with ring-tip breech levers instead of the normal spur patterns.

The original Laidley-Emery Rolling Block was difficult to make, production ceasing in the early 1880s in favour of an even more blatant copy of the Remington. The **New System Whitney** rifle, which lasted until its manufacturer was purchased by Winchester in 1888, had a special pivoting-lever extractor that was more efficient than most Remington patterns. The basic rifle was improved in 1886 by the addition of a main-spring roller and a mechanical firing-pin retractor, but few of the perfected guns were made before Whitney's enforced demise.

One poor feature of the Remington-type Whitneys was the universal omission of a locking bar, which in most Remingtons prevented the hammer falling from full cock unless the breech piece was shut. If the Whitney trigger was pressed while the breech piece was being shut, the hammer would fall onto the firing pin.

The original Laidley-Emery Whitneys were made in calibres as large as .58. The most powerful cartridges chambered in New System guns, distinguished by a rounded receiver, appears to have been .44-40. Catalogues produced in 1884 by the Meacham Arms Company of St Louis listed them in .22, .32, .38 and .44, with 24-28in octagonal barrels and weights ranging from 5–7lb.

Patented by Eli Whitney III in May 1874, the **Whitney Phoenix** rifle had a side-hinged breech-block that lifted up and to the right for loading – awkward for most right-handed firers, who would rather have loaded with their trigger hand. The rifle had a massive wrought iron receiver with a central hammer, the receiver being cut transversely to accommodate the breech-block. The block, hinged on the right, had an extended thumb-piece on the left and contained the firing pin and its coil spring.

The breech-locking catch shown on the patent drawings was let into the standing breech on the left side of the hammer. Intended to hold the breech closed when the hammer was pulled back to half cock, this catch was soon moved to the front right side of the receiver ahead of the breech-block.

The Phoenix rifle had a mechanical extractor, but still suffered the problems inherent in designs of its type. Consequently, several differing extractor systems were fitted during a production life lasting little more than a decade. The original extractor lay under the breech; as the breech opened, it struck the tip of the extractor – which pivoted around its screw – and pushed the extractor claw back towards the hammer. This, in theory at least, expelled the spent case from the chamber. This system predictably generated too little power and was soon replaced by an improved version containing an additional extractor lever. This in turn was replaced by a strengthened version relying on a rotating stem to operate the spring-loaded extractor claw.

Catalogues produced by Whitney in the early 1880s offered the Phoenix as a 9lb military rifle, with three barrel bands, a tangent-leaf sight, and a socket or sabre bayonet; as a 7lb cavalry carbine, with a single band, a ring and a sling bar on the right side of the receiver; and as a sporting rifle. The sporter was made in a variety of styles and calibres, ranging from a plain hunter's gun, with a 26-inch round barrel and open sights, up to a Schuetzen Rifle with vernier peep-and-globe sights, selected woodwork, and a hooked Swiss-style butt plate. Barrels measured between 26 and 32in, weights ranging correspondingly from 7–10lb.

Military-style Phoenix rifles were offered in .43, .45 and .50; sporters came in .32, .38 and .44 rimfire, plus .38, .40, .44, .45 and .50 centrefire. Individual chamberings included .40-50 and .40-70, together with .44-60, .44-77, .44-90, .44-100 and .44-105. However, the Phoenix action was prone to jamming when fired with heavy loads, and was never particularly successful.

The No. 1½ **Remington Rolling Block**, introduced in 1888 and discontinued in 1897, was a lightweight No. 1, generally encountered with an octagonal barrel but weighing a mere 7.5lb. It was available in a variety of rim- and centrefire chamberings from .22 to .38.

After the Remington Arms Company had assumed responsibility for the moribund E. Remington & Sons, it faced a problem of what to do with large numbers of obsolescent Rolling Block actions. One solution was to perpetuate the Light or Baby Carbine, made from the late 1880s until about 1908. Chambered only for .44-40, these little guns had a 20-inch round barrel and weighed a mere 5.5lb. The finish was blue or nickel, the sights, butt and fore-end were traditional military style, and a sling ring was often anchored to a 'D'-bar on the right side of the receiver.

As the years passed, the Rolling Block began to lose ground to newer guns. There was a concerted challenge from Stevens at the lower end of the market, while the hammerless Sharps-Borchardt (q.v.) threatened at the highest level. Remington countered with the No. 3 or **Remington-Hepburn** rifle, with a dropping block operated by a radial lever on the right side of the receiver. It also had a rebounding hammer.

Undoubtedly more refined than its predecessor, the Remington-Hepburn rifle was patented on 7 October 1879 and introduced commercially in 1880. The standard rifle, touted until 1907, chambered a variety of cartridges ranging from .22 to .45, with others available to order. It had a half- or fully octagonal barrel measuring 26–30in, weight being 8–10lb. The rifles had pistol-grip butts with chequering, and short fore-ends with pewter or German silver schnabel tips. Blade front and buck-horn back sights were standard.

Actions made after 1893 were strengthened to handle smokeless-powder cartridges. The modified No. 3, or 'New No. 3', generally embodying the modified Hepburn-Walker action described below and chambering cartridges as large as .45-105 Sharps, had an octagonal barrel of 26–30in and weighed about 8lb. Double set-triggers and a variety of sophisticated target rifles were available to order.

The No. 3 Hunter's Rifle, dating from 1883, embodied a **Hepburn-Walker** action with the breech lever doubling as a trigger guard. The guns had plain open sights, 26–30in half-octagonal barrels, and chequered pistol-grip butts with curved butt plates. They weighed about 8lb and were available until 1907.

Winchester made a single-shot **Model 1885** falling block rifle, designed by John Moses Browning, the son of the Mormon gunmaker Jonathan Browning. Born in Ogden, Utah, on 21 January 1855, the young Browning quickly showed an aptitude for his father's trade and is said to have built his first gun at the age of 13. However, his rise to fame and fortune was delayed until 1883, when the Winchester Repeating Arms Company purchased rights to a single-shot rifle (protected by US Patent 220,271 of November 1879) and a lever-action design that ultimately became the Winchester Model 1886.

After a career involved in the successful development of firearms ranging from the tiniest blowback personal-defence pistol to one of the best machine-guns ever designed, Browning died in Liége on 26 November 1926 while visiting Fabrique Nationale d'Armes de Guerre. He was undoubtedly the most successful firearms designer the world has ever known.

The first New Haven-made 'Winchester-Browning' M1885 single-shot sporting guns were offered commercially in 1885; by the time production ceased soon after the First World War, 139,725 had been made. Chamberings varied from .22 rimfire to .577 Eley centrefire, small-calibre guns being known colloquially as 'Low Wall' and the larger ones as 'High Wall' owing to the height of the receiver alongside the breech block.

The variants of the Model 1885, universally strong and efficient, ranged from the tiny 4.25lb .44-40 carbine introduced in 1898 to a mighty 12–14lb .32-40 or .38-55 Schuetzen Rifle. A 20-bore shotgun was made for some years, but not until 1914.

Magazine Rifles

In 1878, the Ordnance Department decided on a series of trials and convened a Board of Officers to test magazine rifles. Entries included rifles submitted by or for Andrew Burgess; General W. B. Franklin (Colt); Ward & Burton; the Sharps Rifle Company; Charles Hunt; Lewis, Rice & Lewis; Major Buffington; Bethel Burton; Benjamin Hotchkiss; William Miller; E. Remington & Sons; Frank Tiesing; George Clemmons; James Lee; and Chaffee & Reece.

The Ward-Burton, Miller and Clemmons rifles were submitted by Springfield Armory, the Tiesing and Burgess designs came from the Whitney Arms Company, and Winchester backed the Hotchkiss.

From these, the board recommended the Hotchkiss Magazine Gun, no.19, in a report dated 23 September 1878. Little had been achieved when, in 1881, another Board of Officers was appointed to report on potentially serviceable magazine rifles. By September 1882, 53 rifles had been submitted on behalf of twenty inventors and a final eliminator began. Triallists included the Remington-Keene, submitted by E. Remington & Sons, a rifle designed by Philip Boch of New York City, and a Hotchkiss supplied by Winchester. A Chaffee-Reece was submitted by General James Reece; the Lee was promoted by its inventor; and the Trabue came from William Trabue of Louisville, Kentucky. Guns were sent from Fort Union, New Mexico, by Lieutenant A.H. Russell, and from the Marlin Firearms Co. of New Haven. Charles Dean supplied his gun from Fort Walla Walla in Washington State; the Spencer-Lee was submitted by J.W. Frazier of New York City; the Burton came from W. G. Burton of Brooklyn; the Springfield-Jones was the work of J. Sheridan Jones of Menno, Dakota; and, finally, there was a gun from William Elliott.

The most important of the submissions were the Remington-Keene, the Lee, the Chaffee-Reece and the Hotchkiss. The board, in its report forwarded to the Adjutant-General of the US Army on 29 September 1882, recommended the Lee ahead of the Chaffee-Reece and the Hotchkiss.

The principal technical advances in the Lee lay in its detachable box magazine – an advantage that was far from universally recognised at this time – and in the use of an additional locking lug opposing the bolt handle. The Chaffee-Reece and Hotchkiss actions were locked simply by abutting the base of the bolt-handle rib in the receiver.

Neither Lee nor Chaffee & Reece had backers who could gamble the investment necessary to comply with the government requirements. Benjamin Hotchkiss was in the best position, as he had already enlisted the support of the

Winchester Repeating Arms Company as a result of exhibiting prototypes at the Centennial Exposition in 1876 .

E. Remington & Sons were persuaded to produce the Lee, which, as the victor of the first series of trials, seemed worthy of support; Chaffee & Reece approached Colt, but the price of $150 per gun was unacceptably high. However, General Reece had sufficient influence to persuade the Ordnance Department to use the National Armory. As the unit cost could be reduced to about a third of Colt's demand, largely by modifying machinery on which the Ward-Burton bolt-action rifles had been made a decade previously, the Chaffee-Reece trials rifles were made in Springfield.

The government factory completed 753 Chaffee-Reece rifles by the middle of 1884, though late delivery of 750 Lee and 750 Hotchkiss rifles ordered from Remington and Winchester respectively delayed field trials until the end of the year. 713 examples of each rifle were issued to a wide variety of US Army infantry and cavalry units in 1884–5, especially those that were engaged along the frontiers.

The trials dragged on until, in December 1885, Benét reported to the Secretary of War that although the Lee had proved the most effectual of the magazine guns, respondents firmly favoured the single-shot Trapdoor Springfield! He added:

> 'I have been and am an advocate for a magazine gun, but it would seem the part of wisdom to postpone, for the present, any further efforts toward the adoption of a ... magazine arm for the service. The Springfield rifle gives such general satisfaction to the Army that we can safely wait ... for further developments of magazine systems'.

The first Whitney or '**Whitney-Burgess**' repeating rifle featured a lever action designed by Andrew Burgess, patented on 7 January 1873 (134,589) and 19 October 1875 (no.168,966).

Sometimes known as the 'Burgess-Morse' owing to a most complicated lawsuit then in progress between George Morse and the US Government, the Whitney-Burgess embodied a strong but essentially simple action. The operating lever, which formed the trigger guard, extended upward into the breech. Its short rear face rested against the rear of the receiver while a right-angle arm ran forward along the top inner surface of the receiver. A short breech-block was pivoted to the tip of extension arm.

When the breech lever was depressed, it pulled the locking arm down and away from the rear face of the receiver; at the same time, the right-angle extension pulled the breech-block back from the chamber. The spent case was ejected, an elevator raised a new cartridge to be caught by the lower edge of the returning block, and the gun was ready to fire.

Burgess had exhibited three guns made in his workshop in Oswego, New York, at the Centennial Exposition in 1876. There one of the lever-action rifles caught the eye of Eli Whitney, and a production licence was negotiated in 1877. Two muskets were entered in the US Army breechloading rifle trials of 1878, but one failed during the rust test.

The perfected production gun, introduced in 1880, embodied a cartridge elevator patented in May 1879 by Samuel Kennedy (215,227). As it bore Kennedy's name in the manufacturer's marks, it became misleadingly known as the Whitney-Kennedy instead of the 'Burgess Long Range Repeating Rifle with Kennedy's Improvement'.

The rifle was chambered for all the popular revolver cartridges, including .44-40, and short-case rifle rounds such as .40-60, .45-60 and .45-70. It was made with a round, half-octagon or fully octagonal barrel measuring 24–28in, though carbines were made in small numbers. In common with rivals, Whitney offered double set triggers, long barrels, selected woodwork, engraving and special sights as extras.

The 1880-pattern Whitney-Kennedy was supplemented by the Model 1886 rifle, embodying additional features protected by patents issued in December 1880 (235,204) and December 1883 (209,393). This new small-receiver rifle was made until Winchester purchased Whitney in 1888. It was offered only as a .32-30 sporter, with a 24-inch round, half-octagon or fully-octagonal barrel, or as a .38-40 military-style musket.

A New Model **Evans magazine rifle** of 1877 failed to solve the problems of its predecessor, described in the previous chapter. Offered in the same three basic varieties, the New Model – which had a semi-external hammer and a prominent breech-lever locking catch – chambered the so-called .44 Evans Long centrefire cartridge, which reduced the capacity of the magazine to 26.

Sporters were made with round, half-octagon or fully octagonal 26–30in barrels and weighed 9.5–10lb. Though a few guns were sold to Russia during the Russo–Turkish War, apparently for the imperial navy, the Evans company failed in 1880 after only about two thousand guns had been made.

The **Hotchkiss magazine rifle**, designed by a French-domiciled American, had been exhibited at the Centennial Exposition in Philadelphia in 1876. Protected by US Patent 93,822, granted on 17 August 1869, its action was much stronger than any of the contemporary Winchesters. As the rifle appeared to offer the benefits of good long-range performance and durability, the Winchester Repeating Arms Company bought US manufacturing rights in 1877.

Small quantities of Model 1878 Hotchkiss rifles and carbines were assembled at Springfield Armory by uniting actions supplied by Winchester with government-pattern one-piece stocks. The Hotchkiss had a tube magazine in the butt, running down from the receiver ahead of the trigger. Cartridges were loaded into the tube through a butt-trap, rather in the manner of the Spencer carbine. The magazine held five rounds, though a sixth could be placed directly in the chamber. They were fed forward by the follower spring. Cartridge stops connected to the trigger ensured that, when the trigger was pressed, one round moved forward until its nose contacted the underside of the bolt. Opening the bolt to the limit of its backward stroke allowed the rim of the cartridge to spring upward far enough to be caught by the lower edge of the bolt as it returned. Closing the bolt pushed the cartridge forward into the chamber. A cut-off mechanism permitted single shots to be fired while the magazine was held in reserve.

About 2500 Model 1879 Hotchkiss rifles were acquired by the US Navy in 1879–80. These differed principally in the design and position of the combination safety catch/cut-off lever, which was let into the stock of the army guns – beneath the rear of the receiver – but projected above the stock of the navy pattern.

Regulation Hotchkiss rifles had one-piece walnut stocks, their barrels being held by two sprung bands. An 1879-pattern buck-horn back sight lay on the barrel ahead of the bolt mechanism. They had split-bridge receivers and were locked by the bolt-handle rib abutting the front edge of the receiver bridge.

The Hotchkiss was not successful enough to shake the army out of its basic conservatism, even though some officers reported favourably. Late in 1880 the Chief of Ordnance, Brigadier General Stephen Benét, reported perceptively to the Secretary of War:

> The Hotchkiss has met with ... reverses, due to hasty manufacture and imperfect design in some of its minor parts, which can hardly be charged to the invention. It is believed that these defects, in which the mechanical principles ... were not involved, have been corrected in the new model, and more favorable results may now be anticipated. The manufacturer's experience with this gun proves that difficulties are ever to be met and overcome in perfecting a new invention that has to stand the severe test of field service. The principle of the Hotchkiss is a good one, but there seems to be some prejudice existing in our service against the bolt system and its awkward handle that time and custom may overcome.

Small numbers of the so-called First Pattern (1879–80) and Second Pattern (1880–3) sporting rifles were made at a time when the US Army was actively considering the Hotchkiss as an issue weapon. However, neither was particularly successful in a market dominated by lever-action guns and only 22,521 Hotchkiss-type rifles were made in 1879–83.

The improved 1883-pattern Hotchkiss was similar to the guns made at Springfield in 1879, its most obvious characteristic being the two-piece stock.

Unlike its predecessors, which were loaded by removing the magazine spring and follower through the butt trap, the M1883 was loaded through the top of the open action.

Cartridges could be inserted into the feedway, rim first, and pressed back and down into the magazine tube. The changes enabled the 1883-pattern magazine to hold six cartridges instead of five. The bolt lock and the magazine cut-off lay on the side of the receiver.

The success of the rifle in the 1882 trials, when the Hotchkiss placed third behind the Lee and the Chaffee-Reece, persuaded the Ordnance Department to order 750 1883-type guns at $15 apiece from the Winchester Repeating Arms Company. Unfortunately, the field trials failed to generate enthusiasm in the army for bolt-action magazine rifles; in addition, the Winchester, though overhauling the more complicated Chaffee-Reece, was still judged to be inferior to the Lee.

Seeking to recoup some of the investment in the abortive government rifles ordered after the trials of 1882–3, Winchester offered the perfected Hotchkiss commercially. The January 1884 catalogue, containing the first large-scale promotion of the Hotchkiss Model 1883, stated that the gun resulted from 'the experience of six years of manufacturing and the valuable suggestions of many experienced officers who have used it in the field. It is a most simple and solid repeating gun, capable of doing good service under the most disadvantageous circumstances'.

The Hotchkiss Sporting Rifle was offered with a 26-inch round, half-octagon or fully octagonal barrel, and weighed about 8.5lb. Guns generally had pistol-grip butts, while set-triggers were supplied to special order.

Unfortunately, the sporting market was still far more accustomed to lever-action rifles. With the appearance of the Browning-designed Winchester Model 1886, which could handle high-powered cartridges with equal facility, the Hotchkiss bolt-action sporter was relegated to comparative obscurity.

The M1883, made in rifle, carbine and musket forms, was exclusively chambered for the regulation .45-70-405 cartridge. It has been stated that a .40-65 version was also available but, though announced in Winchester catalogues in the summer of 1884, there is no evidence that suitable guns were made in anything other than prototype form.

The six-shot 9lb M1883 musket – made with a 32-inch barrel until 1884 and a 28-inch pattern thereafter – proved popular in militia circles even though it had been rejected by the Board of Ordnance; by far the majority of the 62,034 examples made before assembly ceased in 1899 had taken this form. In 1913, however, Winchester scrapped all the remaining Hotchkiss parts.

The **Remington-Keene rifle** was never adopted by the armed forces, although the US Navy bought 250 for shipboard trials in 1880 and the US Army acquired a similar number in 1881 for trials against the Remington-Lee and the Winchester-Hotchkiss. Others were purchased in 1884 to arm the reservation police maintained by the Indian Bureau. Unlike the military versions, these were half-stocked and marked 'U.S.I.D.'.

Made by E. Remington & Sons under patents granted to James Keene of Newark, New Jersey, in February and March 1874, January and September 1876, and March and July 1877, the 8.5lb bolt-action repeater had a nine-round tube magazine beneath the barrel. Government guns chambered the regulation .45-70-405, though others accepted .40-70 Remington and .43 Spanish ammunition.

Introduced as a sporting rifle in 1877 and offered until 1888, by which time about 5000 had been made, the Remington-Keene had several unusual features. Unlike most other tube-magazine guns, it could be loaded from above or below the receiver at will. The cartridges were only transferred from the magazine to the elevator (or carrier) when the breech was opened; in addition, they were held securely in position while on the carrier. Most other lever actions operated badly when inverted, but the Remington-Keene worked satisfactorily in these circumstances.

One of its most interesting features was that the gun was left at half-cock after the action had been cycled. It was necessary to thumb back the cocking piece before pulling the trigger, which at the time was considered a great advantage in certain military circles. The half-cock system could be disabled merely by removing the 'hammer fly', let into the tumbler.

The standard rifles were about 43.5in long and had 24-inch barrels. As they proved inferior to the Lee, so Remington ceased promoting them in the mid-1880s.

The failure of the **Lee** single-shot rifle in the US Army trials, even though 145 had been made at Springfield in 1875, was a great disappointment for the inventor. James Paris Lee had been born in the small Scottish town of Hawick in 1831, but emigrated with his parents to Canada when just a child. Lee was apprenticed to his clockmaker father before starting out on his own account. Settling first in Janesville, Wisconsin, and then in nearby Stevens Point, Lee began his gun-designing career in the early 1860s.

A breechloading conversion of the regulation Springfield rifle-musket was followed by a pivoting-barrel design, and then by the dropping-block rifles. Lee's attention subsequently turned to a simple turning-bolt rifle protected by US Patent no. 221,328 of November 1879. After the short-lived participation of Sharps, exploitation of the design was entrusted to by E. Remington & Sons; not only did the rifle prove good enough to attract the US Army and the US Navy, but it was also ultimately to serve the British Army in two world wars. James Lee was responsible for the US Navy 'straight-pull' (q.v.) rifle of 1895, made by Winchester, and died in retirement in Short Beach, Connecticut, in 1904.

The first turn-bolt Lee action was locked by a shoulder on the bolt handle abutting the receiver and a small opposed lug engaging a seat cut in the inner receiver wall. The lug was added after prototypes locked only by the bolt-handle rib abutting the face of the receiver had failed during trials. The perfected rifle had a rotating extractor and a detachable box magazine; a cut-off allowed it to be used as a single-loader.

The Lee Arms Company was formed in 1879 in Bridgeport, Connecticut, sharing premises (and possibly some of the financial backing) of the near-moribund Sharps Rifle Company. Early prototypes had included several Sharps-Borchardt components, and the bolt handle lay behind the receiver bridge.

Lee rifles included in the September 1882 trials chambered regulation .45-70 cartridges. Gun No. 10, submitted by E. Remington & Sons, was a standard M1879; No. 36, also entered by Remington, had an 'improved bolt' (usually identified as the model of 1882). The Spencer-Lee rifles, No. 24, 31 and 35, amalgamated Lee-type box magazines with an idiosyncratic slide-action loading mechanism.

The US Army showed so little enthusiasm for the Lee magazine rifle that matters were left to the navy. As early as 1876, the US Navy Bureau of Ordnance had recommended the adoption of a magazine breech-loader; M1879 Hotchkiss rifles had been acquired in 1879–80, whilst 250 examples of the M1880 Remington-Keene and a similar number of Remington-made M1879 Lee rifles were acquired in 1881–2. These were purchased not only to arm newly commissioned warships, but also to allow long-term testing to be undertaken.

Though marked as the products of the Lee Arms Company of Bridgeport, Connecticut, the Lee-type bolt-action guns were made by E. Remington & Sons. Virtually all guns purchased by the navy bore distinctive inspectors' marks – e.g., 'WWK' or 'WMF' – together with an 'anchor/US' marking. They had a one-piece walnut stock, two spring-retained barrel bands, and swivels ahead of the magazine and on the nose-band. The only safety feature was the half-cock notch on the cocking piece.

The rifles were 48.5in overall, had 29.5-inch five-groove barrels, and weighed about 8.5lb. The tangent-leaf back sight was graduated to 500 yards on the base and 1200 on the leaf. US Navy guns all chambered .45-70 government cartridges, but a few sporting rifles in .43 Spanish, .44-77 Necked and others were made to order.

The navy consensus favoured the Lee, though most of the purchases were of the later 1885 pattern. However, more than 200 1882-type guns were bought from a Boston wholesaler in 1891 for the Massachusetts Naval Brigade.

In March 1884, Lee and his employee Louis Diss received US Patent 295,563 to protect a ribbed sheet-steel magazine that retained cartridges when detached from the gun. The patent was assigned to Remington and incorporated in the

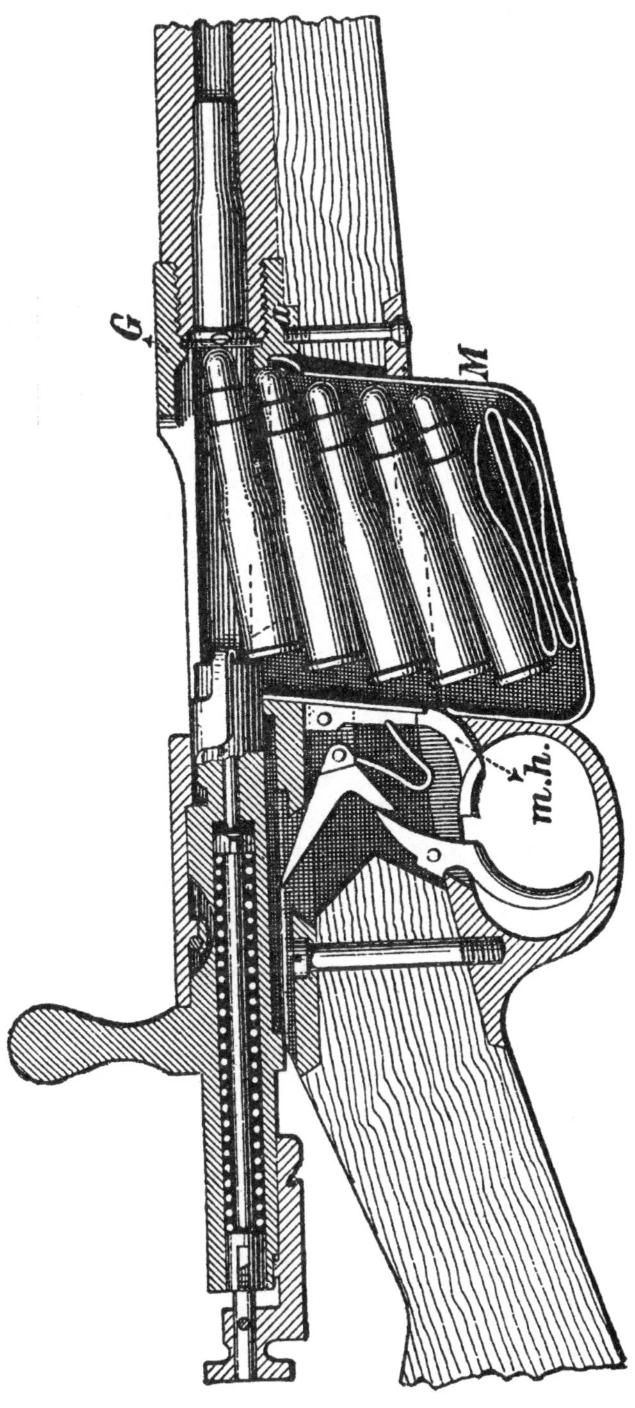

The 1879-type Lee action

improved 1885-pattern rifle, which also had a separate bolt-head with a non-rotating extractor and a greatly enlarged cocking-piece head.

Military-style rifles still chambered standard .45-70-405 cartridges, measured 52in overall, had five-groove 33.5-inch barrels, and weighed about 8.5lb. They were stocked and sighted similarly to the M1882, lacking an upper hand guard, and were made exclusively by Remington. Rifles made after 1888 were marked 'Remington Arms Company', as a result of the collapse of E. Remington & Sons two years earlier. Those purchased by the US Navy display 'U.S.' beneath an anchor, together with an inventory number and inspector's initials; 1610 were ordered in August 1888 to arm newly commissioned warships, pending the introduction of a small-calibre rifle. The last deliveries were made in the 1890s, totalling about four thousand.

The Remington-Lee was surprisingly successful on the export markets, particularly in south and central America. Consequently, many thousands had been made by the end of the nineteenth century. Yet the bolt system was never popular on the North American commercial market, where its strength and an ability to fire ballistically efficient cartridges (at least in box-magazine form) were reckoned inferior to magazine capacity and speed of action. The Remington-Lee challenged this perception, but could not break the mould.

Marlin was one of the few makers of lever-action rifles to remain independent; most of the others either failed in the 1880s or were purchased during Winchester's periodic disposal of troublesome rivals.

The **Marlin Model 1881** repeating rifle was based on patents granted in the USA to Andrew Burgess on 7 January 1873 (134,589), 19 and 26 November 1878 (210,091 and 210,181) and 3 June 1879 (216,080), plus an improved cartridge elevator designed by Burgess in collusion with John Marlin (patent 250,825 of 13 December 1881). It also acknowledged elements of Henry Wheeler's February 1865 patent (46,286), reissued in November 1880; no. 167,712 granted to Emil Toepperwein in September 1875; and two of Marlin's – 222,414 and 234,309 – issued on 9 December 1879 and 9 November 1880 respectively.

The Burgess patents were essentially those used by Whitney and Colt. The Wheeler patent was assigned to Marlin, while Toepperwein's was purchased simply to avoid an embarrassing infringement.

The M1881 rifle was another ultra-simple design, in stark contrast to contemporary Winchesters. It locked by using the breech-lever extension as a prop for the longitudinally sliding breech-block. When the gun fired, the strain was taken by the breech-lever pivot pin – in theory less than perfect, but in practice quite able to handle the pressures of most cartridges of the day. Indeed, the M1881 soon proved capable of handling the .45-70 government round, performing surprisingly well in the US Army repeating rifle trials of 1881–2, and was an instantaneous commercial success.

Many of the earliest rifles were distributed to Schoverling, Daly & Gales of New York as dealers' samples in the early spring of 1881. They had octagonal barrels of 24–30in and chambered .40-60 or .45-70, plus .45-85 from 1885. Their under-barrel tube magazines contained 8–10 rounds.

Heavy barrels, double set-triggers (from 1883), select woodwork, engraving, and a variety of sights were available to order. There were also a few special 'Light' rifles, weighing about 12oz less than normal; made only in .40-60 and .45-70, most of these guns apparently went to Britain. In addition, fifteen smooth-bore shotguns were made in 1884–8.

A small-frame adaption of the M1881 was introduced in 1884 to handle the .32-40 Ballard cartridge, followed in 1886 by another variant chambering the .38-55 Ballard version. Production ceased in October 1891 after 21,716 M1881 rifles had been made in series with other Marlins; consequently, numbers ran as high as 51233.

The genius of Andrew Burgess, harnessed by Whitney and Marlin, was also exploited by Colt. The **Colt-Burgess rifle** was an improved Whitney-Burgess, embodying five patents issued to Burgess in 1873–82 and a sixth granted to Burgess & Marlin in December 1881. The barrels were marked as the product of Colt, together with 'PAT. JAN. 7, 73, OCT. 19, 75, APR. 1, 79, DEC. 7, 80, DEC. 13, 81, JAN. 3, 82'.

Colt introduced the first .44-40-200 centrefire sporting rifles and a short-barrel carbine in November 1883. The rifles offered 25-inch round, half-octagon or fully octagonal barrels, had tube magazines containing fifteen rounds, and weighed 8.5–8.8lb. The carbine had a 20-inch round barrel, weighed 7.3lb and had a twelve-round magazine. Prices ranged from $24 for the carbine to $27 for the octagon-barrel rifles, an additional dollar being charged for each extra barrel-inch. Decoration and specially selected woodwork were available to order, but rarely used on Colt-Burgess guns; production life was very short.

The entry of Colt into the lever-action rifle business threatened the sales of the inferior 1873- and 1876-pattern Winchesters, which lacked the strength of the Colt-Burgess. Winchester simply let it be known that its promising experimental revolvers would be put into production to compete against the Colt Single Action Army pattern. As Winchester had also purchased rights to yet another of Burgess's designs – an improved 1873-pattern rifle, patented in December 1883 – Colt stopped making lever-action guns in 1884, after only 3810 rifles and 2593 carbines had been made.

Designed by Reuben Chaffee and General James Reece of Springfield, Illinois, the principal patent (US no.216,657) being granted in February 1879, 753 examples of the **Chaffee-Reece rifle** were made at Springfield Armory in 1884. They bore an appreciable external resemblance to the 1879-model Hotchkiss; the stock, bands and back sight, for example, were practically identical. Internally, however, Chaffee & Reece relied on a bolt-actuated oscillating rack instead of a conventional magazine spring.

As the bolt moved back, the mobile rack was pushed back down the magazine and its retainers slipped under and behind the rims of the cartridges. The fixed rack simply held the rounds in place. As the bolt was closed, the mobile rack pulled the cartridges forward. The bolt face caught the rim of the first cartridge, raised by an elevator, and fed it into the chamber.

The Chaffee-Reece action was very interesting, as it separated the cartridges and was virtually immune from the perennial (and dangerous) flaw of tube magazines in which the nose of a cartridge rested against the primer of the round ahead of it.

Unfortunately, the oscillating rack system was much more complicated than the Hotchkiss spring, and its advantages were hidden among a welter of breakages. Tube magazines predictably proved to be inferior to the Lee-pattern box in the service trials, when the Chaffee-Reece rifles were particularly prone to failure.

The troops were not particularly fond of the Chaffee-Reece, partly owing to excessive breakages, partly to tortuous dismantling and reassembly, and partly because closing the bolt lifted the weight of all the remaining cartridges in the magazine. The rifle had one brief resurrection – in .30 calibre – during the trials of 1892–3, but was otherwise ignored by posterity.

The handsome and extremely sturdy lever-action **Bullard rifle** was patented by James Bullard on 16 August 1881 (245,700) and 23 October 1883 (287,229), and made by the Bullard Repeating Arms Company of Springfield, Massachusetts, in 1884–9.

The action relied on levers and rack-and-pinion gear to move the breech bolt, being locked at the rear by a variant of the Remington Rolling Block. It rapidly attained a reputation for an extremely smooth operating stroke, one gun allegedly firing twelve shots in five seconds in a trial where its nearest rival – presumably a Winchester – managed only eleven shots in seven seconds.

Bullard repeaters were made in a variety of sizes. According to adverts in *Forest and Stream*, dating from 1884–5, these included 26- or 28-inch round, half-octagon or fully-octagonal barrels, giving weights ranging from 8–9.75lb. Magazine capacity was generally eleven cartridges, though a twelfth could be carried in the breech.

The standard rifles were made with straight-wrist stocks, pistol grips being just one of the many optional extras. There were half-length magazines, specially-selected butts or fore-ends, chequered to order, and receivers were often colour case-hardened. Beach and Lyman sights were offered, though even the standard Bullard rifles were expensive; the .32 version, with a 26-inch round barrel, cost $33 in 1885. Bullards were customarily offered in proprietary chamberings such as .32-40, .38-45, .40-75, .40-90, .45-60, .45-75, .45-85 and .50-115, but a few were also made for the .45-70 US Government cartridge.

An advert in the July 1884 issue of *Forest and Stream* challenged rival manufacturers to '. . . produce a Repeater that can compare with ours in ease of operation, safety, workmanship, style, finish, rapidity of fire, trajectory, penetration and accuracy'. Unfortunately, though the guns were sturdy enough to handle the .50-115 Express cartridge (one example being owned by Theodore Roosevelt), they were unable to withstand competition from Winchester and Marlin, particularly after the introduction of the former's 1886-model rifle. This was at least partly due to Bullard's reluctance to chamber guns for Winchester and other popular cartridges, and so the Bullard Repeating Rifle Company had failed by 1890.

The Colt-Burgess was succeeded by the **Colt Lightning** or 'New Model Lightning' slide-action repeater, locked by a Burgess-type pivoting wedge beneath the breech bolt. The subject of patents granted to William Elliott on 29 May 1883 (278,324) and 18 September 1883 (285,020), the Lightning was well made and worked efficiently once initial ejection problems had been overcome. It could be fired merely by operating the slide handle with the trigger held back.

The medium-frame Lightning was sold commercially from the end of 1884 until 1900. The standard chamberings were .32-20, .38-40 and .44-40, the rifle magazine holding fifteen rounds to the carbine's twelve. It is said that a .25-20-86 version was offered commercially, but no survivor has yet been found.

Medium-frame Lightnings were offered in rifle form, with a 26-inch round or octagonal barrel and a fifteen-round magazine; as a twelve-shot carbine with a 20-inch round barrel; and as a scarce Baby Carbine (chambered for .44-40 and experimentally for .32-20) with a 20-inch barrel, a twelve-round magazine and a weight of just 5.25lb. A selection of sights, finishes and woodwork was available.

The small-frame .22 rimfire and large-frame Express rifles appeared in 1887, their barrels bearing additional patent acknowledgements – 26 May 1885, 15 June 1886 and 22 February 1887. Apart from the differences in size, their most obvious feature was the breech cover: pre-1887 medium-frame guns had an exposed breech bolt.

Handling cartridges such as .38-56-256, .40-60-260, .45-60-300, .45-85-285 and .50-95-300, the Express Rifle (1887–94) presented better-established lever-action guns with a worthy rival. Ten-shot Express rifles were made with 28-inch round or octagonal barrels and weighed 9.5–10lb. There was a 9lb carbine with a 22-inch barrel, and an uncommon 'Baby Express Carbine' weighing 8lb.

A set-trigger patented by Frederick Knous in December 1885 will be occasionally encountered, in addition to an unsuccessful auxiliary bolt-locking arm patented by Carl Ehbets in April 1885, but the Lightning was discontinued in 1900 after 89,777 standard medium frame and 6,496 large-frame Express rifles had been made. A few had been acquired by the San Francisco Police Department, but orders of this type had been rare.

Shotguns

Scatterguns were popular in the West, especially in the hands of railroad, bank and stagecoach guards – the origin of the phrase 'riding shotgun'. Guns will still be found with the marks of companies such as Wells Fargo, or the Southern Pacific Rail Road.

The ability to hit a target without necessarily aiming accurately was a great bonus, while two-barrel guns could deliver a second shot faster than any revolver. American-made guns came in great variety, including single-shot designs, double-barrel patterns, and mechanically operated repeaters. Others were built on well-proven rifle actions such as the Sharps, the Remington or the Whitney Phoenix.

Among the earliest of the simple single-barrel shotguns, with box locks and exposed central hammers, was the 'American' made by **Hyde & Shatuck** of Hatfield, Massachusetts (1876–80), and then until 1908 by their successors C. S. Shatuck & Company.

Patented by Joshua **Stevens** and made in Chicopee Falls, Massachusetts, the **Stevens** double-barrel hammer gun of 1877 was offered in 10 and 12-bore with 24–32in barrels. A 'locking trigger' in an auxiliary guard operated a sliding under-bolt mechanism. Rifle-shotguns, a combination popular in North America, were added from c.1880 in accordance with Stevens' patent of 28 January 1879 (no. 211,642).

Stevens products were often simply and weakly made, but were cheap enough to sell in substantial numbers. By contrast, the '**Colt** Breech-Loading Shotgun, Double barrel, Hammer Model 1878' was made only in 10 and 12-bore – albeit with barrels measuring 28–32in and a variety of chokes to choose. Weight ranged from 7.5 to 11.5lb. The Colts had side locks with rebounding hammers, Purdey-type under-lugs, and a top lever. The barrel-blocks were imported from Birmingham, including damascus, laminated, and fine-twist patterns. Straight-wrist or half pistol-grip butts were English or Circassian walnut.

The Colt shotguns were based on patents granted to Andrew Whitmore and William Mason. Production ceased in 1889, after 22,683 had been made; a few more were assembled from parts in the early 1890s, together with about 40 double rifles sharing the same action. The rifles were customarily chambered for .45-70, .45-85, .45-90 and .45-100 centrefire cartridges.

Other manufacturers took an easier route, preferring not to dabble too greatly in the production of these highly specialised items. Consequently, the **Sharps** Rifle Company marketed English-made 'Old Reliable' guns in 1879–81; most were the work of P. Webley & Sons of Birmingham. The first or 1879-pattern shotguns to bear **Winchester**'s name were made in England by C. G. Bonehill and W. C. Scott & Sons, though they bore nothing but Winchester marks on the barrel ribs. They were side-by-side 10 or 12-bore doubles, ranging from the plain 'D' to a deluxe 'Match Gun'.

Cocked by a thumb lever on the right side of the breech, the 12, 16 or 20-bore **Fox** single barrel semi-hammerless shotgun was made in 1882–1900 by the American Arms Company. This partnership of Henry Wheeler and George Fox moved from Boston to Milwaukee in 1893, but the business was purchased by Marlin in 1901 and work ceased.

Many companies made two-barrel hammer shotguns. One of the original partners of W.H. Baker & Sons Company, **Lyman Smith**, bought the business in 1880 and immediately renamed it 'L. C. Smith & Company'. Alexander Brown of Syracuse – apparently L. C. Smith's works superintendent – received US Patents 274,435 (March 1883) and 289,062 (November 1883) to protect a rotary self-compensating locking bolt and an improved hammer mechanism. Smith then substituted Brown-pattern actions for the Baker-patent side locks.

William H. Baker and Lyman Smith's brother set up the rival **Ithaca** Gun Company in Ithaca, New York, in the early 1880s. This made an improved Baker box-lock action with a radial top lever patented on 25 May and 1 June 1880 (228,020 and 228,165).

The **Lefever** hammer and semi-hammerless doubles included a self-compensating action to minimise the effects of wear. The first guns were patented in June 1878 (205,193) and June 1880 (229,429), then perfected with the grant of US Patent 264,173 to Daniel Lefever and Frederick Smith on 12 September 1882. The 1882 patent protected the Lefever Ball Joint, a short hemispherical-tip bolt acting on the cup-faced barrel under-lug. Wear in the action could be cured simply by tightening the bolt.

The perfected or 1882-pattern double-barrel **Parker** shotgun had a top-lever with a doll's head bolt, though the original rocking-bar mechanism retained much of its popularity for a few years prior to 1890.

Offered until 1910, the **Remington** New Model 1882 had a top lever breech-lock, distinctive 'Circular Hammers' and rebounding locks. It came in 10, 12 and 16-bore, and in seven grades ranging from exceptionally plain to highly ornate. The 28–32in barrels were rolled or damascus-twist steel and had matted ribs. The guns had chequered half-pistol grip butts, double triggers, and weighed 6.5–10.5lb. A few 10-bore New Model Heavy guns were made in 1883–95, with extension ribs and weights as great as 11lb.

The market for good-quality **hammerless** shotguns was initially satisfied by importing guns from Britain and Belgium. However, the US manufacturers were quick to compete; Harrington & Richardson began to make Anson & Deeley guns as early as 1881, and the first hammerless Colt dated from 1883.

Derived from patents issued to Andrew Whitmore & William Mason on 22 August and 19 September 1882, made only in 10 and 12-bore with damascus-twist 28–32in barrels, the box-lock M1883 **Colts** had top levers. The cheapest gun – plain finish, English walnut stock, damascus barrels – sold for $80 in 1893, but specially finished examples could cost $300. Demand was surprisingly meagre. When the last guns had been sent into store in 1896, only 7366 had been made.

Daniel **Lefever** of Syracuse was offering his Automatic Hammerless gun as early as January 1885. Easily recognisable by the thumb-catch on the tang, this double-trigger gun was sold in seven grades ranging from plain 'F' ($75) to special 'AA' ($300). An 'Optimus' super-deluxe pattern was introduced some time prior to 1893, selling for $400. Lefever also made a few double rifles and combination guns prior to 1890, but the quantities involved were small. The guns all had compensated actions, compensated cocking levers and a host of other advanced features.

The first **L. C. Smith** hammerless shotgun appeared in 1886, but Smith sold the business to John Hunter in 1888. It transferred to Fulton, New York, in 1890; however, output was still marked 'The L.C. Smith Shot Gun'.

Among the many other types of **single-barrel hammer guns** sold prior to 1890 were the 'Champion' – made in 1885–90 by the John P. Lovell Arms Company of Boston, Massachusetts – and a large series of unnamed guns made in 1887–1902 by Forehand & Wadsworth and their successors, Forehand & Company of Worcester, Massachusetts. Others may be encountered with 'Side Snap' marks applied by Iver Johnson of Worcester and then Fitchburg, Massachusetts. The Massachusetts Arms Company of Chicopee Falls and the Davenport Arms Company of Norwich, Connecticut, both made guns of this type; some bore the marks of 'A. J. Aubrey', which showed that they had been made by the Meriden Arms Company for Sears, Roebuck & Company.

Single-barrel hammerless shotguns made for Amos **Dickerman** of New Haven, Connecticut, were among the earliest of their type to be made in North America, though never as popular as exposed-hammer patterns prior to 1900. They were protected by US Patent 369,437, granted on 6 September 1887. Work was apparently sub-contracted to Marlin.

Among the lesser manufacturers of **single-barrel hammerless guns** were Forehand & Wadsworth and the Forehand Arms Company, whose guns dated from c.1887–1902. Iver Johnson made the 'Top Snap', while others will be found with the marks of the Crescent Gun Company or the Baker Gun & Forging Company.

An alternative approach to providing extra shots was taken by Christopher Spencer and Sylvester Roper, who patented a **slide-action repeater** in the USA on 4 April 1882 (255,894); Roper received a patent of addition on 21 April 1885 (316,401) for a modification of the basic design. A stubby fore-grip was used to pivot the breech-block, ejecting a spent case and feeding a cartridge into the chamber each time the cycle was repeated. Five rounds were carried in a tube magazine beneath the barrel, though a sixth could be inserted directly into the chamber if required.

A Spencer-Roper rifle was offered unsuccessfully to the US Army in 1882, but, by 1884, a variant was being touted as a 12-bore shotgun with a 30 or 32-inch barrel. Opinions of the gun differed. Bannerman made much of a successful test by the US Army in 1884, but others drew attention to the ease with which unfired cartridges could be ejected in rapid fire. When the Spencer Arms Company failed in 1889, its assets passed first to Pratt & Whitney and thence to Francis Bannerman & Sons of New York.

Seeking a repeating shotgun to compete with the Spencer-Roper pattern, Winchester initially chose the **lever-action** Model 1887 designed by John Browning. Chambered for 10 and 12-bore cartridges, the M1887 was available with barrels ranging from a 20-inch 'riot pattern' to 32in. Chokes, finish and decoration were often dictated by individual clients. About 64,855 guns had been sold by 1901, when the M1887 was superseded by an 'M1901' version that had been suitably strengthened to handle smokeless-powder 10-bore ammunition.

Handguns

Revolvers

The largely overlooked M1875 was followed by the improved **Remington Model 1890**, differing principally in the removal of the under-barrel web. Indeed, the 'new gun' may simply have been a way of ridding the newly formed Remington Arms Company of many 1875-pattern components. The M1890 also underwent military trials, emerging most favourably, but gate loading was being challenged by the swinging cylinder; assembly ceased in 1894 after little more than 2000 had been made.

The **Colt Peacemaker** or 'Single Action Army Revolver' was very popular commercially from the mid-1870s onward, though the notion that it was touted by every outlaw, lawman and frontiersman is far from the truth. In the truly lawless days of the West, the Colt was simply one of many cap-lock or cartridge guns on offer. The myth of its supremacy is attributable to Hollywood's love affair with this particular revolver and the Winchester lever-action rifle.

A combination of blued and case-hardened parts was standard, grips were walnut, and the back sight was a simple groove milled along the frame-top. 'Ejector-case' barrels varied between 4.75 and 16in, while those lacking ejectors

PAT GARRETT

Patrick Floyd 'Pat' Garrett was born in Alabama in June 1850. Raised in Louisiana, he became a cowboy and buffalo hunter in Texas before marrying in 1879 and settling in Lincoln County, New Mexico. Appointed deputy sheriff and then sheriff of the county, Garrett is best known for killing Billy the Kid (1881). After working as a lawman and rancher, he was then appointed Collector of Customs in El Paso in December 1901 but left the customs service in 1906 to return to ranching. Garrett was fatally shot on 29 February 1908 near Las Cruces, New Mexico; his killer, Wayne Brazel, alleged self-defence although many local people suspected that Garrett's death owed more to revenge than chance.

Pat Garrett used .44-40 WCF Colt Single Action Army revolver no. 55093 to kill Billy the Kid. The gun, which had a 7.5-inch barrel, was shipped from Hartford to Benjamin Kittredge & Company of Cincinnati in April 1880. Among the many 'testimonial guns' subsequently presented to Garrett by grateful citizens were a .41 Colt double action (no. 138671), given by friends in El Paso perhaps to mark his birthday in June 1903. Shipped 'soft' from Hartford in October 1902 in readiness for engraving, the revolver had a 4.5in ejector-case barrel, engraved gold-washed nickel plating, and gold-washed white metal grips.

Garrett was also given a cased .38 folding-hammer Merwin & Hulbert, no. 16648, with his name in gold on the case-lid and in black enamel on the grips. Forehand & Wadsworth 'Swamp Angel' revolver no. 4318 was another gift, with a gold-plated cylinder, silver plating on the frame and barrel, and grips of ivory; .32 Hopkins & Allen Model XL no. 3164 was by comparison extremely plain.

ranged from 2–7.5in. Gutta-percha, ivory or mother-of-pearl grips were to be found, while decoration ranged from the most elegant damascening to pure vulgarity.

Minor variations were to be found in the design of the ejector assembly, the ejector rod and the ejector-rod head. The most obvious external change concerned the cylinder-pin retainer, originally a pointed screw running diagonally up under the pin. On 15 September 1874, William Mason had been granted US Patent 155,095 to protect an improved pin retainer embodying a transverse bolt locked by a spring. This was added to the Single Action Army Model at the end of 1893, in the region of no.153000, and introduced gradually until incorporated in all guns numbered above 165000 (1896).

In addition to a minor target-shooting 'Flat Top' derivative (c.1888–95), which had a special open back sight on a raised strap above the cylinder, Colt made a target version known as the Bisley from 1894 until the First World War. Barrels measured 4.75–7.5in and the grip was moved upward to bring the axis of the barrel nearer the hand, enabling the sights to be brought back onto the target after each shot with minimal trouble. Bisley guns – occasionally made with flat-top frames – also had a special hammer with a lower spur. This enabled the sights to be seen; on normal Single Action Army revolvers, the tip of the hammer obstructed the back-sight when the groove was down.

The short-barrel ejectorless gun, often known as the Sheriff's or Bartender's Model, was introduced in the early 1880s. Widely favoured for personal defence, on both sides of the law, these Single Action Army revolvers usually had barrels of 3–4in.

The 'Buntline Special', conversely, was largely created by myth. No trace has been found of an order for five special long-barrel revolvers said to have been placed by Edward Judson, a write of pulp fiction and a dubious biography of Wyatt Earp under the pseudonym 'Ned Buntline'. These were allegedly presented early in the twentieth century to leading lawmen: Bat Masterson, Earp, Charlie Bassett, Neal Brown and Bill Tilghman. A few long-barrel Single Action Army revolvers had been made shortly after the 1876 Philadelphia Centennial Exposition, but they were considered as light carbines or 'Buggy Rifles' and had skeletal wire stocks.

Peacemaker chamberings varied from .22 Short to .476 Eley. The standard Single Action Army Model (total production 310,386 in 1873–1940) was most commonly encountered in .45 Long Colt (150,683) and .44-40 (64,489); most of the standard Bisley guns (44,350, 1894–1915) came in .32-20 (13,291) and .38-40 (12,163).

Among the most popular chamberings were .32-20, .38-40 and .44-40 Winchester, allowing purchasers, including many Westerners, to have an identically-chambered rifle and revolver. This was paramount where communications were very poor. By the time production ceased in 1940, approximately 357,859 revolvers had been made on the basis of the Single Action pattern; serial numbers had reached about 182000 by the end of 1898. Some commercial guns in .44-40 were marked 'COLT FRONTIER SIX-SHOOTER'; others bore the address of the London sales office, 14 Pall Mall.

Hopkins & Allen's solitary contribution to the large-calibre military revolver market was the Model 1877, based on patents granted to Benjamin Williams of New York in April 1874 (150,120); Daniel Moore in December 1874 (157,860, assigned to Merwin, Hulbert & Co.); and William Hulbert of Brooklyn, New York, in March 1877 (187,975).

The guns were marketed exclusively by Merwin, Hulbert & Company and their successors, Hulbert Brothers & Company, sporting-goods distributors of New York City.

The revolver barrel, integral with the upper part of the frame, was attached to the standing breech by the cylinder axis pin and a lock on the frame ahead of the trigger guard. When the catch was released, the barrel could be swung laterally and drawn forward. This pulled the cylinder forward until a star-plate extractor, attached to the breech, pulled spent cases (but not unfired rounds) out of the cylinder until they fell clear. A sliding gate on the right side of the frame beneath the hammer permitted reloading.

A .44 centrefire gun with a seven-inch barrel was tried by the US Army in 1877, but the comparatively weak open frame was unfit for service – though small quantities were bought by Kansas. Merwin & Hulbert military revolvers are very rare. Most of them chambered either .44-40 WCF, being marked CALIBRE WINCHESTER 1873, or .44 Merwin & Hulbert. The latter rarely bore marks.

The first top-strap revolver, a five-shot .38 centrefire pattern with a sheath trigger, appeared in 1879–80. It was followed by the .44 Pocket Army Model, with a $3\frac{1}{4}$-inch barrel and a bird's head butt. The earliest Pocket Army revolvers lacked the top strap, probably to use existing components, but a revised pattern was available by 1882.

The first double-action revolver was announced in the spring of 1883. By 1884, the range had been expanded to include a .44-40 Double Action Army revolver, with a 7-inch barrel and a weight of 41oz; the .44-40 Double Action Pocket Army weighing 36oz; and the .38 S&W-chambered Triumph, a five-shot gun with barrels of $3\frac{1}{2}$ or $5\frac{1}{2}$in. The Army pattern had a conventional lanyard ring on the butt heel, while the Pocket Army had a lanyard hole bored through the extended bird's head butt beneath the grips. Pocket Army revolvers could be converted to Army length simply by substituting the barrel and top-strap assembly. Later Triumph-type revolvers may even be encountered with a folding hammer.

The efficient Merwin & Hulberts were all available in blued or nickel-plated forms, and had chequered gutta-percha grips. Made under contract by Hop-

BASS OUTLAW

The large-calibre Merwin & Hulbert was popular in its short-barrel guise, one .44 Pocket Army gun (no. 195) being taken from Bass Outlaw in El Paso on 15 October 1892. Not to be confused with the better-known desperado Sam Bass, killed by Texas Rangers in 1878, Bass Outlaw was eventually killed in El Paso by lawman John Selman in 1894.

He also owned a professionally converted Colt Single Action Army revolver, no. 42870, which had been altered to allow it to be 'fanned'. The grip had been replaced and the trigger removed, the aperture in the frame being welded shut. The trigger-guard bow was reduced to a spur, a special quick-release cylinder pin was fitted, and the barrel (which lacked an ejector case) was cut to 3in. The changes allowed the hammer to be pulled back simply by sweeping it with the palm of the non-firing hand, allowing extremely rapid fire once the technique had been mastered.

kins & Allen, they offered much better quality than the manufacturer's own guns.

A top-break adaption of the original **Smith & Wesson** Model No.1$\frac{1}{2}$ was made experimentally in 1870, but had had no lasting influence on the company's activities at that time. Work began again in 1874 on the basis of the highly successful Russian Model No.3. The new revolver, chambering a new centrefire cartridge, became known as the .38 Single Action or 'Baby Russian'. After the introduction of modified designs, it was renamed '.38 First Model Single Action'.

The rack-and-pinion extractor of the Model 3 Russian was retained, but sheathed triggers were standard. The first .38 Single Actions were supplied to distributors in the spring of 1876; barrels originally measured 3$\frac{1}{4}$ and 4in, a five-inch variant being added in 1877. They were accepted instantaneously, and nearly thirteen thousand had been made by the end of 1876; 9023 of them were nickel-plated, the remainder being blued. The most popular grips were chequered gutta-percha with 'S&W' moulded into a cartouche at the neck. Only fifteen sets of ivory or mother-of-pearl grips were made in this period.

The original .38 Single Action was modified in 1877 to simplify machining and reduce cost. Most importantly, the extractor mechanism and the cylinder retainer were modified. The retainer was patented by Daniel Wesson and James Bullard in February 1877 (no. 187,689).

Production of the .38 New (or Second) Model Single Action began immediately, the first guns being assembled in July 1877. Numbers reverted to 1, work on the earlier model ceasing after 25,548 had been made. The New Model was a great success, production in 1877 alone amounting to 12,000. Nickel plating and chequered gutta-percha grips were preferred, wood grips being discontinued in 1879.

Few changes were made to the New Model prior to its demise in 1891, apart from the substitution (in 1881) of a slide-bar extractor cam actuator patented in May 1880. 108,225 New Model .38 Single Action revolvers were made.

The third .38 SA Smith & Wesson, the Model 1891 or 'New New Model', was a particularly handsome gun in its long-barrel forms. The greatest external change was the reversion to a conventional trigger guard. Barrels ranged from 3$\frac{1}{4}$ to 6in, finishes remained blue or more popular nickel-plate, and the grips were moulded gutta-percha with a decoratively bordered chequer panel.

The elegant appearance of the new gun did not accelerate sales, however, owing to a rise in enthusiasm for double-action revolvers, and only 28,107 were made in 1891–1911. Many were assembled after 1893 as single-shot target pistols and, amusingly, the company even had to develop an optional sheath-trigger unit – known as the 'Mexican Model' after the market in which it was most favoured.

The success of the .38 Single Action inspired development of a .32-calibre version, embodying a rebounding hammer protected by US Patent 198,228 granted to Daniel Wesson and James Bullard on 18 December 1877.

The first .32 Single Action revolvers were completed at the beginning of 1878. Moulded gutta-percha and plain walnut grips were offered during the first year, but wood was abandoned during 1879. More than ninety per cent of the guns produced in 1878–81 were nickel plated instead of blued. Barrels measured 3–10in, the longest options (8 and 10in) being used sparingly. Production ceased in 1892, after 97,599 guns had been made.

On 1 January 1877, Colt announced the introduction of a .38 Double Action Revolver. Now generally known as the '**Colt Lightning**' – a trade name originally applied by Benjamin Kittredge & Company of Cincinnati – this was soon followed by a .41-calibre version known as the 'Thunderer'. An improved .45 derivative, built on a differing frame and generally known as the Double Action Army & Frontier Model of 1878 or 'Omnipotent' (another of the many names devised by Kittredge), appeared a year later. These guns had an entirely new lock credited to William Mason.

The delicate appearance of the Lightning, which had a frame not unlike that of the Single Action Army matched to a slender bird's head butt, was complemented by similar delicacy in the action. A range of finishes was offered, though many surviving guns are nickel-plated. Grips were made from a single piece of rosewood or, alternatively, chequered gutta-percha. Barrel lengths varied from 1½ to 10in, ejectors being omitted from guns with barrels shorter than 4½in and, on request, from longer examples. In addition, a few revolvers were chambered for .32 centrefire ammunition instead of the more popular .38 or .41.

Accepting a variety of cartridges – including .32-20, .38-40 and .44-40 Winchester, .450, .455 and .476 Eley – the Double Action Army & Frontier Model was very similar internally to the Lightning. However, minor changes had been made in accordance with William Mason's patents of 20 September, 4 and 11 October 1881 (247,374 and 247,379, 247,938 and 248,190), and the rear of the frame differed greatly; the classical outline of the Single Action Army was replaced by a sinuous curve sweeping into the top strap, which gave a much heavier appearance.

Most guns were blued, with walnut grips; options included nickel plating with rubber, ivory or pearl grips. Barrels ranged from 3–7½in, the shortest lacking the ejector case. A few guns – usually short-barrel ejectorless 'Sheriff's' or 'House' patterns – were also made with spurless hammers; these could not be thumb cocked, but were less likely to snag on clothing.

The lock of the Lightning and Thunderer was fragile by comparison with the robustness of the Single Action Army; however, in the hands of an experienced firer who had adapted to the additional effort required to pull through on the trigger, double-action revolvers often paid dividends. Not

JOHN WESLEY HARDIN

Born in Texas in March 1853, John Hardin is generally reckoned among the most callous of gunfighters and the best shots. Beginning at the age of fifteen, he killed about twenty men. Captured in Pensacola, Florida, in 1877 he was tried in Texas and sentenced to twenty-five years hard labour in Huntsville State Penitentiary. Pardoned in 1892, he abandoned his second wife in 1894, headed for El Paso and became a partner in the Wigwam Saloon. Hardin was killed in the Acme Saloon on 19 August 1895 by one of four shots fired by John Selman Sr, armed with .45 Colt Single Action Army revolver no. 141805. Selman himself was subsequently slain by George Scarborough.

Hardin had a variety of revolvers, beginning with a .36-calibre Navy Colt and including ivory-grip Smith & Wesson .44 first pattern (or 'Old Old Model') Russian revolver no. 25274, which he used to kill Deputy Sheriff Charley Webb in Comanche, Texas, in 1874 – a crime for which his brother Joseph was subsequently lynched. Sheriff John Carnes is said to have helped John Hardin escape justice, lending the gunman a double-barrel shotgun to further his cause.

Among Hardin's other guns were a derringer of unknown type, mentioned in 1872, and .44 S&W Double Action revolver no. 352. He also owned a .38 Colt Lightning, no. 84304, which had been presented by James B. 'Killin' Jim' Miller; the backstrap was suitably engraved 'J.B.M. TO J.W.H.'. This particular gun had mother-of-pearl grips, a 2.5in barrel, and lacked an ejector. Most of the playing cards shot by Hardin during the grand opening of the Wigwam Saloon in July 1895 were apparently the work of this gun. However, on 6 May 1895, Hardin had surrendered an engraved 5in-barrelled .41 Colt Thunderer no. 73728, which he had bought a month previously from El Paso dealer A. A. Kline.

Two additional Colt revolvers were found on Hardin's body, but doubt remains whether one was an ivory-grip .45 Single Action Army (no. 126680) and the other was a .41 double action Thunderer. The proprietor of the Acme saloon, Bob Stevens, reported that both were double-action guns.

surprisingly, they were favoured by many famous Westerners – and some noted more for infamy.

Persistent criticism has been levelled at these Colts, overlooking that they were surprisingly successful: 166,849 .38-calibre Lightnings and .41 Thunderers were made from 1877 until 1909, plus 51,210 .45 Double Action Frontier Revolvers (1878–1905). A total approaching 220,000 compared favourably with the production of Single Action Army revolvers, approximately 270,000 of which were made from the beginning of 1878 until the end of 1909.

Despite occasional experimentation, no double-action **Smith & Wesson** revolver was made in quantity until the Colt pattern appeared early in 1878.

Daniel Wesson and James Bullard then strove to perfect a rival, Bullard completing the design of a .32 revolver in February 1879 and a .38 in October.

As the Colt was available in .38 and .41, Smith & Wesson initially concentrated on the .38 Double Action. The company's 1880 catalogue offered the new five-shot .38/100 revolver, which weighed 18oz, with barrels of $3\frac{1}{4}$, 4 and 5in; 6, 8 and 10-inch options were added at later dates. Blue or nickel finish was available, the latter, which was much preferred, having the trigger guard and barrel latch in blue. Moulded black or red gutta-percha grips were standard and optional respectively.

The detachable side plate fitted to the original Double Action revolver ran completely across the frame, weakening it perceptibly. After about 4000 guns had been made, the frame was changed to accept a smaller side plate. This second pattern was extremely successful, about 115,000 being made in 1880–4. The third pattern had an improved cylinder stop, which eliminated the distinctive double row of cylinder-stop slots. About 203,700 guns of this type had been made by 1895.

The first eleven .32 Double Action revolvers were assembled in May 1880, production of the five-shot 14oz guns amounting to 9881 by the end of the year. The original barrel-lengths were 3 or $3\frac{1}{2}$in, a 6-inch option being offered in 1882; 8 and 10-inch barrels were available for a few years from 1888. Nickel plating was even more popular than on the larger .38, as less than 200 blued .32 guns were made in the first year.

Only about thirty of the first pattern were made in the summer of 1880, with a full-width side plate. This was abandoned as soon as it was realised that it weakened the frame. The second variation had the smaller plate, about 22,140 guns being made in 1880–2. The action of the third model included an improved cylinder stop, but its life was short: 21,230 guns were made in 1882–3.

The principal change in the fourth pattern, introduced in the summer of 1883 and made until 1909, was the substitution of an oval trigger guard for the original reverse-curve design. The cylinder stop and sear were modified, though this could not be detected externally. The fourth model was by far the most popular, production amounting to 239,600.

About 54,700 .44 Double Action revolvers (originally known as the 'New Model Navy No. 3') were made from 1881 until 1913 in their own number sequence. Offered in blue and nickel, the guns weighed 2lb 3oz and had barrels of 4–6in. Later options included $3\frac{1}{2}$ and $6\frac{1}{2}$in, but no major mechanical changes were made during their production life. The only clue to date, excepting the serial number, was a change in the cylinder length about 1900. Original cylinders measured 1.44in, whereas later ones were 1.56.

About 1170 examples of the so-called .44 Favorite revolver, numbered in the same series as the standard .44, were made in 1882–5. Efforts were made to lighten the weapon by tapering the barrel, reducing the diameter of the front part of the cylinder and thinning the frame and side-plate walls. The grips were generally chequered wood, finish invariably being nickel plate.

The Old Hickory series of **Iver Johnson** revolvers, introduced in 1877, included solid-frame double action revolvers with conventional trigger guards and single-action sheath-trigger patterns. The double-action guns were made as seven-shot .22 Long or six-shot .32 Long rimfires, with 2½ or 4½-inch barrels, nickel plating and rubber grips; the sheath-trigger guns included a five-shot .32 Long centrefire version, generally encountered with a round barrel and a rubber gripped saw handle. However, fully-fluted cylinders, octagonal barrels, and grips of pearl or ivory could all be obtained. The standard guns cost $35–$60 per dozen in 1881.

Johnson & Bye began identifying their guns with their own name in 1879. The first new gun to be affected was the Eagle, a double-action .38 centrefire six-shot solid-frame revolver with a 3-inch barrel. This was joined in 1881 by the British Bull Dog, a rarely-encountered double-action pattern, and then a year later by the American Bull Dog – another double-action design, with a five-round cylinder, an octagonal barrel and nickel plating. Bull Dogs could be obtained in .32 and .38, rim- or centrefire.

Forehand & Wadsworth made a .32 Russian Model which was made to capitalise on the good reputation of the Smith & Wesson Russian Model. Nothing more than a small-calibre sheath-trigger Bulldog (q.v.), it was sold with a rounded butt, bone grips and a 2½-inch barrel. Most surviving specimens are lightly engraved.

Forehand & Wadsworth also marketed compact 'Bulldog' revolvers from 1877, as British Bull Dog, Swamp Angel and Terror. The first guns were .38 five-shot single-action solid-frame pocket patterns with hexagonal barrels and sheath triggers. Based on patents granted to Ethan Allen in October 1861 (33,509) and Forehand & Wadsworth in April 1875 (162,162), they cost $4.75 apiece in 1881.

Later Bulldogs were .44 calibre five-shot revolvers with longer butts, trigger guards and double-action lock work. Many appear to have been made by Hopkins & Allen (see below). The final version was a .38 gate-loading hand ejector, with a bird's head butt and the legend 'BRITISH BULL DOG' on the top strap above the cylinder.

The .44 Forehand & Wadsworth Russian Model was a large six-shot single-action revolver marketed briefly from 1877. It had a solid frame, a loading gate, and a spring-loaded ejector rod beneath the barrel. It weighed about 40oz and measured 13½in overall.

Sullivan Forehand and Henry Wadsworth died in 1898 and 1892 respectively. Their manufacturing activities had gradually reduced, revolvers being purchased when necessary from Hopkins & Allen. Finally, in 1902, the assets of the Forehand Arms Company were acquired by Hopkins & Allen and the once-famous name disappeared.

By 1876, **Harrington & Richardson** had introduced a new revolver with a removable cylinder axis pin; it was extremely simple and easily made. The first double-action revolver was introduced in 1878 and, by 1908, three million revolvers bearing the Harrington & Richardson trademarks had been made. **Marlin** also made a series of Smith & Wesson-style top-latch .32 and .38 centrefire double-action revolvers in the 1880s. However, production of all handguns had ceased by the end of the century.

The five-shot **Colt New House Pistol**, announced in 1880, was a variation of the New Line with a long-flute cylinder, locking notches on the rear face of the cylinder, a lateral cylinder-pin lock, and a loading gate on the right side of the frame behind the cylinder. Offered in .38 and .41 centrefire, with the standard 2¼-inch barrel, it was characterised by a squared butt heel. Grips were walnut, rosewood, or chequered gutta-percha with 'COLT' moulded into the neck.

The .38 centrefire New Police Pistol of 1882 was a variant New Line gun with a barrel ranging from a scarce ejectorless 2¼-inch pattern up to a 6-inch version with a Lightning-pattern ejector case. Owing to the design moulded into the gutta-percha grips, the New Police revolver is often known as the 'Cop-and-Thug' model.

The 1877-vintage **Remington No. 4** revolver chambered .38 Short centrefire cartridges and had a 2½-inch round barrel. Unlike the other guns in the series, it lacked an ejector rod; the elongated cylinder axis pin was used to punch spent cases out of the detached cylinder.

The seven-shot .22 rimfire Iroquois was similar to the No. 4, though much more lightly built. It weighed a mere 7½oz: half as much as the .38 pattern. About 100,000 Smoot-type revolvers were made from 1873 until the demise of E. Remington & Sons in 1886, more than half the total being rimfire Iroquois examples.

Repeating Pistols

Cartridge derringers continued to be used in large numbers – especially the double-barrelled Remington – but one of the strangest of all the personal-defence weapons of the West was the turret-type **Protector** palm pistol, patented in the USA by Frenchman Jacques Turbiaux on 6 March 1883 (273,644). A patent of improvement was granted to Peter Finnegan of Austin, Illinois, in August 1893 (504,154).

Marketed by the Minneapolis Fire-Arms Company and then by a successor, the Chicago Fire Arms Company, the seven-shot .32 Short rimfire Protector was made by the Ames Sword Company of Chicopee Falls, Massachusetts. Catalogues issued by Hartley & Graham in 1892 indicate that the Minneapolis variant existed in three patterns, nickel-plated or blued, with rubber or pearl 'sides'.

A flat disc-like magazine housing provided a rudimentary frame, and a short barrel protruded between the firer's fingers. The trigger, a spring-loaded plate at the back of the disc, was simply pressed against the base of the firer's palm. The pistols were usually found with two or three finger spurs on the front surface, alongside the barrel. Minneapolis guns customarily had a manual safety lever, whereas Chicago patterns relied on an automatic safety on the finger spur to disengage when the trigger-lever was squeezed. Loading was simply a matter of removing the side plate, which was retained by a small bolt.

CHAPTER 5

A MANTLE OF GREATNESS

From Isolation to the War with Spain, 1890–98

'The only sound came from the dice as they rolled over the bar, and Hardin remarked "You have four sixes to beat". Without warning, Selman fired his sixshooter. Hardin toppled and fell.'

Patrick McGeeney, witness to the killing of John Wesley Hardin by John Selman Sr. in the Acme Saloon, El Paso, August 1895.

1890, the year of the Wounded Knee massacre and official declarations that the Wild West no longer existed, also heralded the end of US isolationism. New-found confidence could be seen in the World's Columbian Exposition, held in Chicago in 1893 to mark the quartercentenary of Columbus and his discovery of America. No venture of such a size had been mounted in the New World, and the fair attracted 24 million ticket holders from a population which – according the 1890 census – numbered only 63 million.

Though it was fashionable for European observers to deride the products of the USA, from railway locomotives to agricultural implements, their views were not always objective. When scrutinised, a hint of envy was often betrayed. By 1883, the USA had overhauled Britain as the world's leading steel maker and, from 1899 onward, was also the leading producer of coal. Exports grew in the last quarter of the nineteenth century, whereas the introduction of protectionist tariffs by the McKinley and Dingley Acts (1890 and 1897 respectively) restricted imports.

The US economy grew steadily and strongly at the expense of longer-established European countries. Yet the State of the Union was still not all its proponents would have wished. Though the worst of the Indian troubles had receded into history with the final surrender of the Lakota (Sioux) nation in January 1891, a new problem had arisen in the West: the subjugation of individual freedom to the incorporators – the ranchers, the land-grabbers, the railroads, the town builders.

The key to the problems lay in the continual 1880s bickering between cattlemen and the farmers, which came to a head in the Range Wars that are now often seen as an integral part of a greater Western War of Incorporation. This still raged when the First World War began in Europe.

The final phase of the War of Incorporation was basically a conflict between capital, represented by mine-owners, cattle barons and their political supporters, and labour personified by share-croppers, homesteaders and mineworkers.

The Wyoming Range War – which may be taken as typical – began as a conflict between large-scale ranching interests, backed by the local political establishment (whose careers the ranchers largely bought and sold), and a confederation of independently minded smallholders, homesteaders and cowboys. The independent faction drew comfort from successes bought during the Johnson County War of 1892, at a considerable cost in lives and property, but the establishment replied with a campaign of terror typified by the 'bounty hunter' Tom Horn. Fighting eventually ceased in 1901.

Equally typical was the so-called Thirty Years War in Colorado (1884–1914), fought by the Western Federation of Miners and its supporters against mine-owning oppressors backed by politicians and the state militia. Flashpoints such as Leadville (1894) and Telluride (1901) presaged the dynamiting of Cripple Creek railroad station in 1904, killing thirteen strike-breakers.

Conflict rumbled on at the muzzle of a gun or the point of a knife, from the mining camps of Idaho to the logging camps of Oregon. It raged from Mussel Slough in California – a conflict between the Southern Pacific Railroad and local farmers – to the jousting between outlaws and lawmen throughout Kansas, Oklahoma, Missouri and Arkansas. And though the incorporators eventually won, they did so only in the face of significant resistance.

BAT MASTERSON

Bartholomew 'Bat' Masterson – alias William Barclay Masterson – was born in Henryville, East Canada, on 27 November 1853, but was raised in New York, Illinois and Kansas. After serving as a buffalo hunter and scout, Masterson killed a gambler and a dance-hall girl in the Texan settlement of Sweetwater in January 1876. Returning hastily to Dodge City, he served as sheriff of Ford County and then as a deputy US marshal before eventually becoming a saloon-keeper. His career as a professional gambler came to an end when he was run out of Denver in 1902. Returning to New York City, where he was made a deputy marshal by Mayor Theodore Roosevelt, Masterson ended his days as sport editor for the *New York Morning Telegraph*. He died at his desk in October 1921.

Bat Masterson owned several Colt cartridge revolvers, including a .45 Single Action Army gun, no. 109319, with a nickel finish and a special front sight. It was bought directly from Colt on 19 October 1885. He has also been linked with Colt Peacemakers numbered 58684, 88438 and 112737.

The Dalton Gang, the Wild Bunch and the 'social bandits' of the 1890s, whose robbing of banks and holding-up of trains were often seen as spiting the establishment, soon gave way to a new type of folk hero – the gunfighters hired by both sides in the Wars of Incorporation; or American Federation of Labor militants John and James McNamara, who dynamited the buildings of the *Los Angeles Times* in September 1910 with the loss of twenty lives.

The War of Incorporation rumbled on until the end of the First World War – the first time so many American servicemen had fought and died away from their native soil – but sowed seeds of resentment which still lie dormant in some parts of the Old West.

If the War of Incorporation had an important effect on the Wild West, a confrontation between the Old and New World provided an impetus for change on an international scale. This came when the USA, confident in its industrial growth and the development of a 'blue water' navy, took on the might of Spain.

US interest in central and south America was a constant source of friction with Old World powers, particularly when the brutality with which the Spanish put down a rebellion in Cuba in 1895 provoked a hostile reaction in the leading US newspapers.

The destruction of USS *Maine* during a visit to Havana harbour on 15 February 1898 was ascribed in many war-mongering quarters of the USA to sabotage, overlooking that it was far more likely to have been due to negligence and sweating cordite. Concerned that the *Maine* incident played into the hands of a US government spoiling for war, the Spanish promised the Cubans limited autonomy. However, Congress demanded that Cuba be granted total independence, which meant the removal of Spanish troops; believing that the Spanish were unlikely to concur readily, the legislators also granted President McKinley the right to use force to free Cuba from Hispanic domination.

War between Spain and the USA was declared on 24 April 1898. European commentators anticipated that the Spanish would not surrender easily, but Spain was a fading glory on the world scene, little more than a prop for the remnants of a once-grand colonial empire. The campaigns proved to be ridiculously one-sided.

A US Navy squadron commanded by Commodore George Dewey destroyed the Spanish Pacific squadron during the Battle of Manila Bay (1 May 1898) – at minimal cost – while the Spanish Caribbean squadron, forced to put to sea by the threat posed by US troops landed on the Cuban coast, was annihilated on 3 July. The surrender of Santiago to General William Shafter (17 July) effectively brought fighting to an end.

The war had been remarkable principally for the unexpected results of the naval actions, and for the well-publicised participation of Theodore Roosevelt and the 1st Volunteer Cavalry. Nicknamed the 'Rough Riders', this unit attained notoriety for its participation in the battle of San Juan Hill.

The Treaty of Paris, signed on 10 December 1898, ended Spanish colonial rule in Latin America and the Pacific. Spain renounced all claims to Cuba, ceded Guam and Puerto Rico to the USA, and transferred sovereignty to the Philippine Islands to the USA in return for 20 million dollars in gold. It elevated the United States of America to the status of a world power, with a far-flung colonial empire, and undermined Hispanic domination of Latin America.

Even though Spanish power had been waning for years, the American victory in the war – and the ease with which it had been achieved – was genuinely unexpected outside North America. Obligatory parades and celebratory backslapping were followed by inevitable squabbling over the glory, but for the USA there would be no turning back.

Firearms

The last decade of the nineteenth century brought consolidation. The products of Winchester, Colt, Smith & Wesson, Marlin, Stevens and many other gunmakers dominated the market-place, but, though advances had been made, the lever-action rifle and the single-action revolver remained supreme west of the Hundredth Meridian.

The beginning of the twentieth century coincided with the commercial introduction of efficient auto-loading pistols, but production had only just begun in Europe by the time of the Spanish–American War. Few North American inventors produced viable designs prior to 1898, though Carl Ehbets received patents protecting gas-operated and aberrant blow-forward guns (US no. 570,388 and 580,935 respectively). John Browning constructed a prototype blowback pistol chambering a .32 semi-rimmed cartridge made by Winchester, successfully demonstrating it to representatives of Colt in the

THE WILD BUNCH

This name was applied collectively to an irregular grouping of outlaws – said to have numbered 200 or more at its peak – which was formed in Brown's Hole on 18 August 1896 (according to legend) and remained active in Wyoming, Colorado, Utah and neighbouring states into the early 1900s. The members of the group never acted as a unit, but rather in small bands or even pairs based on hideouts such as Brown's Hole, Hole in the Wall (in north-central Wyoming) and Robbers' Roost in east central Utah. The principal figures included Robert Parker ('Butch Cassidy'), Harvey 'Kid Curry' Logan, William Ellsworth 'Elzy' Lay, Harry 'Sundance Kid' Longbaugh, Ben 'Tall Texan' Kilpatrick, George 'Flat Nose' Curry, O. C. 'Camilla' Hawks, and Will Carver.

Most of the Wild Bunch had either been killed or captured by 1900, although Butch Cassidy and the Sundance Kid escaped to South America.

summer of 1895. A patent application was filed in September 1895 and granted on 20 April 1897.

In May 1896, Browning delivered three additional guns to Colt – a modification of the 1895-type blowback, a recoil-operated gun locked by dropping the barrel on two swinging links, and a third locked by rotating the barrel. The rotating-barrel gun (US Patent 580,925) was abandoned after a prototype had been made, and the small blowback was rejected by Colt after Browning had applied for what became British Patent 22,455/98 of 25 October 1898. The simplest gun was subsequently exploited in Europe by Fabrique Nationale d'Armes de Guerre, but no Colt-made pistols were distributed commercially prior to 1900.

Longarms

Single-Shot Patterns

No sooner had the 1880-pattern **Springfield** rifles been delivered than experiments with universal-issue guns began in the hope that they would remove the need for separate infantry rifles and cavalry carbines, as well as their differing cartridges. In February 1882, the Board on Magazine Guns recommended a 'modified Springfield, calibre .45' with a barrel of 28in, a lock with a shorter hammer fall, and a full-length stock. With one dissenter, the report also recommended the trial of a 30-inch barrel on a Sharps action.

The **Model 1882** Short Rifle, sometimes confusingly identified as a carbine, was made with a 27.75-inch barrel. The earliest guns had swivels curved to fit the contours of the stock, to prevent them catching in the saddle-scabbards, but they were soon abandoned. The barrels tapered to the same muzzle diameter as the M1873 rifle and accepted the standard socket bayonet.

A modified short rifle was equipped with a triangular-section rod bayonet and a trap in the butt to house the shell ejector and dismantling tool. However, production was minuscule – only a little over fifty of the short rifles being made – and trials with the cavalry at Fort Leavenworth were not successful enough to persuade sceptics of the value of a universal rifle.

Experimental 1882-model carbines were made with 23.75in barrels, the first pattern being stocked almost to the muzzle. The muzzle band was held with a screw rather than the conventional spring, while a distinctive web separated the muzzle from the ramrod. The shell ejector and the dismantling tool were carried in the butt-trap, while a saddle ring was anchored in a plate on the left side of the breech opposite the hammer.

Next came a greatly modified gun with a heavy large-diameter barrel, retained by a single band immediately behind the rounded stock tip. A curved swivel lay beneath the band with a more conventional fitting on the under-edge of the butt. The barrels measured 23.75in, the saddle ring slid along a bar anchored in the left side of the stock alongside the breech, experimental Buffington wind-gauge back sights were fitted, and the three-piece cleaning rod was carried in a butt trap.

The failure of the contemporaneous magazine-rifle trials to provide a real challenge to established single-shot weapons allowed the introduction of new Trapdoor Springfields in 1884. The **Model 1884** rifle introduced the Buffington-pattern wind-gauge back sight to service, the first regulation design that ordinary soldiers could adjust to counteract projectile drift. The lower band was grooved to accommodate the elongated sight leaf.

Changes were made internally in January 1885, with alterations to the sear and tumbler, and new front sights for rifles (.653 high) and carbines (.738, changed to .728 late in 1890) were adopted to correct a universal tendency to shoot high at short ranges. The front sight cover became a permanent fixture from March 1886. In August of that year, improvements were made to the Buffington sight. The heads of the finger-screws on the wind gauge were enlarged to provide a better grip, and also support the folded leaf laterally by overlapping the base. The security of the binding screw was improved, and the movable base and slide were case-hardened.

Minor alterations were made to the action in December 1886, when the firing pin was changed from steel to aluminium bronze, and the rear edge of the rifle front-sight block was rounded from August 1887 onward. A new front-sight protector was introduced in February 1888, and a protector band for the back sight was fitted to the carbine from October 1890.

Production of a thousand M1884 rifles fitted with cylindrical rod bayonets was authorised by the Secretary of War on 17 December 1884; 1003 were made in 1885 and issued in the spring of 1886 to test 'the bayonet fastening and ... its effect upon the accurate shooting of the arm'. It was also suggested that an 'improved rear sight with a detachable front sight cover, similar to the front sight protector on the rod bayonet rifle, be approved and manufactured in sufficient quantity for issue to the troops'.

Rod-bayonet guns were issued to three artillery and ten infantry regiments, but they were not successful enough to displace the standard Model 1884. The **Model 1889** was the last single-shot rifle to be approved as a regulation US infantry weapon. However, ordnance records reveal it to have been expedient, to be made only until a magazine rifle had been perfected.

The quest for a suitable bayonet shuttled back and forth between Springfield Armory, the Tactical Board, the Chief of Ordnance – Brigadier General Benét – and the Acting Secretary of War, Major General Schofield, until a cylindrical rod pattern was approved on 5 August 1889. The perfected rifle and its accoutrements were adopted eleven days later.

Many commentators have criticised the adoption of another Trapdoor Springfield at a time when the US Army was so actively seeking a small-bore magazine rifle. A more balanced view is to be found in a reply by Colonel Buffington, commanding the National Armory at Springfield, to questions raised by the Chief of Ordnance and the Acting Secretary of War:

> [August 1889] The statement that the Army is to be rearmed soon with a .30 caliber magazine rifle is unfortunate. The elements for a .30 caliber rifle have been practically worked out, but the main element, viz; the powder, is wanting, and all efforts thus far abroad and at home, to produce it have been unavailing. American powder makers, although furnished with the best known foreign brown or black powder and an analysis of the same, have not been able to reproduce it satisfactorily, and the Ordnance Department has not yet been able to penetrate the veil of secrecy that surrounds the manufacture abroad of smokeless powders ... It would not do, even were a suitable black powder available, to proceed with the production of a .30 caliber rifle, because it would be inferior to foreign arms using smokeless powder ... A smokeless powder is, therefore, a necessity, and until it can be procured the .30 caliber arm must remain as it is, incomplete as a model arm, and without plant to make it.

Magazine Rifles

The Model 1876 **Winchester rifle** remained structurally similar to the Model 1873, embodying the toggle-joint lock that had graced the Henry. By the 1880s, however, single-shot Sharps, Remington and similar rifles were handling bullets as heavy as 550 grains, loaded ahead of huge charges of black powder in three-inch cases. Cartridges of this length would not feed through Winchester actions. Though necking could reduce case length, the 1876-pattern lever action was not strong enough to handle high pressures in safety.

Winchester's management then chanced upon gunsmiths John and Matthew Browning in the small town of Ogden, Utah. Interest centred on a promising single-shot dropping block gun, which became the Model 1885, and also on an improved lever action in which sturdy vertically sliding locking bars replaced the secure-but-weak toggle pattern. The Browning brothers surrendered rights to the patents for a cash payment, allowing work to begin in New Haven to refine the prototypes for series production.

The **Model 1886 Winchester rifle** was an instantaneous success. By the time it had been superseded by the modernised Model 71 in 1936, 159,994 had been made. More than a dozen chamberings were offered during the long life of the M1886 rifle, including .38-56, .45-70, .45-90, .50-100-450 and .50-110 Express. Barrel lengths, finishes, triggers and decoration were tailored to the whims of the customer.

The merits of the so-called Express cartridges were described in 1880s-vintage Sharps Rifle Company promotional literature:

> The whole secret of the term 'Express' consists in using large charges of powder with a light projectile, which is given so great an initial velocity that gravity is largely overcome, and the bullet will fly 150 to 175 yards without a perceptible fall toward the earth, thus making a very flat trajectory.
>
> The Bullet is made with a hollow point, in order to give, with the same amount of lead, additional bearings upon the grooves of the barrel, and to properly adjust its balance ... The hole in the point of [an] Express Bullet is made to take a .22 caliber rim fire cartridge blank ... so that the hunters of Grizzlies and other ugly game can use them as explosive bullets.

Owing to the power of the cartridges, most 1886-type Winchesters were made with barrels of normal length, carbines being rare. A full-stock carbine was described in the company's 1887 catalogue, but may never have been made. The standard short-barrel carbine, with a half-length fore-end, was pictured from the summer of 1889 onward. A 'take-down' gun, intended to dismantle quickly, was offered in 1894 but was unsuccessful: production is believed to have totalled a mere 350.

Theodore Roosevelt, a long-time champion of Winchester rifles, replaced his Model 1876 with .45-90 M1886 no. 9205. Many hunters concurred, taking the guns all over North America and across the Atlantic to Africa and beyond. The last grizzly bear in California was allegedly killed with an M1886 near San Juan Capistrano, and many a trophy-head gained by courtesy of Winchester graced study walls.

The advent of the Model 1881 lever-action rifle had given Marlin an important advantage over Winchester, a rival with whom relations were strained, but the advent of the Browning-designed Winchester M1886 redressed much of the balance. Next came the **Marlin Model 1888**, chambering some of the most popular handgun cartridges up to and including .44-40. This rifle embodied improvements made in the Burgess-Marlin action by Lewis Hepburn, designer of the Remington-Hepburn sporting rifle. It locked by sliding a bolt vertically into the breech-block – not unlike the system employed in the contemporary Browning-designed Winchesters – and was protected by patents granted on 7 December 1886 (354,059) and 11 October 1887 (371,455).

The 1888-type rifle remained in production for little more than a year. It was replaced by the **Model 1889** rifle and carbine, the first of the series to feature side ejection. This facilitated the attachment of telescope sights; until comparatively recent years, these had to be offset to the side of the receiver on top-ejecting Winchesters.

For most normal purposes, the Winchester Model 1886 was too expensive. In the early 1890s, therefore, the company's engineers produced the **Winchester Model 1892.** This was simply a diminution of its predecessor, offered in rifle and carbine form with an occasional military-style musket. A few take-down variants were made prior to the First World War, but were never popular.

Barrel lengths ranged from 14 to 36in – the latter on special order only – while half- and threequarter-length magazines, selected wood, set-triggers and pistol-grip butts were among the options offered to the customer. Some guns were engraved, though apparently not in such great quantity as 1876-pattern guns had been. The Model 1892 was offered in .32-20, .38-40 and .44-40, plus, from 1895 onward, .25-20. Rifle 53,614 had been made for Theodore Roosevelt, while another had been carried by explorer Robert Peary during his Polar expeditions.

1893 brought a major redesign of the Marlin M1881, necessitated by the introduction of the 1886 and 1892-pattern Winchesters. The **Marlin Model 1893** (1893–1936) was simply the 1892-pattern action enlarged to handle .32-40 and .38-55 ammunition. The rifle was an instantaneous commercial success, offered in a variety of barrel lengths from 20in for the carbine to a special 32in option for the rifles. Standard guns – weighing 7–8lb – had 26-inch round or octagonal barrels, open sights, and a straight-wrist butt. Magazines held ten rounds.

Variants of the Model 1893 included a 6.75lb Model 1893 Carbine in .30-30 and .32-40 only, with a 20-inch round barrel and a seven-round magazine. The Model 1893 Musket, offered with a socket bayonet until about 1915, had a thirty-inch barrel and a full-length fore-end. A cleaning rod lay beneath the barrel.

Next came the **Marlin Model 1894**, which was simply the 1893-type gun reduced to take handgun cartridges. The M1894 was initially offered in .25-20, .32-20, .38-40 and .44-40. It had a ten-round tube magazine, a 24-inch round or fully octagonal barrel, a straight-wrist butt, open sights, and weighed about 7lb. It became so popular that the original 1889 pattern was discontinued about 1900.

The 1892-pattern Winchester rifle was followed by the **Winchester Model 1894**, a John Browning design specifically intended for cartridges loaded with smokeless powder. The rifle was intended to compete against the 1893-pattern Marlin, chambering the same .32-40 and .38-55 cartridges.

The Model 1894 has been made in rifle, carbine and musket forms, and also as a take-down rifle. The variety of barrel lengths, finishes and decoration has been all but boundless. Chamberings have included .32-40 and .38-55 on introduction in 1894, followed by the high-velocity .25-35 and the legendary .30-30 a year later. A few guns were made for the short-lived .32 Winchester Special, but not until 1902.

The success of the Model 94 Winchester persuaded Marlin to adapt his 1893-pattern rifle for the new .30-30 Winchester cartridge, add .25-36 Marlin

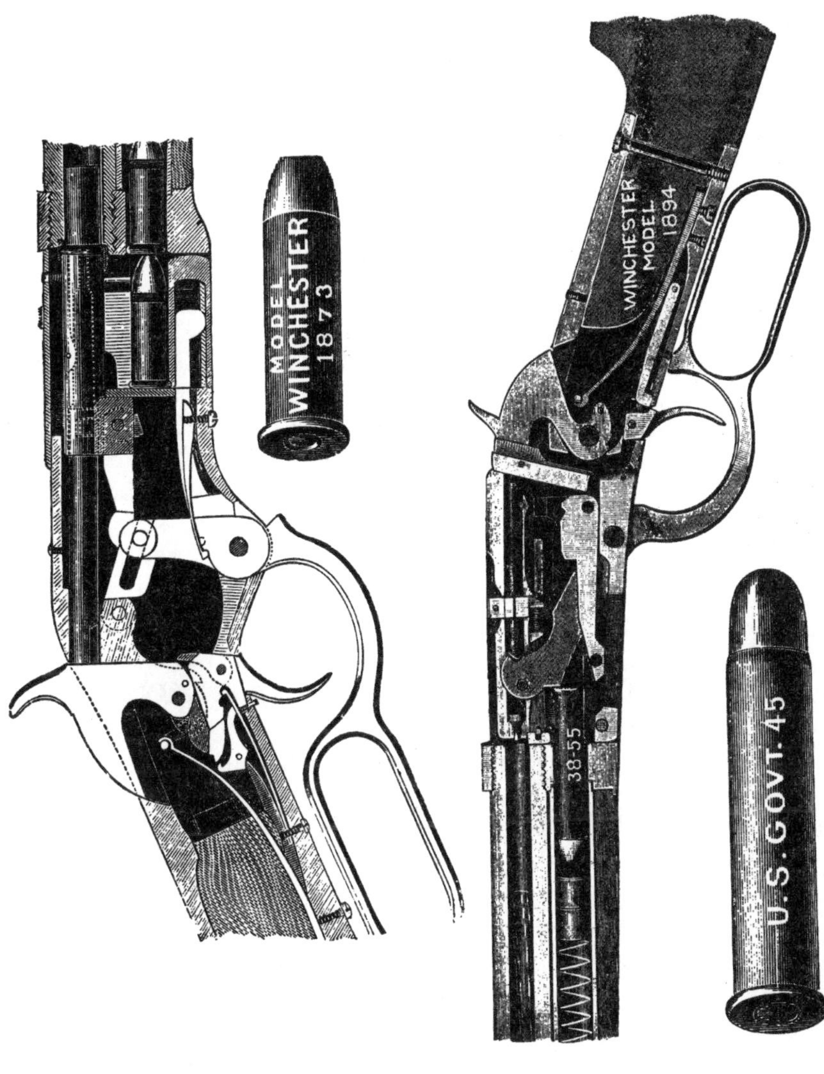

The 1894-type Winchester-Browning action contrasted with the weaker 1873 pattern (top). From Greener's The Gun and Its Development *(1910)*

to rival Winchester's .25-35, and then create the **Marlin Model 1895** to handle cartridges as large and powerful as .45-90. The standard rifles were offered with 24-inch round or octagonal barrels, straight-wrist butts and open sights. They weighed about 8lb.

The **Winchester Model 1895**, once again the work of John Browning, was the first lever-action rifle to incorporate a box magazine. Apparently intended specifically to handle high-power small-calibre smokeless cartridges with sharply pointed noses – a dangerous liability in tube magazines – it also proved to have appreciable military potential. This was evident in some of the cartridges it chambered, beginning with .30-40 Krag and .303 (British). These co-existed with a variety of sporting rounds.

Production began in 1895 at no. 1, and had reached 425,881 by the time the M1895 was finally discontinued in 1938. About 5000, almost all with low numbers, were made with a flat-side receiver. Much sought by collectors, this lacks the rebated lower receiver of the perfected rifles.

Not surprisingly, in view of his previous affections, the Model 1895 was popular with Theodore Roosevelt; 'Teddy' owned one rifled chambering .30-40 Krag cartridges and two .405 examples. Others were used by the renowned big-game hunter Stewart Edward White.

The 1895-pattern Winchester, approved by the National Rifle Association of America for use in shooting competitions, was equally popular with militia and volunteer units participating in the Spanish–American War. The Winchesters were infinitely superior to the converted single-shot Trapdoor Springfields being carried by other units.

By 1890, the US Army realised that the single-shot 'Trapdoor Springfield' was obsolescent. On 16 December 1890, therefore, a Board of Officers chaired by Lieutenant Colonel Robert Hall of the 6th Infantry met in New York City to decide the rules for a **repeating-rifle competition**. The closing date was originally set at 1 June 1892, notice of the competition was published, and circulars were sent to interested parties. During the summer of 1892, Frankford Arsenal delivered 100,000 .30 rimmed cartridges firing a 220-grain bullet at about 2000 ft/sec.

More than fifty guns were tested in New York Arsenal, a report being made on 19 August 1892. The submissions had included a variety of well-known designs in addition to the work of many lesser lights. There were six Krag-Jørgensens; five .30 Mausers, based on the Belgian Mle. 89; two 8mm Austrian-style and one 6.5mm Romanian Mannlichers; a 7.9mm Gewehr 88; a Portuguese 8mm Kropatschek; a 8mm Japanese Murata; a 7.5mm Swiss Schmidt-Rubin; a 7.62mm Russian Mosin-Nagant; three French Berthiers submitted by the Hotchkiss Ordnance Company, Washington; an M1888 Schulhof; and a Swiss Rubin rifle.

The Lee-system rifle, which had enjoyed success in the US Navy, included an

1885-model .30-calibre ten-shot gun submitted on behalf of the Lee Arms Company of South Windham, Connecticut; two similar rifles submitted by the Remington Arms Company of Bridgeport, Connecticut, .303 No. 25 and .30 No. 26; and a .303-calibre British Lee-Metford rifle No. 1 masquerading as the 'Lee-Speed', entered – like all foreign service weapons – by the Chief of Ordnance.

The Krag No. 1 was the 8mm Danish m/89; No. 2 was a similar gun in .30-calibre with a Mauser-type safety, a pivoting ejector and a different cocking piece; No. 3 was identical to No. 2, but had greater head-space; No. 4 was No. 2 with a dust cover over the bolt and a downward-opening loading gate; No. 5 was the same as No. 4, without the dust cover; and No. 6 was a variant of No. 5 chambering a rimless .30 cartridge.

Three single-shot .30 Springfields were submitted by the Chief of Ordnance as control weapons. Even at an early stage, the trials board decided on rimmed cartridges – easier to make than rimless varieties – as well as to seek a rifle that was basically a single-loader with a magazine held in reserve. These restrictions effectively eliminated many promising designs.

Trials resolved in favour of the Lee No. 3, the Belgian-type Mauser No. 5 and the Krag-Jørgensen No. 5; the Krag was victorious largely because fresh cartridges could be inserted in the magazine even when the bolt was shut and cocked on a loaded chamber.

The **Krag** was a turning-bolt repeater with a single lug, on the head of the one-piece bolt body, which locked vertically in the receiver behind the chamber. This potentially weak system ultimately prevented the US Army developing high-velocity cartridges prior to the adoption of the Mauser-pattern Springfield rifle in 1903. Ironically, Krag & Jørgensen developed a twin-lug gun in the early 1890s – US Patent 492,212 of 21 February 1893 – and one gun survives in the Smithsonian collection.

The standard US Krag magazine was adapted from the then-experimental Norwegian trials rifle, the gate swinging down to serve as a loading platform rather than pivoting forward.

The **Model 1892 Krag rifle** was officially adopted on 15 September 1892, but production of the new 'US Magazine Rifle, Caliber .30, Model of 1892', scheduled to begin in 1893, was soon deferred. Although the acting Secretary of War had approved its adoption, and regardless of the fact that the original trials had been undertaken with scrupulous honesty, the American inventors were outraged by the adoption of a foreign rifle. They successfully petitioned Congress to withhold approval for the Krags until another series of tests could be undertaken. Springfield Armory, meanwhile, continued to tool for the new rifle.

Convened in March 1893, the new Board of Officers tested fourteen guns – a Spencer-Lee, a Lee, a Savage, four Dursts, two Blakes, three Russell-Livermores, a Hampden and a White – and reported on 16 May 1893 that none of the triallists had approached the efficiency of the Krag.

The first two M1892 rifles were assembled in Springfield Armory on 1 January 1894, but the first issues, to men of the 2nd and 4th Infantry, were not made until 6 October.

Problems were reported as soon as the guns entered service. As the sights had been calibrated in the depths of the New England winter, the Krags shot high and to the left in warmer conditions until corrections were made. The original flat butt-plate was replaced by a rounded pattern from 23 December 1895, as the toes of many stocks broke when they were struck on the ground during 'Order Arms'. By the end of 1896, nearly forty changes had been made to the M1892, though few guns received all the minor modifications.

The standard US Krag-Jørgensen had an elegant straight-gripped walnut stock, with a grasping groove in the fore-end and a hand guard running from the breech to the barrel band. An open stacking swivel was attached to the nose cap, which had a solid upper surface prior to 16 August 1894. A lug beneath the nose cap accepted the M1892 knife bayonet, copied from the Swiss M1889, and a full-length cleaning rod protruded below the muzzle.

24,562 Model 1892 Krags were made at Springfield Armory, though most were subsequently converted to M1896 standards by eliminating the cleaning rod, reversing the operation of the cut-off and substituting the 1896-pattern back sight.

Though placed in production in December 1895, the **Krag Cadet Rifle** was officially christened 'M1896'. It was essentially similar to the standard M1896, but the barrel band was retained by a spring and sling swivels were omitted. Only 404 were made; 398 survivors were returned for the installation of swivels in November 1900, and 1901-pattern back sights were fitted in 1902.

The **Model 1896 Krag rifle** was standardised on 19 February 1896 – though the decision was arbitrary and there was little to distinguish the last of the much-modified 1892- and the first 1896-type guns apart from the radically different back sight and the three-piece cleaning rod carried in a butt-trap. 61,897 true M1896 rifles was made.

Many 1892-pattern Krags were converted to 1896 standards by filling the ramrod channel in the fore-end, modifying the butt to accept the three-piece rod, substituting the Model 1896 back sight (often later replaced by the M1901), and adding a bolt hold-open notch in the receiver for the extractor pin. Work started in March 1897 and, by 1902, 18,559 of the 24,562 original M1892 rifles had been transformed. These do not bear 'MODEL 1896' marks on the side plate and still simply read '1892'.

Approved on 14 March 1898, the **Model 1898 Krag rifle** was the first major revision of the basic US Krag-Jørgensen pattern. Several changes were made in the bolt mechanism, the receiver and the magazine loading gate to

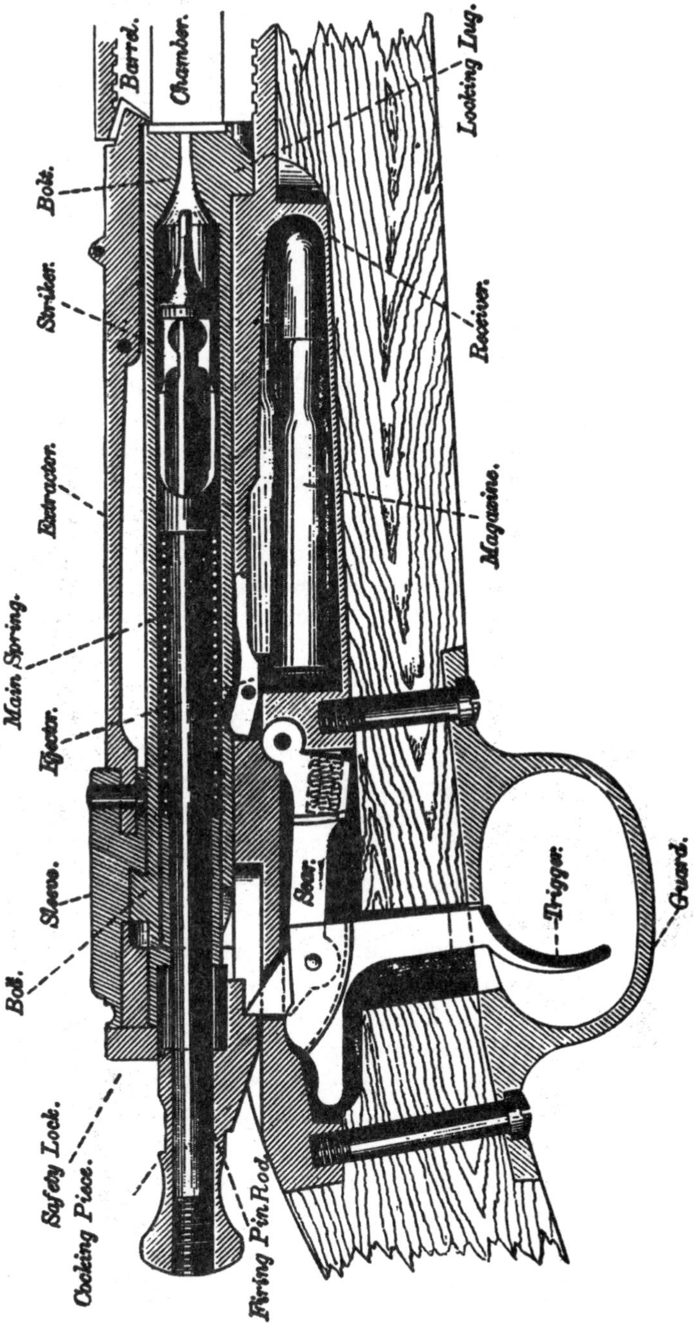

A longitudinal section of the Krag action

simplify production, and the bolt-handle seat was milled flush with the receiver to make stock inletting easier. The 1898-pattern back sight had a knurled drum on the left side of the slider block to control wind-drift adjustments.

The first true M1898 rifles were delivered from Springfield on 9 July 1898, but none saw service during the Spanish–American War. Several different back sights were fitted to M1898 rifles, and many guns made between 28 April 1899 and 11 October 1900 had the headless cocking piece (often wrongly associated solely with carbines) introduced in an unsuccessful cost-cutting exercise. Total production amounted to 324,283, making the M1898 the most commonly encountered US Krag-Jørgensen.

The original sight (M1892) was a tangent-leaf pattern, graduated from 300 to 1900 yards, with a stepped base and no drift adjustment on the leaf. This was replaced by the essentially similar M1896, which had a stepless or continuously curved base; lateral adjustments were still absent, though a binding screw was added to the slider. The rifle sight was graduated to 1800 yards; the carbine pattern, distinguished by a large 'C', ran up to 2000.

The only new sight to be introduced prior to the Spanish–American War was the short-lived M1898 or Dickson Sight, a tangent pattern for 200–2000 yards, with an azimuth adjustment on the three-notch back sight block in addition to a binding screw on the slider. An essentially similar carbine sight was marked 'C'.

Identifying Krags is complicated by the periodic changes of sights. For example, the first M1898 rifles were made with M1896 sights until supplies were exhausted in December 1898. A few M1892 sights were fitted until the perfected M1898 sight became available in April 1899, but the failure of the high-velocity cartridge led to the reappearance of the 1896 pattern in September 1899. This was retained until August 1901, when the 1901 or Buffington pattern was adopted; the M1902 was eventually substituted from August 1903.

The authorities were never entirely satisfied with the Krag-Jørgensen, particularly as the single-lug action proved too weak to cope with higher velocities and rising chamber pressures. Experiments were underway to find a better gun by 1900; after only a decade's service, the Krag was replaced by the Mauser-action M1903 Springfield. Ironically, the smoothness of the Krag action was such that it was readily accepted by sportsmen, thousands being converted to NRA Carbines in the 1920s.

The first experimental **Krag carbines**, made in 1893, were simply rifles with 22-inch barrels and reduced nose caps without the bayonet lug. A cleaning rod was carried in the stock and a saddle ring appeared on the left side of the stock-wrist.

Though the Chief of Ordnance directed carbine production to start in May 1895, development had not commenced until a mere three months previously.

A pattern gun was approved on 17 May 1895, production carbines being designated 'M1896'. The first **Model 1896 Krag carbines** had thin-wrist stocks, a saddle ring-and-bar assembly on the left side of the stock above the trigger guard, and a two-piece cleaning rod in the butt.

An oiler was carried in the butt after February 1897, but most guns subsequently received the 1899 carbine stock. Cut-offs were reversed in 1900. The carbines were relegated to militia cavalry after the summer of 1901, and about 9000 were refurbished for sale to the Guardia Rurales in Cuba in 1912.

The **Model 1898 Krag carbine** was essentially similar to its predecessor but incorporated the improved 1898-pattern rifle action. Manufacture was confined to 1898, owing to the trouble with the high velocity cartridges for which the 1898 tangent-pattern back sight had been graduated. Many guns were subsequently fitted with 1899-type stocks and a selection of sights, but a new carbine appeared in 1899. Production amounted to 22,493 M1896 and 5002 M1898 Krag carbines, plus nearly forty thousand 1899-pattern guns.

Although appreciable numbers of .45-70 1885-pattern Remington-Lee (q.v.) rifles had been acquired, the US Navy Bureau of Ordnance was well aware of the small-calibre experiments being undertaken in Europe. Specifications for a new small-bore rifle were issued in 1892, continuing even though the US Army adopted the Krag-Jørgensen.

The success of the M1885 rifle favoured Lee, encouraging a series of US patents for bolt actions and improved magazines. The most important were 506,319–506,323 – three of which protected a straight-pull bolt – together with the similar 506,339 granted to Francis Richards and assigned to Lee. These were followed by 513,647 of January 1894, granted to Lee to protect a straight-pull bolt-action rifle with a magazine containing a clip and a special cartridge-lifter arm; 547,582 of 8 October 1895, for a perfected five-round clip system; and 547,583 for the final straight-pull system. Twelve **Lee 'straight-pull' rifles** rifles were tested at the US Navy's Torpedo Station in Newport, Rhode Island, on 2 October 1894.

Competitors in the trials included a Miles turn-bolt rifle with a side magazine; a Briggs-Kneeland; five turn-bolt Remingtons with side magazines; a slide-action Van Patten, with a tube magazine beneath the barrel; two turn-bolt French Daudetau rifles with box magazines; a turn-bolt Russell-Livermore with a box magazine; and a prototype straight-pull Lee. Three latecomers were also admitted: a Luger, a Durst and another Briggs-Kneeland, all of which appear to have embodied turning bolts.

It seems that the navy authorities – mindful of problems that had arisen with the Krag – had already decided to favour the Lee, and that the competition was as much to humour American inventors as ensure that no better design appeared unexpectedly.

In May 1895, the Board convened at Newport and officially recommended the Lee Straight-Pull Rifle, which was adopted as the **Model 1895 navy rifle**. An order for 10,000 was immediately placed with Winchester and the first guns were delivered the following year; 19,563 were made in 1896–8, but not all appear to have reached the navy.

The .236 (6mm) M1895 was the first ultra small-calibre rifle to be adopted for service in the USA. A clip containing five semi-rim cartridges could be inserted in the magazine with the bolt open, automatically releasing tension on the case rims so that the clip fell out of the action after the first or second round.

The M1895 navy rifle had an extraordinary wedge-type locking block beneath the bolt. Pulling back on the bolt handle disengaged the wedge and the entire mechanism could be retracted. However, though potentially fast when well lubricated, the inclined operating stroke was awkward when the rifle was shouldered. The Lee was unpopular in service; in addition, the curious floating extractor/ejector (which worked only when the bolt had been partially retracted) gave constant trouble. The firing-pin lock and bolt-lock actuator also proved ineffectual, and the tension in the ammunition clips was difficult to regulate.

The rifle was handy – 47.6in overall, 8.5lb with sling and bayonet – and had a conventional one-piece pistol-grip walnut stock. There was a single barrel band and a most distinctive nose cap. The .236 cartridge was powerful for its day, the jacketed bullet penetrating 23in of pine at fifty yards compared with eighteen for the Austrian 8mm cartridge and only ten for the .45-70. The back sight leaf was graduated from 800 to 2,000 yards, battle sights being provided for 300 and 600 yards; there was no bullet-drift adjustment.

The Lee navy rifle was also offered in sporting guise, apparently to rid Winchester of as many sets of components as possible after the failure of the gun in service, but the tiny .236-calibre (6mm) bullet – despite developing an extremely high velocity for its day – had very poor knock-down capabilities on game. Only about 18,300 navy muskets and 1700 sporting rifles were made before the Lee was discontinued in 1904.

The **Savage** rifle, the last major lever action to be introduced prior to 1917, appeared on the market in 1896. Savage's first patent had been granted in July 1887 to protect a modification of the Peabody-Martini rifle loaded from a tube magazine in the butt. One prototype was made in .45-70, followed by another in .44-40 and then by at least one more. However, hinged-block actions of the Peabody-Martini class were unsuited to magazine feed; Savage, defeated, turned instead to a tilting-block action feeding from a magazine ahead of the trigger.

Work on the perfected lever-action rifle began in the late 1880s, Savage lodging an application for what became US Patent 502,018 in April 1889 even though the patent itself was not granted until 25 July 1893. Two 'M1892' rifles had been entered in the US Army magazine rifle trials, featuring 30-inch barrels and nine-shot rotary magazines with radial arm-type followers. Weighing a little over 10lb, they were stocked to the muzzle, had two barrel bands and would accept a sword bayonet.

Though the experimental rifles worked satisfactorily, they were not good enough to beat the bolt-action Krag-Jørgensen. Savage, meanwhile, had been granted Patent 491,138 on 7 February 1893 to protect a refinement of the rotary magazine in which each cartridge was carried in a separate cradle.

Eager to exploit his design, Savage incorporated the Savage Repeating Arms Company of Utica, New York, in April 1894. His backers are presumed to have been the Utica businessmen – Morris Childs, Richard Reynolds and Edwin Risley – to whom the principal patents were assigned. The succeeding Savage Arms Company, formed at the end of 1897, remained independent until its assets were acquired by the Driggs-Seabury Ordnance Company in 1915.

The **Savage Model 1895** was made by Marlin in several styles. Chambered for a unique smokeless .303 Savage cartridge, the rifle soon presented a serious rival to Winchester and Marlin. The military M1895 chambered .30-40 Krag cartridges, had a six-shot magazine and weighed a mere 8lb 11oz. The carbine was similar, excepting for its 22-inch barrel, half-stock and saddle ring. A sporting rifle, offered only in .303 Savage High Velocity, was made with a selection of round, half-octagon or fully octagonal barrels. It had walnut woodwork and weighed 7–8lb.

The Model 1895 was moderately successful, five thousand sporters selling by 1900, but Savage made continual improvements in the basic design which resulted in the Model 1899.

Savages were operated by depressing the finger lever, withdrawing the support of a long curved extension from under the rear of the breech-block. This allowed the rear of the breech-block to drop down and clear of the 'recoil' or locking shoulder in the top of the receiver behind the magazine. The finger-lever extension withdrew the block back clear of the magazine. The reverse stroke closed the breech, loading a fresh cartridge, and finally tilted the breech-block up into the receiver.

The system was simple and very sturdy; though theoretical objections could be made to the amount of metal placed under stress during firing, the Savage proved eminently capable of handling the most powerful of the contemporary high-velocity cartridges. In addition, unlike rival lever-action rifles with tube magazines, it could handle pointed-nose bullets in perfect safety.

Shotguns

The work on single- and double-barrel guns begun in the 1880s continued as the twentieth century beckoned, with an increasing emphasis on hammerless patterns at the expense of the exposed-hammer types. Interest grew in the repeating shotgun, typified by the slide-action Winchesters, but this was not reflected in sales figures until the decade preceding the First World War.

Available in quantity from 1890, the Model 1889 **Remington** was an improved 1882-type double-barrel hammer gun distinguished by recurved hammer shanks. Offered in 10, 12 and 16-bore, with barrels of 28–32in and weighing 7.5–10lb, it was usually sold with a pistol-grip butt and Remington Arms Company barrel marks. Production ceased in 1908.

The **Crescent** Arms Company of Norwich, Connecticut, one of the makers of 'bargain' or 'budget' guns in huge quantities, marketed box-lock non-ejectors retailing at $10 or less. These were distinguished by brandnames ranging from 'Faultless' to 'Square Deal'. Crescent was purchased in 1893 by H. & D. Folsom Arms Company of New York, but continued to make guns under the same names for many years. Wholesalers Sears, Roebuck & Company of Chicago sold guns named 'A. J. Aubrey' after Albert Aubrey, the first superintendent of the Sears-created Meriden Fire Arms Company.

Hammerless Baker-patent hammer doubles, associated prior to 1890 with the Syracuse Forging Company, were made in 1890–1919 by the **Baker** Gun & Forging Company of Batavia, New York – often under a 'Batavia' brandname, which identified budget-price products. Post-1890 Baker guns differed from contemporaneous Ithaca Gun Company patterns (which were made to earlier Baker patents), but were similar externally to L. C. Smith products. The first hammerless side-lock Bakers did not appear until 1899.

Parker Brothers & Company introduced their first high-quality hammerless box-lock doubles about 1890. The manufacturer was eventually acquired by Remington, but not until 1934.

Production of the Spencer **slide-action repeater** – described in the previous chapter – recommenced under the control of Francis Bannerman & Sons in Brooklyn, the first or 1890-model Bannerman-Spencers being differentiated from the preceding 1882 pattern largely by their ribbed cylindrical operating handles. The last or 1900 model had an improved dismantling system.

When the first slide-action Winchester appeared in 1893, Bannerman sued Winchester's New York agent on the grounds that the 1885 Roper patent was being infringed. After protracted wrangling over the existence of earlier patents in Britain and France, the case resolved in Winchester's favour in 1897; Bannerman appealed, but the case was finally dismissed in 1900. Ironically, it was the existence of the *original* Spencer & Roper patent that finally ruined Bannerman's chances.

Competition afforded by slide-action Winchester and Marlin guns forced Bannerman out of production at the turn of the century. The Brooklyn factory was still being offered for sale in 1907.

The **Remington** No. 3 of 1893–1902 was a simple single-barrel semi-hammerless design, with a radial top-lever breech lock and a cocking lever on the left side of the frame. Made in 10, 12, 16, 20, 24 and 28-bore, with barrels of 30–34in, the ultra-plain shotgun weighed 5.7–6.5lb.

Andrew **Burgess**'s sliding-grip gun was adapted from patents including 210,091 of 19 November 1878, 213,866 of 1 April 1879 and 216,080 of 3 June 1879. Burgess sued Sylvester Roper for patent infringement in the mid-1880s, when it was established that Burgess had been responsible for the first slide-action guns ('Haveness Actions' as he called them) ever made in the USA. The case was lost on a technicality, as Burgess had mistakenly claimed against the 1885 Roper patent instead of the original Spencer & Roper patent of 1882.

The perfected Burgess shotgun was loaded by sliding the pistol grip down the underside of the butt, then returning it to chamber a fresh cartridge and close the bolt. When the gun was fired, the bolt opened automatically to eject the empty case. Cycling the pistol grip then reloaded and closed the bolt ready for another shot.

The Burgess Gun Company was organised in Buffalo, New York, in 1892 and the first 12-bore slide-action shotguns were assembled in 1893. Work continued until Burgess sold out to Winchester in 1899. A rifle had been introduced in 1896, and a folding rifle – chambered for .30-30, .30-40 or .44-40 – was offered fleetingly in 1897.

An improved **Lefever** top-lever double-barrelled hammerless shotgun, introduced in 1894, remained in production until Daniel Lefever sold the Lefever Arms Company to the Durston family in 1901. The first ejector guns were made in 1891, and a single-trigger system had been developed for double-barrel guns about 1898.

The box-lock '**Remington** Hammerless Double Barrel Shot Gun' or Model 1894, made until 1910, had a top lever, automatic ejectors and an automatic safety. It was supplied in 10, 12 or 16-bore, with 28–32in rolled or damascus-twist steel barrels, and weighed 7.5–10lb. The best grades were delicately engraved, with finely cut chequering on the half pistol-grips and the Purdey snap-on pattern fore-ends.

Winchester's **Browning**-designed Model 1893 slide-action gun had an exposed hammer and a five-cartridge tube magazine beneath the barrel. Made exclusively in 12-bore, generally with barrels of 30–32in, it could be obtained with a selection of decorative finishes. Production was confined to 1894–7, a little over 34,000 being made. It was replaced by the Model 1897, made only in 12-bore (solid frame) or 12- and 16-bore ('Take Down'), which was offered until 1957. Serial numbers, which had continued where the 1893 pattern had stopped, eventually reached 1058850.

Right at the end of the period under review, **Marlin** introduced a 12-bore 'Take Down' slide-action shotgun. Known as the Model 1898 and made only until 1905, this was offered in four grades ('A'–'D') with a 26–32in barrel and a five-cartridge tube magazine. It weighed 7–7.5lb.

Handguns

Revolvers

The last decade of the twentieth century saw the eclipse of the original solid-frame sheath-trigger 'Suicide Specials' by cheap double-action revolvers which, though shortcuts were often evident in construction, could embody surprisingly advanced features. Now often also labelled as 'Suicide Specials', these guns deserve much more praise than they customarily receive.

The best of them were as sophisticated as anything Colt or Smith & Wesson could offer, and were even made of first-class materials. The principal weakness of many otherwise promising designs was simply that the manufacturers sometimes lacked the production capacity of the large-scale gunmaking businesses; though they could often compete on price, they could not always compete with the established distribution networks.

Among the finest guns were those produced in the 1890s by the **American Arms Company** of Boston, Massachusetts (1872–93), and then Milwaukee, Wisconsin (1893–1901). These were made to a patent granted to George Fox and Henry Wheeler on 11 March 1890 ('firearm lock', 422,930), which protected a hammer that could be rotated to full-cock and then released by a second pull on the trigger. The guns had a selector on the side of the frame to allow the firer to revert to conventional double-action at will.

The **Foehl & Weeks** Manufacturing Company of Philadelphia, Pennsylvania, made a selection of solid-frame and break-open revolvers under names such as 'Columbian' and 'Perfect' in 1891–4. Some included a removable cylinder system patented by Charles Foehl on 17 December 1889 ('firearm', 417,672). Foehl had been granted an earlier patent to protect the cylinder-rotating pawl incorporated in revolvers made briefly by Henry Deringer & Company of Philadelphia.

Otis Smith of Middlefield and later Rock Fall, Connecticut, originally made solid-frame sheath trigger revolvers in accordance with a patent granted in April 1873 to protect a quick-release cylinder catch. These were superseded by a break-open auto-ejector patented in conjunction with John Smith on 20 December 1881 (251,306). These guns were marketed as 'Model 83 Shell Ejectors', with sheath triggers and bird's head grips, and were in turn replaced by conventional solid-frame hammerless gate-loading guns chambered for .38 rim- or centrefire cartridges. The five-shot revolvers had a double-action trigger system and a unique exposed cylinder stop that could be depressed by the thumb to allow the cylinder to rotate freely.

Model 1892 Smith revolvers were handled by the sporting-goods suppliers Maltby, Henley & Company of New York City, and may be encountered under misleading manufacturers' names such as 'Columbia Armory', 'Spencer Revolver Company' or 'Parker Revolver Company'.

Maltby, Curtis & Company of New York City and its 1889-vintage successor, Maltby, Henley & Co., marketed rim- and centrefire revolvers under the 'Metropolitan Police' brandname. Distinguished by the design of the safety system, these were protected by patents granted to William Bliss of Norwich, Connecticut, on 23 April 1878 (202,627), 28 August 1883 (283,854) and 3 March 1885 (313,048).

The company also promoted a double-action five-shot revolver with a brass frame cast integrally with its brass barrel shroud, relying on a rifled steel liner for strength and accuracy. This was patented by John Smith on 24 January 1889 (376,922) and 28 October 1889 (413,975).

Maltby, Curtis & Company's revolvers were made by the Norwich Pistol Company, formed in Norwich, Connecticut, in 1875. Operations ceased on liquidation in 1881, but the assets were bought back by Maltby, Curtis & Company, business was reorganised, and production began again as the 'Norwich Falls Pistol Company'. Operations failed again in 1887, no doubt linked with a decline in the sporting goods market that caused Maltby, Curtis & Company to enter a temporary eclipse.

Hopkins & Allen began trading in 1868 with cheap sheath-trigger guns disguised by names ranging from 'Acme' to 'Universal'. Large numbers of revolvers were made for Merwin, Hulbert & Company (later Hulbert Brothers & Company), sporting goods dealers based in New York City from 1874–5; Hopkins & Allen-made, but 'Merwin & Hulbert'-marked revolvers were sold until Hulbert Brothers entered liquidation in 1896.

The solid-frame 'XL'-series Suicide Specials described in the previous chapter were supplemented in the 1880s by the 'XL DA' series, with conventional trigger guards, folding-spur hammers, and enlarged butts which offered a better grip. The XL No.3 DA was a five-shot $2\frac{1}{2}$-inch barrelled gun chambering .32 Short rimfire; XL No.6 DA was a similar six-shot .32 and .38 centrefire weapon; and the XL Bulldog chambered .32 or .38 Merwin & Hulbert centrefire ammunition.

The 'Forehand Model 1891' was made for Forehand & Wadsworth (q.v.) on the same machinery as the XL No.6 DA. Offered in hammer and hammerless forms, this five-shot .32 or .38 centrefire revolver was a cheap solid-frame non-ejector. A safety catch on the back strap prevented the hammer going to full-cock except when the trigger was pressed. The Acme, made for Hulbert Bros. & Co., duplicated the hammerless Forehand Model 1891.

The Automatic Model, dating from 1885, had a simultaneous ejector actuated when the barrel was tipped downward. One praiseworthy feature of this particular gun was the efficient latch that locked the barrel/cylinder unit to the frame.

Hopkins & Allen was reorganised in 1898 as the Hopkins & Allen Arms Company, surviving a disastrous fire in 1900 to acquire (in 1902) the assets of

Forehand & Wadsworth – for whom Hopkins & Allen had been making revolvers under sub-contract.

Iver Johnson & Company was created in 1883, becoming the 'Iver Johnson Arms & Cycle Works' within a year. The Model 1879 revolver, despite its designation, appeared on the market at about this time. Initially chambered only for .38 Smith & Wesson cartridges, it was the first American-made double-action revolver with a laterally swinging cylinder. The action was protected by patents issued to Andrew Hyde of Hatfield, Massachusetts, on 4 November 1879 (221,171) and 6 March 1883 (273,282). Unfortunately, it was expensive for an Iver Johnson product and failed to find large enough markets to remain in production for more than a few years.

The Boston Bull Dog, introduced in 1887 in .22 rimfire, .32 and .38 centrefire, was a minor adaption of the double-action American Bull Dog of 1882. The Improved Defender of 1889 was a single-action solid-frame gate loader, almost always displaying 'DEFENDER 89' on the top strap above the cylinder. The Swift was the last revolver to be introduced before Iver Johnson moved to Fitchburg, Massachusetts, in 1891. It was a double-action .38 centrefire pattern, made in hammer and hammerless versions.

The first 'Hammer-the-Hammer' gun appeared in 1892–3, though the catchy advertising slogan was not used until c.1904. The safety system relied on a spacer between the hammer and the firing pin to transmit a blow only when the trigger was deliberately pulled. It was so trustworthy that the hammer could be struck in perfect safety. Introduced in .32 and .38 centrefire, the revolver was joined by a Safety Hammerless Model in 1894.

Introduced c.1897, the **Harrington & Richardson** Automatic Ejecting Model – a break-open pattern resembling contemporary Smith & Wessons – was made as a five-shot .38 or a six-shot .32. It was offered with barrels measuring 2½–6in and blue or nickel-plate finish. The grips were customarily moulded gutta-percha, bearing the H&R pierced target trademark registered in May 1889.

The otherwise identical Police Automatic had a spurless hammer patented by Homer Caldwell of Worcester, Massachusetts, on 4 October 1887 (370,926). It was possible to thumb back the hammer manually, but only after the trigger had been pulled to raise the hammer to half-cock. H&R also made a truly hammerless gun in two forms: a small-frame five-shot .32 weighing a mere 13oz, with barrels ranging from 3–6in, and a larger gun (offered as a six-shot .32 or a five-shot .38) with barrels of 2½–6in.

The .22 or .32 Premier double-action revolver was another break-open pattern, locked by a latch at the rear of the back strap. Finished in nickel or blue, with a choice of 3–6in barrels, it weighed a mere 12oz in short-barrel guise. The Police Premier was essentially similar, but made with a spurless 'Safety Hammer'. The Bicycle Revolver – a seven-shot .22 or a five-shot .32 –

was made with a 2-inch barrel, though otherwise following the standard H&R double-action simultaneous ejecting pattern. The Police Bicycle Model simply had a spurless hammer.

One of the stranger variants of the .32 or .38 Automatic Ejecting Model had a folding knife blade beneath its 4-inch barrel, whilst the 'American' double-action revolver had a solid frame and a pivoting loading gate behind the cylinder. Offered in .32 (six shots) , .38 and .44 (five shots each), the guns were sold in blue or nickel with barrels of 2½–6in. The 'Safety Hammer American' had a spurless hammer, while the .22 or .32 rimfire 'Young America' (with an optional Safety Hammer) was another similar gun with barrels of 2–6in. Vest Pocket revolvers had spurless hammers and ultra-short barrels of 1⅛ or 2in. They weighed merely 8–9oz depending on barrel length.

The fourth variation **Smith & Wesson** .38 Double Action (1895–1909) was similar externally to predecessors described in the preceding chapter, though the sear had been redesigned to improve its efficacy. 216,300 were made.

The .44-40 **Double Action Frontier** revolver was introduced in 1886 to persuade purchasers of rifles chambering Winchester ammunition to buy a Smith & Wesson revolver. By the time it was discontinued in 1913, however, only 15,430 had been made. Offered in blue or nickel, with a 1.56-inch cylinder, DA Frontiers had barrels of 4–6½in. There was also a .38 Winchester Double Action, but only 276 were made in 1900. Sales were so poor that guns were still being offered in Smith & Wesson catalogues as late as 1910; available in blue or nickel, they had barrels measuring 4–6in.

Developed by Joseph Wesson, the **hammerless Smith & Wessons** – they were really enclosed-hammer guns – were based on the contemporary double-action designs. Raising the frame at the rear, above the handgrip, allowed it to entirely envelop the hammer. The finalised design, dating from 1886, also featured a spring-loaded safety plate set into the back strap and an inertia firing pin.

A .44 version was abandoned after prototypes had been made, the first to be made in quantity being the .38 **Safety Hammerless**. The first nickel-plated samples dated from midsummer 1886.

The first pattern had a 'Z'-bar latch in the top strap above the cylinder. About 5250 guns were made in 1886–7. The second variation had an improved barrel latch on the top rear of the frame. Production continued until 1890, reaching about 37,230, but perpetual problems with the barrel-latching system led to more improvements. The third Safety Hammerless revolver had a knurled thumb piece pinned into the top strap, and an auxiliary safety to prevent the gun firing as it was being opened. About 73,520 were made in 1890–8. The fourth model of 1898–1907 had a distinctive knurled-head barrel latch. About 104,000 guns were made in this pattern, the most common of the five .38 variants.

ROBERT PARKER

Better known as 'Butch Cassidy', Robert LeRoy Parker was born in Beaver, Utah, on 13 April 1866. A cattle-rustling and gunslinging career occupied Parker in 1884–7, followed by cattle-droving and a spell in the Wyoming State Penitentiary in 1894–6. Released from jail, Parker pursued a life of bank- and train-robbing, usually in company with fellow 'Wild Bunch' member Elzy Lay (1868–1934). When Lay was captured in October 1899 after an unsuccessful train robbery in Folsom, New Mexico, Parker teamed up with Harry Longbaugh – the Sundance Kid – and continued his criminal activities.

Parker and Longbaugh escaped to South America in 1901, in company with Longbaugh's mistress, Etta Place, and spent some of the years prior to 1906 ranching in Argentina. Returning to their train- and bank-robbing careers, the outlaws were caught in 1909 by a troop of Bolivian cavalry during a raid on the Concordia Tin Mines in San Vicente. In the ensuing gun battle, Longbaugh was fatally wounded and Parker apparently shot himself to evade capture. However, doubts remain to this day; an alternative 'final shoot out' has been placed in Uruguay in 1911, and other sources claim that Parker died in obscurity in Spokane, Washington, in 1937!

Little is known about Parker's preference for firearms, though he is believed to have used Colt Single Action Army revolvers and 1886- or 1894-type Winchesters.

The .32 Safety Hammerless model, also known as the 'New Departure' or 'Lemon Squeezer', appeared in the spring of 1888. It was little more than a reduced-scale .38, sharing similar characteristics. The first pattern resembled the third-model .38 (see above), though lacking the internal safety. A small button-type barrel latch protrudes from the top strap. Production was confined to 1888–1902, 91,417 revolvers being made in their own series. Offered in blue or nickel, the latter predominating, they had been originally offered with gutta-percha grips. Barrels measured 3 and 3½in, though a 2-inch option was introduced in 1902 and a 6-inch version followed in 1904.

The earliest double-action **Colts** were not durable enough to attract military interest. As contemporary hinged-frame auto-ejecting revolvers were far more advanced, Colt determined to develop a gun that offered the advantages of the Smith & Wessons without their comparative fragility.

The project was entrusted to William Mason, who received a patent on 6 December 1881 (250,375) to protect a solid-frame revolver with a cylinder that swung out laterally. The prototypes suggested several improvements: Mason's simplified hammer and spring mechanism was patented on 29 August 1882; Jean Warnant's lever ejector on 8 July 1884; Carl Ehbets's improved star-pattern ejector plate on 5 August 1884; and Horace Lord's improved cylinder

HARRY LONGBAUGH

Better known as the Sundance Kid, Longbaugh was born in Phoenixville, Pennsylvania, in 1870. He became an outlaw in his mid-teens, but was imprisoned for horse-stealing in Sundance in 1887–9. He drifted to Hole-in-the-Wall, Wyoming, about 1890 and later became associated with the Wild Bunch. Longbaugh was reputedly the best shot and 'fastest gun' in the group. Associated with Robert Parker, alias 'Butch Cassidy', after the capture in 1899 of Elzy Lay, Longbaugh accompanied his confederate to South America.

After briefly returning to the USA in 1907 with his ailing mistress, Etta Place, Longbaugh continued his bank- and train-robbing career. He is said to have been fatally wounded by Bolivian cavalrymen in 1909, during an unsuccessful raid with Parker on the pay-office of the Concordia Tin Mine in San Vicente, but rumours still abound; killed in Uruguay in 1911, for example, or death in obscurity in Wyoming at any time between 1930 and 1957. It is assumed that Longbaugh favoured Colt revolvers and Winchester rifles, but nothing definitive is known.

retainer on 5 August 1884. These were followed by a minor improvement granted to Ehbets in October 1884, and then, on 6 November 1888, by the second major patent protecting the Colt swinging-cylinder revolver.

Five thousand .38-calibre **Colt Navy Model 1889** revolvers were ordered after a series of competitive trials. These were made with the long-fluted cylinder that had characterised the Lightning (q.v.) and could be identified by the absence of external locking notches. The cylinder was carried on a yoke, unlocked by retracting the recoil shield on the left side of the frame. When the cylinder had been pulled out of the frame to the left, backward pressure on the cylinder axis pin, to which the extractor plate was anchored, expelled the spent cases.

Externally, the guns resembled the preceding .45 Double Action Army & Frontier model, but lacked the ejector case and had straight-bottom frames. Navy revolvers were made with 6-inch barrels and wood grips, though commercial examples of the 'Double Action Navy Model Revolver' had barrels of varying length.

Unfortunately, the cylinder of the 1889-pattern navy revolver rotated to the left. As the cylinder yoke also swung leftward, wear eventually loosened the action until the bore and chambers no longer aligned satisfactorily.

In 1890–1, 100 Navy-pattern revolvers were tested by the US Army against a similar number of .38 Smith & Wesson Safety Hammerless auto-ejectors. The trial board, while appreciating the safety features of the Smith & Wesson, expressed concern about its complexity; though the Colt had failed the dust test, which its rival had negotiated easily, the Smith & Wesson had been completely disabled by rust.

The rebound spring of the Colt was strengthened, the trigger was combined with the cylinder bolt, and a separate cylinder lock was added to prevent the cylinder rotating with the hammer down. These changes answered the principal objections raised by the army trial board.

Cavalrymen had asked for a cylinder that swung to the right for loading, as men were taught to hold their reins in the left hand and it was easier to transfer the gun to the left hand for loading than switch the reins to the right. The request was rejected, however, and the first of orders for 68,500 **M1892 army revolvers** was received by Colt in the summer of 1892. The new short-flute cylinder had two sets of locking notches, preventing the cylinder rotating when the gun was holstered.

Model 1892 revolvers were acquired by the US Army and the US Navy, differing only in their markings. Navy guns displayed 'U.S.N.' over an anchor on the butt strap, together with the calibre, serial number, inspector's initials and the year of acceptance – e.g., '38 DA', 'No.2332' and 'P' over 'WWK' over '1889'. Army guns bore marks such as 'US', 'ARMY', 'MODEL', '1896', '14436' and 'LW' in six lines. Original guns acknowledged the patents granted on 5 August 1884 and 6 November 1888, but subsequently also those of 5 March 1895 and 9 April 1901.

Accidents soon showed that the Model 1892 could be fired before the cylinder locked into the frame. Colt engineer Frederick Felton developed a special interlock to release the trigger only when the cylinder latch was properly seated, creating the Model 1894. However, 7490 M1892 guns were rebuilt to 1894 standards at Springfield Armory in 1895–6.

Commercial 1889- and 1892-type revolvers had barrels of varying length; the most popular variant was the Target Model, which had chequered walnut grips and a special flat-top frame with adjustable sights. Many were offered as 'New Model Double Action Navy' and 'New Model Double Action Army' revolvers. Army patterns had chequered gutta-percha grips with 'COLT' in an oval, while the navy commercials displayed an additional rampant colt motif. In addition to the regulation .38, these revolvers were also offered in .41 with barrels of 3 or 4½in.

The **Colt New Service Revolver**, which appeared in 1897, was an improved New Model Double Action Army pattern. The name was registered with the US Patent Office in February 1899 but appeared only on the earliest guns, encircling a rampant colt motif on the left side of the frame. A reversion to clockwise cylinder rotation was made, the frame was enlarged to accept .45 Colt or .476 Eley cartridges, and the grip was suited to a large hand. Standard frames had sighting channels cut in the strap above the cylinder; rarer Target Models had flat-top frames with adjustable back sights. Several changes in the trigger mechanism were made during the lengthy production life of the New Service revolver, but none occurred prior to 1900.

Colt introduced the first of its modern double-action pocket revolvers in 1893. The .32-calibre six-shot **Colt New Pocket Model**, chambered for .32 Colt, .32 Smith & Wesson or .32 New Police ammunition, filled the void left when Colt's management declined to compete with the legion of 'Suicide Specials' and abandoned the New Line series entirely.

The New Pocket Model shared many features with the contemporary .38 Double Action Army Revolver (M1892), though its six-round cylinder rotated clockwise. Only 31,000 were made prior to 1905. The guns had small frames and barrels measuring $2\frac{1}{2}$–6in. Few changes were made during their life, apart from minor improvements in the lock, the advent of reeded ejector-rod heads, and a new chequered cylinder latch. The original walnut grips were soon replaced by chequered gutta-percha with 'COLT' moulded into the neck. The New Pocket revolver was superseded in 1905 by the .32 Pocket Positive Model.

The introduction of Colt swinging-cylinder revolvers did not concern Smith & Wesson greatly, as sales of double-action break-open revolvers were booming. When the US Army adopted the .38 Colt in 1892, however, Smith & Wesson were forced to act.

The .32 **Smith & Wesson Hand Ejector Model** and its .32 S&W Long cartridge were introduced in 1896. A split-spring cylinder lock was let into the top strap above the six-chamber cylinder, which swung out to the left of the solid frame after the head of the ejector rod had been pulled forward to release the yoke. Finish was blue or nickel; barrels measured $3\frac{1}{4}$–6in. Adjustable target-pattern sights could be supplied to order, while the maker's marks lay between the flutes of the cylinder.

The new Hand Ejector was not an instantaneous success, partly owing to Colt's lead but also to the enthusiasm with which break-open Smith & Wessons were still being received. Sales were stimulated by orders from the Philadelphia police, but only 19,712 guns had been made when the improved .32 Hand Ejector Model 1903 was substituted.

APPENDIX 1

AMMUNITION

Rudiments of the perfected metal cartridge could be seen in a number of separately primed designs made in the USA prior to the Civil War – e.g. the Burnside and the Maynard patterns, which relied on black powder charges ignited by a separate percussion cap on a nipple struck by a conventional side hammer.

The first truly successful self-contained ammunition, however, was the tiny .22 Smith & Wesson rimfire round, patented in prototype form in 1854 and chambered in the Model No. 1 revolver. Though toylike, this represented a considerable technical advance. Priming compound was spun into the rim of the copper case, which was then turned over and sealed to leave an annular ring of fulminate. The manufacturing process took some time to perfect, restricting calibre until the near-simultaneous introduction of the .32 Smith & Wesson, .44 Henry rimfire and .56 Spencer rimfires.

Although the rimfire cartridges rapidly grew in size and power, they had several drawbacks. Most of these related to the annular ring of priming. Some individual rounds had gaps in the ring, owing to inconsistency in the centrifugal filling process, and others had 'hot spots' – where excessive priming had gathered – which could blow out the base rim and, in particularly badly loaded rounds, detonate when struck a hard blow on the rim during transportation.

Once the Civil War had ended, the impossibility of reloading rimfire cartridges in small Western towns or farmsteads caused their popularity to wane in all but the smallest calibres (e.g. .22, .25 and .32) where factory-loaded ammunition was plentiful enough to use on a throwaway basis.

Some of the attempts to evade the Rollin White 'bored-through cylinder' patent controlled by Smith & Wesson created some unusual cartridges. Typical of these were the teat-fires, loaded from the front of the cylinder, but these had a particularly serious drawback. Fouling in the chamber, if it accumulated sufficiently, could make cartridges difficult to seat; if force was used, there was always a chance that the teat would crush and detonate the fulminate. Damaged eyes and lost fingers soon showed the dangers in teat-fire ammunition and it passed into history.

The cartridges of the Crispin revolver had mercuric-fulminate priming around the periphery of the case, but these were also prone to ignition if struck externally and were rapidly abandoned.

Popular in Europe, the pinfire made no impact in North America, apart from a few thousand Lefaucheux revolvers imported from France during the Civil War and a few small-calibre French and Belgian personal defence weapons sold on the Eastern seaboard. Pinfire cartridges relied on a small vertical rod being struck downward into a cup-like primer, which then ignited the main charge. The one-piece copper cases were durable and waterproof, but the exposure of the pin was a source of potential danger; though pinfire ammunition was still being loaded in Europe in the 1920s, it was rarely if ever loaded in North America.

The ultimate answer was found in the centrefire cartridge. The first US-made examples were primed internally, but could not be reloaded. Eventually, ways were discovered of fitting replaceable primers externally, which was a great leap forward; spent primers could simply be punched out of the cases with a special tool, then replaced with a new primer, a fresh powder charge, possibly a wad or two, and then a new bullet.

The first US centrefire .50-70 cartridges were made in Frankford Arsenal in 1865, using an inside-primer system credited to Colonel Stephen Benét, the commandant.

Cup-primer cartridges were replaced by the earliest Martin designs, made in 1867, which contained a bar of iron pressed tightly against the inside of the case head. Priming composition was held in cavity in the underside of the bar, against the case-metal.

The bar anvil was superseded by the Benét copper cup, retained by crimping the walls of the case. Two flash-holes at the edge of the recess containing the priming compound allowed the flash to pass into the main charge. The copper case, slightly tapered to facilitate extraction, had a sturdy rim. Separated from the charge by a fibreboard wad, the bullet was sunk to more than half its length in the case mouth, to protect the tallow/beeswax lubricant in the circumferential groove, and the case mouth was pressed tightly shut around the bullet to prevent the entry of moisture.

An improved Martin cartridge was tested by the Ordnance Department in 1870, differing in the substitution of a small copper anvil inside a corrugated dish for the previous cup. The design was claimed to reduce the tendency of the case-head to swell or bulge on firing, and to be an ideal way of anchoring the anvil.

The inside-primed cartridge was not the final answer, however, as it was rapidly superseded by a replaceable or 'external'-primer type. This is often credited to Hiram Berdan, but Frankford Arsenal staff were keener to credit Stephen Benét, whose 1866-vintage design had been shown to Berdan; the latter, Frankford's men averred, had even taken samples away with him. Berdan subsequently patented a separate-cap cartridge in 1871.

The British honoured Colonel Edward Boxer, Superintendent of the Royal Laboratory in Woolwich, where a separate-cap cartridge had been developed for the Snider rifle in the mid-1860s. There was, however, a fundamental difference between the Berdan and Boxer methods of priming: the former used a single flash-hole and a separate anvil, whereas the latter used two flash-holes and made the anvil integrally with the base of the case. Ironically, the Boxer primer gained wide acceptance in the USA whereas the Berdan primer has been preferred in many parts of Europe!

The improvements in cartridge design were mirrored by improvements in the manufacturing process. The makers of the earliest rimfire cartridges were often comparatively small businesses. Among the companies which produced ammunition anonymously – marked only on box labels – were the New Haven Arms Company of New Haven, Connecticut; Sharps & Hankins of Philadelphia, Pennsylvania; Smith & Wesson of Springfield, Massachusetts; and the Spencer Repeating Rifle Company of Boston, Massachusetts. Others headstamped their cartridges individually, including Crittenden & Tibbals of South Coventry, Connecticut (mark: 'CT'); Fitch & Van Vechten & Company of New York ('FVV', 'FVV & Co.'); Jacob Goldmark of New York City ('JG', sometimes underlined); C. D. Leet of Springfield, Massachusetts ('CDL'); and the D. C. Sage Company Ammunition Works of Middletown, Connecticut ('SAW').

The huge growth of the ammunition-making business after the introduction of commercial centrefire patterns in the early 1870s led to a marked change in the structure of the manufacturing industry, as the small makers of rimfire cartridges were swept away by companies such as the Winchester Repeating Arms Company and the Union Metallic Cartridge Company (UMC, later incorporated with Remington). These conglomerates were capable of making millions of cartridges weekly in a tremendous variety of styles, and set trends that extended past 1898 to the present day.

The Cartridge Register

.22 BB Cap. The Bulleted Breech Cap was introduced in the 1840s to accompany French Flobert saloon pistols. Originally comprising a small copper or tin case loaded with priming compound and a small round ball, many later examples (especially those made in North America) contained a small black powder charge and a conical projectile. Most BB Caps are capable of killing rats, mice and small vermin at close range, and should never be underestimated.

.22 CB Cap. Conical Ball Caps, apparently originating in the USA, are a more powerful version of the BB Cap (above), generally loaded with the 29-grain bullet associated with .22 Short Rimfire. Originating in the 1880s, CB Caps are still loaded in Europe; the last US-made version was discontinued in 1941. The CB Cap was never as popular as the BB version, as it was too powerful for saloon use yet vastly inferior to .22 Short Rimfire on small vermin.

.22 Extra Long Rimfire. Introduced about 1880 and chambered in a variety of single-shot rifles – Ballard, Remington, Stevens, Winchester and others – this appears to have preceded .22 Long Rifle rimfire, which differs primarily in case length. The Extra Long case was originally loaded with six grains of powder, but length made it unsuitable for most repeating actions: .22 Extra Long gradually lost favour to .22 Long Rifle and was discontinued in the 1930s.

.22 Long Rimfire. This was the predecessor of .22 Long Rifle, adapted from .22 Short in the late 1860s. It offers the same 29-grain lead bullet, but in a substantially longer (.615) case. The earliest known listing is for a Standard revolver of the early 1870s, but Remington, Stevens and others had announced rifles chambering .22 Long by 1875. Unfortunately, .22 Long had neither the accuracy of .22 Short nor the additional hitting power of the later .22 Long Rifle.

.22 Long Rifle Rimfire. Said to have been developed for or by the Stevens Arms & Tool Company in 1886–7, this cartridge was introduced for several single-shot Stevens rifles in 1888 and then rapidly adopted by rival manufacturers such as Marlin (for Ballard single-shots), Remington and Winchester. The standard pattern relies on a 40-grain round-nose lead bullet loaded in a .615 rimmed straight brass case. Rim diameter is usually about .280, the case mouth measuring .225. A typical Remington-UMC black powder loading gave 1103 ft/sec at the muzzle, equating to an energy of 108 ft-lb.

.22 Short Rimfire. Introduced by Smith & Wesson in 1857, this comprises a small round-nose lead bullet – normally weighing about 29 grains – in a straight rimmed brass case. The case is about .420 long, the rim diameter being .280 and those of shoulder, neck and bullet measuring about .225. Performance includes a muzzle velocity of 1050 ft/sec (71 ft-lb).

.22 Winchester Rimfire (.22 WRF, .22 Remington Special). This rimmed straight-case cartridge, with a flat-nosed 45-grain bullet, was chambered initially in the Winchester Model 1890 slide-action rifle and then in a selection of Colt, Remington, Stevens and Winchester guns. .22 WRF was a notable attempt to improve the performance of the .22 Long cartridge, its case being longer and of larger diameter, but had been superseded by 1959. A typical pre-1915 Remington-UMC smokeless loading gave only 1036 ft/sec at the muzzle (107 ft-lb), but Winchester figures gave 1137 ft/sec (129 ft-lb) in the M1890 rifle.

.22 Winchester (.22 WCF). Generally containing a 45-grain bullet in a rimmed brass case with a long shallow neck, this cartridge was introduced with the Model 1885 Winchester rifle. An attempt was made to chamber it in the Model 1873 lever action rifle, but the elongated case was too fragile;

except for a short-lived variant of the Remington No. 7 rolling-block rifle, made in the early 1900s, .22 WCF was confined to the single-shot Winchesters. A pre-1915 Remington-UMC black powder load gave a velocity of 1563 ft/sec at the muzzle, equivalent to 244 ft-lb.

.22 Maynard (.22 Extra Long). Similar to .22 Extra Long rimfire, but with a centrefire primer, this cartridge offered a 45-grain lead bullet in a straight rimmed brass case. Performance included a muzzle velocity of about 1100 ft/sec. Introduced to accompany the 1882-model single-shot sporting rifle, it had a short and unspectacular life in Ballard, Maynard and Stevens rifles before being overtaken by .22 WCF (q.v.).

.22-15 Stevens (.22-15-60). Allegedly designed in the early 1890s by a Massachusetts gunsmith named Charles Herrick, this was announced by Stevens in 1896. Chambered in the company's No. 44 and 44½ sporting rifles, it had an unusually slender rimmed brass case. After enjoying a short vogue as a sporting cartridge – thanks to a 60-grain bullet offering better hitting power than most .22 rimfires – it was eclipsed first by .22-21 Stevens and then .22 WCF.

.236 Lee (6mm Lee Navy). Adopted for use in the Lee Straight-Pull Navy Rifle of 1895, this cartridge featured a 112-grain jacketed round-nose bullet in a necked rimless brass case. Muzzle velocity of the service cartridge was in the region of 2565 ft/sec, giving a muzzle energy of 1635 ft-lb, though the Winchester commercial loading gave only 2550 ft/sec (1618 ft-lb). However, owing to the poor quality of contemporary propellants, .236 Lee was not especially successful; 15,000 rifles were made for the navy, but were soon discarded in favour of the Krag-Jørgensen and then the Springfield. A very few were offered commercially, but achieved no great success. Winchester, Remington and Blake also made rifles in this chambering.

.25 Short Rimfire (.25 Bacon & Bliss). Introduced for a gun patented by F. D. Bliss in the 1860s, this was chambered in 'Suicide Special' revolvers and made until the First World War. The loading was originally a 43-grain lead bullet ahead of five grains of black powder, which gave .25 Short Rimfire much the same performance as .22 Long Rifle.

.25 Stevens Rimfire. Apparently first offered in 1895 with the Stevens Favorite rifle, this cartridge was developed by Stevens in conjunction with the Peters Cartridge Company. The load was originally a 67-grain lead bullet ahead of ten grains of black powder, which made the .25 Stevens a good performer on vermin and small game. However, it was more expensive than the .22 rimfires and had faded into obscurity by 1940. A typical pre-1915 Remington-UMC load was rated at a muzzle velocity of 1161 ft/sec (201 ft-lb).

.25-20 Single Shot. Created in the 1880s as a 'wildcat', this necked centrefire cartridge was apparently originally chambered in Remington rolling-block rifles, though Maynard, Stevens and Winchester also used it. Too slender to feed satisfactorily through lever-action rifles, .25-20 Single Shot had lost most of its popularity by 1918. Ammunition was still being offered into the early 1930s; a typical pre-1917 Remington-UMC black powder loading gave 1468 ft/sec with an 86-grain bullet (412 ft-lb), though a Winchester loading of the period gave merely 1304 ft/sec (325 ft-lb).

.25-20 Winchester (.25-20 WCF). Introduced for the short-action Winchester Model 1892 rifle in the mid-1890s, this necked rimmed-case centrefire cartridge was a modified .25-20 Single Shot with a shortened case and a more pronounced neck. It was popular for use against small game until the advent of .218 Bee and .22 Hornet. Loaded with an 86-grain bullet in a 1.33in case with .410-diameter rim and .335 shoulder, its comparatively low power (1500 ft/sec, 430 ft-lb, with a Winchester black powder load) restricted effective range to about 150 yards.

.25-21 Stevens. Designed by Captain William Carpenter of the US Army, this centrefire cartridge had a slender straight rimmed brass case. Introduced for the Stevens No. 44 single-shot rifle in 1897, and later chambered in the Remington-Hepburn, the cartridge briefly capitalised on mistrust of necked cases that cost Stevens sales of .25-20 (q.v.). The regular factory black-powder loading offered by Remington-UMC prior to 1917 fired an 86-grain round-nose lead bullet at 1551 ft/sec, giving a muzzle energy of 459 ft-lb.

.25-25 Stevens. This straight-case cartridge, a predecessor of .25-21, was designed by William Carpenter and introduced commercially in 1895. It was substantially longer, but developed a velocity only 30 ft/sec greater; consequently, the shorter .25-21 case gradually gained favour at the .25-25's expense. It was usually chambered in the Stevens No. 44 and 44½ rifles.

.25-36 Marlin. Derived from an experimental '.25-37' cartridge developed by gunsmith William Lowe in 1893–4, this rimmed necked-case centrefire cartridge was offered with the Marlin Model 93 rifle from the mid-1890s. Similar to .25-35 Winchester, but not interchangeable, .25-36 Marlin survived into the 1920s. A typical Remington-UMC black powder load of the early 1900s propelled a 117-grain bullet at 1855 ft/sec (894 ft-lb).

.30 Long Rimfire. An elongated version of .30 Short rimfire, sharing many of the same vices, this cartridge originated in the late 1860s; by 1873, Colt, Sharps, Standard and other handguns were chambering it, but the advent of better centrefire cartridges ruined its market. Most .30 Long rimfire ammunition had disappeared by 1910.

.30 Short Rimfire. A survivor of the 1860s, when it was introduced for the Sharps four-barrel derringer, the Standard revolver and other close-range defence weapons, this small rimmed straight-case cartridge barely survived into the 1920s. It was loaded with a 55-grain bullet and about six grains of powder, confining it to roles in which its low power was no great handicap.

.30-30 Wesson. Chambered in a single-shot rifle with a tipping barrel, and also apparently in small numbers of falling block patterns, this rimmed brass-case cartridge had so slight a neck that it appeared to be a continuous straight taper from rim to mouth. Franklin Wesson is believed to have introduced it about 1883, but information is lacking. Ammunition was loaded by Remington and Winchester prior to 1900, but never achieved widespread distribution. A typical load comprised a 165-grain round-nose lead bullet ahead of 30 grains of black powder; muzzle velocity was about 1250 ft/sec, which gave an energy of about 573 ft-lb.

.30-30 Winchester (.30 WCF). Introduced commercially in 1895, this rimmed necked-case round is still one of the best-known US sporting rifle cartridges. Widely used throughout North America against medium game, .30-30 is generally loaded with round-nose bullets suited to tube magazines. It is not particularly powerful, nor does its effective range extend much beyond 250yd, but it has an awesome mystique. The case measures 2.01in overall, the rim diameter being .505 and the neck .330. A pre-1917 Remington-UMC black-powder load gave a 170-grain bullet a muzzle velocity of 2020 ft/sec (1541 ft-lb), though a Winchester version with a 220-grain bullet was rated at 1970 ft/sec (1552 ft-lb).

.30-40 Krag. The US Army's first small-bore cartridge, adopted in 1892, the rimmed necked-case centrefire Krag has since built a lasting reputation for accuracy – but only when loaded to moderate pressures. Inferior in virtually every respect to .30-06 except recoil, it is nevertheless considerably better than .30-30. The case is 2.315in long, with a .545-diameter rim, a .425 shoulder and a .340 neck. The pre-1917 Remington-UMC commercial loading propelled a 220-grain bullet at 2005 ft/sec (1964 ft-lb).

.32 Ballard Extra Long. An elongated version of .32 Long Rifle, this was introduced for the No. 2 single-shot sporting rifle shortly after Marlin started making Ballard rifles in the mid-1870s. Remington rolling blocks, Stevens No. 44 and other single-shot rifles have also been chambered for it. The .32 Ballard Extra Long offers a 115-grain round-nose lead bullet in a straight rimmed brass case with a centrefire primer. Muzzle velocity was about 1200 ft/sec, giving an energy of 368 ft-lb. By 1920, however, .32-20 WCF had eclipsed the Ballard round and production stopped.

.32 Extra Short Rimfire. The unusually short case of this stubby little rimmed cartridge was designed specifically for the Remington Magazine Pistol, introduced in 1871, in an effort to increase the capacity of a magazine that would otherwise have held only three standard .32 rounds; the Extra Short permitted an increase to five. Subsequently adopted for other guns in which compactness was an asset – such as the Chicago Fire Arms Company 'Protector' – it lasted into the 1920s, but never achieved widespread distribution. The original loading comprised a 54-grain bullet ahead of about five grains of powder.

.32 Extra Long Rimfire. This cartridge is believed to have originated c.1870, though information is difficult to obtain. It was certainly being chambered in a variety of single-shot rifles by 1876 – Ballard, Remington, Stevens and others amongst them – but had disappeared by the early 1900s. A typical loading consisted of eighteen grains of black powder and a 90-grain bullet; muzzle velocity is estimated to have been about 1050 ft/sec, giving a muzzle energy of 221 ft-lb.

.32 Long Rifle Centrefire. This was simply a derivation of the similar rimfire cartridge, intended to be reloaded. It appeared about 1900, being offered by both Remington and Winchester. However, it achieved so little distribution that it is by no means certain what guns chambered .32 Long Rifle Centrefire – other than suitably modified rimfires.

.32 Long Rifle Rimfire. Apparently dating from the late 1870s, this was an unsuccessful compromise between .32 Long and Extra Long. Loaded with an 82-grain bullet and about thirteen grains of powder, .32 Long Rifle chambered in a variety of single-shot rifles and, later, in the Models 1891 and 1892 Marlin lever-action repeaters. Never universally popular, it disappeared after the First World War.

.32 Short Rimfire. One of the oldest metal-case cartridges, this owed its introduction to the advent of appropriately chambered Smith & Wesson Model No. 1½ and No. 2 revolvers. It was subsequently adapted to many rival designs, including Colts, Whitneys and innumerable 'Suicide Specials', as well as chambering in many Remington, Stevens and Winchester rifles. Popular in its heyday, new .32 Short rimfire ammunition may still occasionally be encountered.

.32-20 Winchester (.32-20 WCF). This venerable cartridge was introduced for the Model 1873 lever-action rifle in 1882. Now comparatively uncommon, its virtues lie in its low power, useful in urban districts, and the ease with which it can be reloaded. .32-20 WCF features a rimmed necked 1.315in centrefire case with a rim diameter of .410 and a neck measuring .325. A typical factory loading offers a 100-grain bullet, fired at about 1700 ft/sec to attain a muzzle energy of 642 ft-lb.

.32-30 Remington. Introduced in 1884 to accompany the Remington-Hepburn No. 3 sporting rifle, this rimmed centrefire cartridge had a necked brass case. .32-30 was never popular, being too long to chamber in most short-action repeaters, and was also somewhat under-powered for use in the Remington-Hepburn. It had been discontinued, apart from dealers' stocks, by 1915. The standard factory load generated only about 1380 ft/sec with a 125-grain bullet (529 ft-lb).

.32-35 Stevens & Maynard. Introduced in the mid-1880s for the Stevens No. 9 and No. 10 New Model single-shot rifles, this was also offered in the later No. 44 and No. 44½. It was regarded as a very accurate cartridge, although eventually forced into obsolescence by Winchester's .32-40. The straight-taper rimmed brass case was originally loaded with a round-nose lead bullet weighing about 160 grains. This developed a muzzle velocity of 1375 ft/sec, equating to an energy of 672 ft-lb.

.32-40 Ballard (.32-40 WCF, .32-40 Winchester). This straight-taper rimmed brass case, 2.13in overall with rim and neck diameters of .505 and .340 respectively, was developed for a Ballard single-shot target rifle. Introduced commercially in 1884, it was subsequently appropriated for Winchester and Marlin lever-action rifles before being abandoned in the early 1940s. A 165-grain bullet attained 1450 ft/sec in pre-1917 Remington-UMC black powder loads, giving a muzzle energy of 771 ft-lb, whereas a Winchester version of the period gave only 1385 ft/sec (703 ft-lb).

.32-40 Bullard. Not to be confused with the similarly named, but quite different .32-40 Ballard, this rimmed necked-case round was introduced with the Bullard single-shot and lever-action repeating rifles in the mid-1880s. The cartridge, loaded with a 150-grain lead bullet, was necked a considerable distance from the case mouth – distinguishing it from .32-40 Ballard, which had a straight-taper case. Bullards were never widely available, and their unique ammunition had disappeared by 1900. Muzzle velocity is estimated to have been about 1490 ft/sec, giving a muzzle energy of 740 ft-lb.

.32-40 Remington (.32-40-150). Introduced in the 1870s to accompany Remington's Sporting Rifle No. 1, this dual purpose hunting/target round also chambered in some of the later Hepburn pattern rifles. It has an odd rimmed brass case described by Frank Barnes in *Cartridges of the World* as 'taper-necked'. It was superseded by .32-40 Ballard and .32-40 Winchester, and had disappeared by 1910. The bullet is said to have weighed about 150 grains, giving a muzzle energy of about 480 ft-lb at an initial velocity of 1200 ft/sec, but details are lacking.

.32-40 Winchester (.32 WCF) – see .32-40 Ballard.

.35-30 Maynard. A straight-case rimmed cartridge, loaded with a 250-grain lead ball and generating a muzzle velocity of about 1280 ft/sec (910 ft-lb), this was introduced for the 1882-pattern Maynard single-shot sporting rifle. It was subsequently chambered in the Maynard Nos. 7, 9, 10 and 16. Although sturdy and reliable, guns of this type had disappeared by the end of the nineteenth century, victims of progress.

.35-40 Maynard. This was a minor adaptation of .35-30 Maynard (above), introduced about 1890. A longer case permitted an increase in powder capacity, raising the muzzle velocity to 1375 ft/sec with a 250-grain ball (1050 ft-lb). Appearing at a time when the Maynard rifles were losing favour, however, .35-40 ammunition was never commonplace and had virtually disappeared by 1910.

.38 Ballard Extra Long. Derived from .38 Extra Long Rimfire (q.v.), this rimmed straight-case design was announced for the single-shot Ballard No. 2 sporting rifle at the beginning of 1886. An efficient and economical cartridge, it was subsequently adopted by many of Ballard's rivals. The original factory load offered a 145-grain bullet capable of attaining 1275 ft/sec (532 ft-lb).

.38 Extra Long Rimfire. Chambered in a selection of single-shot rifles – Ballard, Howard, Remington, Frank Wesson and other designs – this appeared about 1870. Customarily loaded with a 150-grain bullet and 30 grains of black powder in a straight rimmed case, .38 Extra Long Rimfire was neither accurate not powerful enough to maintain popularity after the First World War. A typical load gave a muzzle velocity of about 1250 ft/sec and an energy of 525 ft-lb.

.38 Long Centrefire. Conceived as a substitute for .38 Long Rimfire, specifically to permit reloading, this appeared in the mid-1870s. Chambered mainly in Ballard, Remington, Stevens and other single-shot rifles, it had been overtaken by bigger, better and more accurate cartridges by 1900. The original load comprised a 150-grain bullet and about 20 grains of black powder, muzzle velocity being 950–1000 ft/sec.

.38 Long Rimfire. Introduced during the Civil War, this chambered in a range of single-shot guns from Allen to Wesson patterns – but which seems to have begun with the Remington-Beals sporting rifle. The original Remington revolver rifle and some early revolvers were also chambered for it. Realising that much of its one-time popularity had been lost to .38 centrefire rounds, most manufacturers had discontinued .38 Long rimfire by 1917. Fired from a rifle, the cartridges gave a velocity of about 980 ft/sec at the muzzle, energy equating to about 320 ft-lb.

.38 Short Rimfire. This was introduced during the Civil War, though details remain elusive. A variety of guns were being chambered for it by 1875, including Allen, Colt and Remington revolvers and Ballard, Remington, Stevens and Frank Wesson rifles. Largely superseded by similar centrefire ammunition by 1900, .38 Short rimfire had virtually disappeared by 1920. A typical load, consisting of eighteen grains of black powder and a 130-grain bullet, generated a muzzle velocity of 825 ft/sec in a rifle (197 ft-lb).

.38-35 Stevens. This short-lived rimmed straight-case round, intended for the Stevens single-shot rifles, appeared in the mid-1870s. Most cases were 'Everlasting' patterns, made with specially thickened walls capable of surviving perpetual reloading. However, thickening the walls reduced the propellant space, restricting power; consequently, the larger Everlasting cartridges were much more popular, and .38-35 disappeared in the late 1880s. A typical factory load fired a 215-grain round-nose lead bullet at a velocity of 1250 ft/sec (746 ft-lb).

.38-40 Remington(-Hepburn). Another of the unique taper-necked cartridges, this was introduced with the Remington No. 1 in about 1876 and reintroduced with the Remington-Hepburn at the end of the nineteenth century. It has been suggested that this cartridge was produced to compete with .38-40 Winchester (q.v.) at a time when the necked case was viewed with scepticism. The Remington cartridge offered much the same performance as the Winchester pattern, but ultimately lost favour – its rival chambered in a repeating rifle – and had been discontinued by the beginning of the First World War. Performance included a muzzle velocity of about 1200 ft/sec with a 245-grain projectile (790 ft-lb).

.38-40 Winchester (.38-40 WCF). This appeared in 1874, to accompany the .44-40 version. The rimmed 1.305in brass case could be identified by its neck, which had a diameter of about .417; the base and rim diameters were .470 and .525 respectively. Offered also in Colt and Remington rifles, and once widely distributed, .38-40 had lost much of its popularity by the 1930s. Generally regarded as too powerful for small game, but not good enough for use on larger animals, .38-40 does little that .44-40 cannot do better; its only real advantage lies in a slight reduction in recoil. A pre-1910 black powder Winchester load fired a 180-grain bullet at 1268 ft/sec (643 ft-lb).

.38-45 Bullard. Introduced with the short-lived Bullard rifles in the mid-1880s, this cartridge had a rimmed straight-taper brass case loaded with a 190-grain round-nose lead bullet. Muzzle velocity was about 1375 ft/sec, giving an energy in the region of 815 ft-lb – entirely adequate on small game, but with no real margin of superiority over rival (and better distributed) cartridges such as .38-40 Winchester.

.38-45 Stevens. Another of the so-called 'Everlasting' cartridges, with specially thickened walls to withstand reloading, this rimmed straight-case cartridge was introduced for the Stevens single-shot rifle c.1875. Owing to its comparatively small powder capacity (cf. .38-35 Stevens), it was soon discontinued. The original factory load offered a 210-grain round-nose lead ball, which attained about 1400 ft/sec at the muzzle (945 ft-lb).

.38-50 Maynard. Distinguished by an elongated straight rimmed brass case, and a paper-patched 255-grain round-nose bullet in its original factory loading, this was announced in conjunction with the Model 1882 Maynard single-shot rifle. It was too similar to the .38-55 Winchester to prosper, and had been discontinued by 1900. A muzzle velocity of about 1325 ft/sec gave an energy of about 990 ft-lb.

.38-50 Ballard. Introduced for the single-shot Ballard Perfection and Pacific rifles in the mid-1870s, this rimmed straight-case round was sometimes offered with a thick-wall 'Everlasting' case. Somewhat less powerful and about .2in shorter than its 1884-vintage successor, .38-55, the .38-50 Ballard cartridge fired a 255-grain paper-patched bullet at 1320 ft/sec (990 ft-lb).

.38-50 Remington-Hepburn. Introduced with the Remington-Hepburn single-shot match rifle c.1883, this rimmed 'taper-neck' cartridge offered a 250-grain bullet which could attain about 1320 ft/sec (990 ft-lb). As performance was so similar to .38-55, the Remington round soon lost favour and was discontinued before the First World War.

.38-55 Ballard (.38-55 Winchester). This straight 2.13in rimmed-case centrefire cartridge was introduced for the Ballard No. 4 target rifle in 1884, replacing the older .38-50 round (q.v.) in public favour. Marlin and Winchester subsequently produced lever-action rifles chambering it, while Remington adapted the Lee bolt-action rifle, and many single-shot guns also appeared. Although .38-55 had lost favour completely by 1940, it was returned to production for Winchester commemorative rifles in the 1970s. The rim diameter is .505, with a .390 case mouth; the performance of a pre-1910 Winchester black-powder load included a muzzle velocity of about 1285 ft/sec with a 255-grain bullet (935 ft-lb). A Remington-UMC equivalent attained 1316 ft/sec, or 981 ft-lb.

.38-55 Winchester – see .38-55 Ballard.

.38-56 Winchester. This was the necked equivalent of .38-55 (q.v.), with a larger body diameter. The increase of a single grain of black powder improved performance – a velocity of about 1369 ft/sec being attained with a 255-grain bullet (1061 ft-lb) – but not to the levels demanded by game larger than deer. Chambered in the Model 1885 single-shot and Model 1886 lever-action Winchester, the Model 1895 Marlin and Colt New Lightning rifles, .38-56 was loaded until the mid-1930s.

.38-70 Winchester (.38-70-255). A rimmed necked-case cartridge loaded with a standard 255-grain round-nose lead bullet, at least in its original factory guise, this chambered in the Model 1886 lever-action rifle from 1894 onward. A typical pre-1917 Remington-UMC black powder load gave a muzzle velocity of 1493 ft/sec and an energy of about 1262 ft-lb, but .38-70 offered no great improvement over the small .38-55 and was eventually discontinued.

.38-72 Winchester (.38-72-275). Specifically developed for the Model 1895 lever-action rifle, but also chambered in the Model 1885 single-shot pattern, this rimmed brass-case cartridge had an all but imperceptible neck which was often hidden by a pronounced annular crimp at the base of the bullet. The Model 95 rifle was sturdy enough to withstand high pressures, for its day, yet .38-72 offered little advantage over .38-55 or .38-70; pre-1917 Remington-UMC factory loadings offered a 275-grain round-nose bullet fired at 1483 ft/sec (1343 ft-lb), whereas the Winchester equivalent of the day attained 1443 ft/sec (1272 ft-lb).

.38-90 Winchester Express (.38-90-217). Made only in 1886–1904, this lengthy rimmed brass-case cartridge was introduced for the Model 1885 single-shot rifle. Distinguished by a very shallow neck and a 217-grain lead bullet with a flattened nose, the 'Express' appellation suggested a far greater velocity than the 1600 ft/sec it normally attained (1230 ft-lb).

.40-40 Maynard. Offered with the 1882-pattern Maynard No. 9 and No. 10 single-shot rifles, ideally suited for hunting and target shooting alike, this short-lived cartridge was no longer being loaded by 1905. The factory load offered a 330-grain bullet – round- or flat-nosed – in a rimmed straight case. Muzzle velocity was listed as 1260 ft/sec, giving an energy of 1170 ft-lb.

.40-50 Sharps (.40-$1\frac{11}{16}$). Among the shortest of the Sharps cartridges, dating from c.1875, this necked centrefire cartridge had a rimmed case measuring 1.720in. Rim diameter was about .580, the shoulder measured .490 and the neck behind the case mouth was .425. It originally chambered in Sharps, Remington and similar single-shot rifles. Powerful enough for use on small or medium game, the original 265-grain paper-patched bullet attained a velocity of about 1460 ft/sec at the muzzle (1260 ft-lb).

.40-50 Sharps (.40-$1\frac{7}{8}$). Dating from the late 1870s, this straight-cased rimmed cartridge originally fired a paper-patched round-nose lead bullet with a performance not unlike that of the .40-40 Maynard described above. Remington and Winchester each chambered single-shot rifles for it, but popularity was comparatively short-lived.

.40-60 Marlin. This was dimensionally identical to (and interchangeable with) the .40-60 Winchester, but loaded a little differently to generate a muzzle velocity of 1447 ft/sec with a 260-grain bullet (1209 ft-lb) in the Remington-UMC black powder version or 1419 ft/sec (1163 ft-lb) in the Winchester type. The cartridge was supposed to be confined to the Model 1895 Marlin lever-action rifle, but most .40-60 Winchesters would fire it without protest. Colt also chambered the New Lightning rifle for .40-60, using the Marlin version without altering its designation.

.40-60 Maynard. Another of the dual-purpose hunting/target shooting Maynard cartridges, this was intended for the 1882-pattern Nos. 10, 12, 13, 15 and 16 target rifles. The elongated .40-40 case contained a 330-grain paper-patched bullet, generally with a flat nose, which could attain 1370 ft/sec (1360 ft-lb) at the muzzle. However, as Maynard rifles were not as popular as Savage, Stevens, Remington and Winchester patterns, the guns and their distinctive cartridges disappeared at the beginning of the twentieth century.

.40-60 Winchester (.40-60-210, .40-60 WCF). This was introduced with the 'Centennial Model' Winchester lever-action rifle of 1876 in an attempt to provide a better game cartridge than the preceding .44-40 WCF had been. The Model 1876 rifle was offered until 1897, but the cartridge continued to be loaded as late as 1934. The case is rimmed, with a perceptible taper and a less pronounced neck; loaded with a 210-grain flat-nose bullet, it could generate a muzzle velocity of 1562 ft/sec and an energy of 1138 ft-lb (pre-1917 Remington-UMC black powder load), though Winchester ammunition was customarily loaded to lower levels. This was hardly in the same league as the powerful cartridges chambered in the Remington and Sharps rifles of the day, but was at least a start. See also .40–60 Marlin.

.40-63 Ballard. A factory-loaded thick wall or 'Everlasting' version of the .40-65 Ballard, described below, this differed from the so-called .40-70 Ballard only in its propellant capacity. The rimmed straight-case cartridge, which contained a 330-grain paper-patched lead bullet, was offered for the single-shot Ballard No. 4 and No. 5 rifles after the mid-1870s. Intended principally for target shooting, .40-63 made a passable game cartridge; its muzzle velocity of about 1330 ft/sec gave an energy of 1315 ft-lb, comparable to Sharps cartridges of the same dimensions.

.40-65 Ballard (.40-65 Ballard Everlasting). Intended for hand-loading, but with a slightly greater external diameter than the .40-63 and .40-70 Ballards (q.v.), this round originated in 1876. It chambered in the Nos. 1½, 4 and 5 single-shot rifles, but .40-65 will not chamber in later rifles, owing to its case diameter, though .40-63 and .40-70 will operate satisfactorily in the older guns.

.40-65 Winchester (.40-65-260). Developed in the late 1880s for the Winchester Model 86 rifle, this straight tapered 2.1in case, with an almost imperceptible neck, also chambered in the Marlin Model 95 and some single-shot rifles. It had a .605-diameter rim, and a neck measuring .425 immediately behind the case mouth. A typical Winchester black-powder load fired a 260-grain flat-nose bullet at a muzzle velocity of about 1395 ft/sec (1124 ft-lb). Intended to provide a comparatively hard-hitting round suited to lever actions, .40-65 was discontinued in the 1930s but has recently been resurrected for use in replica guns.

.40-70 Ballard – see .40-63 Ballard.

.40-70 Maynard. Third and largest of a series of three .40 cartridges chambered in the 1882-model Maynard single-shot rifle, this is perceptibly longer than the .40-60 version; the larger rim and base also differentiate between the two otherwise similar rimmed straight-case rounds. Loaded with a 270-grain flat-nose bullet, seated deeply in the case to reduce overall length below that of .40-60 Maynard, the seventy-grain powder charge could generate a muzzle velocity of 1650 ft/sec and an energy of about 1625 ft-lb.

.40-70 Peabody 'What Cheer'. This oddly-named cartridge, commemorating a famous rifle range near Providence, Rhode Island, dates from c.1877. Made for Providence Tool Company single-shot rifles by UMC and Winchester, the distinctive rimmed necked cartridges were originally loaded with paper-patched flat-nose lead bullets weighing 380 grains. The long tapering shoulder was intended to facilitate extraction in the sturdy, but sometimes temperamental Peabody-Martini action. Muzzle velocities in the region of 1420 ft/sec gave an energy of 1710 ft-lb, sufficient for use against most North American game. Few other rifles chambered for this cartridge have been encountered, so it is assumed that its heyday passed with the Providence Tool Company.

.40-70 Remington – see .40-70 Sharps (necked).

.40-70 Sharps (.40-2¼, .40-70 Remington). Introduced in the 1870s, this rimmed necked-case cartridge was popular among hunters and target shooters alike. The case, 2.250in overall with a .595 rim and a .500 shoulder, contained a 330-grain paper-patched round- or flat-nose bullet. A typical Winchester-made black powder load developed only 1220 ft/sec at the muzzle (1091 ft-lb), but Remington-UMC loads were considerably more potent. Remington chambered its No. 1 Rolling Block and No. 3 (Hepburn) rifles for the Sharps cartridge in the 1880s, offering ammunition under the '.40-70 Remington' designation. These cartridges are dimensionally identical to the original Sharps pattern, and will interchange.

.40-70 Sharps (.40-2½). Dating from c.1879–80, this round chambered in Sharps, Remington, Winchester and similar single-shot rifles before being discontinued in the 1930s. It was resurrected in 1989 for Shiloh Sharps rifles. The rimmed 2.5in straight case has a rim diameter of .535 and a neck measuring .420 immediately behind the case mouth. The original factory load contained a 330-grain paper-patched lead bullet, attaining a muzzle velocity of 1260 ft/sec and an energy of 1164 ft-lb.

.40-70 Winchester (.40-70-330). Introduced for the Model 1886 Winchester lever-action repeating rifle in 1894, and also chambered in the company's Model 1885 single-shot as well as the Marlin Model 1895, this rimmed necked cartridge was generally loaded with a 330-grain flat-nose lead bullet. Muzzle velocity of a typical pre-1917 Remington-UMC black powder load was 1457 ft/sec, giving an energy of 1556 ft-lb – adequate for most types of North American game. Winchester loadings were customarily lighter, giving about 1340 ft/sec (1316 ft-lb). Although .40-70 WCF was designed specifically to provide a heavier alternative to .38-70, yet could still be fed through the same action, it was never popular and had virtually disappeared by 1930.

.40-72 Winchester (.40-72-330, .40-72 WCF). Intended to accompany the Model 1895 lever-action rifle, this rimmed straight-case cartridge never found widespread favour owing to the existence of .405 Winchester (q.v.); it was loaded until 1936, but then disappeared. A typical pre-1910 Winchester factory load consisted of a 330-grain bullet offering a velocity of about 1359 ft/sec at the muzzle (1354 ft-lb), but Remington-UMC loads were usually slightly more powerful.

.40-75 Bullard. Identical to .40-60 Bullard in all respects except bullet and powder charge, this was introduced c.1887 for the short-lived Bullard single-shot and repeating rifles. The original 258-grain bullet developed a muzzle velocity of 1510 ft/sec, giving an energy of 1310 ft-lb – suitable for all but the largest North American game.

.40-82 Winchester (.40-82-260, .40-82 WCF). Originally chambered in the Model 1885 single-shot and Model 1886 lever-action repeating Winchester rifles, this rimmed-case cartridge, with an all-but-undetectable neck, was popular against virtually all North American game including elk and grizzly bear. The standard load originally comprised a 260-grain flat-nose lead bullet ahead of 82 grains of black powder, giving a muzzle velocity of about 1490 ft/sec and an energy of 1285 ft-lb.

.40-85 Ballard. This was simply a later form of the .40-90 Ballard cartridge described below, loaded with five grains less powder. It apparently dates from after 1881. Performance with the lower charge was not radically different from the original .40-90 version.

.40-90 Ballard. Apparently introduced in 1878, in 'Everlasting' (i.e. thick walled) form, for the Ballard No. $4\frac{1}{2}$ and No. 5 single-shot sporting rifles, this rimmed straight-case cartridge was originally loaded with a 370-grain paper-patched flat-nose lead bullet. Performance included a muzzle velocity of about 1425 ft/sec, which gave an energy of 1665 ft-lb.

.40-90 Bullard. Chambered in the short-lived Bullard single-shot and repeating rifles made c.1887–91, this rimmed necked cartridge had a notably stubby case. Loaded by both Remington and Winchester for some years, the Bullard rounds had disappeared by the First World War. The original 300-grain flat-nose lead bullet was fired at a muzzle velocity of about 1570 ft/sec, giving a respectable energy of 1650 ft-lb.

.40-90 Peabody 'What Cheer'. This cartridge is essentially a .40-70 'What Cheer' (q.v.) with a thin tubular sheet-metal extension allowing a greater powder charge. It was introduced about 1878 to accompany the No. 3 deluxe Peabody-Martini sporting rifle, enjoying a limited vogue before disappearing soon after the demise of the Providence Tool Company. The standard 500-grain bullet was fired at a muzzle velocity of about 1250 ft/sec, giving an energy of 1730 ft-lb.

.40-90 Sharps (.40-$2\frac{5}{8}$). Never especially popular, this rimmed necked-case centrefire Sharps rifle cartridge appeared c.1876. The case was 2.630in long, with a rim diameter of .600, a .500 shoulder and a neck measuring .435 immediately below the case mouth. The standard pre-1910 Winchester black powder load fired a 370-grain paper-patched lead bullet at about 1357 ft/sec at the muzzle (1513 ft-lb), but the original Sharps cartridges developed somewhat greater power. Many bullets were made to accept a .22 Short rimfire blank in their noses, in the forlorn hope that the blank would explode on contact with a target. .40-90 now chambers only in some modern Sharps-type rifles.

.40-90 Sharps (.40-3¼). Whether this pre-1885 rimmed straight-case round is genuinely a Sharps design has been contested, as Ballard and Remington rifles have also been chambered for it and it has been suggested that this is simply another 'Everlasting' Ballard. The case is 3.245in long, has a .535 rim and measures .420 immediately behind the case mouth. The round-nose paper-patched bullet weighed 370 grains and attained a muzzle velocity of about 1385 ft/sec (1576 ft-lb). Discontinued in the 1930s, it has recently been reintroduced for replica Sharps rifles.

.41 Long Rimfire. Developed from the .41 Short, this was introduced in c.1873 with the Colt New Line revolvers, though many other handguns and even a few single-shot rifles subsequently chambered it. A typical load of fifteen grains of black powder in the short, straight rimless case gave a muzzle velocity of about 700 ft/sec with a 163-grain bullet (180 ft-lb).

.41 Short Rimfire. Though a very weak load by modern self-defence standards, this small straight-case rimmed cartridge was once very popular. It was introduced during the Civil War with the National derringer, designed by Daniel Moore, but was subsequently chambered in a wide variety of handguns. Among the most popular was the Remington Double Derringer, produced until 1935, which persuaded many manufacturers to offer .41 Short ammunition until the Second World War. Muzzle velocity is typically only 425 ft/sec with a 130-grain bullet (52 ft-lb).

.44 Ballard Extra Long ('.44 Extra Long Centrefire'). Introduced for the Ballard No. 2 sporting rifle in the mid-1870s, this was rapidly eclipsed by the .44-40 WCF round and is now very rarely seen. Remington-UMC loaded the straight rimmed case with a 265-grain bullet and about 50 grains of black powder, which gave about 1320 ft/sec at the muzzle (1030 ft-lb).

.44 Evans ('.44 Evans Short'). A short straight-case rimmed round, this was introduced about 1875 for the original Evans repeating rifle. Ammunition was rather surprisingly being offered by Winchester into the 1920s; though Evans rifles were never made in large numbers, enough of them must have survived to make production of cartridges worthwhile. A typical loading of 28 grains of black powder gave the 215-grain bullet a muzzle velocity of 850 ft/sec (350 ft-lb).

.44 Evans New Model (.44 Evans Long, '44-40 Straight', '.44-40-300'). Introduced with the 'New Model' Evans repeating rifle in 1877, this was little more than an elongated version of the .44 Evans Short containing a 40–42 grain powder charge and a heavier bullet weighing 280–300 grains. This raised muzzle velocity to about 1200 ft/sec (895ft-lb with 280-grain bullet).

.44 Extra Long Rimfire. Developed specifically for single-shot Ballard rifles, probably in the early 1870s, this was so rapidly displaced by .44-40 WCF that it had almost disappeared within a decade. Too long to feed through some repeating-rifle actions, the .44 Extra Long was not accurate enough to succeed. A typical loading gave a muzzle velocity of 1250 ft/sec (763 ft-lb) with a 218-grain bullet and a 45-grain powder charge. The .44 Wesson Extra Long was identical, but loaded with a different bullet.

.44 Henry Rimfire ('.44 Henry Flat'). Developed for the Henry rifle, introduced in 1860, this saw extensive use not only in the Civil War but also in post-war days. Ammunition was still being offered in the 1930s, though .44 Henry was never powerful enough for use on anything other than small game and owed its reputation to association with one of the first successful repeating rifles. It was also chambered in Colt revolvers and a few other rifles, but was rapidly eclipsed by .44-40 WCF. A typical charge of 28 grains of black powder in the .815 straight-sided rimmed case gave the 200-grain bullet a muzzle velocity of 1125 ft/sec (568 ft-lb). An excessively rare centrefire version of the .44 Henry rimfire cartridge was made for a short time in the early 1870s.

.44 Long Centrefire. This was apparently another of the Ballard cartridges, introduced in the mid-1870s for single-shot sporting rifles and also used by gunmakers such as Frank Wesson. Rapidly eclipsed by .44-40 WCF, .44 Long soon disappeared. A typical load is believed to have comprised a 227-grain bullet propelled by 35 grains of black powder, giving a muzzle velocity of about 1150 ft/sec (667 ft-lb).

.44 Long Rimfire. This is said to have been introduced by Allen & Wheelock in the early 1860s, chambered in a rifle designed by Ethan Allen, but has also been used in a variety of Ballard, Remington and other single-shot rifles. Loaded with a 220-grain bullet and a charge of 28–30 grains of black powder, .44 Long rimfire was an acceptable small-game cartridge, but rapidly lost favour once the .44-40 centrefire pattern appeared, and had virtually disappeared by 1917. Performance was typically 825 ft/sec in a rifle (332 ft-lb).

.44 Short Rimfire. Usually associated with handguns such as the Hammond 'Bulldog' derringer or Forehand & Wadsworth revolvers, this also chambered in a few single-shot rifles. It is believed to have been introduced during the Civil War, perhaps in 1864, but was never especially popular and was rarely seen when the First World War began. A typical load – a 200-grain lead bullet and fifteen grains of black powder – gave a muzzle velocity of about 500 ft/sec (112 ft-lb) in a typical revolver.

.44 Wesson Extra Long – see .44 Ballard Extra Long.

.44-40 Winchester (.44-40 WCF). Introduced to accompany the Winchester Model 1873 lever-action rifle, and subsequently also chambered in the Colt Peacemaker revolver, this cartridge holds a special place in the history of the Wild West. Very weak by modern rifle standards, it is now restricted largely to handguns and Italian-made Winchester replicas. The rimmed centrefire case, 1.305in long, is perceptibly necked. The rim diameter is about .525, the body measurement being .455 and the neck .445. A typical Remington-UMC black-powder load of the pre-1917 era propelled its 200-grain round-nose bullet at a muzzle velocity of about 1270 ft/sec (716 ft-lb).

.44-60 Peabody 'Creedmoor' – see .44-60 Sharps, below.

.44-60 Sharps (.44-60 Sharps Necked, .44-60-$1\frac{7}{8}$). This was introduced in the mid-1870s for use in an assortment of Sharps and Remington rifles. Very similar to the Russian 4.2-line Berdan carbine cartridge, which may have served as a prototype, the .44-60 fired a 395-grain bullet at a muzzle velocity of about 1250 ft/sec (1375 ft-lb) and was useful on the target range and against medium-size game alike. The .44-60 Peabody 'Creedmoor' and .44-60 Winchester rounds were identical apart from designation.

.44-60 Winchester – see .44-60 Sharps, above.

.44-70 Maynard. Introduced in 1882 for the No. 11 and No. 14 single-shot rifles, this was Maynard's version of the .45-70 government cartridge. It was loaded with about 70 grains of black powder and a 430-grain 'hunting' bullet, which gave a velocity of about 1310 ft/sec (1640 ft-lb) at the muzzle.

.44-75 Ballard Everlasting. Made only in small quantities, this cartridge was introduced in 1876 with the Ballard No. 4, No. 5 and No. 6 rifles, but had apparently been discontinued by 1881. It shared the sturdy thick-wall straight case with the remainder of the 'Everlasting' series, but no details of its original performance have been found.

.44-77 Sharps (.44-77 Remington). Introduced in the mid-1870s for the Sharps rifle, this was also chambered in the Remington-Hepburn. Very popular on the target range, where its accuracy was greatly appreciated, the .44-77 also made an acceptable mid-range hunting round. The rimmed centrefire case, 2.25in long, had a pronounced neck. The rim diameter was .625, comparable measurements for shoulder and neck being .500 and .465 respectively. Muzzle velocity was typically 1460 ft/sec with a 365-grain bullet (1728 ft-lb).

.44-85 Wesson. Apparently loaded only by the US Cartridge Company in the early 1880s, in a $2\frac{7}{8}$-in straight rimmed case, this was destined for the Wesson 'Creedmoor' rifle. The load of 85 grains of black powder and a 390-grain bullet would probably have given a muzzle velocity of about 1400–1450 ft/sec.

.44-90 Remington. Loaded in a 2.6-inch straight rimmed case, this was a minor variant of the .44-100 Remington 'Creedmoor' (described below) with a smaller powder charge. It was apparently destined for a Remington-Hepburn Long Range Creedmoor rifle.

.44-90 Remington Special. Introduced for the rolling-block Remington Creedmoor target rifle in c.1873, this was similar to the .44-90 Sharps pattern except for its $2\frac{7}{16}$in necked case, which was shorter and slightly fatter than the Sharps equivalent. The standard Remington-UMC factory load consisted of a 550-grain bullet propelled by 90 grains of black powder to give a muzzle velocity of about 1250 ft/sec (1812 ft-lb).

.44-90 Sharps. Introduced in 1873, this was originally destined for the Sharps Creedmoor rifle. It is basically a longer version of the .44-77 pattern (q.v.), but had a short life: .44-calibre Sharps rifles were discontinued in 1878, though ammunition was still being made at the turn of the century. .44-90 cartridges now chamber only in some of the replica Sharps rifles. The rimmed centrefire case was $2\frac{5}{8}$in long and had a prominent neck. The rim diameter was about .625, figures for the shoulder registering .505 and .470. Typical performance: 1270 ft/sec at the muzzle, with a 520-grain bullet (1863 ft-lb).

.44-95 Peabody 'What Cheer'. Introduced in the 1875–7 period, this was chambered for the Peabody-Martini Long Range Creedmoor No. 3 target rifle but does not seem to have retained its popularity long after the failure of the Providence Tool Company in the 1880s. The shallowly necked rimmed brass case contained a 550-grain bullet, which achieved a velocity of about 1310 ft/sec (2100 ft-lb) at the muzzle.

.44-100 Ballard. One of the 'Everlasting' patterns introduced in 1876 with the No. 5 and No. 7A single-shot rifles, this was specifically intended for reloading and had a special thick-wall brass case. Discontinued in the early 1880s, the cartridge fired a 535-grain bullet at a muzzle velocity of about 1400 ft/sec (2328 ft-lb). It had a reputation for good accuracy and was powerful enough to down large game, but was superseded by the .45-100 pattern.

.44-100 Remington 'Creedmoor'. Chambered in the Remington-Hepburn No. 3 Long Range Creedmoor target rifle from 1880 onward, this had a 2.6-inch straight rimmed case containing a 550-grain bullet but was never particularly popular and had been discontinued by 1910. Muzzle velocity was about 1380 ft/sec, giving a muzzle energy of 2338 ft-lb.

.44-100 Wesson. Another of the US Cartridge Company loadings, dating from the early 1880s, this had an extraordinary $3\frac{3}{8}$in straight rimmed case, loaded with 100 grains of black powder and a 550-grain bullet. The .44-120 Wesson was outwardly identical, but contained a larger propellant charge. Both were intended for single-shot target rifles made by Franklin Wesson.

.45 Colt Revolver (.45 Long Colt). Introduced in 1872–3, this was the cartridge that tamed the Wild West along with the .44-40 Winchester. It is very accurate, a good man-stopper, and one of the most powerful revolver cartridges obtainable prior to the advent of .44 Magnum. The straight rimmed centrefire case was about 1.285in long, with rim and body diameters of .510 and .480. The standard 255-grain bullet attained a muzzle velocity of about 800 ft/sec (363 ft-lb).

.45-50 Peabody. Possibly adapted from the .45 carbine cartridge developed for the Turkish Peabody-Martini rifle, this necked rimmed-case sporting round seems to date from c.1875. It was never particularly popular and may have been abandoned in the 1880s. Performance included a muzzle velocity of about 1295 ft/sec with a 290-grain bullet (1085 ft-lb).

.45-60 Winchester. One of several cartridges chambered in the Model 1876 lever-action rifle, this straight-case rimmed cartridge appeared in 1879 and was still available in the 1930s. It also chambered in some lever-action Kennedy and slide-action Colt rifles. Firing a 300-grain bullet at a muzzle velocity of 1307 ft/sec, giving a muzzle energy of 1138 ft-lb (pre-1917 Remington-UMC black powder version), made it a better all-round cartridge than .44-40 WCF, though it was not suitable for use against large game.

.45-70 Government. Adopted by the US Army in 1873 for the 'Trapdoor Springfield' rifle, replacing the .50-70 pattern (q.v.), this cartridge had a straight centrefire case – 2.105in long – with a prominent .610-diameter rim. The body diameter tapered from about .505 at the base to .480 at the mouth. Many differing loads were offered, especially commercially, but a typical pre-1917 Remington-UMC black powder load with a military-style 405-grain bullet attained a muzzle velocity of 1361 ft/sec (1666 ft-lb). A 1910-vintage Winchester variant with a 500-grain bullet attained 1179 ft/sec (1544 ft-lb).

.45-75 Sharps. This was identical to the .45-70 government cartridge (q.v.), usually loaded to give similar performance but occasionally with a powder charge of 75 grains instead of 70 ('.45-75-2$\frac{1}{10}$').

.45-75 Winchester. The original chambering of the M1876 lever-action rifle, this had a rimmed brass case with a perceptible neck. Also used in a few Kennedy rifles, the pre-1910 Winchester black powder loading fired a 350-grain bullet at a muzzle velocity of 1343 ft/sec (1402 ft-lb); Remington-UMC versions were often more powerful, typically giving 1470 ft/sec and 1680 ft-lb. The .45-75 cartridge was a good performer on all but the largest North American game at short range. Winchester was still offering ammunition of this type as late as 1935.

.45-82 and .45-85 Winchester – see .45-90 Winchester.

.45-90 Winchester. A longer version of the .45-70 Government cartridge (q.v.), this was introduced for the Winchester Model 86 lever-action rifle – but also chambered in Winchester and possibly some Sharps single-shot rifles. The .45-90 and its near relations .45-82 and .45-85 (which differed solely in powder charges) were adequate on medium game out to 200 yards; however, like most cartridges of the type, they had a looping trajectory that complicated range-gauging. The straight 2.4in centrefire case had a .595-diameter rim, the neck measurement being about .475. A typical pre-1917 Remington-UMC black powder load gave a muzzle velocity of 1554 ft/sec with a 300-grain bullet (1609 ft-lb), though a Winchester equivalent gave merely 1480 ft/sec (1459 ft-lb).

.45-100 Ballard. Derived from the .44-100 pattern, this large straight-case rimmed cartridge was introduced for Ballard single-shot rifles sometime prior to 1882 (though details are still disputed). It was listed in Marlin catalogues as late as 1889, but production is assumed to have stopped by 1900. A typical example fired a 550-grain bullet at 1370 ft/sec (2300 ft-lb), but bullets as light as 285 grains could be supplied to create high-velocity reloads.

.45-100 Sharps. Dating from c.1878, one of a series of similar straight-case cartridges, .45-100 was chambered in Sharps and other single-shot rifles. The 2.6in straight centrefire case had a rim diameter of about .595, the comparable neck dimension being .490. Muzzle velocity was usually about 1360 ft/sec with a 550-grain bullet (2259 ft-lb). Theoretically long obsolete, it has recently been reintroduced for replica Sharps rifles.

.45-120 Sharps. One of the longest of all the cartridges in its class, this was introduced for the Sharps-Borchardt rifle in 1878–9; however, as the Sharps Rifle Company failed in 1881, few guns and only a handful of cartridges were ever made; .45-120 had been consigned to history until resurrected for replica Sharps rifles in recent years. Owing to the great weight of its bullet, the cartridge is entirely satisfactory for all but the largest soft-skinned North American game. However, low velocity gives a notably looping trajectory. The straight centrefire case, 3.25in long, has rim and neck diameters of .595 and .490; performance included a muzzle velocity of about 1520 ft/sec with a 500-grain bullet (2566 ft-lb).

.45-125 Winchester. Introduced in 1886 specifically for the single-shot Winchester rifle, this was still being made when the First World War began. The long rimmed case had a slight neck, positioned well back from the mouth. A standard Winchester black powder loading, with a 300-grain bullet, attained a muzzle velocity of 1638 ft/sec (1788 ft-lb).

.50-50 Maynard. A minor derivative of the .50 Government Carbine cartridge, this was introduced in 1882 for the Maynard single-shot sporting guns.

.50 Government Carbine. Basically a short-case version of the .50-70 rifle cartridge described below, this was normally loaded with a 400-grain bullet and 45–48 grains of black powder. This gave a muzzle velocity of about 1200 ft/sec (1285 ft-lb). Carbine cartridges would chamber in .50-70 rifles, but rifle cartridges were usually too long to seat satisfactorily in the chambers of carbines.

.50-70 Government Musket. This was the official US Army service cartridge in 1866–73, later developing into .45-70 (q.v.). The original cases had a slight-but-perceptible neck, but the current '.50-70' pattern offered is virtually straight-sided. The centrefire case was about 1.75in long. The diameters of rim, body and neck were .660, .565 and .535 respectively. The standard military 450-grain bullet customarily reached about 1260 ft/sec at the muzzle (1587 ft-lb), but a variety of loadings were offered commercially.

.50 Remington Rimfire. Introduced for the Navy-pattern Rolling Block pistol of 1865, this was rapidly superseded by a centrefire version with inside priming. It was comparatively hard-hitting for a rimfire, even though velocity was low. The standard 290-grain bullet, propelled by 23 grains of black powder, gave about 600 ft/sec at the muzzle (234 ft-lb).

.50-90 Sharps (also known as .50-100 or .50-110, depending on individual combinations of bullet weight and powder charge). Loaded in a $2\frac{1}{2}$-inch rimmed case, with a slight neck, the 'Big Fifty' apparently dates from 1874–5. Soon replaced by the .45-calibre Sharps cartridges, a typical .50-90 round fired a 475-grain bullet at 1350 ft/sec (a muzzle energy of 1920 ft-lb).

.50-95 Winchester. This stubby necked-case cartridge was developed for the Model 1876 Winchester rifle, appearing in 1879. Never popular, though chambered in a few rifles such as the slide-action Colt Lightning, it had been abandoned by the 1890s. Performance of Winchester black powder ammunition included a muzzle velocity of 1498 ft/sec with the standard 300-grain bullet (1495 ft-lb), but the Remington-UMC equivalent was more powerful.

.50-115 Bullard. Confined to the Bullard repeating and single-shot rifles of the 1880s, this was made only for a few years. The most distinctive feature is the semi-rim case, the first of its type to be made in the USA, with a slight tapering shoulder close to the neck. The standard factory load is believed to have fired a 300-grain bullet at a muzzle velocity of about 1540 ft/sec (1585 ft-lb).

.50-140 Sharps. This heavyweight straight-case round is believed to have been introduced about 1880, possibly for the Sharps-Borchardt rifle to special order. No other details are known. Performance is estimated to have included a muzzle velocity of about 1350 ft/sec with a 700-grain bullet, giving a muzzle energy of 2850 ft-lb – more than adequate for even the largest North American game.

.50-140 Winchester Express – see .50-140 Sharps.

.55-100 Maynard. The largest of the centrefire Maynard rounds, this appeared in 1882 for the No. 11 Improved Hunter's Rifle. Production of guns and ammunition was comparatively small. A bullet weighing 525 grains attained a muzzle velocity of about 1400 ft/sec, giving a muzzle energy of 2285 ft-lb.

.56-46 Spencer Rimfire. Among the smallest of the Spencer series, this was introduced after the Civil War for sporting purposes. Loaded in the USA until the First World War, the necked 1.035in brass case was too short to hold more than about 42–45 grains of powder; this gave a 330-grain bullet a muzzle velocity of about 1210 ft/sec and a muzzle energy of 1080 ft-lb, but this was much too low to compete with the large single-shot rifle patterns. The .56-46 Spencer had a neck diameter of about .478, the relevant figures for the case-base and rim being .558 and .641.

.56-50 Spencer Rimfire. Designed by Federal Army technicians in Springfield Armory during the Civil War, this was a .50-calibre derivative of the .56-56 Spencer pattern. Developed for the 1865-pattern Spencer carbine, fitted with the Stabler cut-off, the .56-50 round was used in a variety of other military carbines and was still being offered in Remington-UMC catalogues after the First World War. A typical load of 45 grains of black powder gave the 330-grain bullet a muzzle velocity of about 1230 ft/sec (1175 ft-lb). Loaded rounds were about 1.635in long, with a 1.155in case; the diameters of the neck, base and rim were .543, .556 and .639 respectively.

.56-52 Spencer Rimfire. This was a post-Civil War variant of the .56-50 cartridge (q.v.), introduced by the Spencer Repeating Rifle Company but made only for a few years. The original form had a slight neck – Spencer considered the straight-case government round to be crimped too severely – but this was often omitted by individual manufacturers; .56-52 and .56-50 rounds are interchangeable.

.56-56 Spencer Rimfire. The original form of the Spencer rimfire cartridge, first made in 1860, this had a stubby .875in case and a neck/base diameter of .560. It was also chambered in a few Ballard and Joslyn carbines, and was still being offered as late as 1920. Loaded with a 350-grain bullet, the .56-56 cartridge had a muzzle velocity of about 1200 ft/sec (1125 ft-lb).

APPENDIX 2

GUN PERFORMANCE

Myth and Reality

The performance of the rifles and handguns used in the American West has been the subject of heated debate. Some of the Westerners were excellent shots, no doubt, but the modern preoccupation with the mythology of the West – inspired by countless misleading films – has created a belief that not just the men but also their weapons were imbued with supernatural qualities.

This is most evident in stories about the Buntline Special or the Lone Ranger's silver bullets. However, modern-day obsession with reloading and attempts to 'duplicate original performance', using replica guns and ammunition made to modern engineering standards, have often obscured the real capabilities of the Guns of the West.

Reloading equipment used by individual buffalo hunters and plainsmen was often crude by current standards; powder measures were often inaccurate, and backwoods bullet-casting techniques fell well short of the standards of mass-manufacturers who 'swaged' the projectiles – compressed them in dies – before loading them into the cases. The swaging process expelled minute air bubbles from the cast metal. Out on the frontier, particularly in the early days, hand-cast bullets could still contain air bubbles and impurities. Consequently, they were often lighter and more susceptible to fluctuations in weight than machine-made types.

It is generally accepted that the manufacturing standards of pre-1900 black-powder propellant were better than today's, but reliable test data from the pre-1900 period is very difficult to obtain. How well the black-powder propellants of the day were kept in the climatic extremes of the West is another matter entirely. It seems likely that storage conditions were often far from ideal, and that performance suffered accordingly.

The major ammunition manufacturers certainly produced 'laboratory' muzzle-velocity and trajectory figures prior to 1900, but this was not true prior to the 1880s, when ballistic pendulums and chronographs (then confined largely to military test facilities) were in short supply. Consequently, velocity was often given in terms of comparative penetration into wood, thin iron plates or sand.

Variations in the grain and density of wood, particularly, makes it an unreliable arbiter; penetration figures, therefore, should always be regarded as the most general of guidelines. Figures taken from Remington-UMC and Winchester ammunition catalogues published prior to 1910 give the following:

TABLE ONE

Numbers of half-inch dry pine sheets pierced

			Sheets pierced	
Cartridge	*Velocity, ft/sec*	*Bullet weight*	*Lead bullet*	*Jacket type*
.25-20 Winchester	1547	86	9	10
.30-40 Krag	2005	220	15	58
.32-40 Winchester	1505	165	8.5	20
.38-40 Winchester	1325	180	7.5	14
.40-70 Sharps straight	1220	330	11.5	—
.40-90 Sharps straight	1357	270	16	22
.44-40 Winchester	1270	200	9	13
.45-70 Government	1361	405	15	19

Note: all were black powder loads excepting the smokeless .30-40 Krag and .32-40 Winchester types.

Disparity among testing systems makes it particularly difficult to calculate absolute figures, or to compare performance of individual cartridges made by a selection of manufacturers.

Flint- and cap-lock guns were commonly encountered in the early days of the West, left over from military surplus or the many types of Trade Guns and Pennsylvania Long Rifles supplied to the Indians or brought westward with the settlers. Some of the guns were smooth-bores, but rifles predominated in the smaller calibres owing to their proven accuracy. Rifling spun the projectile to provide gyro-stability in flight, which the balls fired from smooth-bores patently lacked. The rate of spin varied greatly, depending on the rifling pitch, but the standard three-groove .45-70 Trapdoor Springfield barrel spun the 500-grain projectile clockwise at more than 44,500rpm.

Methods had to be found to seal the escape of propellant gas around the bullet, which handicapped most smooth-bores, but this was customarily solved by wrapping the projectile in a greased patch to fill the space between the bullet and the bore walls. However, loading often became difficult and, after many unsuccessful experiments, a better answer was found in the self-expanding ball. This utilised the force of the propellant gas to force the hollowed bullet-base outward into the rifling.

Perfected by a Frenchman, Claude-Étienne Minié, the self-expanding ball was a revelation. The effective range of rifled longarms was at least tripled virtually overnight, and accuracy at long range improved out of all recognition. Paradoxically, the muzzle velocity of the new rifle-muskets was substantially less than that of many smooth-bore guns. This was partly due to the weight of the elongated bullet – no longer just a simple ball – but largely to the highly effective gas seal, which, by forcing the bullet to engrave in the rifling, also substantially increased friction between the bullet and the bore walls.

A .45-calibre Long Rifle tested in 1935 by the University of California gave a muzzle velocity of about 2100 ft/sec, but this declined rapidly until the bullet was travelling at only 550 ft/sec by the time the 500-yard mark had been passed. Tests undertaken in Washington Arsenal in the 1840s, using a ballistic pendulum, had credited the .69-calibre smooth-bore flintlock and cap-lock muskets with velocities of 1500 ft/sec at the muzzle and 385 ft/sec at 500 yards. Experiments undertaken in the late 1850s with a .58-calibre M1855 rifle-musket, however, returned about 1000 ft/sec at the muzzle and 670 ft/sec at 500 yards. This showed clearly how well the self-sealing projectile, by engaging the rifling efficiently, improved velocity-retention at long range.

The muzzleloaders were soon replaced by the breechloading guns, many differing types being tried during the Civil War. The earliest designs were often handicapped by ammunition: the combustible paper or linen patterns used in the Sharps, for example, or the externally-ignited tin-foil or copper cartridges chambered by the Maynard and Burnside carbines. The introduction of rimfire ammunition shortly before the Civil War began, by Smith & Wesson and the New Haven Arms Company, then changed all the rules.

Using entirely self-contained ammunition, even though it could not be reloaded, gave an undreamed consistency – not only on a shot-to-shot basis, but also from month to month and even from year to year.

The biggest weakness of the first rimfire cartridges lay in their comparatively small dimensions, which limited the amount of propellant which could be contained in the cases. The small .22 and .32 Smith & Wesson revolver patterns were widely regarded as toys, even though they could inflict a nasty wound at short ranges; far more effective were the .44 Henry and .56 Spencer rimfires chambered in rifles or carbines.

Yet the power of even the Spencer rounds compared badly with expanding-bullet rifle-muskets – especially at long range – and only with the introduction of centrefire priming was some kind of parity restored. The widespread introduction of cartridge cases fabricated from sheets of brass, or drawn in a single piece, was a great catalyst. Brass cases gave good sealing properties ('obturation'), and were sufficiently elastic to spring back to their original shape when chamber pressure dropped. This facilitated extraction in a way copper cases could rarely match.

By the 1870s, therefore, the weak rimfire rounds of the 1860s had been superseded by centrefire patterns offering greater power than the rifle-musket ammunition. This was largely due to the greatly increased strength of centrefire cartridge cases.

As far as the Wild West is concerned, the progress from muzzleloading to the perfected small-calibre rounds of the twentieth century can be seen in a few typical rifle rounds: the .50-70 Government pattern of 1868, the .44-40 centrefire round fired in the first 1873-type Winchesters, the .45-70 Government cartridge of 1873, typical small- and large-case Sharps rounds of the mid-1870s, and the .30-40 Krag of 1892. Except for a few experimental examples, Government-made Krag cartridges always contained a charge of smokeless powder; the earliest commercial equivalents, however, relied on black powder and offered substantially less power.

The accompanying charts are based on material very kindly supplied by Lyman Products, calculated by computer for modern projectiles, and are based on hypothetical muzzle velocities. However, these have been selected to compare as closely as possible with original loadings. For example, according to pre-1910 Remington-UMC and Winchester data, a typical .45-70-405 load was fired at 1361 ft/sec; the bullet of the .40-70 Sharps left the muzzle at about 1220 ft/sec (330-grain bullet); and the appropriate figure for the commercial .30-40-220 Krag cartridge (smokeless propellant) was 2005 ft/sec.

The efficiency of black powder cartridges was limited by the burning characteristics of the propellant, which restricted muzzle velocity to 1850 ft/sec, and by the inability of a plain lead bullet to withstand excessive friction with the bore walls without 'stripping' (failing to engrave in the rifling).

Black-powder cartridges customarily generated comparatively low velocities of 1250–1450 ft/sec, and so a heavy large-calibre bullet was needed to give the required striking power and to 'set up' properly in the rifling.

The ability of a bullet to retain velocity at long range depends greatly on its ability to cut through the air with the least possible resistance. Blunt bullets pierce air far poorer than ogival or pointed versions; and bullets with large cross-sectional areas encounter more resistance than small-diameter ones by presenting a larger surface to the air flow. The rate at which a bullet loses velocity can be calculated if the *ballistic coefficient* (usually known as 'C') is known. This accounts for the weight of the projectile in relation to its cross-sectional area, and also for the shape of the bullet-nose.

The performance details given in the accompanying tables shows the dramatic changes made, in the case of the .45-70 Government cartridge, by substituting a flatnose bullet (case ii) for a conventional roundnose pattern (i); the flat nose encounters such air resistance that velocity declines rapidly and

TABLE TWO

Velocity (ft/sec)

Cartridge	*Bullet ('C')*	*Muzzle*	*100yd*	*250yd*	*500yd*
.50-70 Government	422gn (.250)	1300	1124	964	813
.45-70 Government (i)	426gn (.359)	1400	1256	1094	942
.45-70 Government (ii)	405gn (.141)	1500	1133	886	664
.44-40 Winchester	203gn (.188)	1300	1109	951	805
.40-70 Sharps straight	293gn (.201)	1400	1196	1009	848
.44-90 Sharps	490gn (.384)	1500	1351	1169	989
.30-40 Krag	200gn (.377)	2000	1803	1523	1183

TABLE THREE

Energy (ft-lb)

Cartridge	*Muzzle*	*100yd*	*250yd*	*500yd*
.50-70 Government	1583	1184	871	619
.45-70 Government (i)	1854	1492	1133	839
.45-70 Government (ii)	2023	1154	706	397
.44-40 Winchester	762	555	407	292
.40-70 Sharps straight	1275	930	663	468
.44-90 Sharps	2448	1985	1487	1065
.30-40 Krag	1776	1444	1030	621

Note: black powder cartridge efficiency was limited by the burning characteristics of the propellant, which cut muzzle velocity to 1850ft/sec, and 'stripping' (failure to engage in the rifling).

long-range drift increases spectacularly. The same effect could be achieved firing a bullet which had been accidentally deformed in a pouch or bandolier.

Figures published by the British Army in the 1880s suggested that the .45-70-500 'Trapdoor Springfield' cartridge had a muzzle velocity of 1301 ft/sec; 875 ft/sec at 500 yards; 676 ft/sec at 1000 yards; 523 ft/sec at 1500 yards; and 404 ft/sec at 2000 yards. Extreme range was about 2750 yards.

The average Wild West cartridge was loaded with a short blunt-nosed lead bullet, which was far from ideal ballistically. Projected at velocities only just

TABLE FOUR

Mid-range trajectory (in)

Cartridge	*100yd*	*250yd*	*500yd*
.50-70 Government	3.0	22.8	115.7
.45-70 Government (i)	2.5	18.2	90.0
.45-70 Government (ii)	2.6	23.4	138.4
.44-40 Winchester	3.1	23.4	125.7
.40-70 Sharps straight	2.6	20.3	105.3
.44-90 Sharps	2.1	15.7	79.3
.30-40 Krag	1.2	8.9	47.9

Note: owing to the effects of air resistance, the highest point of the trajectory is actually nearer to the target than the firer, but the mid-point provides an acceptable means of comparison which is also easier to calculate.

above the speed of sound, the bullets lost momentum rapidly and could only describe a high looping trajectory which made accurate range-gauging essential if hits were to be obtained.

The *mid-range trajectory* figures show the height of the bullet above the line of sight. When a .50-70 rifle was being fired to strike a target placed at 500 yards, with the sights set accordingly, the bullet was 115.7in – nearly ten feet! – above the line of sight when it was half-way to the target. The handbook published by the US Navy in 1870, for the .50-70 Remington rifle, suggested that the mid-point trajectory of the projectile was nearly 87 feet above the sight-line when the sights were set for 1050 yards.

Flat trajectories minimise the effects of range-gauging errors, which may be bad enough to result in the bullet passing over the target. However, not until small calibres and ultra-high velocities were combined was any real progress made. Table Four compares the trajectories of the cartridges under detailed review, and it will be noted how the .30 Krag – with the smallest bullet diameter and the highest velocity – performs the best. The Krag was introduced towards the end of the period under review, however, and had comparatively little effect on the distribution of traditional large-calibre black powder designs prior to 1900.

Another important factor was *time of flight*. The slow-moving bullets took a surprisingly long time to cover the distance to targets which stood hundreds of yards away. This presented few problems if the target was inanimate, but even a ponderous-looking buffalo could move a surprising distance in a couple of seconds. So, too, could an Indian on a swift-moving pony.

TABLE FIVE

Flight time of bullet (sec)

Cartridge	*100yd*	*250yd*	*500yd*
.50-70 Government	0.25	0.68	1.54
.45-70 Government (i)	0.23	0.61	1.36
.45-70 Government (ii)	0.23	0.69	1.67
.44-40 Winchester	0.25	0.69	1.61
.40-70 Sharps straight	0.23	0.65	1.46
.44-90 Sharps	0.21	0.57	1.27
.30-40 Krag	0.16	0.43	0.99

Reaching long ranges was surprisingly slow. The 500-grain bullet loaded in the standard .45-70 Government round took 1.46 seconds to reach 500 yards and 3.22 seconds to reach 1000 yards; the figures for 1500 and 2000 yards were 5.95 and 9.23 seconds respectively. For the .577 British Snider, which had a velocity of only 1240 ft/sec, the time taken to reach 2000 yards was a staggering 14.7 seconds. Velocity had dropped to merely 196 ft/sec.

A man moving at walking pace could easily have covered twelve yards in a ten-second period; a running man could have covered sixty yards; and a man on horseback could have travelled 150 yards at a gallop.

And what if there was a *crosswind* ? This adds an additional 'drift' element to a natural tendency of a rapidly rotating bullet to drift slightly towards the

TABLE SIX

Approximate drift in 5mph crosswind (in)

Cartridge	*100yd*	*250yd*	*500yd*
.50-70 Government	1.5	9	34
.45-70 Government (i)	1	7	25
.45-70 Government (ii)	3	17	59
.44-40 Winchester	2	10	36
.40-70 Sharps straight	1.5	10	34
.44-90 Sharps	1	6	24
.30-40 Krag	0.75	5	21

TABLE SEVEN

Approximate drift in 20mph crosswind (in)			
Cartridge	*100yd*	*250yd*	*500yd*
.50-70 Government	6	38	135
.45-70 Government (I)	4	27	100
.45-70 Government (ii)	11	66	236
.44-40 Winchester	7	41	147
.40-70 Sharps straight	6	39	138
.44-90 Sharps	4	25	96
.30-40 Krag	3	19	86

direction of its spin. The effects of winds which howled across the Great Plains were not to be taken lightly; Chicago was not christened 'Windy City' for nothing.

The foregoing information applies mainly to rifles, the most powerful and most efficient of the firearms available in the Wild West. They were significantly magnified in the case of handguns which, essentially short-range weapons, lacked the reserves of power to ensure a kill at ranges greater than a hundred yards. Indeed, the crudity of their sights and the uncertain action of some trigger systems often made a hit doubtful at even a quarter of that distance.

Details in Appendix One, which lists the best-known cartridges used in the West, emphasise the weakness of the smallest rim- and centrefire handgun rounds.

Accuracy

Modern tendencies to exaggerate the prowess of the gunfighters, backed by a dearth of nineteenth-century information, make it difficult to analyse the potential of the pre-1900 gun/cartridge combinations. This is partly because the military authorities – who often pursued trials with great attention to detail – all too often analysed results using methods which now seem to be inappropriate.

A favourite was 'Figure of Merit', which was little more than the mean radius of the best 50 per cent of the shots. Results of this type are virtually impossible to compare with today's method, which is usually simply a circle containing *all* the shots fired in a particular trial. A case can be made for the use of 'mean grouping potential', deliberately disallowing a tiny percentage of shots by considering them as untypical or freakish, but every attempt of this type seems to be based on its own criteria.

The handbook for the 1870-pattern US Navy .50-70 Remington rifle reveals that the 'Absolute Deviations' at 300 and 1050 yards were 7.04in and 32.7in respectively, which suggests 'all shot' group diameters of about 32in and 148in; these give a clue to the performance of a first-generation military breechloading rifle. Comparable figures for the .30-06 cartridge chambered in the M1903 Springfield rifle – 3.4in at 300 yards and 24.8in at 1500 yards ('all shot' group diameters of about 15in and 112in) – show how rapidly performance improved in only forty years.

Results surviving from the second match contested by the USA and Ireland, on the range at Dollymount, near Dublin, in June 1875, bear mute testimony to the accuracy of the long-range target rifles of the day. The US marksmen all used breechloading rifles, whereas the Irishmen used muzzleloaders. The bull's eyes of the National Rifle Association targets measured 8 × 8in for distances up to 300 yards; 24 × 24in for 300–600 yards; and 36 × 36in for distances above 600 yards. The longest range customarily contested in the 1870s was 1000 yards.

Irishman John Pollock scored 59 × 60 at 800 yards in the 1875 match; Colonel John 'Old Reliable' Bodine (USA) achieved a score of 59 × 60 at 900 yards; and James Wilson (Ireland) scored a remarkable 55 × 60 at 1000 yards.

Cleaning the bore before each individual shot was advantageous, as powder residue left in the bore ruined the accuracy of even the finest target rifle after only a handful of shots had been fired. Proper lubrication of the bullet was also essential if fouling was to be kept to a minimum.

The distances claimed for 'kills' in the West present problems of their own. Men swore to have downed buffalo at distances 'attested as 1257 yards' or 'measured at 1568 yards', but the basis for these is rarely clear. The biggest doubt concerns the methods of measurement. Few cowboys carried a theodolite or a measuring chain in their saddlebags, so three possibilities are left.

Countless tests have shown that 'guessed range' is notoriously unreliable – unless local knowledge is so good that (for example) sight settings had already been matched with landmarks. Many buffalo hunters were excellent shots and knew their hunting areas intimately, so doubts raised about performance should first be tested against these proven skills.

Concern can also be raised about 'measurement after the fact', relying solely on recollections of how men were standing or where an animal had fallen. A third possibility is 'paced range'. Practical tests have shown that while many men will count a single pace as a yard, the *actual* measurement (depending on the height of the pacer) is likely to be 27–30in. It is no coincidence that military-rifle sights graduated in paces use distances of this magnitude: e.g. the

Russian *arshin* was 27.99in, and the Austro-Hungarian *schritt* was 28.53in. If a mistake of this type was made with paced measurements, therefore, a claimed kill at 1500 yards would be brought in to 1125–1250 yards and something which had once seemed improbable becomes significantly more plausible.

Long-range target rifles such as the Remington Creedmoor and its rivals demonstrated that occasional kills were possible at extreme distances, assuming that all the favourable factors coincided. They also show, convincingly, that kills of this type could *not* be repeated regularly.

Some evidence of the performance of a military-style rifle survives in the form of a photograph of Denver gunsmith John Lower posing with a target shot with a .45-70 Sharps-Borchardt in January 1882. Fifty shots fired off-hand (i.e. without support) from 200 yards grouped within 23in, with ten shots – and an eleventh 'cutting' – in the 6-inch bull's eye.

As for handguns, information is surprisingly scarce. The guns themselves were almost always capable of putting three consecutive shots on a playing card at 25 feet (the distance across the average saloon!) if the firer took deliberate aim and assuming the sights were fine enough to help. Missing in life-or-death situations, therefore, was usually due to factors other than inherent accuracy: movement, misfiring, fear, or clouds of propellant smoke.

Cards from a faro deck were pierced by John Wesley Hardin, apparently using a .38-calibre Colt Lightning double-action revolver, during the opening ceremonies of the Wigwam Saloon in El Paso on 4 July 1895. The double-action guns had considerable advantages for the practised 'fast-shooter', though the accuracy of a single-action Peacemaker often held an edge in deliberate fire. Hardin undoubtedly fired at comparatively short ranges, but the best of the groups are impressive – often with five shots strung together in a ragged hole. What set Hardin above many of his contemporaries was his cold-blooded approach to gunfighting, which, in the final analysis, was often the difference between life and death.

In 1876, the US Army undertook long-range tests with the .45 Single Action Army Colt revolver, which was then the regulation handgun. The mean absolute deviation at 50 yards (probably fired from a rest) was 3.11in. Competing Smith & Wesson No. 3 American and 1875-type Remingtons returned 4.33in and 4.1in respectively, which gives a good guide to the performance to be expected from guns of this class. Converted to group diameters, these suggest that the shots could be placed within circles measuring 14.1in for the Colt, 18.5in for the Remington and 19.6in for the Smith & Wesson.

Trials undertaken with a .45 Peacemaker in 1898, possibly in comparison with the .38-calibre M1892 revolver, returned absolute deviations of 5.3in at 50 yards, 8.3in at 100 yards and 24.9in at 250 yards. These equate to group diameters of about 24in, 38in and 113in respectively.

Pre-1910 Winchester catalogues listed assessments by the famous marksman A. C. Gould, generalising the accuracy of Winchester cartridges:

TABLE EIGHT

Accuracy at 200 yards
.30 Krag: 8-inch circle
.32-20 Winchester: 6-inch circle
.38-40 Winchester: 6-inch circle
.40-60 Winchester: 8-inch circle
.40-82 Winchester: 8-inch circle
.40-110 Winchester Express: 12-inch circle
.44-40 Winchester: 8-inch circle
.45-60 Winchester: 8-inch circle
.45-70-405 Government: 8-inch circle
.45-90 Winchester: 8-inch circle
.45-125 Winchester: 12-inch circle
.50-110 Winchester Express: 20-inch circle

Although Gould added that his assessments were for the fall of 'nearly all the shots' – and it is by no means clear what he was excluding (one shot in ten, perhaps?) – at least they give a contemporary view of what could be achieved.

Writing in *Modern American Pistols and Revolvers* (1894), Gould also noted that he had seen 'some splendid shots among them [cowboys shooting revolvers], but they never did any good shooting by twirling the revolver around, snapping it in a careless manner, shooting it upside-down, or any other of the absurd ways which stage shots sometimes attempt.'

The consensus among observers was that though buffalo hunters generally and some of the gunslingers individually were extremely good shots, marksmanship among cowboys, soldiers and Indians were often extremely poor. This was customarily attributed to lack of practice – especially in the US Army, where ammunition was often scarce – and to the styles of shooting practised by the Indians, who were usually much better versed in the bow and arrow.

One of Custer's first steps when he took command of the 7th Cavalry was to ensure that his men attended regular target practice, and to make sure that due praise was given to those who passed out as marksmen. Although Little Big Horn overshadowed the value of this training, Custer's men undoubtedly sold their lives dearly as a result of familiarity with their weapons.

BIBLIOGRAPHY

The list which follows consists entirely of books, although details of selected relevant articles will occasionally be found in the text.

As *The Guns that Won the West* concentrates more on the history of guns and gunmaking in the USA, only an occasional book devoted to political, social or economic history appears here. However, a particularly good source of additional information is *The Oxford Book of The American West* (Clyde Milner II, Carol O'Connor and Martha Sandweiss, eds.). Although a conventional bibliography is absent and failure to identify publishers provides an unnecessary irritation, the bibliographical notes to each chapter are helpful.

Ball, Robert W. D., *Remington Firearms: The Golden Age of Collecting*. Krause Publications, Iola, Wisconsin, 1995.

Barnes, Frank C., *Cartridges of the World* ('The Book for Every Shooter, Collector and Handloader'). DBI Books, Inc., Northbrook, Illinois, eighth edition, 1996.

Batty, Peter and Parish, Peter, *The Divided Union* ('The Story of the American Civil War, 1861–65'). The Rainbird Publishing Group, London, 1987.

Beebe, Lucius, *High Iron. A Book of Trains*. D. Appleton–Century Company, Inc., New York, 1938.

Bowman, Hank Wieand, *Antique Guns*. Fawcett Publications, Greenwich, Connecticut, 1963.

—*Antique Guns from the Stagecoach Collection.* Fawcett Publications, Greenwich, Connecticut, 1964.

—*Famous Guns from the Smithsonian Collection.* Fawcett Publications, Greenwich, Connecticut, 1966.

—*Famous Guns from the Winchester Collection*. Fawcett Publications, Greenwich, Connecticut, 1958.

Brophy, William S. (Lieutenant Colonel), *Krag Rifles*. The Gun Room Press, Highland Park, New Jersey, 1980.

—*Marlin Firearms* ('A History of the Guns and the Company that Made Them'). Stackpole Books, Harrisburg, Pennsylvania, 1989.

Brown, Dee, *Bury My Heart at Wounded Knee*. Henry Holt, New York, 1988.

—*Hear That Lonesome Whistle Blow!* Touchstone, 1994.

Browning, John and Curt Gentry, *John M. Browning, American Gunmaker.* Doubleday & Company, New York, 1964.

Butler, David F., *United States Firearms; The First Century, 1776–1875.* Winchester Press, New York, 1971.

—*Winchester 73 & 76* ('The First Repeating Centerfire Rifles'). Winchester Press, New York, 1970.

Campbell, John, *The Winchester Single-Shot* ('A History and Analysis'). Andrew Mowbray, Inc., Lincoln, Rhode Island, 1995.

Cochran, Keith, *Colt Peacemaker Encyclopedia.* Published privately, Rapid City, South Dakota, 1986. A supplement was published in 1989.

Crossman, Edward C. and Dunlap, Roy F., *The Book of the Springfield.* Wolfe Publishing Company, Prescott, Arizona, 1990.

De Haas, Frank, *Single Shot Rifles and Actions.* DBI Books, Inc., Northbrook, Illinois, revised edition, 1990.

Du Mont, John S., *Custer Battle Guns.* Phoenix Publishing, Canaan, New Hampshire, 1988.

Edwards, William B., *Civil War Guns.* Stackpole Company, Harrisburg, Pennsylvania, 1962.

Fuller, Claud E., *The Breech-Loader in the Service, 1816–1917* ('A History of All Standard and Experimental US Breech-Loading and Magazine Shoulder Arms'). N. Flayderman & Company, New Milford, Connecticut, 1965.

Garaviglia, Louis and Worman, Charles, *Firearms of the American West, 1866–1894.* University of New Mexico Press, Albuquerque, New Mexico, 1985.

Gardner, Robert E. (Colonel), *Small Arms Makers* ('A directory of fabricators of firearms, edged weapons, crossbows and polearms'). Crown Publishers, Inc., New York, 1958.

Gluckman, Arcadi (Colonel), *United States Martial Pistols & Revolvers.* Stackpole Company, Harrisburg, Pennsylvania, 1956.

—U.S. Muskets, *Rifles and Carbines.* Stackpole Company, Harrisburg, Pennsylvania, 1965.

Grant, Ellsworth S., *The Colt Armory* ('A History of Colt's Manufacturing Company, Inc.'). Mowbray Publishing, Lincoln, Rhode Island, 1995.

Grant, James J., *Boys' Single Shot Rifles.* William Morrow & Co., New York, 1967.

—*More Single Shot Rifles.* Gun Room Press, Highland Park, New Jersey, 1984.

—*Single Shot Rifles.* Gun Room Press, Highland Park, New Jersey, 1982.

—*Single Shot Rifles Finale.* Wolfe Publishing Company, Prescott, Arizona, 1992.

—*Still More Single Shot Rifles.* Pioneer Press, Union City, Tennessee, 1979.

Greener, W. W., *The Gun and Its Development.* Cassell & Co. Ltd, London, ninth edition, 1910. Reprinted by Arms & Armour Press, London, 1973.

—*Modern Breech Loaders*. Cassell, Petter & Galpin, London, 1871. Reprinted by Greenhill Books, London, 1985.

Hackley, Frank W., Woodin, William H. and Scranton, Edward L., *History of Modern US Military Small Arms Ammunition*. Macmillan Company, New York, volume 1 (1880–1939), 1976. Gun Room Press, Aledo, Illinois, volume 2 (1940–5), 1978.

Hatch, Alden, *Remington Arms in American History*. Remington Arms Company, Inc., Ilion, New York, revised edition, 1972.

Hatcher, Julian S. (Major General), *Hatcher's Notebook* ('A Standard Reference Book for Shooters, Gunsmiths, Balisticians, Historians, Hunters and Collectors'). Stackpole Company, Harrisburg, Pennsylvania, third edition, 1962.

Haven, Charles T. and Belden, Frank A., *A History of the Colt Revolver*. William Morrow & Company, New York, 1940.

Hicks, James E. (Major), *US Military Firearms, 1776–1956*. James E. Hicks & Son, La Vineta, California, 1962.

Hogg, Ian V., *The Cartridge Guide* ('The Small Arms Ammunition Identification Manual'). Arms & Armour Press, London, 1982.

Hogg, Ian V. and Weeks, John S., *Pistols of the World* ('A comprehensive ... encyclopedia of the world's pistols and revolvers from 1870 until the present day'). Arms & Armour Press, London, and DBI Books, Inc., Northbrook, Illinois, 1978.

Houze, Herbert G., *Winchester Repeating Arms Company* ('Its History and Development from 1865 to 1981'). Krause Publications, Iola, Wisconsin, 1996.

Hull, Edward A., *The Burnside Breech Loading Carbines* (Man at Arms Monograph No. 1). Andrew Mowbray, Inc., Lincoln, Rhode Island, 1986.

Jamieson, G. Scott, *Bullard Arms*. Boston Mills Press, Boston Mills, Ontario, Canada, 1989.

Jinks, Roy G., *History of Smith & Wesson*. Beinfeld Publishing Company, North Hollywood, California, 1977.

Kirkland, K. D., *America's Premier Gunmakers*. Bison Books, London, 1990.

Kopec, John A., Graham, Ron and Moore, Kenneth C., *A Study of the Colt Single Action Army Revolver*. Published privately, La Puente, California, 1976.

Lake, Stuart N., *Wyatt Earp, Frontier Marshal*. Boston, Massachusetts, 1931.

Layman, George J., *A Guide to the Maynard Breech-Loader*. Nashoba Publications, Inc., Ayer, Massachusetts, 1993.

Lewis, Berkeley R. (Colonel), *Small Arms and Ammunition in the United States Service, 1776–1865*. Smithsonian Institution, Washington DC, 1968.

Lord, Francis A., *Civil War Collector's Encyclopedia*. Volume 1 published by Stackpole Company, Harrisburg, Pennsylvania, 1963; volume 2 ('Military Matériel, Both American and Foreign, Used by the Union and Confederacy') by Lord Americana & Research, West Columbia, South Carolina, 1975.

McAulay, John D., *Carbines of the Civil War.* Pioneer Press, Union City, Tennessee, 1981.

—*Civil War Breech Loading Rifles* ('A survey of the innovative infantry arms of the American Civil War'). Andrew Mowbray, Inc., Lincoln, Rhode Island, 1987.

—*Civil War Carbines* (Volume 2: The Early Years). Andrew Mowbray, Inc., Lincoln, Rhode Island, 1991.

Macdonald, John, *Great Battles of the American Civil War.* Michael Joseph, London, 1988.

Madis, George, *The Winchester Book.* Taylor Publishing Company, Dallas, Texas, 1971.

Mallory, Franklin B. and Olson, Ludwig, *The Krag Rifle Story.* Springfield Research Service, Silver Spring, Maryland, 1979.

Marcot, Roy, *Spencer Firearms.* R&R Books, Livonia, New York, 1995.

Markham, George (John Walter), *Guns of the Wild West* ('Firearms of the American Frontier, 1849–1917'). Arms & Armour Press, London, 1991.

Mathews, J. Howard, *Firearms Identification.* Charles C. Thomas, Springfield, Illinois, three volumes, 1962–73.

Miller, W. T. (ed.), *Photographic History of the Civil War.* New York, twelve volumes 1911.

Milner II, Clyde A., O'Connor, Carol A. and Sandweiss, Martha A. (eds.), *The Oxford History of the American West*. Oxford University Press, Oxford and New York, 1994.

Myszkowski, Eugene, *The Remington-Lee Rifle.* Excalibur Publications, Latham, New York, 1994.

Neal, Robert J., *Smith & Wesson 1857–1945.* A. S. Barnes & Co., Inc., South Brunswick, New Jersey, 1966.

Parsons, John E., *Henry Deringer's Pocket Pistols.* William Morrow, New York, 1952.

—*Smith & Wesson Revolvers: The Pioneer Single Action Models.* William Morrow, New York, 1957.

—*The First Winchester.* Winchester Press, New York, 1969.

—*The Peacemaker and its Rivals.* William Morrow, New York, 1950.

Pitman, John (Brigadier General): *Breech-Loading Carbines of the United States Civil War Period.* Armory Publications, Tacoma, Washington, 1987.

Poyer, Joe and Riesch, Craig, *The 45-70 Springfield.* North Cape Publications, Tustin, California, 1991.

Ramage, C. Kenneth (ed.), *Lyman Centennial Journal, 1878–1978.* Lyman Publications, Middlefield, Connecticut, 1978.

Renneberg, Robert C., *The Winchester Model 94. The First 100 Years.* Krause Publications, Iola, Wisconsin, 1991.

Roberts, Ned H. (Major) and Waters, Kenneth L., *The Breech-Loading Single-Shot Rifle.* Wolfe Publishing Company, Prescott, Arizona, 1995.

Rosa, Joseph G., *Colonel Colt, London.* Arms & Armour Press, London, 1976.

—*Guns of the American West (1776–1900).* Arms & Armour Press, London, 1985.

—*The Gunfighter: Man or Myth?* University of Oklahoma Press, Norman, Oklahoma, 1969.

—*They Called Him Wild Bill: the Life and Adventures of James Butler Hickok.* University of Oklahoma Press, Norman, Oklahoma, 1974.

— *Wild Bill Hickok: The Man and His Myth.* University Press of Kansas, Lawrence, Kansas, 1996.

Schumacher P. L., *Colt's Variations of the Old Model Pocket Pistol, 1849–72.* Fadco Publishing Company, Beverly Hills, California, 1957.

Schwing, Ned, *Winchester Slide-Action Rifles* ('Volume I: Model 1890 and Model 1906'). Krause Publications, Iola, Wisconsin, 1992.

Schwing, Ned and Houze, Herbert, *Standard Catalog of Firearms.* Krause Publications, Iola, Wisconsin, sixth edition, 1996.

Sell, De Witt E., *Handguns Americana.* Borden Publishing Company, Alhambra, California, 1972.

Sellers, Frank, *Sharps Firearms.* F. W. Sellers, Denver, Colorado, 1982.

Sellers, Frank and Smith, Samuel E., *American Percussion Revolvers.* Museum Restoration Service, Ottawa, Ontario, Canada, 1971.

Serven, James E., *Colt Firearms from 1836.* The Foundation Press, La Habra, California, seventh printing, 1972.

Smith, Walter H. B., *The Book of Rifles.* Stackpole Company, Harrisburg, Pennsylvania, seventh edition, 1968.

Steffen, Randy, *The Horse Soldier, 1776–1943.* University of Oklahoma Press, Norman, Oklahoma, four volumes, 1977.

Sutherland, Robert Q. and Wilson, R. Larry, *The Book of Colt Firearms.* R. Q. Sutherland, Kansas City, Missouri, 1971.

Suydam, Charles H., *The American Cartridge.* Borden Publishing Company, Alhambra, California, 1986.

Swayze, Nathan L., *51 Colt Navies.* Published privately, Yazoo City, Missouri, 1967.

Taylerson, Anthony W. F., *Revolving Arms* (a volume in the 'Arms and Armour Series'). Herbert Jenkins Ltd, London, 1967.

—*The Revolver, 1865–1888.* Herbert Jenkins Ltd, London, 1966.

—*The Revolver, 1889–1914.* Barrie & Jenkins Ltd, London, 1970.

Taylerson, Anthony W. F., Andrews, R. A. and Frith, J., *The Revolver, 1818–65.* Herbert Jenkins Ltd, London, 1968.

Wahl, Paul, *Gun Trader's Guide.* Stoeger Publishing Company, South Hackensack, New Jersey, eighteenth edition (revised John E. Traister), 1995.

Waite, M. D. and Ernst, B. D., *The Trapdoor Springfield.* Gun Room Press, Highland Park, New Jersey, 1983.

Walter, John, *Secret Firearms* ('An Illustrated History of Miniature and Concealed Handguns'). Arms & Armour Press, London, 1997.

Ward, Geoffrey C., *The West, An Illustrated History*. George Weidenfeld & Nicolson Ltd, London, 1996.

Watrous, George R., *The History of Winchester Firearms, 1866–1966*. Winchester-Western Press, New Haven, Connecticut, third edition, 1966.

Webster, Donald D., *Military Bolt Action Rifles 1841–1918*. Museum Restoration Service, Alexandria Bay, New York, and Bloomfield, Ontario, Canada, 1993.

Williamson, Harold F., *Winchester. The Gun that Won the West*. A. S. Barnes & Company, South Brunswick and New York, and Thomas Yoseloff Ltd, London, 1962.

Wilson, R. L., *The Colt Heritage* ('The Official History of Colt Firearms from 1836 to the Present'). Simon & Schuster, New York, undated (1979).

—*Winchester, An American Legend*. Random House, New York, 1991.

Winant, Lewis, *Firearms Curiosa*. Ray Riling Arms Book Company, Philadelphia, Pennsylvania, 1961.

INDEX